SECURITY DESIGN FOR MAXIMUM PROTECTION

Richard J. Gigliotti and Ronald C. Jason

BUTTERWORTHS
Boston • London
Sydney • Wellington • Durban • Toronto

Library of Congress Cataloging in Publication Data

Gigliotti, Richard J.
  Security design for maximum protection.

  Bibliography: p.
  Includes index.
  1. Security systems.   I. Jason, Ronald C.   II. Title.
TH9705.G54   1984   658.4'73   83-25282
ISBN 0-409-95119-6

Published by Butterworth Publishers
80 Montvale Avenue
Stoneham, MA 02180

10 9 8 7 6 5 4 3 2

Printed in the United States of America

To Mr. and Mrs. Kissington, Mr. and Mrs. Victor Gigliotti, Mr. and Mrs. Arnold Jason, Brandy, Lynne, Gina, Vickie, and Richie, Randy, and Barry—our families and our source of inspiration, motivation, and commitment.

CONTENTS

PREFACE

The more we thought about and discussed the issue, the more we felt that a reference work dealing exclusively with the concept of high security would be a valuable addition to the security practitioner's library and a useful contribution to the body of security-related literature that currently exists.

In the area of nuclear security, for example, each facility's safeguard program strives for the ultimate in physical protection of a very sensitive and valuable commodity—strategic special nuclear material—and/or the ultimate in physical protection from radiological sabotage. Because of the sensitivity surrounding all aspects of nuclear power, licensed nuclear facilities fall under the purview of the United States Nuclear Regulatory Commission, which regulates, among other things, a safeguards effort at each installation. We often think of such sites as maximum-security facilities. If we were to list others that could be considered maximum security, certain prisons, banks, military installations, defense contractors, and Fort Knox would no doubt come to mind. But what is maximum security? Is it in actuality the ultimate safeguard condition that one would suppose? Is maximum security a realistic and attainable goal?

In the early stages of our work, we discovered that there appears to be no standard for, or accepted definition of, maximum security. To the bank manager it may be the uniformed security officers who are employed to stand watch in the lobby; to the prison warden it may be the low escape rate enjoyed at his institution; and to the nuclear security director it may be faith in his system of protection. To paraphrase an old cliche, the level of security is in the eye of the beholder.

We feel that a universally accepted standard for the levels of physical security is necessary, considering the state of today's art. We also feel that the subject of high security has been overlooked by a market that offers quite a compendium of publications on virtually every other aspect of security. This book, therefore, is our response and is intended to be an aid and information resource for those who may wish to develop a high-security system or upgrade an existing system by applying high-security techniques and principles. An assumption made throughout this book is that a facility security survey is the first prerequisite to effective protection and should be accomplished prior to implementing any security system. There are many references to surveys and many professionals capable of conducting them. For this reason, discussion of security surveys has been intentionally omitted.

Writing a book about high-level security is not easy. Initially, we attempted to address the contents to all interested persons, but we soon found that we had no appreciation for the magnitude of that approach. After spending considerable time reviewing references, mostly technical manuals and reports, we realized that it would not be easy to draw the line on detail. To some readers there may be too little detail; for others, too much; some will react positively, and others, negatively.

After numerous setbacks and much soul searching, we came to the realization that we were misdirecting our efforts by trying to treat each component of a physical security system as "maximum" in and of itself. Maximum security is not and cannot be applied to an individual component of a system. Rather, maximum security is the result of a total protection system, a concept more than a component. While individual chapters may deal with components, it must remain clear to the reader that each component described and aspect discussed only contributes to the overall level and subsequent effectiveness of the security program. The reader must also bear in mind that when we speak of maximum security, we are in reality speaking of high levels of security, and that although the term implies perfect security, this is hardly realistic, however desirable. We do not pretend to suggest that the principles, techniques, procedures, guidance, and systems discussed will result in the ultimate protection system. What we do guarantee is a better appreciation on the part of the reader of the difficulties and demands involved in achieving and maintaining a high level of security.

We owe a great deal to many people who assisted us in what turned out to be a substantial task. Our sincere appreciation to Sharon Caetano for her very able assistance and outstanding typing support. Our deepest gratitude for their encouragement, support, assistance, and tolerance, to Dennis Crowley, vice president, First Security Services Corporation; Gary French, president, Colt Firearms; Bob Gustafson, corporate security director, United Nuclear Corporation; Dan Harvey, district manager, First Security Services Corporation; Dave Janis, President, Advanced Security Corp.; Ken Jenkins, vice president, First Security Services Corporation; Bob Johnson, president, First Security Services Corporation; Bill Madden, U.S. Nuclear Regulatory Commission; Gene McDonald, vice president, Globe Security Systems; Steve Messemer, assistant manager of security, Colt Firearms; Jerry Remkiewicz and Bob Romanowski, regional manager and corporate security director, respectively, First Security Services Corporation; Walt Thoma, regional manager, Interstate Security Services Division of Globe Security Systems; Don Wanat, vice president, Colt Firearms; and Chip Winslow, manager of the technical services division, First Security Services Corporation.

Our special thanks to Dick Barry, executive vice president, First Security Services Corporation; Joe Bobe, president, Leonard Security; John Cauley and Larry Curran, vice presidents, First Security Services Corporation; Ed Dione, vice president, Leonard Security; Mary Kerin, administrative assistant to the regional manager, First Security Services Corporation; and Ed Leonard, former commissioner, Connecticut State Police and current chairman, Leonard Security.

Last but not least we would like to thank Greg Franklin, editor, Butterworths, for his patience, understanding, commitment, and friendship.

Richard J. Gigliotti
Ronald C. Jason
Waterford, Connecticut
September 1, 1983

FOREWORD

During the past decade the private security industry has undergone significant change in terms of the quadrupling of the number of people working in the field while at the same time substantially upgrading the professional competency of its personnel.

The police community has witnessed and applauded these changes as a welcome assist to the constant effort that we are all engaged in to stem what seems to be the ever increasing tide of crime across the nation. As part of the private security field's increased efforts in education and training the authors of *Security Design for Maximum Protection* have further contributed to improve the skills of practicioners of their profession by documenting in a clear and concise work years of experience and knowledge in providing the highest level of security for properties requiring extreme protection.

This is a highly complex and technical area since the facilities that warrant this level of protection often are among the most heavily government regulated and inspected plants in the nation. However, Richard Gigliotti and Ronald Jason have written a very readable and more importantly useable book that will truly advance the private security profession one more step toward better serving the public and their clients.

William F. Quinn
Chief of Police
Past President
International Association
of Chiefs of Police

CHAPTER 1

Description and Approaches

Protection of one's person and possessions is natural and universally accepted. Unfortunately, there are those who have made it their objective to deprive some of us of one or both of these. In the battle against the criminal element, our resourcefulness in designing and developing more and better methods of protecting our life, property, and livelihood has been unbounded. No system, however, can be made completely secure. Any system conceived by man can be defeated by man.

In other words, no physical protection system is 100 percent defeat-proof. It can be designed to eliminate most threats, but it will have its weak links; for example, the perimeter fence or the alarm system. In any event, if a system cannot fully protect against a threat, it must at a minimum offer enough protection so as to delay the threat until the system can be upgraded, at least temporarily, to the point at which the threat can be defeated (e.g., the arrival of local law enforcement authorities or on-site guard response force, the implementation of contingency measures such as additional physical barriers, the release of noxious gases, etc.).

Maximum security is a concept; the end to the means used to achieve it. Physical barriers, alarm systems, guard forces, and all the other components of a security system do not individually achieve maximum security. The parts of the system cannot realize the ultimate aim unless they are combined in the right proportions.

LEVELS OF PHYSICAL SECURITY

How would one categorize a particular security system? Would one consider protection minimum, medium, or maximum, and what criteria would be used in making this determination? Would a facility be compared to a prison, nuclear reactor, department store, or the average American home? While the initial question may appear to be answered easily, arriving at an intelligent and impartial assessment becomes much more difficult simply because there are no known universally accepted standards by which the security professional may evaluate a security system.

This lack of standards often serves to delude responsible individuals into believing that the protection they provide (or are paying to have provided) is of a higher level than is actually the case. (This, by the way, is not an indictment of any person or organization.) Because of the confusion and lack of cohesive opinion on the subject, this book considers the following five levels (or generic categories) of security systems (also see Figure 1–1):[1]

Level 1—minimum security
Level 2—low level security
Level 3—medium security
Level 4—high level security
Level 5—maximum security

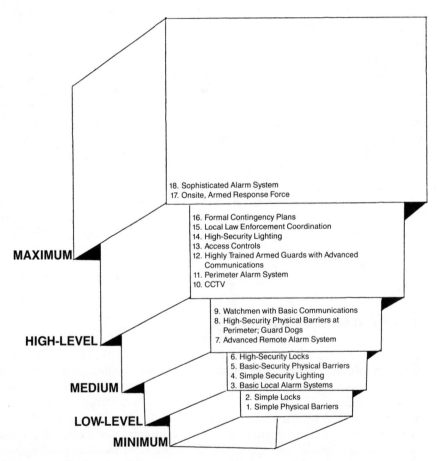

18. Sophisticated Alarm System
17. Onsite, Armed Response Force

16. Formal Contingency Plans
15. Local Law Enforcement Coordination
14. High-Security Lighting
13. Access Controls
12. Highly Trained Armed Guards with Advanced
    Communications
11. Perimeter Alarm System
10. CCTV

9. Watchmen with Basic Communications
8. High-Security Physical Barriers at
   Perimeter; Guard Dogs
7. Advanced Remote Alarm System

6. High-Security Locks
5. Basic-Security Physical Barriers
4. Simple Security Lighting
3. Basic Local Alarm Systems

2. Simple Locks
1. Simple Physical Barriers

MAXIMUM

HIGH-LEVEL

MEDIUM

LOW-LEVEL

MINIMUM

Figure 1-1   The levels of physical security. (Courtesy of *Security Management*.)

Mimimum Security

Such a system would be designed to *Impede* some unauthorized external activity. Unauthorized external activity is defined as originating outside the scope of the security system, and could range from simple intrusion to armed attack. By virtue of this definition, a minimum security system would consist of simple physical barriers such as regular doors and windows equipped with ordinary locks. The average American home is the best example of a site protected by a minimum-security system.

Low-Level Security

This refers to a system designed to *Impede and Detect* some unauthorized external activity. Once simple physical barriers and locks are in place, they can be supplemented with other barriers such as reinforced doors, window bars and grates, high-security locks, a simple lighting system that could be nothing more elaborate than normal lighting over doors and windows, and a basic alarm system that would be an unmonitored device at the site of the intrusion that provides detection capability and local annunciation. Small retail stores, storage warehouses, and even older police stations are examples of sites that could be protected by low-level security systems.

Medium Security

A system of this type would be designed to *Impede, Detect, and Assess* most unauthorized external activity and *some* unauthorized internal activity. Such activity could range from simple shoplifting to conspiracy to commit sabotage. When a system is upgraded to the medium level, those minimum and low-level measures previously incorporated are augmented with impediment and detection capability as well as assessment capability. To reach the medium level of security, it is necessary to:

1. Incorporate an advanced intrusion alarm system that annunciates at a manned remote location
2. Establish a perimeter beyond the confines of the area being protected and provide high-security physical barriers such as penetration-resistant fences at least eight feet high and topped with multiple strands of barbed wire or barbed tape at that perimeter, or use guard dogs in lieu of perimeter protection
3. Use an unarmed watchman (with basic training), equipped with the means for basic communication (e.g., commercial telephone) to off-site agencies

Medium-security facilities might include bonded warehouses, large industrial manufacturing plants, some large retail outlets, and National Guard armories.

High-level Security

A system of this sort would be designed to *impede, detect, and assess* most unauthorized *external* and *internal* activity. After those measures previously mentioned have been incorporated into the system, high-level security is realized with the addition of the following:

1.   Closed-circuit television (CCTV)
2.   A perimeter alarm system, remotely monitored, at or near the high-security physical barriers
3.   High-security lighting, which at a minimum, provides at least 0.02 foot-candles of light around the entire facility
4.   Highly trained armed guards or unarmed watchmen who have been screened for employment and who are equipped with advanced means of communications such as dedicated telephone lines, two-way radio links to police, duress alarms, etc.
5.   Controls designed to restrict access to or within a facility to authorized personnel
6.   Formal plans prepared with the knowledge and cooperation of police dealing with their response and assistance in the event of specific contingencies at the protected site
7.   Varying degrees of coordination with local law enforcement authorities

Some examples of high-level security sites could be certain prisons, defense contractors, pharmaceutical companies, sophisticated electronics manufacturers and the like.

Maximum Security

Such a system is designed to *impede, detect, assess, and neutralize* all unauthorized *external* and *internal* activity. In addition to those measures already cited, it is characterized by:

1.   A sophisticated alarm system with, at a minimum, sufficient redundancy to preclude defeat by a lone individual; remotely monitored in one or more protected locations; tamper-indicating with backup source of power

2. On-site response force of highly screened and trained individuals armed 24 hours a day and equipped for contingency operations; and dedicated to neutralizing or containing any threat against the protected facility until the arrival of off-site assistance

The highest level of physical security protection will be found at nuclear facilities, some prisons, certain military bases and government special research sites, and some foreign embassies.

In order to upgrade a security system to the next highest level, all criteria for that level must be met (see Figure 1-1). It must be remembered that individual criteria from a higher level can be met without the total system being upgraded. For example, if a medium-security facility institutes access controls and installs a closed-circuit television (CCTV) system, the overall level of security has not been upgraded to a high level. In reality, what results is a medium-security system with some high-level characteristics.[2] Depending on its capabilities, a high-level system could achieve maximum security by the addition of a neutralizing capability.

By using modern methods, materials, and technology, a maximum-security system can be developed or an existing system upgraded. The following chapters contain information and techniques that will be useful for accomplishing this end. Some of the methods are simple and inexpensive to implement; others require a great deal of planning, preparation, and expense to install and maintain.

The present state of the art being what it is, the authors have concluded that a highly detailed discussion of every type, model, and variation of a component would be of little real value. Instead, we have chosen to deal with several examples of components that could result in maximum security. When the term maximum security is used, it denotes the high level of physical security offered by the total system. High security refers to characteristics of an individual component. There is little discussion of less than high-security components such as wooden doors, local alarm systems, and simple fences because their presence in a maximum-security environment is incidental and does not significantly contribute to the maximum-security concept.

Maximum security is security in depth—a system designed with sufficient diversity and redundancy so as to allow the strength of one particular component to offset the weakness of another. There is no set rule regarding the number of protective layers; again, it depends on the material being protected. As a general rule, however, the more layers, the more difficult it is to defeat the total system. The Nuclear Regulatory Commission has for years inspected nuclear facilities on a component-specific basis. While such evaluation can certainly point out weaknesses in any component, it by no means attests to the effectiveness of the total system. It must always be remembered that maximum security is dependent on the total system and not on its individual components.

THE PSYCHOLOGY OF MAXIMUM SECURITY

The concept of maximum security is as much psychological as it is physical. To the casual criminal, a maximum-security facility is a target to be given up in favor of a minimum (or zero) security facility. To the security director, maximum security accurately describes the system of protection he has designed and that allows him to go home at night with the conviction, real or imagined, that the assets entrusted to him for protection will still be there in the morning. To the average citizen, maximum security is a state of mind more than physical components.

When designing a protection system, one can capitalize on the psychological aspects of maximum security. If a system can create the appearance of being next to impenetrable, then it has succeeded in deterring some lesser adversaries. The same principle can be seen when one compares a threat dog to an attack dog. The former has been trained to put on a show of aggression while the latter has been trained to carry out his threat—a case of bite being worse than bark.

While the concept of maximum security may deter those who are not up to the challenge, it will not turn aside those who are. Whenever the value of the protected assets exceeds the degree of perceived risk, there will always be takers. For a criminal to act and, for that matter, a crime to be committed, there must be desire and opportunity; the criminal must want to commit the act and he must have the opportunity. The effectiveness of the system can be measured in terms of eliminating the opportunity; the psychology of the system can be measured in terms of eliminating the desire.

Desire to commit a crime can be eliminated or reduced in a variety of ways. The end result is that the criminal feels the risk outweighs the treasure and moves on to another target. The strongest reason for a criminal to lose his desire is the threat of getting caught. The possibility of apprehending him may be increased by the use of lighting that increases observation capabilities, barriers that delay intrusion, alarms that signal an intrusion, and a security force that can neutralize intrusion. For the maximum psychological effect to be achieved, the capabilities of the protection system must be known to the criminal, that is, they must convince him that the odds of getting caught are against him. This can be accomplished by posting signs in and around the facility advertising its protection. While the capabilities of the system should be announced, details should be considered proprietary information and safeguarded accordingly. This is the primary reason that certain details of maximum security, (e.g., radio codes, access controls, locks, etc.) are changed whenever key personnel terminate their employment. It is far simpler and cheaper to attempt to eliminate a criminal's desire than it is to eliminate his opportunity.

There are those who disagree on the value of advertising a security system's capabilities. They feel that maintaining a low profile will somehow contribute to the overall effectiveness of the system and criminals will not know that an attractive target exists. This philosophy can be called the ostrich syndrome; it may have been true before the advent of mass and multimedia, but it certainly is not today. A security director who thinks that he can maintain a low enough profile that a criminal will be fooled is merely deluding himself and risking the assets he has been entrusted to protect. When it is suggested that the system's capabilities be advertised, this is not to mean that full-page display ads are taken out in local and regional publications. Rather, anyone surveilling a protected facility, passively or actively, will understand that action directed against the target will not be "a piece of cake." He will have to plan it carefully and more than likely enlist additional help; this is not in his best interests, as the more people in on a scheme, the more chance of an information leak.

It is important, therefore, that consideration be given to the psychological aspects of maximum security when designing or maintaining a system. An implied presence can do wonders in dissuading criminals from targeting a facility.

THE VALUE OF PLANNING

When setting up a maximum-security system, the best results come from a careful and detailed plan. Two basic questions must first be answered:

1. What is being protected?
2. How important is it? (This is measured in terms of "political" and economic impact, corporate commitment to its protection, and health and safety of the public.)

A third question is sometimes asked: do the costs of protecting it outweigh its value? While this may be a consideration when planning for a security system less than maximum, it is tacitly implied that something calling for maximum security is worth the cost to someone. Once these questions have been answered, planning can commence.

One of the best approaches to take is to list the basic prerequisites of the security system. As was previously stated, maximum security is designed to impede, detect, assess, and neutralize all unauthorized external and internal activity. Under each prerequisite are listed those components that would accomplish it. If the system includes a capability to neutralize, this is stated and provided for accordingly:

Security force

Response force

Coordination with local law enforcement authorities (LLEA)

The next step is to decide which components are going to be used to impede (Table 1–1) detect (Table 1–2), assess (Table 1–3), and (if necessary) neutralize (Table 1–4).

Once the decision is made on the components that will be used to make up the maximum-security system, attention should be directed to developing a design-reference threat.

Design-Reference Threat

The design-reference threat defines the level of threat with which the facility's physical protection system would contend (or is designed to defeat). This is a most important consideration when designing or upgrading a system and is essential for cost-effective planning.

The security director should list all possible threats to a particular facility. For example, a hospital's security director might list the following as conditions or situations the system should be able to defeat:

Disorderly conduct

Internal theft or diversion

Assaults on employees or visitors

Armed attack on facility

Burglary

Robbery

Kidnapping

Auto theft from parking lot

Hostage incident

The next step is to evaluate these threats in descending order of credibility, that is, which are the most credible based on such things as past

Table 1-1 Components to Impede

Physical Barriers	*Locks*
Perimeter fence	Perimeter fence
High-security doors	Openings
High-security windows	Designated doors
Vault	
Security Force	*Access Controls*
Manning levels	Protected areas
Training	Vital areas
Equipment	

Table 1-2 Components to Detect

Alarm Systems
Doors
Perimeter
Protected areas
Vital areas

experience, loss rates, crime statistics, and so on. The hospital in this case could perhaps list as follows, going from the most credible to the least:

1. Internal theft or diversion
2. Auto theft from parking lot
3. Disorderly conduct
4. Assaults on employees or visitors
5. Burglary
6. Robbery
7. Hostage incident
8. Kidnapping
9. Armed attack

In this example, internal theft or diversion is considered a very real possibility (probably based on past experience), followed by theft of automobiles from the hospital's parking lot. Although possible, the threat of armed attack carries low credibility and therefore is of far less concern when deciding on the design of and money to be invested in the security system. Once the credible, realistic threats have been identified and given priority, this information can be used to arrive at the design-reference threat.

The types of adversaries that would likely be encountered by the security system is another area of consideration when determining the design-reference threat. The Nuclear Regulatory Commission[3] describes six generic categories of adversaries and the characteristics of each:

1. Terrorist groups
2. Organized sophisticated criminal groups

Table 1-3 Components to Assess

Lighting	Communications	CCTV
Perimeter	On site	Perimeter
Protected areas	Off site	Protected areas
Vital areas		Vital areas

Table 1-4   Components to Neutralize

Security Force	Response Force	LLEA Coordination
Manning levels	Manning levels	Contingency planning
Training	Training	Training drills
Equipment	Equipment	

3.   Extremist protest groups
4.   Disoriented persons (psychotic, neurotic)
5.   Disgruntled employees
6.   Miscellaneous criminals

The security director should now assess these potential adversary groups in terms of likelihood of encounter, from most likely to least. The hospital's list would probably look like this:

1.   Miscellaneous criminals
2.   Disgruntled employees
3.   Disoriented persons
4.   Organized sophisticated criminal groups
5.   Extremist protest groups
6.   Terrorist groups

The most likely threat group would include petty thieves from within the hospital's work force.

Time, location, and circumstances influence the likelihood of a threat from a particular group. For example, labor disputes could lead to threats by disgruntled employees; hospitalizing an unpopular political figure could lead to threats by terrorists. In any case, extraordinary circumstances should not influence the determination of likely adversaries, but should be considered during contingency planning.

Once the likely threats and adversaries have been determined, it becomes necessary to correlate the two and establish a specific design-reference threat. The process begins by comparing the most credible threats with the most likely adversaries for a particular facility (in this case, the hospital).

1.   *Internal theft or diversion*
     Miscellaneous criminals
     Disgruntled employees
     Organized sophisticated criminals
2.   *Auto theft*
     Miscellaneous criminals
     Organized sophisticated criminals

3. *Disorderly conduct*
   Disoriented persons
   Miscellaneous criminals
4. *Assaults*
   Miscellaneous criminals
   Disoriented persons
   Organized sophisticated criminals
5. *Burglary*
   Organized sophisticated criminals
   Miscellaneous criminals
6. *Robbery*
   Disoriented persons
   Miscellaneous criminals
7. *Hostage incidents*
   Disoriented persons
   Miscellaneous criminals
   Disgruntled employees
   Extremist protesters
8. *Kidnapping*
   Organized sophisticated criminals
   Terrorists
   Extremist protestors
   Miscellaneous criminals
9. *Armed attack*
   Terrorists
   Extremist protestors

There is always overlap among adversary groups to one degree or another, and this fact must be kept in mind when preparing a threat-versus-adversary analysis. In our example, the hospital's security director has defined the primary threat to his facility as being internal theft or diversion, and his most likely adversaries in this area as miscellanous criminals followed by disgruntled employees and organized sophisticated criminals. The protection system must be designed or upgraded to counter his most real threat. The most "worthy" adversary, however, appears to be an organized sophisticated criminal, probably because of the hospital's drug supply. While he is the least likely adversary in this threat, he is the most capable (in terms of desire, resources, and capabilities), and therefore the system must be designed to defeat him. Thus, at the same time, adversaries of lesser capability will also be defeated. A very simple analogy illustrates this principle: a screened door will, if properly installed, keep out flies; it will also keep out wasps, butterflies, and birds.

Continuing the process of determining the adversary most capable of carrying out the most credible threats, the hospital's security director will probably come up with the following results:

1. Internal theft—organized sophisticated criminals
2. Auto theft—organized sophisticated criminals
3. Disorderly conduct—disoriented persons
4. Assaults—organized sophisticated criminals
5. Burglary—organized sophisticated criminals
6. Robbery—miscellaneous criminals
7. Hostage incident—terrorists
8. Kidnapping—terrorists
9. Armed attack—terrorists

Planning a system to address a realistic security concern as well as the adversary most capable of causing that concern allows the system's architect to prepare for the worst possible case and least capable adversary.

Establishing the design-reference threat, therefore, is contingent on determining the groups to which the specific threats or adversaries belong:

1. *Internal Theft (crimes against property)*
    Auto
    Burglary
2. *Violent conduct (crimes against persons)*
    Robbery
    Disorderly conduct
    Assaults
    Hostage incidents
    Kidnapping
    Armed attack

On this basis the hospital's security director knows where he has to channel his resources and the degree of protection his efforts will have to offer. Since internal theft or diversion has been defined as the most credible threat, his system should be designed to counter this crime as it would be perpetrated by an organized sophisticated criminal. This is where much of his budget money will be used. His next most credible threat is auto theft from the parking lot. Again, resources will have to be directed so as to counter auto theft perpetrated by an organized sophisticated criminal. At the other end of the scale, an armed attack on the facility is a very remote possibility: If it were to happen, chances are the act would be perpetrated by terrorists. Since the possibility is quite low, attention and resources (and budget money) will be minimal if any in this area, and more than likely will consist of contingency planning and/or local law enforcement coordination.

The design-reference threat and its supporting analysis become the basis for planning the measures that will be instituted to preclude its occurrence or counter its effects.

Example: A Nuclear Fuel Cycle Facility

Determining the design-reference threat for a nuclear fuel cycle facility, for example, would follow the same process.

1. *Possible threats*
    Internal theft or diversion
    Armed attack
    Hostage incident
    Burglary
    Civil disturbance
    Auto theft
    Sabotage
    Employee pilferage
    Kidnapping
    Robbery
    Assaults
2. *Credible threats (most to least)*
    Internal theft or diversion of nuclear material
    Sabotage (including threats)
    Armed attack (as a prelude to other action)
    Civil disturbance (including antinuclear demonstrations)
    Employee pilferage (of non-nuclear material)
    Assaults
    Auto theft (from parking lot)
    Kidnapping
    Hostage incident
    Burglary
    Robbery
3. *Potential adversaries (most to least)*
    Terrorist groups
    Disoriented persons
    Disgruntled employees
    Extremists or protesters
    Miscellaneous criminals
    Organized sophisticated criminals
4. *Match-up of threats and adversaries*
    a. Internal theft or diversion
        Disgruntled employees
        Disoriented persons
        Terrorists
    b. Sabotage
        Terrorists
        Disoriented persons
        Disgruntled employees

      c. Armed attack
          Terrorists
      d. Civil disturbance
          Extremists or protesters
      e. Pilferage
          Miscellaneous criminals
      f. Assaults
          Disoriented persons
      g. Auto theft
          Miscellaneous criminals
      h. Kidnapping
          Terrorists
          Disoriented persons
      i. Hostage incident
          Terrorists
          Disoriented persons
          Disgruntled employees
      j. Burglary
          Miscellaneous criminals
      k. Robbery
          Miscellaneous criminals

5. *Most credible threat, most capable adversary*
      a. Internal theft or diversion—terrorists
      b. Sabotage—terrorists
      c. Armed attack—terrorists
      d. Civil disturbance—extremists or protesters
      e. Pilferage—disgruntled employees
      f. Assault—disoriented persons
      g. Auto theft—miscellaneous criminals
      h. Kidnapping—terrorists
      i. Hostage incident—terrorists
      j. Burglary—miscellaneous criminals
      k. Robbery—miscellaneous criminals

6. *Basic Generic threat groups*
      a. Theft
          Internal
          Pilferage
          Auto
          Burglary
      b. Violence
          Sabotage
          Armed attack
          Civil disturbance
          Assault
          Kidnapping

Hostage incident
Robbery

We can see that a nuclear fuel cycle facility's number one security concern is the theft or diversion of nuclear material. The most capable adversary (although the least likely) is a terrorist group. While theft may be the most serious concern, other violent actions, including sabotage and armed attack, are very real possibilities. The chance of a fuel cycle facility being burglarized or robbed (in the traditional sense) is negligible due to the heavy protection provided. The security director must therefore base his system on a design-reference threat that reflects his most serious concerns. The *Code of Federal Regulations* requires that nuclear fuel cycle facilities "must establish and maintain . . . a physical protection system. . . . the physical protection system shall be designed to protect against . . . theft or diversion of strategic special nuclear material and radiological sabotage."[4] The *Code* describes the threats the system must be able to defeat[5]:

1. Radiological sabotage (i) A determined violent external assault, attack by stealth, or deceptive actions, of several persons with the following attributes, assistance, and equipment: (A) well trained, (B) inside assistance, which may include a knowledgeable individual who attempts to participate in a passive role, an active role, or both, (C) suitable weapons, up to and including hand-held automatic weapons, equipped with silencers and having effective long-range accuracy, (D) hand-carried equipment, including incapacitating agents and explosives; (ii) an internal threat of an insider, including an employee (in any position).

2. Theft or diversion of formula quantities of strategic special nuclear material. (i) A determined, violent, external assault, attack by stealth, or deceptive actions by a small group with the following attributes, assistance, and equipment: (A) well trained, (B) inside assistance, which may include a knowledgeable individual who attempts to participate in a passive role, an active role, or both, (C) suitable weapons, up to and including hand-held automatic weapons, equipped with silencers and having effective long-range accuracy, (D) hand-carried equipment, including incapacitating agents and explosives, (E) the ability to operate as two or more teams; (ii) an individual, including an employee (in any position), and (iii) conspiracy between individuals in any position.

In summary, a design-reference threat is a systematic analysis of all possible threats and adversaries so that credible threats and adversaries can be identified and this information used as a basis for planning and implementing a physical protection system.

Layering for Protection

It is important that the designer remember the principle of security-in-depth. Protection must be "layered" so as to provide diversity & redundancy (Figure

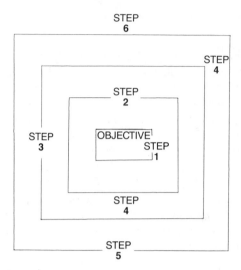

Figure 1-2 Layering. (Courtesy of *Security Management*.)

1–2). Whenever and wherever possible layer components. Conduct a walk-through of the facility and likely threat routes. Start either at a point outside and work in, or, start at the most sensitive point within the facility and work out.

Physical Barriers.   Physical barriers should be checked at the area considered the most sensitive, such as the vault, cell block, tool crib, shipping department. This area will be called the objective.

1.   Provide a high-security barrier around the objective.
2.   Enclose a high-security barrier within another high-security barrier.
3.   Surround the outer barrier with a penetration-resistant fence.
4.   Establish isolation zones on either side of the penetration-resistant fence.
5.   Surround the outer isolation zone with yet another penetration-resistant fence and isolation zone.
6.   Establish an isolation zone on the outside of the outermost fence.

Entry and exit points should be identified and determination made of which ones are vital to the effectiveness of the total system. High-security doors and windows must be installed or upgraded where appropriate. As a general rule, if a window is not needed at a particular location, it should be eliminated. The area containing the objective should be a vault or other such strong room, depending on cost considerations and the effectiveness of the total system. It is important to evaluate the structural components of the facility including walls, ceilings, and floors and determine their ability to withstand a threat equivalent to the design-reference threat.

Physical barriers are not exclusively for keeping someone out; they can also be used to keep someone in.

Locks. After deciding which openings require locks (high-security and otherwise) the types of locks are selected.

Access Controls. Protected and vital areas are designated and decision is made as to who will be admitted to the facility and who will be allowed unrestricted access within it. Generally, the protected area will include the facility itself and the outside area around it up to the first penetration-resistant fence. Vital areas would include the vault or strong room, and could include the alarm stations, emergency generator buildings, or other areas that could be considered vital to the protection of the objective and the facility (one must not overlook the possibility that the facility itself, rather than its contents, could be the target of an action).

Security Force. Appropriate manning levels of the security force for each shift are established, with the amount of training necessary and desirable (some states have mandated training levels for security officers). The force is equipped with resources to handle the design-reference threat.

Alarm Systems. A maximum security system should have a perimeter alarm system capable of detecting an intrusion anywhere on the perimeter. Additionally, all vital areas should be equipped with alarms capable of detecting the presence of an intruder. All doors that contribute to the protection system should be alarmed and all alarms continuously monitored by a person in a remote location on site. Alarm circuits should be supervised so that tampering with the system or its components will cause an alarm.

Lighting. The value of lighting should be considered for impeding as well as for assessing. In deciding where security lighting should be directed; it should be kept in mind that proper placement will avoid silhouetting security personnel. High-intensity glare lighting, positioned so as to illuminate the isolation zone outside of the protected area, is always appropriate in a maximum-security environment. Also, inside areas can be illuminated so as to facilitate the use of normal CCTV, thus saving money on expensive low-light cameras, energy costs notwithstanding.

Communications. The ability to communicate on site is of vital importance to the security force. Consider the alternatives for communications. In addition to commercial telephones, the security force should be equipped with at least one dedicated and supervised hot line to local law enforcement authorities (LLEA) and a two-way radio network. Each officer should have his own two-way radio and the system should have at least a two-channel capability. Additionally, the facility should be able to communicate with LLEA by means of two-way radio.

CCTV. The CCTV cameras should be placed to ensure proper surveillance and assessment. Depending on the type and quality of equipment, the perimeter and protected and vital areas can be effectively monitored. The use of CCTV instead of personnel to serve this function can save money.

Response Force.   If the nature of the security system requires it to neutralize a threat, attention must be directed toward establishing a response force of security personnel that is properly trained and equipped for that purpose. The number of personnel constituting a response force should be sufficient to counter the design-reference threat.

LLEA Coordination.   When a system has been designed or upgraded to safeguard something that requires protection of this magnitude, local law enforcement authorities should be brought into the picture. It always helps to establish liaison very early in the game. Once the cooperation of LLEA is secured, it is helpful to consult with them on contingency planning to meet the design-reference threat, and if possible, to schedule joint training sessions and drills to exercise the plans.

Once the process of analysis has been completed, it is time to plan the security system. It is much easier to incorporate security features when a facility is constructed. In this respect, corporate support is essential. The security director should work with the architects and contractors throughout the construction. When this is not possible and an upgrade to an existing facility is necessary, the security director will more often than not become the chief architect of the upgrade. Whenever this happens, the value of planning as discussed will become evident, as it is the basis for the formal security set-up.

THE SECURITY PLAN

The security plan is frequently contracted out to a consultant who will work with the security director. Before system implementation, it is a necessary building document; after implementation it becomes a necessary reference document. Needless to say, the plan should be treated as proprietary, and access to it should be restricted to those who have a "need to know."

The plan can take many forms and contain much information. In its basic sense, it is a description of the protection system and its components. Detail can be as much or as little as desired by the security director. For use as a building document, however, it should be quite detailed. Much information can be deleted after implementation, but if the facility is regulated by an agency that requires safeguards, the plan may have to retain many details. If this is the case, the document should be treated as sensitive.

The security plan should contain, but not necessarily be limited to the following information:

1.   A description of the facility and its organizational structure
2.   The security organization of the facility
3.   A discussion of the physical barriers used in the system
4.   A discussion of the alarm system used

5.   A description of access controls used to restrict access to or within the facility
6.   A discussion of security lighting at the facility
7.   A description of the communications capability
8.   A description of the CCTV capability and its use
9.   A breakdown of the security force; its organization, training, equipment, capabilities, resources, and procedures
10. A discussion of outside resources including LLEA and others as appropriate.

Depending on the nature of the facility and its commitments to regulatory agencies or if the security director so desires, certain other plans can be developed, such as contingency, training, qualifications plans, and so on.

Justification

When it finally comes down to selling a security design or upgrade to the people who will have to pay for it, the job can be made somewhat easier by following a few basic principles.

There aren't many security directors who have not heard that, "Security contributes nothing to production, is an overhead item, and a necessary evil." Dealing with the "Necessary Evil Syndrome" has been the subject of much discussion since the business of assets protection started. Good security holds losses at a minimum and keeps costs down, thus resulting in increased profits. Fulfillment of the security mission can be called negative profit, compared with the positive profit generated by production. Accordingly, security management personnel must justify many, if not all, systems, expenditures, programs, personnel, approaches, and, at times, their own existence.

Most facilities usually cut costs for security before anything else, therefore a planned, systematic approach is necessary to keep this practice to a minimum and to secure the resources necessary for efficient security operation. Justification should be based on the following steps:

1.   Convincing oneself that a proposal is justified
2.   Convincing others that it is justified
3.   Formulating the approach
4.   Presenting the approach

Convincing Oneself that a Proposal Is Justified

It has been said that a good salesman believes in his product. So too, must the security director believe in his proposal. Before it can be justified to anyone, it has to be justified in his mind. In some cases, this takes only a few minutes and consists of a mental evaluation of the issue. In others, it is a lengthy and detailed examination of alternatives.

As a first step, it is necessary to define the issue—just what it is that is wanted—personnel, equipment, policy, and the like. Then he must consider the pros and cons: do the results justify the expense; is there a cheaper way to accomplish the same thing; is it really necessary and what happens if it isn't done?; is there enough money available to finance it?

Next, he considers the benefit to the company: Will this increase profits? Not likely. Will this reduce overhead? Possibly. Will this make the job easier? Probably. Making the job easier has long-term benefit in that it deters potential complaints.

Turnaround time must be considered, that is, the time it will take to gain a return or realize a benefit from the expenditure or approach.

The security director must rely somewhat on gut feeling. If it is felt that the proposal is logical and rational but there is a negative gut feeling, he should set the proposal aside and reconsider it at a later date. Circumstances could change and the whole proposal could become moot.

Convincing Others that it Is Justified

Once he is convinced that his proposal is sound, it has to be sold to others who may see everything involving security printed in red ink. Generally, any money that can be saved, no matter what the percentage, is a plus when justifying a proposal. Money saved is negative profit and it should be sold as such.

Before an attempt is made to convince others of the soundness of an approach, the security director must research the whole issue, investing amounts of time and effort proportional to the expense and importance of the issue. Research is based on: the company's past experience, personal experience, supporting documentation, and others' perceptions.

Company's Experience

The company may have encountered problems in this area in the past and therefore could be receptive to the idea. There may be a policy that could support the proposal or eliminate it from the start.

The security director should consider any adverse publicity that could result from implementation of, or failure to implement, the approach. Tarnished company image is perhaps one of the most overlooked areas of corporate concern. If a company is in the midst of a problem that threatens its image, its executives and public relations officers will often go to great lengths to preserve its image; however, the inclination to spend money to counter bad press diminishes as time goes by. Very simply, the tendency to prevent reoccurrence of an unfavorable situation diminishes as more time elapses.

An idea is best promoted hard on the heels of a situation in which it would have prevented the occurrence.

Personal Experience

A security director has probably dealt with the same issue before or is familiar with others' handling of a similar issue. He can draw on previous experience to define and analyze possible short- and long-term ramifications and positive and negative results.

It is advisable to pay particular attention to idiosyncrasies that could provide necessary direction to the approach, and if possible, capitalize on them. For example, if the approving authority has a liking for gadgets and the approach calls for the use of gadgetry, this affinity could be parlayed into a successful acquisition.

Formulating the Approach

Armed with the raw data that have been accumulated up to this point, it is necessary to adopt a strategy for communicating arguments in a convincing manner.

Formulation of the approach is based on personal knowledge of and experience with the approving authority. If charts and transparencies are generally well received, they should be used; however, the amount of time that should be spent is in proportion to the magnitude of the project.

If personal experience shows that a concise approach is best, the security director should formulate accordingly. He must decide on the format, written or verbal, and prepare for both. Consistency is important; the odds increase in favor of subsequent approvals if credibility has been established. He should make a list of areas to be covered by priority (Figure 1–3). Certain basic information must be communicated regardless of the format:

1. Definition of the problem
2. Ramifications
3. Alternatives
4. Elimination of each alternative (except his)
5. The solution
6. Support for the solution

Presenting the Approach

Once the issue has been researched and an approach formulated, it must be presented. (It is always a good idea to send a memo regarding the issue

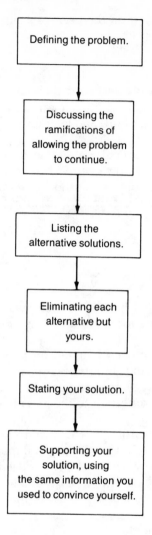

Figure 1-3   The Justification Process. (Courtesy of *Security Management*.)

beforehand.) If a formal presentation is required, it is recommended that the presentation be tested on affected individuals who should be encouraged to offer their critiques.

The first consideration in this respect should be timing. An appropriate time is important. If past experience says that the first thing in the morning is the wrong time, it makes sense to choose another. If there are problems with another aspect of the business, the presentation can be deferred until a more opportune time.

Once the presentation commences, the approach should be presented as formulated and include the basic information already discussed. The security director must be concise and consistent; and anticipate any questions and be prepared to answer them. Depending on time and importance, audiovisual aids can be effective, as can handouts; it may be no more than a single page outline but it helps to leave something for later reference. Above all, he must not oversell. If he has convinced himself that what he is asking for is necessary, it is probably because it is necessary and this will come through.

If after this effort the proposal is not approved, and if the security director thinks it necessary to protect himself, he should do so with memos-to-file and other such correspondence so that if problems result from the proposal's disapproval, it can be shown that he tried.[6]

NOTES

1. Richard J. Gigliotti, Ronald C. Jason, and Nancy J. Cogan, "What Is Your Level of Physical Security?" *Security Management*:46. © 1980. Copyright by the American Society for Industrial Security, 1655 N. Fort Drive, Suite 1200, Arlington, VA 22209. Reprinted with permission from the August 1980 issue of *Security Management* magazine.
2. Ibid., pp. 46–50.
3. "U.S. Nuclear Regulatory Commission, *Generic Adversary Characteristics Summary Report* (Washington, D.C.: The Commission, 1979), p. 11–12.
4. *The Code of Federal Regulations*, title 10, part 73.1, Washington, D.C., 1982.
5. Ibid.
6. Richard J. Gigliotti, "The Fine Art of Justification," *Security Management*:30–34. © 1980. Copyright by the American Society for Industrial Security, 1655 N. Fort Drive, Suite 1200, Arlington, VA 22209. Reprinted with permission from the November 1980 issue of *Security Management* magazine.

CHAPTER 2

Physical Barriers

When we speak of physical barriers, most people tend to think in terms of reinforced concrete walls, chain link fences topped with barbed wire, modern bank vaults, and such other apparent applications of maximum security. We can think back, however, to the Roman Empire, whose power and influence extended over what was then almost all of the known world. The continuance of this power was guaranteed by the establishment of outposts throughout the conquered territories manned by elements of the powerful Roman legions. These outposts were actually fortified garrisons—an example of using physical barriers for protection of a base of operations.

This same principle has been used throughout recorded history: the British and Colonial fortresses during the Revolutionary War; the U.S. Army forts in the Indian territories during the last half of the nineteenth century; the French Maginot Line in World War II; and even the protected base camps established by American forces in Viet Nam. It is interesting to note that the last were actually a variation of the system of forts used during the Revolutionary War to which forces could retire with a relative degree of safety for rest and reequipping.

The concept of physical barriers is not unique to man. When a monkey climbs a tree, he is taking advantage of a natural barrier in his environment, which provides a form of physical security. While in the tree, he is out of danger from the carnivores that prowl the jungle floor, though not completely safe from attack by other natural enemies.

Man has used barriers to enhance physical security throughout his history. When his earliest forebears started down the path that forever separated him from the lesser bipeds, he took with him the instinctive need for physical security in its most primitive form—the cave and the tree. Certainly, the need for some edge in the game of survival was crucial to man's continued existence. He could not outrun the saber-toothed tiger and giant wolf; he had no protective shell like that of the giant tortoise; he could not intimidate his enemies by sheer size as could the mastodon; and his reproductive capacity was limited. Only by using the security provided by climbing the nearest tree or taking shelter in a handy cave was man allowed the necessary time to continue his progress along the evolutionary path.

As prehistoric man's intelligence increased over the centuries, he was able to see and understand that certain changes and improvements could be made to the natural shelter available. There was not much that he could do to a tree, but by dragging rocks, boulders, and fallen trees across the mouth of his cave, he could erect rudimentary walls and fences, physical barriers that enhanced the natural protection. The eventual addition of animal skins to cover the openings in his cave dwellings was another sign of the march toward civilization and was another component in the physical security envelope he was developing.

DOORS

The modern equivalent to the caveman's animal skin is the door. The function of a door in physical security is to provide a barrier at a point of entry or exit. The function of a door in maximum security is still to provide such a barrier, however, the barrier must also be impenetrable by ordinary means, and offer the maximum delay time before penetration by extraordinary means (i.e., by the use of cutting tools, hand-carried tools, and some explosives).

During construction of a maximum-security facility, it is necessary to define the function of all doors and their relationship to the total protection system. When an existing door is evaluated, the function must again be defined and must include the area or material protected.

It is not necessary to make all doors maximum security, only those that are essential to the effective functioning of the total security system. Once a particular door is designated to be incorporated into the overall system, it must be upgraded to provide maximum security. There are two options in this respect: one can replace the door with a commercially available, penetration-resistant model, or upgrade it to provide the necessary resistance. Obvious areas of concern when dealing with maximum-security doors are door hinges and hardware. This chapter discusses hinges and other door hardware, and locks and locking mechanisms are covered in detail in the next chapter.

Personnel Doors

The average industrial personnel door is a hollow steel composite door with 18-gauge metal facing. It is usually hung on butt hinges with nonremovable pins, and may open in either direction. It may have ventilation louvers or glass panels. According to the *Barrier Penetration Database*,[1] the hollow steel door can be penetrated in one minute or less by various methods, including:

1.   Defeat of the locking mechanism, if a knob is accessible, by using a half-pound pipe wrench to break it (0.4 ± 0.08 minutes)

2. Prying the door open using a 15-pound pry bar (0.2 ± 0.04 minutes)
3. Penetration using a 10-pound fire axe (3.8 ± 0.08 minutes)

Hollow steel doors can be made more penetration-resistant by a variety of methods:

1. Bolting or welding a steel plate to the inside and/or outside of the door (especially if louvers or glass are present)
2. Installation of several dead bolts that go into all four sides of the door frame[2]
3. After removing the metal back, welding quarter-inch steel louvers on the inside of the front panel of the door, three to four inches apart from top to bottom and replacing the back door panel (Figure 2–1)
4. Replacing hardware with more penetration-resistant types or upgrading existing hardware[3]

By upgrading the hollow steel door, additional weight is added and will be a consideration when evaluating hinges and hardware. In most cases, hinges will have to be reinforced to compensate for the added weight.

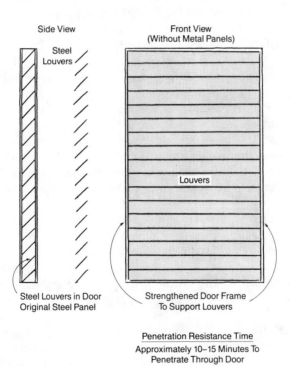

Figure 2-1 Hardened door. (U.S. Army Material Systems Analysis Activity.)

Substantial steel doors or security-class doors are commercially available and are made of three-quarter-inch steel on one side and eighth-inch steel on the other, and filled with 3 inches of fiberglass or similar material. Ten pounds of bulk explosives take 1.5 ± 0.3 minutes to penetrate this type of door.[4]

In addition to the door-hardening techniques mentioned above, there are ready-made security panels that have been marketed under the name DELIGNIT® by Blomberger Holzindustrie of Blomberg, West Germany. This product is highly tempered plate material consisting mainly of hardwood veneers (primarily beech) cross-laminated and bonded under pressure with phenolic resins. The material is available in thicknesses of 20, 30, 40 and 50mm in a variety of standard sizes, as well as specially ordered sizes and thicknesses, and is suitable for construction of bullet-resistant and burglar-impeding doors, partition walls, and so on.

Tests conducted by official agencies in West Germany and in Britain indicate successful resistance of a sample 30-mm panel to a limited variety of small-arms fire up to and including .357-caliber magnum and 12-gauge shotgun. In addition, a test was conducted wherein two 30-mm sections of DELIGNIT® panel were spaced 150mm apart and subjected to fire from a military rifle firing the 7.62 NATO standard round. The result of a series of five shots was that no bullet penetrated the inner of the two panels.

While the manufacturer does not provide a finished door, it can provide the names of door fabricators who have had experience with their material. The manufacturer claims it can be worked by any carpentry shop equipped to handle hardwood veneers, although use of carbide-tipped cutting tools is recommended.

Frames for maximum-security doors should be anchored to the wall in such a manner that penetration resistance is at least equal to that of the door itself. If at all possible, hinges should be inaccessible from the side of the door that would face the likely threat. As an alternative, individual hinges should be case-hardened or replaced with a heavy-duty, case-hardened piano hinge and the hinge pins made unremovable by welding or pinning (Figure 2–2).

Additionally, some consideration should be given to installing quarter-inch steel plate over exposed hinges, which will offer an additional barrier to cutting and require somewhat more explosives to defeat. Another way to increase the resistance of hinges is to mortise them into the door jamb and door, thus exposing little if any of the hinge pin. The installation of a piano hinge on the outside of the door and jamb would provide a barrier to the support hinges.

A simple yet effective application of the dead bolt principle previously mentioned is to install half-inch steel rods, equidistant between support hinges, on the inside of the door. On the inside door jamb, install a quarter-inch steel plate that has been drilled to accept the rod. If the hinges are defeated, the arms will continue to hold the door secure.

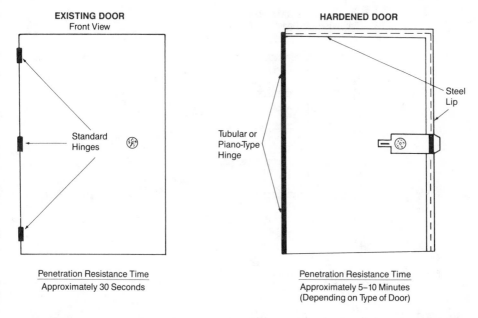

Figure 2-2 Hardening door jamb seam, hinges, and locking devices. (U.S. Army Material System Analysis Activity.)

An existing security-class door can be hardened to increase penetration time from 1 to 2 minutes to 20 to 30 minutes by "welding heavy angle iron or small structural I-beam to form a 14 inch or smaller grid on the inside of the front door panel (without interfering with the locking mechanism)"[5] (Figure 2–3).

No high-security door should have its hardware and hinges accessible from the side from which a threat is likely. Doors should open toward the likely threat direction.

In addition to the solid maximum-security doors discussed thus far, several companies make turnstile-type doors. These are useful for controlling access, however, they have no use as high-security barriers.

Retrofit Upgrading Existing Doors

In situations where it is desired to harden an existing door against tool attack, the customary practice is to clad the attack side with heavy-gauge sheet metal or steel plate. This solution has as its principal merit the fact that it can be implemented quickly with materials that can be purchased locally. Cladding should be applied only to solid or laminated wood or to substantial hollow metal doors. The thinnest recommended cladding material is 12-gauge steel sheet. It must be securely fastened to the door by using carriage bolts with

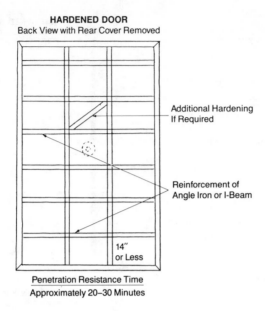

Figure 2-3   Hardening fire-class or improving security-class doors. (U.S. Army Material System Analysis Activity.)

the nuts applied from the protected side. The nuts should be tack-welded to the bolts to prevent removal or, alternatively, the ends of the bolts can be peened to serve the same function. Bolts should be not less than 5/16 inch in diameter and should be spaced from 6 to 10 inches apart and as close to the edge as the door frame will allow, preferably not more than 1 or 2 inches. If the cladding is applied to an outward-opening door, it will probably be necessary to provide protection to the free edge of the cladding to prevent its being pried up and peeled off the substrate. This can be accomplished by forming the sheet metal cover so that it wraps around the door edges, or it may be practical to build up the outside face of the door frame with a steel guard that will deny access to the edge of the cladding. Experiments were conducted at the Navy Construction Battalion Civil Engineering Laboratory[6] in the use of 9-gauge low-alloy, high-strength steel sheet and three-quarter inch plywood to build up a laminated veneer for retrofit hardening. They showed that a two-inch laminated panel consisting of exterior steel layers, one central steel layer, and two plywood layers (S-P-S-P-S) was found to have the added merit of stopping all calibers of pistol fire and high-powered rifle fire up to and including .30-06 military ball rounds. A door constructed by this system would have the merits of both attack and bullet resistance.

With retrofit cladding, it is necessary to take into account the effects of the door fit due to the additional thickness and the problem of additional weight. To install this heavy door it is necessary to provide for mounting with heavy-duty hinges and protect against hinge-pin removal and hinge destruction if resistance against attack is to be accomplished.

The door recommended for this application is a hollow door with a skin of 12-gauge cold-rolled steel reinforced by internal channel stiffeners of 22-gauge or thicker steel. The hollow spaces between the stiffeners may be filled with suitable material as needed for thermal insulation.

Door Frames

The high-security door system will not present full resistance to attack and penetration unless the frame is hardened to a level similar to that of the door itself. Similarly, the attack resistance of the frame means little without commensurate strength of its attachment to the surrounding wall and the door. In fact, to be effective the doors, frames, and wall attachments must be designed as attack-resistant assemblies.

The frame should be fabricated of 16-gauge or thicker steel. To strengthen and support it against being spread apart or crushed by hydraulic jacks or other tools, the frame (jambs and head) must be filled with a suitable cement grouting, and bonded to and backed by the wall structure surrounding the door system.

Hinge Vulnerability and Common Countermeasures

Door installations in which the hinges are located on the exterior side of the frames are vulnerable to unauthorized entry through attack on the hinges. It is frequently possible to use a drift punch and hammer to drive out the hinge pin and then open the door from the hinge side. Alternatively, the hinge knuckle can be cut off with a hacksaw, cold chisel, or torch, and entry then made.

The most common countermeasures to that threat are to inhibit or prevent the removal of the hinge pins. This is most frequently done by peening over or tack-welding the ends of the pins. Another approach is to install a set screw in the knuckle so that it locks the pin in place. Peened and welded hinge pins can be freed by filing off their ends and then driving them out. Set screws are seldom effective in resisting an attack with a drift pin and hammer. Still another technique is the use of a continuously interlocking hinge system running the full length of the door (piano hinge).

Some manufacturers make hinges in which the knuckles completely cover the ends of the hinge pins and thus prevent their being driven out with a drift pin. Regardless of how the pin is protected, if the knuckle is exposed on the outside, it is generally possible to saw off or otherwise remove and/or destroy the assembly and thus gain entry by prying open the door from the hinge side.

Door and Frame Interlocking

Various countermeasures have been used to prevent entry through destruction or removal of the hinge pin and/or knuckle assembly. The most common of these is to install a substantial protruding steel dowel pin in the hinge edge of the door or frame and a mating socket or hole in the frame or door so that the pin engages in the socket when the door is closed (see Figure 2–6). In this manner the door and frame are interlocked automatically whenever closed and the removal of the hinge will not allow opening of the hinge side. Using this basic approach, one can devise a variety of pin-in-socket, tongue-in-groove, or other similar devices to provide interlocking on the hinge side of the door. In the case of large fabricated steel doors, it is simple to orient the channel-iron-framing member (on the hinge side) so that it creates a cavity (groove) into which a corresponding angle iron (tongue), which is welded to the door frame, can engage. In view of the relatively simple nature of the design and installation of positive interlocking hardware (i.e., internal steel dowel pin-in-socket or tongue-in-groove) for coupling the hinge sides of the door to the frame, it is recommended that this practice be used wherever highly valuable, critical, or sensitive assets are secured. The following is quoted from the Sandia Laboratories' *Barrier Technology Handbook*[7]:

> Doors, due to their functional requirements and associated hardware, impose design restrictions and are, in many cases, one of the weakest links in a structure. For barrier purposes, the principle of balanced design requires that doors with associated frames, hinges, bolts and locking mechanisms be strengthened to afford the same penetration delay as is provided by the floors, walls, and ceilings of the parent structure. Conversely, if the door structure cannot be enhanced, it may not be cost effective to upgrade the existing structure. No currently available standard or commercial doors or hardware provide significant resistance against determined adversaries.

Hinges Appropriate for Door Weight

In designing the hinge system, the weight of the door must be considered. For example, a door designed for resistance against tool attack only might weigh 10 to 15 pounds per square foot, and could be hung on butt hinges, particularly if the door is used infrequently.

Vehicle Doors

The standard security vehicle overhead door found in many facilities is usually of the corrugated steel, roll-up variety. These doors are ordinarily constructed of 16-gauge steel with a stiffness required to withstand 20 pounds per square foot of wind pressure and can be easily penetrated. Using a 6-foot pry bar and a 2×4 plank weighing 20 to 25 pounds, penetration time is 0.8 ± 0.2 minutes. Hardening this type of door is difficult; therefore its use in a maximum-security environment should be kept to a minimum. Specifically designed vehicle doors are usually constructed of at least quarter-inch steel plate and are more penetration resistant.[8] Table 2–1 shows estimated penetration times for standard vehicle doors. Corrugated roll-up and hollow steel panel doors offer little resistance to explosive attack; delay time is governed by the set-up, retreat, return, and crawl-through times. Thermal cutting by torch or oxy-lance (burn bar) affords the same delay as for a personnel door. The material thickness of the panel door requires more time than does the corrugated door material.[9]

Hand-carried tools, for example, jimmy bars and axes, can be used to penetrate a vehicle door. A vehicle itself may be used to effect penetration quickly when the noise associated with such an attack is not a major consideration. Where there is any large door opening, the threat of vehicular attack is always present.

Certain techniques exist for hardening and thus upgrading vehicle doors. Rubber tires could be installed directly behind the outer vehicular door (with a portion below ground level) for greater penetration resistance, or a door clad with sheet metal could be used to resist vehicular penetration. Redwood could be inserted into a panel door to increase resistance to penetration by thermal tools. In this case, however, increased weight necessitates the use of correspondingly upgraded hardware, which, as an added benefit, enhances protection of the door against tool and vehicular attack. Alternately laid steel channels welded together and covered by sheet metal could be used as a door and could provide significant penetration resistance.[10]

Where lateral wall space is not a consideration, the use of a manual or mechanically actuated sliding door should be considered. The door should be constructed (or hardened) to the same standards and by the same methods as specified for personnel doors. In addition, the top runner track must be reinforced and a substantial and well-anchored channel must be provided for the bottom of the door to travel in.

The sliding door presents definite security advantages over those offered by the corrugated steel roll-up door. For example, the structural steel members

Table 2-1   Estimated Penetration Times for Standard Vehicle Doors

Barrier	Countermeasure	Countermeasure Weight (pounds)	Penetration Time (min)
Corrugated steel	Jet Axe, JA-I	20	0.8 ± 0.2
	Pry bar and 2 × 4 plank	23	0.9 ± 0.2
Hollow steel	Pry bar	15	0.2 ± 0.4
	Fire axe	10	3.8 ± 0.8
	Bulk explosives	10	About 1

U.S. Nuclear Regulatory Commission.

needed to support a roll-up door adequately are of greater bulk and complexity than those required by the sliding door. The joints necessary in the corrugated steel roll-up door present a weakness in overall structure and are vulnerable to attack. By its very nature, the sliding door is a single, solid entity. Because of its method of mounting, it is almost impervious to forced entry by use of a pry bar, especially when the top track rail is hardened.

Aside from being rammed with a vehicle, the main vulnerability of the sliding door would be to prying against its opening edge. This method of attack can be forestalled by installation of several manually activated drop-pins similar to the familiar barrel bolt, although of much larger and sturdier construction. These drop into receiver holes drilled into the inner rail of the bottom track or into the floor. An intruder attempting to cut through these drop-pins would have to make a lateral cut the entire width of the door (unless he was able to determine the approximate location of the pins by either spotting the heads of their mounting bolts that protrude through to the outer door surface, or by simply estimating that the pins have been situated on and equidistant from the door's center line). To prevent this, drop-pins must remain undetectable from the outside of the door and they should be spaced at random intervals along the lower door. While the upper track anchoring points would ordinarily be subject to tool attack, their protection by a steel plate or apron on the outside, or attack side of the door, would discourage anyone concerned with effecting a stealthy entry.

The third type of vehicle door that may be encountered in a high-security installation is very similar to that used in the average homeowner's garage. This consists of a series of rigid panels that are joined together along their horizontal edges by hinges so that when the door is raised, it rolls up along a track and usually stores itself under spring tension, parallel to, but approximately eight feet off the floor. There is similarity between these doors only in a generic sense. The home garage door usually has panels constructed of tempered Masonite® or similar product set into wooden framing, with each panel joined to those adjacent by three hinges and usually with a series of glass panes replacing one of the lateral panels. This door can be defeated with nothing more sophisticated than a rock or a shoe. Even without the glass, the panels can be quickly broken out of their support framing.

The high-security articulated vehicle door, however, is usually constructed of panels composed of a corrugated metal stiffener sandwiched between aluminum plate or special steel alloy panels. The hinges are often of the continuous or piano-type and the track has been reinforced to resist external force and to carry the door's extra weight when in the retracted or stored position. As previously stated, however, this type of door is susceptible to vehicle attack or forced entry by lifting with a pry bar.

Vault Doors

By their purely functional design and often massive construction, vault doors serve instantly to discourage attempts at forced entry by all but the most determined adversaries. This is probably the ultimate application of the psychology of maximum security as a deterrent. Prior to opting for the construction of a vault, however, careful consideration must be given to the following questions that are (or certainly should be) of valid concern:

1. What is the expected maximum period that vault protection will be required?
2. Are there federal, state or local governmental regulations that require vault protection of these assets?
3. Are the assets being protected of a size and configuration that would make their unauthorized removal extremely difficult without the use of heavy or special equipment not generally available in the area?
4. Can the assets being protected be rendered unusable by removal of key components? (Separate storage of these components would be required, however, the size of the resultant security system could be reduced with appropriate corresponding dollar savings.)
5. Will movement of the assets being protected be kept to a minimum?
6. Are there large numbers of persons requiring daily access to these assets during the course of their duties?
7. Would theft of these assets have an adverse effect on:
    a. The company's continued ability to remain in business (a trade secret or nonpatented process, material, machine, etc.)?
    b. Health and welfare of the general public?
    c. The environment?
    d. National security?
8. Will construction of a vault lower insurance premiums?
9. Can a vault be constructed within the existing facility without extensive renovation and/or reinforcement?
10. In the event of company growth, would the present facilities be sufficient to accept this growth and provide the room for expansion, or would a move elsewhere be necessary?

Strong Room Doors

If, after considering the pros and cons of vault acquisition, it is decided that the cost of protection would be prohibitive in comparison to the benefits, serious consideration should be given to construction of a vault-type room or strong room.

A strong room is defined as an interior space enclosed by or separated from other similar spaces by walls, ceiling, and floor constructed of solid building materials, with no windows and only one entrance. Strong room doors should be of heavy-gauge metal construction or of solid hardwood reinforced with a metal plate on the inside. Door louvers and baffle plates (if used) should be reinforced with no. 9-gauge, two-inch-square wire mesh fastened on the interior side of the door. Heavy-duty hardware should be used in constructing a strong room door, and all screws, nuts, bolts, hasps, hinges, pins, and the like should be securely fastened. The door should be set into a suitable frame in the same manner as previously described for installation of personnel doors. Where air-conditioning or heating ducts pass over or through the strong room, or where sewers or tunnels may pass under this space (and they are of a size and shape large enough to accommodate a small person), they should be equipped with personnel barriers. Duct barriers should be constructed of heavy-gauge wire mesh securely fastened to the duct by welding. For sewers and utilities tunnels, effective barriers can be constructed of steel bars or rods, half-inch in diameter, extending across the width of the pipe or tunnel with a maximum spacing of six inches between the bars. The ends of these bars or rods should be firmly anchored to prevent removal and, where the vertical and horizontal bars or rods meet, they should be welded together. In effect this will form a very substantial grillwork that cannot be easily defeated.

Emergency Doors

While some may argue that emergency doors have no place in a maximum-security setting, their use is mandated most of the time. If a facility is of a certain size and/or employs a certain number of people, it must by statute provide a specific number of emergency exits. In the maximum-security environment these should be kept to the minimum required by law. Their number and location depends on many variables such as the type of work being performed in the building, the work space configuration (or partitioning) within the building, and so on. To ensure that emergency exits do not diminish the effectiveness of the maximum-security measures in place, the following questions must be answered:

1. Where are the emergency exits located with respect to the assets being protected?
2. What type of emergency exit door (including hinges, locking mechanism, frame, anchoring, etc.) will be installed?
3. Into what areas will the emergency exits allow personnel to pass?
4. Will the doors be alarmed?

If particularly valuable or strategic material is processed or ordinarily handled near an emergency exit, the possibility of a diversion of this material through the door is very real. It would be relatively easy for a dishonest employee to hide quantities of the material on his person during an emergency evacuation or drill and cache it outside the facility for later retrieval. The possibility must be considered.

There are no hard and fast rules relative to the construction of emergency doors and hinges and methods of mounting. The obvious choice would be doors, hinges, and frames of construction and quality equal to the other security doors in use at a facility. It naturally follows that if a high-security door is procured, the method of mounting should not negate the money spent on its purchase. The only element of an emergency exit over which there is little if any control is its locking mechanism. Most ordinances covering the use of emergency exits and devices are fairly specific in requiring the use of a panic bar locking mechanism. The type of panic bar usually encountered on emergency exit doors is most susceptible to defeat by an adversary using a simple wire hook or coat hanger. In order to maintain security of the exit, some people have chained or otherwise locked (from both sides) emergency exits. This can have disastrous consequences such as those experienced during the fire at the Coconut Grove nightclub in Boston, where nearly 500 lives were lost because the exit doors were locked.

Methods are available, however, to ensure that exit doors keep people out and also allow the safe exit of those inside. One system provides overlapping sections fastened to stiles that meet and overlap when the door closes. The stiles close the gaps around the door so that prying tools cannot be forced through to trip the panic bar. None of the equipment is exposed, so would-be intruders are not able to push it out of the way. When the panic bar is depressed, however, the barrier springs free and the door opens easily. As added security, the hinges are tamper-resistant, which makes defeat by removing them quite difficult.

Another type of panic-bar emergency device eliminates the bar that can be easily tripped and replaces it with a rim device that is not as likely to be snagged by a coat hanger.

At most facilities, emergency exits allow personnel to exit into parking lots, alleyways, or city streets. When evacuation is necessary, however, people should be channeled by physical barriers to a central assembly area that is under the control of the security department. Personnel should not be allowed to exit into a parking lot, alley, or street. To allow this could facilitate employee theft or diversion of the assets being protected, or could lead to a breach in the security system by an insider who would allow accomplices to enter the facility and plunder it. In addition to employing physical barriers to move evacuating employees to a controlled safe area, the security department should be organized to provide some sort of monitoring of the evacuation process and routes to ensure that stolen or diverted material is not passed through or thrown over a fence to an accomplice or for later retrieval.

Alarming of emergency exit doors should be mandatory. Not only should the door have a locally annunciating alarm, but it must be tied into the facility's central alarm station. In this way, each of the alarm systems serves to back up the other. To ensure positive performance, these alarm systems must be periodically checked. It is suggested that a check at least twice a day of both systems be implemented. In addition, each emergency exit door should have a tamper-indicating seal (or seals) affixed (Figure 2–4) and these should be checked each time the alarm system is checked.

ROOFS

In arriving at a design for a maximum-security roof (or ceiling), the most obvious and simplest solution would appear to be to use the same specifications and technology employed in construction of the high-security walls in this space or building. There are, however, considerations that must be made that are not instrumental in wall design.

1. How much loading will this roof or ceiling be subjected to?
2. If this is a ceiling in a multistory facility, will the space directly above the protected area be covered by a trained suitably equipped member of the security force or by a sophisticated alarm system that annunciates locally and at a remote monitoring station that is manned around the clock?
3. Will the integrity of the roof or ceiling be broken by piping, ductwork, or access hatches?
4. Will any portion of the roof be accessible from outside the protected area, or conversely, grant access outside the protected area from inside it?
5. Will the roof or ceiling be alarmed; monitored by security officers or CCTV; equipped with adequate lighting to permit proper assessment; not provide places of concealment for intruders such as air-conditioning units, exhaust fan hoods, charlie nobles (smoke pipes), etc.?

These and many more site-specific questions must be worked out between the building architect or room designer and the person responsible for

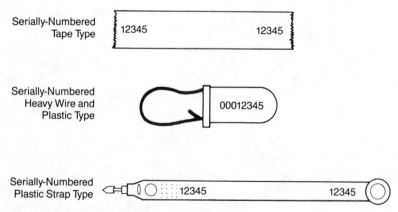

Figure 2-4 Tamper-indicating door seals.

ensuring that the degree of security necessary will be provided. Officials involved in the preliminary planning stages of the construction of a new facility or upgrading of an existing one into the maximum-security class must include the company security director. This individual should be prepared to discuss these matters with his staff and obtain the input of the personnel who will have the day-to-day responsibility for being sure that the system works. If the facility is part of a corporation that may have installations of this type in other locations, a visit to one or more of these sites by the security staff would pay handsome dividends in avoiding mistakes that may be plagueing others. Careful and imaginative planning will eliminate costly (and embarrassing) oversights that may require considerable time, effort, and expense to rectify.

The prime requisite of any roof in a maximum-security setting is its ability to withstand or defeat attempts at forced entry. The roof most commonly selected is usually constructed of poured concrete, approximately $5\frac{1}{2}$ inches thick with steel reinforcing rods on 8×12-inch centers embedded in the center of the concrete slab. In tests of resistance to forced entry, it was found that 4 pounds of bulk explosives and 20-pound bolt cutters required only 2.8 ± 0.4 minutes to effect penetration.[11] Another type of roof construction often found in industry and government buildings consists of 16-gauge sheet metal placed on ribbed steel decking, covered by 2 inches of insulation followed by a final covering of a half-inch of asphalt and gravel. Using a 10-pound fire axe and a five-pound shovel, penetration was achieved in 2.3 ± 0.7 minutes. In a test of this same type of roof construction, 20 pounds of Jet-Axe JA-I charge and equipment effect penetration in 0.8 ± 0.2 minutes.[12] The conclusion reached in the study from which these results are drawn is that while there are quite a few variations in the types of materials and the manner in which they may be assembled, they can all be defeated in about a minute with a few pounds of appropriate explosive. The obvious answer therefore, is to construct the best roof possible, but to prevent anyone from reaching it by establishing a protected area around the building, then providing adequate assessment capabilities, alarms, and the like to detect anyone who may have managed to penetrate the protected area.

If the construction of a strong room is being considered within an existing maximum-security setting, there are several combinations of commonly available materials from which to fabricate a homogeneous roof or ceiling that will provide significant resistance to forcible entry.

The creation of this roof or ceiling is well within the capabilities of any commercial carpenter with an assist from a sheet metal shop. In tests conducted by the Civil Engineering Laboratory of the Navy Construction Battalion Center, the best composite material consisted of 0.10-inch sheets of 6061-T6 aluminum over half-inch plywood on both sides of an 18-gauge 304 stainless steel sheet. In laboratory tests[13] a panel constructed in this manner was subjected to attack by a $7\frac{1}{4}$-inch circular saw equipped with a metal cutting blade and an oxyactelylene torch; the average rate of linear progression was

3.06 inches per minute. Switching over to the circular saw with metal cutting blade, 22 seconds passed without complete penetration. In all cases, large quantities of smoke were generated, as the saw blades and stainless steel sheet became extremely hot. Subsequent tests indicated that an abrasive blade on the saw was ineffective.

To defeat attempts simply to disassemble the roof when the composite is assembled into standard-sized panels and then used as conventional building materials, the substrate should be laid in a random pattern to avoid the neat layering of edges through all the various materials. The components can be bonded together through the use of nuts and bolts, screws, tempered screw-nails, or ringed nails; however, the nuts and bolts should be peened to prevent removal and the heads of the screws should be ground for the same purpose. Although it would be possible for someone to shear off the nail heads, the holding action of the nail shanks would still present a formidable task to anyone inclined to attempt to peel the roof. If this type of composite is used, it must be remembered that it would be covered by insulation and probably several different layers of weatherproof roofing. This additional material would add substantially to the penetration resistance of such a roof. Its use is not recommended, however, in the construction of a roof that is not alarmed, not easily visible to the guard force or well lighted, or that is close to or part of the protected area perimeter. As previously indicated, this material would be suitable inside an already protected installation, or could be used in small low buildings located well within a protected area.

Upgrading Existing Roofs

When the company security department is faced with the task of upgrading an in-place facility, the task becomes many times harder. The installation of alarms, lights, doors, walls, gates, and many other security responsibilities must be considered.

Before upgrading the roof of an existing facility, the security director must climb up there and have a first-hand look for himself. What does he see? Are there fire escapes that allow access to the roof? Are there roof hatches, skylights, ducts, piping, air-conditioning units, strong and firmly attached downspouts, coamings (which could anchor a grappling hook)?

Once he has made an assessment of the roof's liabilities, he must consult the individual responsible for maintaining plant services (usually the chief of maintenance or of the physical plant), and ascertain which of these potential access points are essential to plant operations. If the plant site is an old building, it will often be found that many of these potential problems can be eliminated as the elements are nonfunctional, having been replaced by more modern equipment but remaining in place simply because they plug a hole that would be left in the roof by their removal. Once a decision is made as to which of these appurtenances can be removed, the subsequent hole should be rehabilitated so that the physical integrity and strength of the repair is not less than that of any other part of the original and undamaged roof structure.

Low, flat roofs that might be susceptible to scaling through use of a grappling hook should have shielding installed behind the coaming to prevent the hook from finding a secure anchoring point. This need not be anything more exotic than panels of heavy-gauge sheet metal. These can be anchored to the lip of the coaming and roof and angled back toward the roof to form an inclined plane up which the hook will ride, right back over the edge (Figure 2–5).

Another possibility that may be worthy of consideration, especially for facilities situated in remote areas, would be attack by helicopter. If the roof of the main building, or the building that would be the attackers' objective, is flat and thus suitable for landing a helicopter, or even if it is not flat but is suitable for landing an attack force from a hovering helicopter, consideration should be given to installation of one or more tall lightweight metal light poles to the roof. These will prevent the helicopter from landing or coming close enough to the roof to discharge personnel. These poles could also support area floodlights that would light the protected area and rooftop. In addition, flagpoles, radio communications antennas, tall chimneys and exhaust stacks, or guy wires serve to prevent attack by such a strategem.

FLOORS

In most buildings, the floor is probably the least thought of part of the total security package. It exists for the purpose of providing a smooth dry working surface and as a base on which the building may be erected floor by floor. True? Ordinarily, this would be a good thumbnail description of the purposes

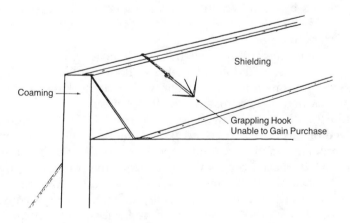

Figure 2-5   Grappling hook shielding.

of flooring, however, in a maximum-security installation, the same amount of thought that has been devoted to design of the walls and roof must be alloted to the floor. A typical floor is usually constructed of poured concrete, 6 to 8 inches thick, reinforced with rebar steel rods or 6-inch square mesh of no. 10 wire. Floors constructed in this manner are adequate for most facilities, however, the average penetration times by one or two adversaries using explosives, sledgehammers, and bolt cutters in any combination averages two to four minutes.[14]

This penetration time does not take into account the time spent in arriving at the site, setting up for the penetration, retreat time (if explosives are to be used), and crawl-through. If the target is located in a multistory building, the attempted penetration may come from above or below, and therefore the floor in the space above the target site must provide an amount of resistance equivalent to that of the other security features.

How can existing floors similar to what is described be afforded an additional measure of penetration resistance? The most obvious answer would be to increase the floor's thickness by adding additional layers of rebar, reinforcing wire, and poured concrete. This simplistic solution should not be implemented lightly, as the addition of what may amount to quite a number of tons of weight to a structure that was not originally designed for this additional weight could present a very real personnel safety hazard. If this is the only feasible solution, a competent engineering firm should analyze the situation and design the necessary additional supporting columns or beams to ensure an adequate margin of safety.

If the cost of accomplishing a complicated building redesign and renovation as briefly described above is not possible, an alternative may be to relocate the objective to a ground floor or perhaps even into a below-ground location. If the target is relocated to ground level, it should be placed away from exterior walls, preferably toward the center of the structure with several intervening walls between it and any exterior wall (that is, layered; see Figure 1–2). If there is a basement or utility space under the site selected for relocation, it should be sealed off or provided with sophisticated alarms to preclude entry from that point.

An interesting method of tremendously increasing the penetration resistance of a wall that would be adaptable to floors (and ceilings) would be to anchor steel I-beams into the concrete walls, interlocking as many additional beams as necessary across the width of the floor (or ceiling). These beams could then be covered with a simple overlaid wooden floor, which could be tiled or carpeted as required. The accompanying illustration shows how this hardening method would appear in cross-section (Figure 2–6).[15] Properly installed, these I-beams would increase the penetration resistance time to approximately two to four hours. The additional weight, however, restricts the use of such a hardening or protection method to new construction or to a facility in which the proper steps have been taken to ensure the total system has been properly engineered.

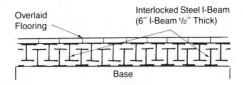

Figure 2-6 I-beam application to floors. (U.S. Army Material System Analysis Activity.)

FENCES

Fences are used to:

1. Define a particular area
2. Preclude inadvertant or accidental entry into the area
3. Prevent or delay unauthorized entry
4. Control (or channel) pedestrian and vehicular traffic

In a maximum security-setting, fences are not the ideal barrier (Table 2–2); walls of solid construction should be used for the purposes described above. It is recognized, however, that walls are an often undesirable or impractical, and fences are the most viable alternative.

The type of fence used in a maximum-security setting should be chosen after careful analysis of many factors. Based on determination of the objectives it will serve, additional questions should be answered:

1. Will one fence be enough, or will two or more in a series be required?
2. Will there be vehicle barriers in conjunction with the fence?
3. How far will the fence be from the area of chief concern?
4. What will be the closest area of concealment to the fence?
5. Will the fence be alarmed?

Environmental conditions will certainly affect the design of a fence system and should be considered; for example:

1. Will erosion under the fence be a problem?
2. Will corrosion of the fence be a problem?
3. What natural features or vegetation around the fence might interfere with detection or assessment of activity in the area?

Selection of the kind of fence will not stop at a choice of fabric; decisions must be made as to height, the means of anchoring the posts and bottom, and the type of topping. If two or more fences are to be installed, what, if anything, will be placed between them, and what will be the distance between

Table 2-2 Penetration Aids

Item	Description	How Used
Canvas sheet	6' × 8' folded sheet	Thrown over top of fence to aid climbing
Cutters	Bolt cutters, wire cutters, tin snips	To cut fence fabric, barbed wire, or tape
Steps	18" iron rods bent into step form	Hooked into fence fabric and used as climbing aids
Wire hooks	6" to 12" lengths of stiff wire bent into hooks	Hold barbed tape to fence to aid climbing
Long hooks	3" rods bent into hooks	Pull down barbed tape toppings to aid climbing
Ladder	7' step ladder	To jump over fence
Extension ladder	20' ladder hinged in the middle to form an A	To cross over combination barbed tape-fence barriers
Pry bar	10' 2 × 4 or piece of 2" pipe	Lift fence fabric to aid crawling underneath fence
Plywood	4' × 8' sheet of ⅜" plywood	Put over barbed tape to aid crossing
Carpet	4' × 15' heavy carpet rolled up on a 5' 4 × 4	Throw over fence to aid climbing
Plank	Two 8' 2 × 2 planks with a nail in one end	To lift carpet roll over fence

U.S. Department of Commerce, National Bureau of Standards.

them? Finally, considering the kinds of tools likely to be required for penetration, what will be the total penetration time for all fences and obstacles? Once these questions are answered, planning can commence. The type most frequently encountered is no. 11 American wire gauge or heavier, with 2 inch mesh openings, 7 feet in height, topped by three strands of barbed wire or tape evenly spaced 6 inches apart and angled outward 30 to 45 degrees from the vertical.

This type of fence can be breached in 4.3 ± 0.3 seconds using no material aids, but with the assistance of one person not crossing.[16] To increase the penetration time of this fence to 8.4 ± 1 second, it is necessary to install V-shaped overhangs with concertina barbed wire or tape inside the V.[17] The types of fences described can be driven through in a light pickup truck in 2 ± 1 seconds with no significant damage to the truck.[18]

Less frequently encountered fences include the V-fence, which consists of 3-inch posts set at an angle of 60 degrees in 30-inch diameter by 24-inch high concrete footings 12 inches below grade. The posts are in 10-foot centers and staggered 5 feet front to back. The chain link mesh is 10 feet high with a cable installed at the top. Corrugated steel sheet is placed on the outside posts to prevent crawling under. Nine rolls of GPBTO (general-purpose barbed tape obstacle) are used inside the V to delay crawl-through.

All rolls are secured to the chain link mesh with wire ties. Cutting through this fence takes about four minutes. Climb-over takes only 40 seconds, using ladders and bridges as breaching aids.[19] This same fence can be equipped with razor ribbon instead of GPBTO, with a second sheet of corrugated steel attached to the inside posts to form a V-shaped trough filled with 2- to 5-inch rocks and 9-inch diameter telephone poles, and with six rolls of barbed tape concertina. Thus outfitted, it offers penetration resistance of 10 minutes for digging and crawling under. Climb-over times are similar to those of the V-fence previously described. While personnel penetration cannot be prevented, breaching by a vehicle is almost impossible for the latter type of V-fence.[20]

Regardless of how elaborate fences may be, they still offer only a modicum of security. Fences are necessary, but investments in this area should be kept to a minimum as the money can be better used on other components of the total system.

In a maximum-security environment, there are certain things that must be kept in mind regarding the use of fences. Height should be a preliminary consideration. The higher the fence, the better the chances of defeating a climb-over by personnel using most simple breaching aids. Whenever a fence is used in a maximum-security system, the method of anchoring it is very important. No matter how sophisticated the fence may be, if the fabric can be pried up from ground level using a 2 × 4 or similar breaching aid, it is nearly useless. "The time required to go under a fence is only slightly longer than the time required to climb a fence without a barbed tape topping but is significantly shorter than the time required to climb a fence with a barbed tape topping when only limited aids are used."[21]

Penetration time can be doubled by the addition of a bottom rail (Figure 2–7).[22] Many fences are constructed so that the bottom of the fabric either touches the ground or is no more than two inches above grade level. Without some method of anchoring this fabric, crawl-under is quite simple. If cost is no obstacle, burying the lower portion of the fabric (about three to six inches) in concrete would virtually preclude crawl-under. Another alternative would be to anchor the bottom of the fence fabric with 3-inch reinforcing rods to precast concrete sills that are $8\frac{1}{2}$ feet long, 10 inches high, and 3 inches wide. Each sill is buried under the fence fabric, between posts, with three inches of sill above ground and the reinforcing rods from the sill bent around the fence fabric. This method is effective in that it takes less time to cut through or climb over the fence than it does to separate the fabric from the reinforcing rods.[23]

Topping a fence with barbed wire or tape is another consideration. The U.S. Nuclear Regulatory Commission (NRC) requires protected area fences to be topped with at least three strands of barbed wire, angled outward at a 30- to 45-degree angle. As previously mentioned, this particular topping does very little to preclude climb-overs. A somewhat better topping is GPBTO, often called razor ribbon. It is intimidating in appearance and thus offers a psychological deterrent to less than determined adversaries. In actuality,

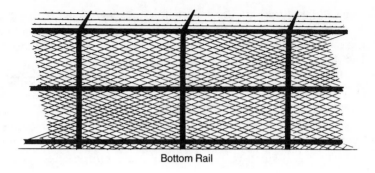

Bottom Rail

Figure 2-7   Bottom fence rail.

however, the use of breaching aids generally improves penetration times for barbed-tape-topped fences. "The fastest penetration times for barbed tape-topped fences were achieved when a piece of carpeting was thrown over the fence. The carpet was made by nailing the end of 4 feet wide by 15 feet long heavy carpet to a 5 feet long 4 × 4 and then rolling the carpet around the 4 × 4."[24] Generally, the addition of any barbed wire or barbed tape topping does not significantly increase penetration resistance. If an intruder is discouraged from climbing over and crawling under, he will probably choose to go through the fence.

Cutting through the fence generally takes more time than climbing over and crawling under. Once again, the fact that the bottom portion of the fabric is securely anchored increases penetration time. If the bottom is not anchored, "it takes only a single row of approximately 12 to 15 cuts to make a man-sized opening. Anchoring the fence in concrete doubles the cutting time."[25] To double the cutting time through chain link fence, it is necessary to fasten another layer of fabric to the inside of the fence.[26]

Yet another way of increasing cut-through time would be to interlace metal or wood lattice in the fabric. This technique, however, significantly reduces visibility and should not be used when the fence is the single component of a perimeter protection system. (Fences should never be the single component of a perimeter protection system in a maximum-security environment.)

Entry and Exit Points

Entry and exit points must be considered when erecting a security fence. The first criterion should be that the integrity of all gates and doors be the same as or better than that of the fence in which they are installed. They should be kept to the minimum number necessary to maintain compliance with governmental and/or company mandates.

Gates should open out if at all possible. Many swing in and out and should be modified accordingly. They should be equipped with a jamb or frame to strengthen the integrity of the opening. The most common types are swing gates and sliding gates with variations.

Most vehicular gates have access roads aimed directly at them, thus facilitating vehicle intrusions. Penetration resistance of most fabric-type gates is equivalent to that of the fence in which they are installed. Vehicle drive-through is easier at a gate than at any other part of the fence. The use of metal doors set in jambs rather than gates offers a somewhat higher degree of penetration resistance but the cost is usually not worth it, although for emergency fence doors this should be mandatory. For any emergency door in a perimeter fence, opening should be facilitated by a panic bar on the inside. Emergency doors should be locked and the panic bars installed so that an intruder cannot use the bar to open the door from the outside. Although access controls are discussed later (Chapter 8), it should be noted that any opening of perimeter fence doors or gates should be controlled and monitored.

Another method of controlling pedestrian traffic through fences is by use of turnstile gates. Penetration time (by deactivating electrical controls or forcible entry) is approximately one minute. When installed in a common chain link fence, an adversary would probably choose to breach the fence rather than the turnstile gate.

The weak link in a gate is usually the hardware—hinges and locks. Fence gate locks should be accessible only from the inside. Built-in locks depend on fence alignment for effectiveness and should be supplemented with a piece of case-hardened or stainless steel chain and padlock. The chain should be wrapped around the fencepost and gatepost until it is as tight as possible, and padlocked; there should be no slack left in the chain. Where possible, stainless steel cable should be used, as it tends to flatten out when attacked with bolt cutters and is somewhat difficult to defeat. A bridle can be made from three-eights- to half-inch stranded stainless steel cable, looped on both ends using NiccoPress fasteners (Figure 2–8). Bridles can be used in conjunction with case-hardened padlocks for a variety of purposes.

A double-leaf swing gate should be securely anchored where both leaves meet by a solid foot bolt, several feet long, on each leaf that is dropped into a steel anchoring hole in the ground (Figure 2–9). The addition of a chain or cable and padlock will also enhance the gate's security.

Because fences are not the ideal physical barriers in a maximum-security environment, their usefulness is limited. Their primary function should be to simply define a particular area.

WALLS AND MOATS

In designing a maximum-security perimeter barrier system where cost is no object, the most penetration-resistant structure would be a thick, high wall.

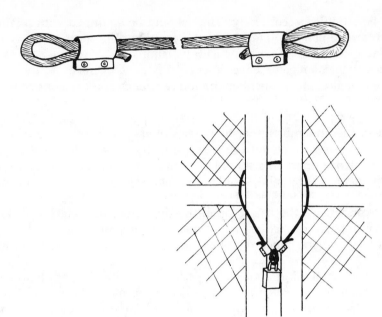

Figure 2-8 Bridle.

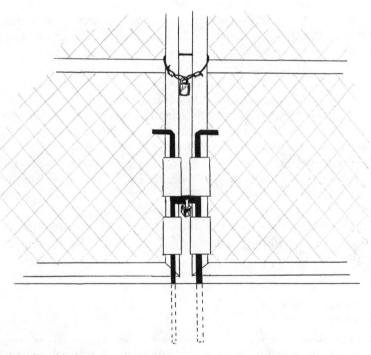

Figure 2-9 Double-leaf gate drop bolts.

Walls, however, do not allow free visual access to the area outside. A possible alternative is the modern equivalent of the medieval moat. It completely surrounds the protected area, and all entry and exit points are bridged with either fixed or movable structures. These points can be kept to the absolute minimum and controlled around the clock. They can also be equipped with methods of preventing breach by ramming with a vehicle.

The moat would be of the dry type and equipped with a suitable drainage system. It would be at least 8 feet deep and measure a minimum of 10 feet from edge to edge. To increase protection, a standard chain link fence topped with an outrigger equipped with three strands of GPBTO would be positioned at the inner edge. This would be attached in such a way that there would be little or no lip that could be used to support a ladder or serve as a working platform for someone attempting to cut through the fence fabric. The fence posts would be a minimum of three inches in diameter and concrete filled. Top rails would not be used. The strong fence posts would maintain the longitudinal rigidity required, but by omitting the top rail stiffener, a degree of instability is introduced that would increase protection by making it difficult for someone to secure a good anchor point for a bridge or from which to work to penetrate the area.

The bottom edge of the fence fabric would be embedded in the concrete at the time the moat lining is poured to prevent entry by prying up the fabric and crawling under.

The specification of moat depth and width can only be reached when integrated into the total barrier design. A minimum depth of eight feet is recommended as this would require a larger ladder to reach from the moat bottom to the top of the fence. Such a ladder would be bulky and difficult to maneuver and could not easily be hidden if it must be brought to the planned penetration site on foot. An eight-foot depth would also serve as a definite deterrent to anyone contemplating penetration by crashing through the fence with a vehicle. Any commonly available tracked vehicle, including a bulldozer, would be unable to climb out of the moat due to this depth and the 90-degree wall angle. A minimum width of 10 feet is recommended as this would preclude the use of uncomplicated bridges such as a four × eight-foot sheet of three-quarter-inch plywood. To prevent a ladder (modified by the addition of hooks or steel rods to one end) from being used as a bridge by hooking or inserting the modified end into the fence, an aluminum or galvanized steel sheet would be attached to the outside of the fence to a height of three feet. This ladder could still be used as a bridge by hooking it into the fence fabric above this plate, but the angle and the unsteadiness would provide a very unstable work platform. The easiest way to bridge this type of perimeter barrier would be with a 20-foot extension ladder modified so that the upper end has a hook attached to the end of each leg. To use, the ladder would be extended to its full height then allowed to fall across the moat so that the hooks would fall behind the top of the fence fabric. Once the hooks were in position, the ladder would form an inclined plane over which the adversaries could climb or crawl and drop to the ground inside the protected area.

This type of entry can, however, be defeated by a double moat system, which is nothing more than a second 8-foot × 10-foot (or larger) moat immediately adjacent to the first with the previously specified fence installed between on a 12 to 15-inch-thick reinforced concrete wall. The fence would be topped with a Y-type of barbed tape standoff with concertina tape installed in the center of the Y as well as on either side of the outrigger arms.

On either fence, a motion detection system would be required, as would a detection system located between 10 and 15 feet beyond and parallel to the second moat. To prevent the inadvertant entry of personnel and wildlife, an outer-perimeter chain link fence eight feet high and topped with three strands of GPBTO would be installed. Depending on the amount of property available, this fence would be located a minimum of 25 feet from the outer edge of the first moat.

In our example, cost *is not a factor*; the objective is to use fencing and other physical barriers as a first line of defense. As previously mentioned, our preference is the use of walls rather than fences.

TOPOGRAPHY

The natural deterrence offered by topography, while of often limited value, should be taken into consideration when designing or upgrading a facility to the maximum-security level. Rivers and other large bodies of water, swamps, escarpments, deserts, and so forth are all examples of natural obstacles that may be used in various ways.

Probably the most famous examples of the optimal use of natural barriers were the prisons on Alcatraz Island in California and the French penal colony on Devil's Island located off the coast of (then) French Guiana. The physical barriers used to contain the prisoners in these facilities were usually enough to discourage escape attempts. Even if they might be defeated, however, the escapee was still left with no way off the island except by whatever means his wits could devise using materials at hand or (in the case of Alcatraz) attempting to swim to freedom. It is an interesting point that although both of these prisons were in operation for many years, only a very few escapes were ever successful.

When a facility has a river or other large body of water as a boundary, the natural obstacle may be used in conjunction with more traditional fences as a deterrent. The clear view of the approach route across these areas would serve to discourage an adversary from attempting an approach from that direction, especially if after crossing, he was faced with sophisticated alarms and man-made barriers around his objective. In a remote or isolated area, a river or large body of water abutting the site could also serve as adversary approach or escape routes, thereby turning these nominal topographic barriers into liabilities against which additional protective means or procedures must be provided.

The advantage offered by a desert environment would be similar to that provided by a natural water barrier. As with water obstacles, the possibility of an unseen approach across a barren landscape would be very slim. The advantages of isolation and early detection could be outweighed by the fact that approach and/or escape might be accomplished across the very feature that seems to offer some degree of protection, from any direction.

Swamps, while not usually a consideration in a maximum-security setting, could conceivably be encountered. The principal advantage offered by marshy terrain is its impenetrability to usual forms of ground transportation. The most practical setting for a facility in a swampy area would be at the center of the swamp with only one access road. In the event of successful penetration of the facility, this access road could be blocked to contain the adversaries until outside assistance arrives at the scene.

The security offered by a deep forest should also be considered. When a facility is located in a remote area of dense forest, with very limited and controlled access routes, this remoteness serves to discourage all but the most determined adversaries. As with the natural barriers provided by swamps, forest locations would require adversaries to forego the usual methods of transportation when access routes are limited and controlled. This might mean they would have to walk in, carrying all the equipment and arms they believe necessary for the successful completion of their mission. In addition, their escape plan must be structured to require, as the last resort, escape by foot. Depending on the remoteness of the objectives, the terrain to be encountered, and the climatic conditions prevailing, these difficulties, when considered above and beyond the resistance to be expected from the on-site security personnel, could force the adversaries to choose another course of action and shift their attention to a more vulnerable target.

In summary, natural barriers may be efficiently incorporated into a total security system only when effective, round-the-clock monitoring of these approach areas by a security guard or CCTV system is provided.

NOTES

1. *Barrier Penetration Database*, Revision 1 (Upton, N.Y.: Brookhaven National Laboratory, 1978), p. 17.
2. Ibid., p. 18.
3. *Hardening Existing SSNM Storage Facilities, Preliminary Report* (Aberdeen, Md.: U.S. Army Materiel Systems Analysis Activity, 1979), p. 33.
4. *Barrier Penetration Database*, p. 18.
5. *Hardening Existing SSNM Storage Facilities*, p. 31.
6. *Technical Memorandum No. 61-78-9.* (Port Hueneme, Calif.: Civil Engineering Laboratory, Naval Construction Battalion Center).

7. *Barrier Technology Handbook, 77-0777* (Albuquerque, New Mexico: Sandia Laboratories, 1978).

8. *Barrier Penetration Database*, p. 17.

9. *Barrier Technology Handbook*.

10. Ibid.

11. Ibid.

12. Ibid.

13. *Technical Memorandum No. 51-78-04* (Port Hueneme, Calif.: Civil Engineering Laboratory, Naval Construction Battalion Center, 1977).

14. *Hardening Existing SSNM Storage Facilities*, p. A-6.

15. Ibid., diagram 5.

16. *Barrier Penetration Database*, p. 8.

17. Ibid., p. 9.

18. Ibid., p. 8.

19. *Barrier Technology Handbook*, paragraph 3.5.4.

20. Ibid., paragraph 3.7.4.3.

21. Ibid., pp. 78–79.

22. Ibid.

23. Ibid.

24. Ibid., p. 77.

25. Ibid., p. 79.

26. Ibid., p. 80.

CHAPTER 3

Locking Devices and Systems

If, despite one's best efforts, an adversary manages to penetrate perimeter barriers without being detected, he should encounter yet another obstacle in his path—locks. Locks may be sophisticated and engineered to perform as part of a total system such as the Mul-T-Lock, which incorporates four steel deadbolts locking into a door casing in four different directions when the lock is activated. They may be as simple as a keyed padlock and hasp.

The old adage "locks only keep honest people honest" is no less true today that it was when originally conceived. With the ever increasing crime rates and sophistication of criminals and their tools, it is false economy and self-deception to believe that an inexpensive or even moderately priced lock will provide adequate protection to any item or area of extraordinary value or sensitivity.

Over the centuries, many ingenious locks have been developed, some becoming standards while others were elaborate one-of-a-kind devices. These, and indeed all locks, have one thing in common—they were the result of someone's thinking, and it has been history's hard lesson that whatever one man can do, another can un-do. The defeat of these ingenious locks often required equally ingenious methods to open them surreptitiously. Some of the methods were quick and easy while others demanded considerable time and effort. The bottom line for any lock regardless of type, cost, construction features, and installation methods is that it can be defeated by force and the use of certain tools. We will consider our primary goal to be the provision of maximum protection against surreptitious entry, with a close secondary consideration being maximum impedance to forced entry.

A lock is but one of many considerations in the designing of a maximum-security environment. For example, a maximum-security lock installed in or on a wooden hollow core or standard glass door is of little value. While the lock provides excellent protection when properly used, its value in this case is negated by the ease with which the door can be penetrated. The average burglar will always seek to gain entry by attacking the weakest portion of the total security envelope around his objective. If it appears the lock cannot be easily defeated, he will look at the hinges to see if they might be his entry ticket. If the hinges provide penetration resistance equal to that provided by the lock and door construction, he will look at the door frame and at the

53

walls, floor, and ceiling. Only when each component of this door and its surrounding structure provides a degree of penetration resistance equal to that of the installed maximum-security lock, can the basic barrier be reasonably depended on to impede or prevent surreptitious or forced entry.

The efficient use of any locking device in a maximum-security application is contingent on its successful integration into the total overall structural component. Therefore a lock is defined as: "A mechanical device attached to or mounted within the physical structure of a door, gate or other closure, capable of securing the closure to its surrounding structure through a conscious, physical manipulation of an actuating mechanism. . . .

"To estimate a suitable degree of security for any given situation can be an intricate process of reasoning. Many other factors, besides the difficulty of picking or compromising security, enter into the decision of what device is most suitable. The customer thinks first of cost then appearance. Also, the lock must be easy to operate, especially if it is used often by people who have difficulty with mechanical manipulations. And it must have a degree of durability consistent with the frequency of use and the load factor under which it must perform. A cheap lock won't last long on a high-traffic door, though it might serve adequately on a seldom used bedroom or storeroom door. Sometimes it is necessary to launch into a lengthy explanation that if an intruder can get in without visible signs of break-and-entry he is not technically a burglar—just a thief. And to prosecute him it is necessary to catch him 'red-handed' with the goods and prove that he took them without permission. Even then he faces only a petty theft count. But a burglar who enters by force leaving visible signs of forcible entry automatically faces a burglary rap that is much more onerous, whether or not he acquired anything in his depredations."[1] "The fact is, however, the overwhelming number of burglaries will not be affected by more sophisticated keying mechanisms because these entries are usually accomplished by brutalizing the lock or breaking in some other way. Few illegal entries are traceable to a picked lock. Nevertheless, there are certain needs for the super-sophisticated keying arrangements—most notably to guard against surreptitious entry."[2]

Moderately priced locks make up the greatest percentage of any manufacturers product line and the inventory of the average locksmith. Therefore the purchase of padlocks, flush-mounted locksets, knob inset locks, and so forth must not be left to the discretion of the company purchasing department with only vague guidelines to assist it. It must be the responsibility of the security department to evaluate intelligently the various types of locks available that appear to possess the basic required features necessary for the environment or structure in which they will be installed, and to draft a list of ones that meet the standards, complete with manufacturers' names and model numbers. This list must specify that substitutions will not be accepted unless they provide a greater degree of protection than that of the item originally specified.

The initial step in assembling this information, where there is no time factor involved, would be to contact the various manufacturers and suppliers of locking devices for complete information packages on their products. Once this background information is assembled, a decision must be made on which type of lock would best serve the intended purpose. This decision will undoubtedly eliminate many models and, in some cases, complete product lines may be removed from contention. Those manufacturers who survive this initial cut may be queried on certain specific details that are not usually contained in their literature. It is recommended several individuals participate in compiling this list of questions. They should attempt to visualize every conceivable threat to which the structure holding the lock could be subjected. Questions or problems arising or uncovered by this method are then specifically addressed to the manufacturer(s). Only when there are no longer any questions or doubts about the ability of the lock (or locks) being considered, should purchase procedures be initiated, with the purchasing department being constrained by the aforementioned list of specific make(s) and model(s).

It goes without saying that the above procedure could take several months. Where timing is critical, the assistance of a reputable locksmith will be invaluable. Without being overly specific, he can be acquainted with the basic needs and his recommendations solicited. It is suggested that the possible application of any devices recommended by the locksmith also be subjected to theoretical attacks by a committee of individuals directly involved in on-site physical protection. This will uncover weak spots that could be exploited successfully by an adversary. Again, only after responsible individuals are satisfied that they have intelligently arrived at an acceptable choice, should purchase procedures be initiated.

Whenever possible, it is highly desirable to consider the security of an opening while the opening is in the design stage. George E. Wheatley[3] states:

The following checklist should always be used in approaching the security of an opening:

1. Make sure that the door and frame are adequate.
2. Select a lock which provides maximum security, meets code requirements and functions to the owners requirements.
3. Plan the master keying to provide adequate security.
4. Use a key section which is not of the stock type that is easily duplicated by any locksmith.
5. Have one person in complete control of the system and responsible for the issuance of all keys.
6. Have all locks furnished as "construction master keying" and have all keys delivered directly to the owner.
7. Where extra security is required use special security cylinders with all keys registered and available only from the lock manufacturer.

Wheatley also offers a list of American National Standards Institute (ANSI) standards that are available for consideration regarding locks, doors and hardware. They are:

A 156.1	1970	Butts and hinges
A 156.2	1975	Locks and door trim
A 156.3	1972	Exit devices
A 156.4	1972	Door control closers
A 156.6	1972	Architectural door trim
A 156.7	1972	Template hinge dimensions
A 156.8	1974	Door controls

PADLOCKS

There is no such thing as a pick-proof lock; however, a lock may be pick-resistant. Most burglars are not deterred by sophisticated locks. If one desires entry through a locked closure, he will usually brutalize the lock, closure, and/or closure hardware.[4] It is for this reason, therefore, that a lock must be thought of as only part of a system, and the devices used in conjunction with it—hasps and hardware—must be of sufficient penetration resistance.

While the use of padlocks should be kept to a minimum in a maximum-security environment, they are often effective for specific applications. There are two basic padlocks, combination and key-type.

Combination Padlocks

Combination padlocks are most often encountered when the area or space being protected is infrequently entered. They provide an adequate means of protection from forced entry (without the use of heavy tools and provided the locking hardware is of sufficient penetration resistance) and, in addition, there are no keys to lose. The principle reluctance to use of combination padlocks appears to stem from the inherent time factor required to open them. Many individuals are too impatient or seem to lack the manual dexterity and good eyesight required to ensure proper manipulation of the numbered dial. Despite these shortcomings and where time is not a factor, the use of a high-security combination padlock is recommended whenever one must be used. An additional advantage of the combination over the key padlock includes the capability to change combinations quickly and easily whenever necessary without incurring an extra expense. It must be remembered, however, that any record of lock combinations has to be afforded a sufficient degree of protection to preclude its falling into the wrong hands.

"It is desirable that a combination lock afford a choice of a large number of combinations. The number of combinations is determined by the number of tumbler wheels in the lock mechanism and the number of graduations on the dial. High-quality locks usually have one hundred divisions on the dial and three tumbler wheels; such a lock is capable of providing a theoretical 10^6 combinations which in practice reduces to tens of thousands. Some combination locks are made with four tumblers but it is considered that the added number of combinations possible does not proportionately improve the security of the lock and does increase the inconvenience of dialing the combination.

"It is desirable for a combination lock to be designed so its combination can be easily changed but at the same time be tamper resistant. Combinations can be changed by:

1. Disassembly of the tumbler wheel pack and relocation of screws or pins
2. Taking apart the wheel pack and resetting an insert in each wheel
3. Use of a special key which requires minimal training of the operator and provides a maximum number of combinations—this is the most convenient.

"The combinations of some locks can be covertly determined by using a radiographic technique. Resistance to this form of attack can be increased by utilizing materials in the mechanism that are not easily radiographed, e.g., plastics. Combination locks are vulnerable to compromise if the back of the lock is readily available, e.g., when the lockable access cover is open. Removing the back cover from the lock usually allows the combination to be determined. For this reason it is desirable to protect the back of the lock by back plates or other devices. High quality combination locks are designed for use in two basic forms: (1) in a lock case to be mounted on or into a door such as a mortise lock and (2) as a padlock. Combination padlocks are not vulnerable to usual rapping techniques and are usually resistant to manipulation. The most important aspect of lock control for combination locks is the protection of the combination. It is desirable to change the combination of a lock every time that a person who knows the combination no longer requires it.

"Losing the combination of a manipulation-resistant, well-designed lock in a high-rated door is an expensive situation. This can be prevented by keeping a record of the combination in another location which is as secure as the place protected by the lock. Combination locks can be set to a single number to simplify the daily chore of opening, but this is a very poor practice since it reduces the security of the lock. Frequently, four-wheel locks are set to only three different numbers for ease of opening. This defeats the purpose of the fourth wheel but it is not considered serious since the number of remaining combination choices is considered adequate. It is not recommended that one select combinations in common sequences and multiples of ten. It is also not recommended that the last number of a combination be set close to zero because in some cases the lock can jam.

"A standard for three- or four-tumbler combination locks is issued by Underwriter's Laboratories, UL-768, 'Combination Locks.'"[5]

Many commonly available combination padlocks are susceptible to manipulation. There are scenes in old movies where the safecracker brushes his fingertips on his jacket lapel, places his ear against the safe door and proceeds to twirl the dial several times in each direction, then triumphantly pulls down on the door handle and swings it open. While these scenes were over-dramatized, the basic concept was correct. Brushing the fingertips on a coarse material or even lightly passing them over a strip of sandpaper sensitized them so that minute vibrations of cogs, levers, and tumblers settling into place could be more easily detected. The ear-to-the-door method served the same purpose, although the use of a physician's stethoscope was usually preferred. While ordinary safes can still be found with this type of combination lock, modern office safes are equipped with manipulation-resistant combination locks. These are designed so that the opening lever does not engage the tumblers until the entire correct combination has been set. They are available both built in or as padlocks and provide a high degree of protection.

Key Padlocks

The Army's *Physical Security Field Manual* states, "Most key locks can be picked by an expert in a few minutes. The possibility of the loss and compromise of a key and the possibility of an impression being made should be considered in determining the security value of a key-type lock."[6]

Another concern voiced in the manual is the possibility of an identical padlock with a known key (or combination) being substituted for a lock in use. For this reason, it must be stressed that any padlock when not in use should be snapped shut around a locking eye or hasp. Some padlocks can be equipped with a key-retaining feature that makes it impossible to remove the key unless the padlock is shut. This is a good feature and should be incorporated in a maximum-security environment.

"As in the case of combination locks, it is desireable for a key lock to be capable of being set for a large number of different keys.

"A high-quality six-pin lock with ten key cutting levels per pin potentially permits 10^6 different keys to be used. However, this large number of key cuts is not as useful as a large number of combinations because less time-consuming techniques for defeating key locks are available. It is important that the key cut required to open a lock (bitting of a lock) be changeable to permit changes whenever keys are lost or anyone having access to the key is reassigned or terminated. Changing the bitting of a lock can be accomplished usually by changing pins, wafers, or levers. To ease the task of a bitting change, some locks have cores that are removable for replacement by means of a special key called a 'control key.' If all locks in a facility are keyed to the same control key, the locks are virtually master keyed because, with the core removed, the problem of opening the lock is elementary. Master keying is undesirable from a security point of view because disassembly and inspection of any lock in the system by a competent person provides access to all the other locks in the master-keyed system, and because termination of a person who had access to a master key would require changing the bitting of all locks set for his master key. The changing of the bitting of a large number of locks can be costly, but the convenience of master systems is such that there is strong pressure for using them. A compromise in this conflict between convenience and security may be to use a nonmastered set of locks for protected areas and to permit master key sets for other less sensitive areas."[7] This is not to deny the use of a removable core system in a maximum security environment. These shortcomings of any master key system must be considered before its application in a maximum-security setting.

The most commonly encountered keyed padlock uses a key similar to that used to open the door to a home. When this type of key is used in a lock equipped with a six-pin tumbler, pick resistance would be adequate for most applications. Some lock makers now also offer keyed padlocks using keys with randomly spaced shallow holes placed along the shaft at different angles. The lock pins engage certain of these holes to activate the mechanism. The latest adaptation of this system uses a four- rather than a two-sided key for what the manufacturer claims are over 40 billion different combinations. Another type of key lock occasionally encountered is the tubular lock. "The tubular lock has been widely used on vending machines, parking meters, and burglar alarm switches. The tubular lock's position as a high-security lock has been eroded by a proliferation of 'picks' for the lock. One version of the lock, which uses concentric sets of pins, is U.L. approved and is still commonly used in high security applications."[8] Many less than high-security padlocks can be picked. Various devices and techniques have been used in the past and will undoubtedly be used in the future.

Moderately priced padlocks usually offer a greater degree of protection against "slipping" with thin metal strips or the easy fabrication of a master key; however, they can also be easily picked by an experienced person, and the lock cases and shackles are still susceptible to tool attack.

Where esthetic considerations are of no concern, the usually less expensive security padlock (meeting military specifications) and a high-security hasp may be sufficient. Any padlock used in a maximum-security setting should at a minimum be a six-pin tumbler type with a hardened steel shackle and case-hardened body. Additional features would be a hidden shackle or a shackle designed to prevent defeat by a hacksaw through the incorporation of a free-rolling covering over the portion of the shackle that may be exposed to attack. A free-rolling covering should not allow the saw teeth to gain a purchase on the metal.

Most reputable manufacturers of locks and locking hardware offer high-security padlocks in a variety of sizes that can be used with keys or combinations. In addition, because of constant demand for better locks and locking devices, new companies are formed every year by individual inventors to produce and market a limited line of items in this field. Many of these companies fail because their products are either not up to requirements of the anticipated market or, less often, because of failure to market the product aggressively. The point is that when shopping for new locks or locking equipment, consideration should be given to the reputation of the manufacturer; the track record of the equipment or items being contemplated for purchase; the results of independent tests of the product by government or trade organizations; and the local availability of parts and repair service, as well as the user's needs.

When contemplating the purchase of new locking devices, one should not depend exclusively on past experience or knowledge. With the advances being made in design and construction, new and more effective locks are continually being developed. Most reputable manufacturers and suppliers will be happy to demonstrate their product lines and can supply invaluable advice and assistance. If there is uncertainty about the suitability of a certain lock for your purposes, it is wise to ask the salesman if it is on a General Services Administration (GSA) schedule. If it is, then it has been adopted for federal government use. A complete copy of the GSA specifications should be available, and it is very worthwhile to check them. They will often be very detailed as to construction and performance requirements, and may even indicate the levels of security or materials the lock may be suitable for protecting. It is important to be flexible—having always used brand X does not mean sticking with it; when the need arises to replace or upgrade locks, one should check out the entire field. A note of caution, however, before purchasing any new locks: it is important to make sure it has been proved in service and that it carries the Underwriters Laboratory or other approved independent testing certification.

Some padlocks are equipped with a steel cable shackle rather than a solid type. Cable is sometimes more difficult to saw through and, when attacked with bolt cutters, tends to mash or flatten, thus increasing its resistance to attack (individual strands could, however, be attacked using a pair of high-quality wire cutters, but this method requires additional time).

Hasps

Security hasps are marketed by several manufacturers and are of two basic types (Figure 3–1)—the normal hinged hasp and staple and a sliding hasp and staple. Both models are constructed of hardened steel at least three-sixteenths of an inch thick, with hinge pins incapable of being driven out or with a track strong enough to prevent the sliding hasp from being pried out. These are most effective when used on steel doors by welding them directly to the door and door jams.

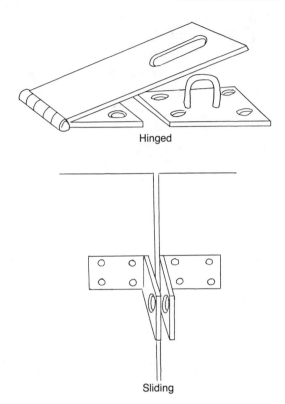

Hinged

Sliding

Figure 3-1 Hinged and sliding hasps.

Any padlock, regardless of quality and cost, is useless unless the hasp it is used with is equally impervious to attack.[9] It makes absolutely no sense to put a high-quality (and expensive) padlock on a dime-store hasp secured in the conventional manner with wood screws. "A $60.00 high-security padlock attached to a 50¢ hasp provides only 50¢ worth of security."[10]

There are several brands and types of hasps currently available for maximum-security applications. "The Army Natick Laboratory MIL-H-43905A High Security Hasp is made of carbon steel and is available in six styles. Two of these styles, No. 8 and No. 9, are available in stainless steel specifically for Navy shipboard use. A new shrouded hasp (Figure 3-2) has been developed (by CEL) and is in limited procurement for nuclear weapons security applications. This is the MIL-H-29181 (YD) 'Hasp, High Security, Shrouded, for High and Medium Security Padlock.' It is available in two styles. The hasps are investment cast from ASTM A 296, grades CA-6NM alloy."[11]

The *Belsaw Bulletin* (July 1981 issue) features the Sargeant and Greenleaf line of hasps "that can be suited to meet just about any type of application."[12]

On metal doors it is always best to weld a hasp to the door. If the door is wooden or it is otherwise impossible to weld the hasp, the next most secure

Figure 3-2 High-security shrouded hasp. (Civil Engineering Laboratory, Naval Construction Battalion Center, Port Hueneme, Calif.

method of mounting is to use hardened bolts and nuts through the door. The least favorable method is the use of screws. If it is necessary to attach the hasp to the door using bolts or screws, special types are recommended. "The 'clutch-head' or 'one-way' screw is designed so that it may be tightened but once in place, it cannot be removed."[13]

Another type of screw/bolt "is the 'twist-off' type (Figure 3–3). This bolt has a 'hex' head and once the bolt has secured the hasp to the door or wall, additional turning pressure causes the hex head to twist off. This leaves only a flat head bolt that cannot be turned and, therefore, removed.[14]

The CEL (Civil Engineering Laboratory) of the Naval Construction Battalion Center has developed some new hasp designs worthy of mentioning. Their design is "based on the use of commercially available Type 304 stainless steel $3 \times 3 \times \frac{1}{4}''$ angle and $\frac{1}{4}''$ plate using ordinary machine and welding shop practices. A 304 welding rod should be used in welding the weather cover to the right-hand hasp leg; alternatively, a 309 or 310 welding rod may be

Clutch-Head Screw

Twist-Off Screw

Figure 3-3 "Clutch-head" screw and "twist-off" bolt. (Courtesy of Belsaw Bulletin.)

used for assembling hasp components. If the hasp is to be welded to a steel door, a 309 or 310 welding rod must be used. The hasp can also be drilled and mounted using studs plug-welded in counter-sunk holes in the hasp."[15] (Figure 3–4)

The CEL cautions that certain adjustments may have to be made to accommodate the varying shackle lengths found on different brands of locks. "Hasp installations should be made only after the doors are hung to insure that the shackle holes will be in alignment if the door sags."[16]

Figure 3-4   CEL-developed hasp. (Civil Engineering Laboratory, Naval Construction Battalion Center, Port Hueneme, Calif.)

INDOOR LOCKS

According to Wheatley,[17] there are only four basic types of locks—mortise, cylindrical (or bored), unit, and rim. Wheatley states that mortise locks have been in use for nearly 150 years and are predominant in commercial construction usage. To provide proper service in a maximum-security setting, he states the mortise lock latch bolt should have a projection of at least five-eighths of an inch. While the dead bolt, often an integral part of a mortise lock, has a half-inch projection, it is available with a one-inch projection that can be furnished with two hardened steel inserts for protection against attack by saw.[18]

Mortise Locks

Mortise locks are designed to fit within the existing door structure with only the cylinder face and knob normally visible when the door is closed. Maximum security potential can be realized when a well-made mortise lock is installed in a heavy-duty steel or steel-clad door, and it can also provide effective (albeit more easily penetrated) protection when installed in a sturdy, solid wooden door. As previously explained, use of a highly penetration-resistant lock in a door of only moderate penetration resistance would generally be considered a waste of money. Obviously, however, if this solid wooden door were located within several outer layers of security protection, and if the only threat likely to be encountered would be that presented by an insider who would attempt surreptitious entry through defeat of the locking mechanism rather than physical assault on the door itself, its use would indeed be justified.

Because its design requires it to be sandwiched between the door's inner and outer veneers, the lock case presents a considerable cross-sectional area to anyone attempting defeat by drilling or simply applying well-directed sledge hammer blows around the lock cylinder and knob in an attempt to break the mechanism out of the door. In a steel (or heavy-duty steel-clad) door, this would not be a problem as the lock case would be very effectively protected by the door structure. A mortise lock in a wooden door can be provided a measure of protection through the installation of a hardened steel faceplate of greater height and width than the lock mechanism (Figure 3–5). The greater size would shield the lock from hammer blows by allowing the force of the blows to be absorbed by the solid door structure rather than by the lock case. The fact that this faceplate would be fabricated from hardened steel would also aid in resisting drilling attempts.

Cylindrical Locks

Cylindrical locks are somewhat similar to mortise locks in that their operating mechanism is contained within the door structure with only the knob(s) vis-

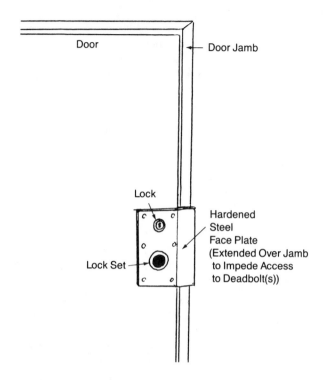

Figure 3-5   Steel face plate installation.

ible. Because the cylindrical lock design is more compact that that of the mortise lock, the lock keyway is incorporated into the knob face. The lock may be set from inside the space by a button in the inside knob face. Although cylindrical locks are generally supplied only with a common latch bolt, separate dead bolts are available from some manufacturers that are incorporated with the cylindrical unit in a single housing (these then can no longer be considered cylindrical locks).

Unit Locks

Unit locks, like mortise and cylindrical locks, are installed in rather than on a door. While the working mechanism is also concealed within the door structure, it is installed more simply than mortise and cylindrical units are. Because the unit lockset leaves the factory as a complete, ready-to-install package, anyone of average mechanical ability with commonly available tools should have no problem fitting one to a wooden door. Using the template provided by most manufacturers, the installer marks the door and then cuts a U-shaped opening in the stile. The completely assembled lockset is then slipped into this opening and secured in place by a faceplate fitted over the latch and screwed to the door. The installer then marks where the latch touches the door frame and installs the strike plate there to complete the installation. Because of the unusually generous faceplates provided on unit locksets and their rather small cross-sectional density, they are considered fairly resistant to defeat by use of a sledge hammer to drive the unit out of the door.

Rim Locks

As mentioned by Wheatley, the last type of lock commonly encountered is the rim lock. Rim locks are available with simple snap latches, with deadbolts, and with interlocking bolt-type latches. George E. Wheatley states that rim locks are "used for the most part as a supplemental lock after the initial installation." He goes on to say, "It requires no mortising in the door, merely a hole for the cylinder. . . . For maximum security, the best type of lock is a rim lock with interlocking bolts."[18]

While the rim lock with interlocking bolts appears to offer a high degree of protection, its use in a maximum-security environment should be carefully considered. Because the unit is designed as an add-on, its method of attachment to the door structure can vary from wood screws to stove bolts. As with the other three types of door locks that have been discussed, the protection provided can be substantially improved through use of a hardened steel faceplate sandwich, which overlaps the lock mechanism. When contemplating such a modification, however, the overall thickness of the door and steel faceplates must be considered to ensure that the proper size lock is procured.

ELECTROMECHANICAL LOCKING SYSTEMS

While the treatment of locks and locking devices has centered thus far around padlocks and other types of locks activated by physical manipulation, this section deals with the activation of a locking device by an electrical impulse.

An important consideration when contemplating the use of an electromechanical locking device is its susceptibility to the introduction of a bogus electrical current to activate it. It should be impossible for an adversary to defeat the device by cutting wires or rewiring circuits without doing so much damage to the structural housing that forcible entry would be a more expedient way of defeating the system. With any electromechanical system, all components and wiring should be contained within a physical barrier (wall, floor, ceiling, etc.).

Another important consideration is its "fail" capability (i.e., what happens if power is lost). In a maximum-security environment, electromechanical locking devices should fail in a closed or locked position. (It must be stressed that this is strictly from a security viewpoint. Safety considerations could rule out a fail-closed system.)

The locking portion of the system is the electric strike plate or electric throw (or dead) bolt. This type of lock can be activated by remote control or by use of a local access-control device (access-control devices are more fully covered in Chapter 8). The electrical strike or dead bolt is what keeps the door or closure locked. As soon as an impulse is received, the strike opens or the bolt retracts.

Many electrical strikes are inadequate when it comes to providing maximum security. The latch is the weakest point and, depending on installation and protection, the likely point of attack by an adversary. There are, however, some exceptions.

ELECTRIC THROW OR DEAD BOLTS

Electric throw or dead bolts provide more physical security than do most electric strikes, however, their electrical systems are just as vulnerable unless proper safeguards are provided (fail-closed, for example).

"Almost all electronic locks have certain mechanical features. Some will magnetically release a pin from a slot or hole in the bolt itself via a solenoid coil, allowing the user to then move the bolt with a second key. Others are powerful enough to operate the bolt totally by solenoid electromagnetic action. Power is usually 12 or 24 volts DC, obtained from a 115-volt step-down transformer and rectifier. To assure operation when electric power has failed, a rechargeable battery is (usually) incorporated into the unit."[19]

Generally speaking, surface mounted dead bolts, unless they are secured to a closure by welding or bolting (with steel plates in between) (Figure 3–6) should not be thought of as providing a high level of security.

MECHANICAL LOCKING SYSTEMS

There are several types of combination mechanical locking systems on the market. Depending on installation and application, some may be used to provide high security but their value in a maximum-security environment lies chiefly in the area of access control (access control and associated hardware for controlling access are covered in Chapter 8).

With any type of combination lock, be it dial or push-button, care must be exercised when opening it so as to avoid compromise of the combination. If compromise is even suspected, the combination should be changed.

The U.S. Atomic Energy Commission (now the Nuclear Regulatory Commission), in its regulatory guide entitled *General Use of Locks in the Protection and Control of Facilities and Special Nuclear Materials* says of push-button

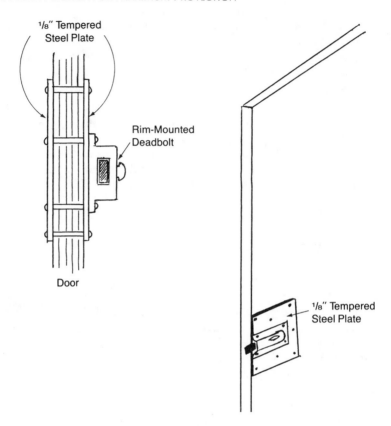

Figure 3-6   Hardened rim-mounted deadbolt.

mechanical locks, "The mechanical locks appear to be fairly resistant to concealed attack; however, more information is needed on their resistance to forcible attack."[20] The regulatory position is that such locks are not recommended for use due to the lack of comprehensive standards and specification against which evaluation can be made. Tests conducted subsequent to the regulatory guide indicate that some locks are quite resistant to forcible attack. They can be made more so by shielding techniques as described under Padlocks.

PANIC HARDWARE

No matter how maximum the security environment at the particular facility may be, certain contingencies have to be built into the system to ensure the safety of personnel. While there may be some exceptions, safety takes precedence over security in virtually 100 percent of cases. For this reason, it becomes necessary to provide a means of emergency egress even in a maximum-security setting. The most common and in fact the only logical way to do this is by use of panic-type locking hardware.

A general rule of thumb indicates that, whenever and wherever possible, the emergency exit should not be the primary entry into or exit from an area. All panic or emergency exits should be alarmed, they should not be subject to routine use, and they should be inspected frequently for security and operation.

Panic-type hardware should always be installed on an emergency door, gate, or other closure. This hardware should be capable of securely locking the closure from the outside and should be protected from defeat from the outside. A typical panic bar commonly encountered in many buildings and on many personnel gates can be defeated from the outside by using a wire coat hanger bent into a hook. For this reason, panic closures should be of solid construction, as should the surrounding structure to a distance of at least four feet on all sides, and alarmed, both remotely and locally. Whenever possible, the use of bar-type exit devices is to be avoided.

The door should be adjusted from the inside so that maximum pressure (consistent with local ordinances) is required to open the locking device. All such devices should be equipped with a deadlocking latch to preclude slipping from the outside.

KEY CONTROL

Thus far we have discussed the importance of selecting the proper locking devices for service in the maximum-security environment. Emphasis has been placed on the mechanical apparatus—good features, bad points, susceptibility to defeat, methods of modification to prevent defeat. No mention has yet been made of perhaps one of the most sensitive areas associated with a locking system—key control.

For our purposes, we will assume that the reader has established a key control system. It may be a procedure as simple as issuing new employees a set of keys that gives them free access to all parts of the building or offices; it could be as restrictive as giving no one a key but having security officers open and lock doors with a key (or keys) for which they are held strictly accountable; or it could be somewhere between these two extremes.

It must be remembered that a lock is a nondiscriminating device—it will open for anyone who possesses the correct key or combination. Ideally, in a maximum-security setting, keys to sensitive or vital areas are stored, under rigid control procedures, in a locked cabinet, physically located in a security post that is manned around the clock. If there is no continuously manned post, the keys may be stored on site in a container with greater penetration resistance than that of any single sensitive or vital area. Making penetration resistance of this key repository greater than that of any single area definitely increases the time and probably the personnel and equipment needed to gain forced entry into it. If entry into the key repository were as easy as forcing any single door, an intelligent adversary would naturally concentrate his attention there, knowing that for the expenditure of only the amount of effort necessary to force his way into the key safe, he could obtain the means easily and quickly to gain unimpeded access to all sensitive or vital areas.

There are strong and compelling reasons for issuing keys to certain individuals such as those in a supervisory or management position. Are the reasons valid? Are the keys issued because that person's duties require frequent passage through certain doors or access points, or have they been issued for the sake of convenience only? There will be individuals who will argue that their duties require they have access to the facility during non-working hours. Some of these, such as the maintenance department supervisor, head of the security department, and plant manager are legitimate, while others will be found very infrequently to require after hours access. In any organization, being issued keys seems to serve a special ego need. It says that this person is someone special, he can come and go as he pleases. It is all well and good to massage egos with such a simple "perk," but is it really wise? We read frequently about the loyal employee who takes his trusting employer to the cleaners by embezzling large sums of money, stealing the formula for a secret process, or acting as the inside man for a gang of burglars. Granted, such incidents are thankfully infrequent, but in a maximum-security environment it scarcely seems worth the risk.

A point was made that the issuance of keys is often an unconscious management "reward" for faithful service. Perhaps the ultimate extension of this is the issuance of a master or grand master key. The loss, theft, or unauthorized duplication of a single master key negates the entire system, whereas loss of a key to a lock (or several locks) within a system has only comprised that lock or locks. It is granted that where an individual has a legitimate need for access to several different areas in the execution of his duties, the use of a master or grand master key would be convenient, but this convenience would not be worth the possible compromise of the system were a loss, theft, or unauthorized duplication to occur. Compromise of the key control system for the sake of convenience or accommodation is unpardonable.

When establishing a new key control system (it is hoped with all new equipment), it is important to ensure that no key that is to reach the hands of any person outside the security management staff bears manufacturer's cut code numbers or keyway ID information. If these are the only keys available, the information should be recorded and stored in a secure space as if it were an actual key. If these numbers were obtained by an unauthorized individual, it would be a relatively simple matter to have a less than ethical locksmith duplicate the key. Once the information has been recorded and properly stored, the numbers may be ground off the keys or obliterated in some other manner. Unauthorized duplication would be somewhat more difficult if the keyway used a controlled key blank available only from the manufacturer and then only to the registered owner of the system. Unfortunately, more and more independent suppliers of key blanks are turning out blanks that often negate the precautions taken by the original lock manufacturers. Because there are just so many ways to configure the guide cuts in a blank, the unprincipled locksmith may find one that needs only a few minutes work with a needle file to make it fit an altogether different keyway from the same manufacturer than that for which it was made.

Of course, these are not foolproof measures. If an individual is determined to obtain an unauthorized copy of a key, he may do so in several ways. The first (and most obvious) is to steal the key from someone to whom it has been legitimately issued. This is often even easier than it sounds. How many times have we seen personnel in positions of responsibility toss their keys into an unlocked desk drawer or onto a locker shelf where they remain available to almost anyone for most of the work day? If this avenue is blocked by proper security precautions by the keys' authorized possessors, there are several alternatives. If the door on which this lock is installed is left open during the business day and if no one is posted or working in the area, it would be only a few minutes work for someone to remove the lock and replace it with an identical one. The legitimate lock is then taken to a locksmith who disassembles it, reads or measures the depth of the pins, determines what blank will fit the keyway, and cuts the necessary key. The legitimate lock is then returned to its rightful place in the door (another short job), and key control inventory has now been increased by one—an unauthorized and soon to be very costly one. There are easier methods, such as borrowing a key and, if the custodian is nonchalant about its return, running out and having it duplicated in a very short time. If the key custodian is conscientious, he will demand its return as soon as possible. The "borrower" gets around this minor obstacle by using the old movie ploy of taking an impression in wax, clay, or even putty for later reproduction. All of these possibilities have a common thread running through them: disregard for responsibility by personnel entrusted with maintaining an aspect of a total security envelope.

Some individuals may feel that, because they have stamped Do Not Duplicate on their keys, the possibility of unauthorized replication is eliminated. This would be the same as posting No Trespassing signs on a piece of undeveloped property, then walking away firmly believing that no one will ever set an unauthorized foot on it. While the majority of locksmiths will honor a Do Not Duplicate stamp, this admonition could be temporarily obliterated by tape or some other covering that could cause it to be missed by a hurried craftsman. This stamp, however, holds no special concern for the person with a key duplicating machine who is only interested in the quick and easy dollar.

So far, the subject of master keys has only been touched on. Ideally, master keys will not be used in a maximum-security environment. Many individuals who serve as company chief operating officers, executive heads of departments, or even company owners firmly believe that they should be provided master keys because their duties may require access to any part of the facility. While the premise is sound, the practice certainly is not! The possibility for loss or theft of a master key is just as good as those for any other key; the chances of unauthorized duplication is only slightly less than that for any other key.

There are many small sites where maximum security is necessary because of valuable merchandise or material sold, used, or processed at the facility. Often the size of the site or its business volume makes 24-hour on-site guard service impractical. We will assume that the premises are protected with all the usual burglar-resistant devices—bars or grillwork over the windows; steel or steel-clad doors; sophisticated alarms; adequate perimeter lighting; and so on. The alarm system requires a key to activate and deactivate, but what kind of protection is provided for this key? Typically, it is placed on a key ring or in a case and kept in someone's pocket or purse. If it is kept in the pocket of clothing that is being worn, a skirt or trousers, for example, the key is reasonably secure; however, if it is left in a jacket pocket or purse, or thrown into a desk drawer, one of security's cardinal rules is violated. Some individuals, especially those whose duties require frequent passage through many locked doors, maintain their keys on a belt-model key reel. These are available in two styles. One has a closed loop through which the belt must be threaded, and which offers a high degree of probability that it cannot be lost or surreptitiously removed. The second model has a clip-type holding device that slips over the belt and is held on by spring tension. This type of key reel is more easily removable and should not be trusted too much. Key reels are convenient, but because they are constructed of lightweight materials, the chain and its attendant hardware can be broken and the keys lost in an emergency. Anybody contemplating the use of a belt key reel will have to decide if the reduction in key security is worth the convenience.

What happens to these keys once their owners leave the business premises? Are they tossed into the auto glove compartment or left on the dashboard? Are they left on a bedroom dresser until the next business day? Again, typically, this is probably exactly what happens, but is this good security procedure? Keys must be given the maximum amount of security available; which then means they will not be left in unattended vehicles or homes. They must either be secured in a safe place or constantly carried by their owners.

Many individuals, mindful that there is a possibility that their keys may be lost, will often attach an owner identifying information tag in the hope that they will be returned by the finder. This is certainly not a wise practice. Anyone finding keys with owner ID tags would literally have this person at their mercy. Our recommendation is that no owner identifying data be used on a key ring or case. This would minimize the chances of anyone using found keys in an unlawful manner. It would not, however, eliminate this possibility because some makers of duplicate keys will stamp their shop name into the cut blank and it is conceivable that an owner's could be traced through this shop. Of course, in a maximum-security setting, the loss of keys would mean that all locks those keys operate should immediately be changed.

While it is recommended that in a maximum-security setting keys not be indiscriminately issued, the realities of the situation demand that certain management or supervisory personnel have keys to aid in the execution of their duties. When this is required, a careful assessment must be made to ensure that these personnel are given only the absolute minimum number. The keys should be issued on a signature receipt form on which the individual receiving them acknowledges his responsibilities; which include assurance that the keys will be stored in a proper penetration-resistant container when not in use or carried on the individual's person. He must signify that the keys will never be loaned to anyone, no matter the reason (except of course in the event of a major emergency where failure to yield the keys could result in loss of life or major property damage). The receipt should indicate that these keys remain company property, shall not be duplicated, are subject to audit and recall at any time, and must be surrendered upon termination of employment or when there is no longer a need for them by the individual. An additional consideration would be the requirement that replacements for keys damaged in use will be strictly on a one-for-one basis.

Key Accounting Procedures

In the maximum-security environment, the majority of keys necessary for limited day-to-day operations will be stored in a penetration-resistant container that is located in a continuously manned security post. Proper accounting procedures require that an inventory of these keys be posted inside the container and that the keys be counted at every security shift change. The on-coming officer must assure himself that the number of keys remaining in the container and the number still signed out on the key issue/receipt record agree with the authorized container inventory. Only then can he sign the record indicating his acceptance of the count.

There are two schools of thought on the method of implementing this record. When a bound book is used for the record, the key accounting procedure is enhanced, as the removal of a page is easily detected, especially if each page is sequentially numbered before the book is placed into service. Where a member of the security management staff audits the daily security paperwork, this method would require that he physically go to the security station to ensure proper accounting procedures are being maintained. The second method uses a printed form that should be sequentially numbered for accounting purposes. This method allows the auditor to check key issue and receipt records without leaving his desk, and offers the additional advantage of allowing the record to be filed daily with all the other security operations paperwork.

Figure 3–7 is a simple format for a key issue/receipt record. It would

Date: _____

CHECK-OUT				CHECK-IN		
Key number	Key to:	Signature(s) of person(s) accepting key(s)	Time out	Issuing guard's signature	Time in	Receiving guard's signature

We certify that a complete inventory of the controlled key container has been performed and all keys are present except for number(s): _____

(*When applicable*)

☐ The above exceptions are still legitimately checked out and are therefore accounted for as indicated by transference of check-out data to the issue/receipt record for _____
                                                                                                        (Date)

☐ The above exceptions cannot be accounted for. The last receiver of record has been contacted with the following results: _____

Off-going Guard: _____ On-Coming Guard: _____
                         (Signature)   **(Signature)**

Figure 3-7 Key issue receipt record sample.

function as follows:

1. A new record is started at 12:01 am each day.
2. A person needing a key to a particular lock comes to the security station and request the key.
3. Officer on duty checks the key access list to ensure this person is authorized to check this key out.
4. If the person is authorized, he fills in the necessary information in the first three columns of the issue/receipt record.
5. The issuing officer enters the necessary information in columns four and five

6.   When the key is returned, the receiving officer completes the transaction by entering the necessary information in columns six and seven.

A written plant procedure should be established requiring all keys checked out to be returned to the security station immediately after use.

When one security officer relieves another, after completing the required inventory and reconciliation, the on-coming officer indicates his acceptance of the key count as correct by entering the work "ALL" in the first column, running a horizontal line through the next five columns and entering his signature in the last one.

At midnight, the off-going and on-coming officers conduct a complete physical inventory of the key container and record their results in the space(s) provided at the bottom of the form. (If a bound book format is being used, this certification could be on a separate form that is transmitted to the security manager daily.) It would not be inappropriate for a member of the security management staff to audit all keys randomly, both those in service and those in storage.

For access to vital or sensitive areas, the access authorization list should indicate that two authorized individuals must sign for the key. This ensures that no one person will have unescorted access there. Ideally, the entry to the area should also be under the observation and control of yet a third person in the security organization. For example, two authorized individuals check out the keys to the emergency generator building. The door to this building is under continuous CCTV observation by an officer at a fixed post. After these individuals have identified themselves to him (by means of door intercom, telephone, radio, etc) and he recognizes them as authorized persons, he would actuate a remote-control electric strike to allow entry after the mechanical locks have been opened. The interior of this space should also be under CCTV observation so that not only would both persons in the space be checking on the other, but a third person (the officer monitoring the CCTV) would check on them both. Because the electric strike would lock the door behind these persons, they would have to contact the officer for exit. If there is a possibility that some item could be surreptitiously removed from this area, the officer would not activate the door-release mechanism until another officer arrived to search the personnel exiting. The monitoring officer can also ensure (with a reasonable degree of certainty) that these persons have properly secured the area when they exit.

Some facilities have found it advantageous to use one brand (or model) of lock for all exterior locations that are not part of a vital or sensitive area, with a different brand (or model) reserved for these. This avoids the possibility of inadvertently using a lock on a vital area that may have been used on a remote gate, and which might have been compromised at some point in the past. Ideally, whenever a lock is moved from one location to another, its core should be changed or it should be recombinated. In this manner, the possibility that the lock may have been compromised in the past would present no problem with its use at a new location.

The last item to consider is controlling access to the supply of key blanks and key machine (if there is one on site). The possibilities of unauthorized duplication of keys are great enough without making it even easier by providing the means and the method right on site. This equipment and supply of blanks should be stored in a safe or strong room when not in use, and should be under the exclusive control of the security manager. Carrying this concept to its logical conclusion, the entire lock and key system should be under security department control.

ADDITIONAL CONSIDERATIONS

Some additional thoughts are offered here regarding locks and locking systems.

- It must be reiterated that the integrity of a door, gate, or other such closure must be equal to the integrity of the lock or locking device and vice versa.
- In a maximum-security setting, the more impenetrable the barrier, that is, the closure and its surroundings, the better the lock that is required to maintain impenetrability.
- Wherever possible, the simplest, strongest locking device should be used. A 2 inch by 4 inch steel I-beam, padlocked on the inside at both ends across an inward-opening metal door will certainly provide high penetration resistance and may be just what is needed under certain conditions.
- Consideration must be given to lock, combination, and key control so as to avoid compromise.
- Depending on circumstances, an entrance equipped with a wooden door can be upgraded by installing another door, constructed of steel plate at least quarter-inch thick (with associated high-strength hardware) on the opposite side of the entrance jamb.
- If an adversary cannot get at a lock to attack it, just about any high-quality lock can be used. For this reason, consideration should be given to protecting the lock and its keyway by boxing it with steel plate (as previously described).
- Tools and keys to vehicles should be locked up or otherwise secured to preclude their use against a lock, door, or barrier.
- Sliding doors generally should not be used in a maximum-security environment unless they are modified or designed for maximum-security application (i.e., deep, reinforced steel tracks, barbed locking bolts, dead bolts at the top and bottom of both ends, etc.).
- "The 'Key Grabber' is a technique that is used when an unauthorized person has a key and pays surreptitious visits. With this method, the

lock is changed to accept a new key that is slightly different. The suspect key will turn a fraction of the way in the lock and then it will stop, unable to move ahead or back or be removed. The only thing that can be done is to abandon the key in the lock. It is necessary to enter at another point and to dismantle the lock in order to fix it."[21]

"A pin tumbler lock can be adapted so that a key will only lock the dead bolt but cannot open it again. The authorized key works both ways."[22]

NOTES

1. A. T. Grumback, "Locks and Locking—Pertinence," *Security World* (May 1978):34.
2. A. T. Grumbach, "Locks and Locking—Lock Sophistication," *Security World* (October 1978): 55.
3. George E. Wheatley, "Locks and Keying," in *Handbook of Building Security Planning and Design*, ed. Peter S. Hopf (New York: McGraw-Hill Book Company, 1979), p. 15–10. Materials used with permission.
4. Grumbach, "Locks and Locking—Lock Sophistication," p. 34.
5. Atomic Energy Commission, *General Use of Locks in the Protection and Control of Facilities and Special Nuclear Materials* (Washington, D.C.: The Commission, 1973).
6. *Physical Security, U.S. Army Field Manual 19-30* (Washington, D.C.: Department of the Army, 1979), p. 4-29.
7. Atomic Energy Commission, *General Use of Locks*, p. 5-12-3.
8. Richard C. Rhodes, "Technical Notebook: Lock Security, part 1," *Security Management* (March 1978):p. 66. 1978. Copyright by The American Society for Industrial Security, 1655 N. Fort Myer Drive, Suite 1200, Arlington, Va 22209. Reprinted with permission from the March 1978 issue of *Security Management* magazine.
9. Belsaw Machinery Co., *Belsaw Bulletin—Locksmith Shop Notes* 54, no. 4 (1981):p. 52.
10. *Techdata Sheet 77-07R* (Port Hueneme, Calif.: Civil Engineering Laboratory, Naval Construction Battalion Center, 1979).
11. Ibid.
12. *Belsaw Bulletin*, p. 52.
13. Ibid.
    14. Ibid.
15. *Techdata Sheet 76-08R* (Port Hueneme, Calif.: Civil Engineering Laboratory, Naval Construction Battalion Center, 1977).
16. Ibid.
17. Wheatley, "Locks and Keying," p. 15–2.
18. Ibid., p. 15-3.
19. W. E. Osborne, "Access through the Locking Barrier," *Security World* (July 1978):p. 35.
20. Atomic Energy Commission, *General Use of Locks*, p. 5-12-4.
21. A. T. Grumbach, "Locks and Locking—Fulfilling Special Locking Requirements," *Security World* (February 1979:p. 39.
22. Ibid.

CHAPTER 4

Advanced Alarm Systems

When someone says "alarms," the immediate thought is of bells ringing, sirens blasting, and lights flashing. But alarms are much more than the signals that are generated to attract the attention of the person who will investigate and correct the problem. The alarms just described are all relatively modern signaling devices, but what came before and what led to their development?

Alarms are not a recent addition to the quest for better and more efficient means of alerting us to danger. Prehistoric man more often than not was the hunted, not the hunter. In order to survive, he had to adapt his primitive intelligence to recognize signals that meant the difference between life and death. The crack of a twig, a rustle in the leaves, a sudden cessation of animal sounds were all alarm signals that he had to be smart enough to interpret. As his intelligence grew, he realized that nearly all creatures in nature possessed senses greater than his own. For example, the ancestral dog's keen sense of smell and hearing extended the range at which man could detect danger.

As civilizations developed and became more sophisticated, animals were increasingly used as alarms. Peacocks and hens were, and still are, used effectively to warn of the intrusion of unknown animals and humans into the area the bird has established as its own. Siamese cats seem to have a penchant for getting near the face or neck of a sleeping person. This allegedly goes back to their development in the royal households of certain Indian Ocean empires where the cats were bred and trained to sleep draped around the necks of the royal family members. In this way, if someone attempted to cut their throat in the dark while they slept, the unfortunate cat would suffer the brunt of the attack, but his cry would awaken the intended victim and hopefully summon the palace guard.

Geese and swans have been popular early warning systems from the days of the ancient Chinese, through the European Dark and Middle Ages, up to the present period. Certain species of hogs have even been used successfully in this capacity, with the added advantage that if undomesticated, they backbreed to a wild state, or if allowed to become feral, will often attack and rout intruders.

Members of the bird family have not escaped man's attention in his quest for efficient alarm systems. A custom that supposedly originated in

Welsh coal mines is still used in some small operations today. A canary in a cage is taken into the tunnels with the work crew. Because the bird's higher metabolism demands a higher concentration of oxygen in its atmosphere, its untimely demise warns the miners that deadly gases are accumulating in the tunnel and gives them time to escape before they too are overcome. Canaries were ostensibly chosen for this task over other birds because their warbling (or sudden lack thereof) would keep the miners in the area aware of the prevailing conditions, without having to constantly keep an eye on the bird.

All of these biological alarm systems have one thing in common—they alert the human presence to impending danger. Man must still take the decisive step in avoiding or neutralizing the danger. When animals were not present or where their presence was not desirable, man came up with some very simple alarm systems, often making do with whatever was at hand to improvise. Bells and gongs with trip wires have been used for centuries. With the advent of the food canning industry in the latter half of the nineteenth century, frontier soldiers and settlers alike found the empty containers and a couple of small stones could be substituted for bells when used with a piece of string or twine as a trip. There were many variations on the theme, but all involved action by the intruder that in turn resulted in a warning sound.

As we entered the electric age, it was only natural that this mighty leap in technology would be recognized and used to provide new and better systems for protecting valuables. No longer was man forced to rely on his own senses or those of some other living creature. Now he had a mindless servant who could be depended upon (considering the reliability of the existing power supply at the time), to be on the job around the clock and who didn't get sick, old, or have to be fed and otherwise cared for. Naturally, the earliest electrical alarm systems were thought of as modern miracles, however, it wasn't long before ways were found to defeat them. This forced scientists back to the drawing boards to design newer and more sophisticated systems. This has been the continuing story—as soon as a new system is developed and placed into service, the forces against which it is supposed to protect immediately start looking for ways to defeat it, usually with success. This then forces development of a newer and better system, ad infinitum.

While seeming marvels of electrical gadgetry were developed up until the early 1950s, it was with the electronic age and the transistor that today's state-of-the-art alarm systems finally came into their own. Granted, there have been some false starts; however, it can generally be agreed that the products available today are better than anything that has ever come before. This same statement will probably be just as true 20 years from now as it is today. Research now going on holds great promise for the future of the alarm industry with benefits that everyone connected with the field of security can instantly recognize.

For example, at the National Research and Resource Facility for Submicron Structures laboratory in Ithaca, N.Y., scientists are working in the field of microelectronics. One of the researchers of this facility has built a device that can detect changes in the earth's magnetic field produced by the wink of an eye.[1]

A mechanism using this principle as the trigger in an alarm system would certainly bear close scrutiny, as it would appear virtually undefeatable. Naturally, this technology is still in the experimental stage and it will be several years at least before it begins reaching the commercial world. Until twenty-first-century technology comes up with the new equipment, we will have to make do with the very best available today. The following pages discuss some of the more sophisticated alarm systems we now have and how they may be used in a maximum-security setting.

ALARM SYSTEMS IN THE MAXIMUM-SECURITY ENVIRONMENT

Two major characteristics of alarm systems in the maximum-security environment are diversity and redundancy. Diversity, that is, the use of different types of systems, is not only highly desirable, it is mandatory to preclude defeat and offer necessary protection. Ideally, microwave, ultrasonic and infrared, to mention a few, are integrated into the total system to serve a specific function and to offer the required degree of diversity. The same principle of diversity can be equally applied to the physical barriers and locking systems previously discussed. The Maximum Security practitioner does not rely exclusively on walls or fences to deter intrusion. He does not rely exclusively on the same types of locks to secure sensitive areas. The principle of layered security applies equally to all components of a system, and alarms are not exceptions.

Alarm systems use various principles of operation, each of which is subject to limitations and has advantages over the others. The maximum-security practitioner should attempt to capitalize on the advantages of a particular system by careful integration of different types of alarms, the advantages of each offsetting the disadvantages of the other. A perimeter should never be protected by a single alarm system, be it microwave, infrared, or seismic. Diversity occurs when one intrusion-detection system is used in conjunction with another that operates on a different principle.

Redundancy implies a fail-safe or backup capability. The example of microwave and seismic intrusion detection systems being used in tandem to provide diversity illustrates redundancy. No single area should be protected by a single component. An intruder must defeat two separate, independent, and redundant systems in order to penetrate the electronic fence around the perimeter.

The *Code of Federal Regulations*[2] states that for fixed-site and in-transit protection of nuclear material, "A physical protection system . . . is designed with sufficient redundancy and diversity to assure maintenance of the capabilities described." These capabilities include:

1.   Preventing unauthorized access
2.   Permitting only authorized activities and conditions
3.   Permitting only authorized placement and movement of strategic special nuclear material
4.   Permitting removal of only authorized and confirmed forms and amounts of strategic special nuclear material
5.   Providing for authorized access and assuring detection of and response to unauthorized penetration
6.   Providing a response capability to assure numbers 1 through 5 above are achieved and that adversary forces will be engaged and impeded until off-site assistance forces arrive

The *Code* goes on to require "assurance that a single adversary action cannot destroy the capability of the security organization to notify off-site response forces of the need for assistance."[3] It is therefore a prime requisite that diversity and redundancy be built into any maximum-security system and, in this case, an alarm subsystem.

In order fully to integrate the principles of diversity and redundancy into a maximum-security alarm system, it is necessary to understand some of the different types of alarms and their basic methods of operation. Robert P. Lee, Vice President of Sonitrol Security Systems of Providence, Inc. spoke before the Warwick, Rhode Island Chamber of Commerce and the American Society for Industrial Security. He very neatly outlined what for many security practitioners is a most confusing subject, that is, alarm systems. Lee stated, "Any alarm system, from the device hung on a door knob to the complex system guarding nuclear facilities, can be described with a three-part equation:

"Detection devices + Alarm controls = Alarm signaling."[4]

There are basically two types of detection devices. The first protects a space and the second protects a point. Lee refers to these as space protection and point protection, and further groups space protection into two classes: active and passive. His description, taken from that speech, is as follows.

"Active devices transmit energy, such as ultrasonic, microwave, and photobeam. While photobeam devices detect an interruption in a line-of-sight beam, ultrasonic and microwave offer volumetric detection by sensing a shift or disruption in a transmitted pattern of energy. Passive devices are those which receive energy, such as microphones and passive infrared sensors. Microphone sensors for use in audio-detection systems are either direct transmission, which transmit sound instantly, or audio accumulators, which require a number of counts or repeated impacts prior to activation. Passive infrared sensors essentially look at a room, optically breaking the view area into one or a multitude of viewing zones, depending on the sensor design. Abrupt changes in received infrared energy in relation to the background cause the sensor to trip. People emit infrared energy and are detected."[5]

Lee explains point detection:

"Safes, money rooms, doors to critical areas, and areas in the vicinity of highly valuable objects are often covered by specific sensors. Magnetic or mechanical closed-circuit contacts, pressure-sensitive mats, capacitance alarms, as well as other devices can fall into this category."[6]

The second part of Lee's equation, alarm controls, is the heart of the system. The device used to power protective loops and detection devices also controls zoning, delays, and operation. Additionally, it is responsible for output signals and annunciators, indicators, and other alarm signaling devices. Standby power systems for alarm controls are suggested by Lee. Their use in a maximum-security environment is, of course, mandatory.

Alarm signals are broken down into two types, according to Lee: local and remote. A local alarm signaling device is located on site and serves to alert someone in the vicinity of the affected area that an intrusion has been detected. The type of local alarm device is typically a bell, siren, or horn that is sometimes used in conjunction with a visual display such as a rotating beacon. A remote alarm signal transmits the alarm signal to some other location such as on-site or off-site monitoring station (central station monitoring) or local law enforcement headquarters.

There are several ways to achieve remote alarm signaling. Two of them were described by Lee.

The first involves signal transmission over the regular dial-up telephone network. This can be done by an automatic dialer, which plays a prerecorded message over the phone to the police or a neighbor. Another more advanced way to use the dial-up network is with a digital communicator, which would send a coded signal to a special receiver at a remote station.

The second basic method of remote signaling uses direct leased lines. These are currently leased from the telephone company and essentially provide a direct connection between the alarm control and the alarm receiving company. Signals are constantly sent by the alarm control, which allow the receiving company to tell if someone has cut or tampered with the telephone lines. This leased supervised line connection is currently the most secure way to transmit data [to an off-site alarm monitoring company].

"Two additional methods of alarm signal transmission involve radio transmission and cable TV line transmission. Both involve transmission of digital signals by a digital communicator to a special receiver in a remote location. Neither method is currently in widespread use. Cable networks are still in the future for many neighborhoods. Radio transmission is basically line-of-sight FM signaling, and is greatly affected by terrain.

"It is interesting to note that you can combine local with remote signaling or use remote signaling alone to have a silent alarm."[7]

Alarm systems in the maximum-security environment must of necessity be much more sophisticated than illustrated here. The basic requirements for any such system include defeat resistance, dependability, and tamper indication, in addition to diversity and redundancy.

Defeat Resistance

The basic purpose of an alarm system, regardless of its degree of sophistication, is to alert a guardian to unauthorized access. If the system can be defeated or circumvented without the guardian's knowledge, it has failed.

One of the easiest ways to defeat an alarm system is to interrupt its power, which turns the system off. A maximum-security alarm system should therefore have its power source protected from interruption. Additionally, the system must "announce" that it has lost power whenever that is the case. To ensure continuous operation, a maximum-security alarm system should have at least one, and preferably two or more, backup sources of power, that is, commercial AC power, emergency generator, and batteries (these are required at nuclear sites). In the event of a power failure or interruption by design, one of the backup sources will keep the system in operation.

Several other methods of defeating alarm systems exist, including bypassing components and even the system itself. In the maximum-security environment, one alarm system should protect another. This has been previously expressed to a certain degree under redundancy. On a perimeter, for example, there should be at least two intrusion-detection systems, primary and secondary. While the primary system may be susceptible to defeat, it should be next to impossible for the attempt to go unnoticed by the secondary system (assuming that both are functioning properly) and vice versa. When redundancy is achieved by using systems in tandem, the possibility of an intruder bypassing a system or its components is greatly reduced (Figure 4–1).

Tamper Indication

Yet another method of defeating an alarm system is by the introduction of a bogus secure signal from the sensor or detector to the control unit. This can be precluded by enclosing alarm system components in housings or structures that are themselves alarmed. For example, the housing of an exterior microwave intrusion alarm transmitter has an access cover or other means by which access can be had to the electronic components within. The means of access must be protected or the system can be compromised. "Surreptitious attacks on the detection system should be detected. Tamper protection will minimize the threat from anyone escaping detection while attempting to open a detector enclosure. To be effective, the tamper protection should be monitored on a

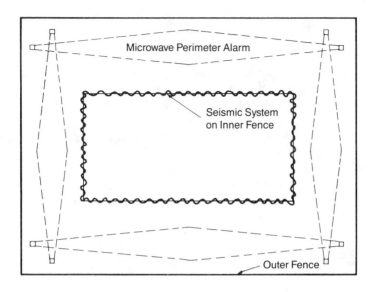

Figure 4-1   Redundancy in a perimeter alarm system.

24-hour schedule. Too often protection circuits of this type are connected to the primary alarm circuit. In this type of hookup, the circuits are only monitored when the overall detection system is in the 'secure' mode during non-working hours. There should be little need to monitor the protection circuits during secured hours if the facility is adequately protected because presumably no one could reach the detector or signal lines without being detected. Therefore, for maximum protection, tamper circuits should be monitored continuously, especially during working hours when the system is in 'access.'"[8]

All components of the system must be protected so that unauthorized tampering will in all cases generate an alarm. The usual method is through a mechanical switch of some sort that will activate if a component is moved or disturbed. Another method, excellent when used in conjunction with conventional tamper protection, is to position detectors where each can "watch" another. Depending on the type used, this could result in false alarms, so a competent alarm installer should be consulted prior to using this approach.

Supervised Circuitry

Power and signal lines must also be protected or they can be compromised without alerting the system. The best indication of trouble somewhere along a power line is in the loss of commercial, or purchased, power. Indicators of this condition are fairly numerous: alarm system failure, lighting failure, communications failure, and so on. Signal line security, however, is a different story. "If a signal line is compromised, the control unit will not receive an alarm signal even if the detector is functioning properly. The *minimum* acceptable line supervision should detect an open or shorted signal line. Since most signal transmission system transmitters recognize an open circuit as an alarm signal, the line supervision circuit need only detect someone trying to compromise the detection device by electronically short-circuiting the alarm contacts. To minimize signal line compromise, the signal line supervision should be monitored on a 24-hour schedule."[9]

Maximum security requires a different approach to signal line protection. At a minimum, high-security signal lines should have an end-of-line impedance device that will detect and send an alarm in any event of impedance changes. Changes on the order of 5 to 25 percent should cause an alarm.[10]

In any event, supervised circuitry and lines are a must in maximum-security applications.

Signal Splitting

A top-of-the-line maximum-security alarm system will have at least two on-site monitoring stations manned by the facility's security organization. Many times, the secondary station is "slaved" off of the primary station, that is, it is an extension of the primary station in that alarm signals must pass through the primary station on their way to the secondary station. This principle can be easily seen when Christmas tree lights are wired in series. The power passes through the first light and into the second, third, and so on. Because of this arrangement, a "slaved" secondary station provides a check on the primary station. If the primary station is disabled, so too is the secondary station. The arrangement is tantamount to placing another security person in the primary station so as to have a "two man rule."

A much better and more secure (although more expensive) system of alarm monitoring is to operate each of the two stations independently by splitting the alarm signal. Signal splitting occurs when a sensor detects an intrusion and sends a signal to the alarm station. The usual signal path would be to the primary station. If, however, the path is blocked, for example by disabling the primary station, the alarm signal will reverse its direction and travel to the secondary station, thereby annunciating the alarm. In effect, alarm sensors are monitored by two stations capable of operating independently of each other. This method is referred to as multiplexing.

The Nuclear Regulatory Commission's physical protection upgrade rule requires such splitting so that both primary and secondary monitoring stations are able to receive signals such that a single adversary action cannot defeat the overall system.

Dependability and Simplicity

One of the chief failings of intrusion detection systems, some more than others, is lack of dependability. This is usually translated into an excessive number of false alarms, continual malfunctions, and poor service records. It goes without saying that a system that continually alarms loses its effectiveness regardless of the cause. False alarms are caused by a variety of things, some of the most common of which are improper application, faulty installation, improper calibration or sensitivity, and inherent component and/or system design weaknesses. For the purposes of this discussion, it must be remembered that a false alarm is just that, false or unexplained. A person or animal inadvertantly, or by design, setting off the alarm cannot be considered to have caused a false alarm. In practice, any alarm caused by anything other than an unauthorized intruder is usually referred to as false, however inaccurate that may be.

The Nuclear Regulatory Commission (NRC) states, "The mode of installation of the perimeter alarm system influences its effectiveness."[11] This is a particularly thought-provoking statement. Some companies will go to great lengths to select an excellent security alarm system and then turn its installation over to the maintenance department. This is tantamount to asking a high school physics class to take over operation of a nuclear reactor. While such an installation may be within the capabilities of some maintenance departments with a well-trained and well-equipped electronics section, the majority do not have the expertise, equipment, or interest in taking on a task of this magnitude. It is therefore in the best interests of the company security manager either to arrange for the manufacturer to supply installation or to contract independently for this service with a professional installer. The advantages of an independent installer's services include:

1. The job must be done right or he won't be paid.
2. He will usually guarantee and stand behind his work.
3. Most installers also service alarm systems, and if problems develop, the man who installed the devices would seem to be the logical choice to perform the repairs, as he would be thoroughly familiar with the system.
4. If system components must later be relocated, or if the system requires expansion, the original installer would again appear to be the logical choice to do this.

The NRC goes on, "In general, dividing the site perimeter into segments that are independently alarmed and uniquely monitored assists the security organization responding to an alarm by localizing the area in which the alarm initiated. Segmenting of the perimeter alarm system also allows testing and maintenance of a portion of the system while maintaining the remainder of the perimeter under monitoring. It is generally desirable that the individual segments be limited to a length that allows observation of the entire segment by an individual standing at one end of the segment."[12]

Whenever and wherever possible, the perimeter intrusion-detection system should be segmented to ensure that failure of a component causes only a portion of the total system to become inactive rather than losing the entire system. Based on the previous description, many manufacturers have designed their alarm systems to operate within this stratagem. When a manufacturer states his system is zoned or employs zones, he is speaking of segmenting. It is recommended that the length of each segment be limited to what can be monitored effectively by an individual standing at one end of the segment. This deals with compensatory measures that may be taken in the event of a segment failure to ensure that perimeter intrusion-detection capability remains intact. As with any piece of capital investment equipment, an effective preventive maintenance program is a must. Much of the equipment currently available is state-of-the-art, and while manufacturers generally take great pains to engineer long life and trouble-free service into their products, no device man has yet been able to build remains failure-proof.

When constant false alarms are generated, the value of the system becomes questionable. Pierce R. Brooks lists 10 deadly errors that police officers commit. One of these, "relaxing too soon," usually results from "those 'phony' silent alarm calls."[13] It is fairly obvious that frequent false alarms cause those charged with responding to them to become complacent; however, complacency is one thing that is best left out of a maximum-security environment. It therefore behooves security professionals to eliminate false alarms to the extent it is humanly and physically possible. A medium-sized manufacturing facility in the Hartford, Connecticut area experienced over 250 alarms during 1981. Of these, one resulted in the apprehension of an intruder; the others were all caused by malfunctions, rodents, employees, wind, weather, and the like. Fortunately for the company, the security force did not allow itself to become complacent. It routinely and thoroughly investigated all alarms so the apprehension of an intruder was no surprise. The security force must be made to understand that a full and proper response to each and every alarm is mandatory within a certain specified period of time, no matter what the cause may be. In any case, minimal or no false alarms is the standard in a maximum-security setting. Dependability therefore becomes a prime requisite during the selection of an alarm system.

Simplicity in design is yet another consideration. It must be remembered, however, that many "simple" systems require only "simple" means to defeat them. There are times when this is not the case. Take, for example, a balanced magnetic door contact. Relatively simple in principle and design, it can be quite difficult and sometimes impossible to defeat. The false alarm rate for balanced magnetic contacts is quite low, based on the authors' experience, thereby making their use desirable. While certain characteristics such as simplicity are important, they cannot be the determining factors when selecting a maximum-security alarm system.

Very often, improper application or use of a particular type of alarm system sensor results in an excessive false alarm rate. Microwave, for example, penetrates beyond the area to be protected if it is enclosed by thin partition walls and/or windows. Movement close to the outside of the microwave-protected area may cause an alarm. Additionally, a microwave motion detector mounted on a flimsy wall that allows considerable movement will cause false alarms. The Defense Industrial Security Institute in Richmond, Virginia has published guidelines (Table 4–1) that are useful in determining the type of sensor to use to avoid improper applications.

A very important consideration when contemplating any product, including alarm systems and components, is its track record. It is always advisable to research this subject thoroughly before investing. Some systems do not stand up as well as others and should be eliminated from consideration. Checking with past and present users of the system can help one to determine whether or not an installation's weak points would be a major drawback. For example, a certain component may have a notoriously high rate of failure when used in an outdoor setting. It could, however, be just the thing for an interior application. When considering the track record of the product, it is also important to know the qualifications of the installer and quality of his continued service after the purchase has been made. Far too many sellers of security equipment lose interest after the sale has been consummated. This is unfortunate, as any alarm system only provides protection when it is "up" and working. If it malfunctions, and if service is inadequate or in some cases, nonexistent, the system itself creates a security breach and is totally worthless. It is therefore incumbent on the purchaser to ensure that a system will be maintained. When he does not know the seller, it is a good idea for him to assess the seller's service record, preferably by checking with others who use the same system and services. Such research should not be based exclusively on a list of references provided by the seller, but should extend to others who use or have experience with the seller and his product. Based on their input, a decision can be made accordingly.

MAINTENANCE

Once an alarm system has been purchased and correctly installed, it must be maintained. As previously stated, a piece of equipment that is not working is worthless. All systems, alarms included, must be maintained in an operable and reliable state. Some federal agencies require this.

The term maintenance is many times thought of in an active sense, that is, when something is broken, it is fixed. More important, maintenance must be thought of in a passive sense, that is, preventive maintenance. All security systems, alarms included, must be scheduled for regular routine maintenance. A preventive maintenance program should consist at a minimum, of:

1. Visual inspection of all components for damage, wear, and tear
2. Tests for operability and effectivity

Table 4-1 Volumetric Sensor Selection

Environmental and other Factors Affecting Sensor Usage	(Encircle one)		Effect on Sensor			Recommendations and Notes
			Ultrasonics	Microwave	Passive I/R	
1. If the area to be protected is enclosed by thin walls, or contains windows, will there be movement close by the outside of this area?	Yes	No	None	Major	None	Avoid using a microwave sensor unless it can be aimed way from thin walls, glass, etc., which can pass an amount of microwave energy.
2. Will protection pattern see sun, moving headlamps, or other sources of infrared energy passing through windows?	Yes	No	None	None	Major	Avoid using a passive I/R sensor unless its pattern can be positioned to avoid rapidly changing levels of infrared energy.
3. Does area to be protected contain HVAC ducts?	Yes	No	None	Moderate	None	Ducts can channel microwave energy to other areas. If using a microwave sensor, aim it away from duct openings.
4. Will two or more sensors of the same type be used to protect a common area?	Yes	No	None	None (see note).	None	Note: Adjacent units must operate on different frequencies.
5. Does area to be protected contain fluorescent or neon lights that will be on during Protection-On period?	Yes	No	None	Major	None	Microwave sensor, if used, must be aimed away from any fluorescent or neon light within 20'.

6. Are incandescent lamps, that are cycled on-and-off during Protection-On period, included in the protection pattern?	Yes	No	None	None	Major	If considering use of passive I/R sensor, make a trial installation and, if necessary, redirect protection pattern away from incandescent lamps.
7. Must protection pattern be projected from a ceiling?	Yes	No	None, but only for ceiling heights up to 15'.	Major	Major	Only *ultrasonic* sensors can be used on a ceiling, but height is limited to 15'. At greater ceiling heights, either (1) use rigid ceiling brackets to suspend sensor so as to maintain 15' limitation, or (2) in large open areas try using a microwave sensor mounted high on a wall and aimed downward.
8. Is the overall structure of flimsy construction (corrugated metal, thin plywood, etc.)?	Yes	No	Minor	Major	Minor	*Do not* use a *microwave* sensor. Where considerable structural movement can be expected, use a rigid mounting surface for ultrasonic or passive infrared sensor.
9. Will protection pattern include large metal objects or wall surfaces?	Yes	No	Minor	Major	Minor (major if metal is highly polished).	1. Use ultrasonic sensor. 2. Use passive I/R sensor.
10. Are there any nearby radar installations?	Yes	No	Minor	Major when radar is close & sensor is aimed at it.	Minor	Avoid using a microwave sensor.

Table 4-1   (Continued)

Environmental and other Factors Affecting Sensor Usage	(Encircle one)	Effect on Sensor			Recommendations and Notes
		Ultrasonics	Microwave	Passive I/R	
11. Will protection pattern include heaters, radiators, air conditioners, etc.?	Yes No	Moderate	None	Major, when rapid changes in air temperature are involved.	1. Use ultrasonic sensor, but aim it away from sources of air turbulence. (Desirable to have heaters, etc., turned off during Protection-On period). 2. Use microwave sensor.
12. Will area to be protected be subjected to ultrasonic noise (bells, hissing sounds, etc).?	Yes No	Moderate, can cause problems in severe cases.	None	None	1. Try muffling noise source and use an ultrasonic sensor. 2. Use a microwave sensor. 3. Use passive infrared sensor.
13. Will protection pattern include drapes, carpets, racks of clothing, etc.?	Yes No	Moderate, reduction in range.	None	Minor	1. Use ultrasonic sensor if some reduction in range can be tolerated. 2. Use a microwave sensor.
14. Is the area to be protected subject to changes in temperature and humidity?	Yes No	Moderate	None	Major	1. Use an ultrasonic sensor unless changes in temperature and humidity are severe. 2. Use a microwave sensor.
15. Is there water noise from faulty valves in the area to be protected?	Yes No	Moderate, can be a problem.	None	None	1. If noise is substantial try correcting faulty valves and use an ultrasonic sensor. 2. Use a microwave sensor.
16. Will protection pattern see moving machinery, fan blades, etc.?	Yes No	Major	Major	Minor	1. Have machinery, fans, etc., turned off during Protection-On period.

Question	Yes	No				Corrective Action
						2. Use careful placement of ultrasonic sensor. 3. Use passive infrared sensor.
17. Will drafts or other types of air movement pass through protection pattern?	Yes	No	Major	None	None, unless rapid temperature changes are involved.	1. If protection pattern can be aimed away from air movement, or if air movement can be stopped during Protection-On period, use an ultrasonic sensor. 2. Use a microwave sensor. 3. Use a passive I/R sensor.
18. Will protection pattern see overhead doors that can be rattled by wind?	Yes	No	Major	Major	Minor	1. If protection pattern can be aimed away from such doors, use an ultrasonic sensor. 2. Use a passive I/R sensor.
19. Are there hanging signs, calendar pages, etc. which can be moved by air currents during Protection-On period?	Yes	No	Major	Major	Moderate, can be a problem.	1. Use ultrasonic sensor, but aim pattern away from objects that can move or remove such objects. 2. Use passive infrared sensor.
20. Are there adjacent railroad tracks that will be used during Protection-On period?	Yes	No	Major	Minor	Minor	A trial installation is required if using an ultrasonic sensor.
21. Can small animals (or birds) enter protection pattern?	Yes	No	Major	Major	Major (particularly rodents)	Install a physical barrier to prevent intrusion by animals or birds.
22. Does area to be protected contain a corrosive atmosphere?	Yes	No	Major	Major	Major	None of these sensors can be used.

Source: ADT Sensory Survey Checklist Form 2269-00, with approval by ADT.

3.   Checks of backup power sources (including routine replacement of batteries if necessary)

When preventive maintenance programs for alarm systems are being formulated, the following guidelines are suggested:

1.   Inventory all system components as completely and accurately as possible. Depending on the number and nature of components, it may be wise to categorize and develop a separate program for each.
2.   Compile the necessary manufacturer's recommended preventive maintenance schedules and procedures.
3.   Set up a schedule for routine recommended preventive maintenance checks by category of component, e.g., all microwave intrusion detectors on the first work day of the month; all mechanical door contacts on the second work day of the month, etc. (assuming that preventive maintenance is done on a monthly basis). In a maximum-security environment, depending on the size of the facility and security systems, preventive maintenance should be performed at least once a month, and for sensitive areas, more often.
4.   Whenever and wherever batteries are used, they should be replaced at regular intervals in accordance with manufacturer's recommendations.
5.   If backup power is supplied by other means, e.g., emergency generator, it should be tested for operability and checked to ensure that the fuel tank and crankcase are full. An emergency generator should be a separate item in the preventive maintenance program. Immediately after each use, the fuel tank should be refilled or topped off.
6.   Light emitting diodes should be checked and replaced if defective.
7.   All components of the alarm system should be function-tested during preventive maintenance. Defective components must be repaired immediately or replaced or appropriate compensatory measures instituted until repairs can be effected.

If, after a careful program of preventive maintenance, a component of the system fails during routine operation, it should be replaced or repaired immediately. If this is impossible, compensatory actions must be taken to maintain the required levels of security until the component is functioning again. The most effective such measure is a member of the security force, equipped with two-way communications (and a duress system or alarm) and posted so as to provide the same information as the defective part. If, for example, a portion of a perimeter alarm system is out of service, a security officer may be posted in the area to observe visually and report on the affected area. Depending on the nature of the breakdown, closed-circuit TV could be used to monitor an area or entry as a compensatory measure.

A comprehensive testing program must be maintained for all systems, including alarms. The Nuclear Regulatory Commission outlines requirements for testing at fixed nuclear sites:

"1.   Tests and inspections during the installation and construction of physical protection-related subsystems and components to assure that they comply with their respective design criteria and performance specifications.
2.   Preoperational tests and inspections of physical protection-related subsystems and components to demonstrate their effectiveness and availability with respect to their respective design criteria and performance specifications.
3.   Operational tests and inspections of physical protection-related subsystems and components to assure their maintenance in an operable and effective condition, including:

   i.   Testing of each intrusion alarm at the beginning and end of any period that it is used. If the period of continuous use is longer than seven days, the intrusion alarm shall also be tested at least once every seven days."[14]

In the maximum-security environment, repairs and maintenance must be performed by at least two persons working as a team, both of whom are technically competent to service the defective component. This is yet another NRC requirement. Additionally, the NRC requires that the on-site security organization be notified prior to and on completion of repairs and maintenance. Once repairs are complete or preventive maintenance performed, the security organization must test the component to ensure its operability and performance.

While budgetary constraints may preclude the use of two-man maintenance teams, it is essential, regardless of who performs maintenance and/or repairs, that the system be tested by the security force on completion of repairs. It is also not a bad idea to double-check the system, after securing appropriate approval, sometime after the initial performance check. This is to preclude a time-delay disabling device left by a bogus serviceman.

Maintenance Documentation

Whenever a piece of equipment breaks down, it must, of course, be repaired. The form used to initiate repairs is usually referred to as a work order or work request. Whenever an item of security equipment or a security system component requires repair, a work order must be generated by the person responsible for security or his designee. No repair work other than approved and scheduled preventive maintenance should be allowed to occur without the security organization's knowledge and approval. No one other than the chief security officer or his designees should be able to authorize maintenance of any type on security systems or equipment. It is therefore essential that the security organization initiate the work order that bears the signature of the official requesting service. A copy of the work order should be retained and filed by the security organization.

The work order should be forwarded to the appropriate service personnel and, after repairs are effected, signed off by those performing the maintenance. The work order should also be signed by those security personnel conducting the after-service performance check. The completed form must then be returned to the security organization for retention for a suitable period of time (as determined by regulatory agencies or security management).

In addition to the documentation provided by the work order, security logs or journals must also record the fact that maintenance was performed, the time and date it was performed, the persons performing it, time that the system was checked for performance after maintenance, the persons performing the check, and the time and date the system was placed back into service. The logs or journals should also be used to note any type of maintenance performed on security systems or equipment, scheduled or otherwise.

ALARM SYSTEM OPERATION

Most alarm system sensors operate on the following principles, either singly or in conjunction with another:

1.   Breaking an electrical circuit
2.   Interrupting a light beam
3.   Detecting sound
4.   Detecting vibration
5.   Detecting motion
6.   Detecting a change in capacitance due to penetration of an electrostatic field[15]
7.   Detecting heat

Breaking an electrical circuit can be accomplished in a variety of ways, metallic foil and/or wire, grid wire sensors, pressure mats, and door contact switches, to name a few. There is no application for these types of sensors in a maximum-security environment if they are used alone—remember, diversity and redundancy. Each can be used to advantage and to the limits of a practitioner's imagination when they are supplemented with other types of sensors.

Interrupting a light beam is the basic principle behind photoelectric sensors. They may be susceptible to occlusion by snow, rain, smoke, or dust, and can be bypassed if an adversary has knowledge of its location and application. Photoelectric sensors should never be used exclusively but may be incorporated into the overall protection system.

Detecting sound can be quite effective in a maximum-security setting when used in conjunction with other types of sensors. Sound detectors are limited in their application, however, to areas where natural background noise is minimal and where discussions of classified information is prohibited.

Vibration-sensitive sensors are used on barriers, including ceilings and floors. They are designed to sense vibrations associated with a penetration attempt. They too have their drawbacks in that their use is restricted to areas where excessive vibrations are not normally encountered.

Detecting motion can be accomplished in a variety of ways. Two of the most common security applications of this capability are ultrasonic and microwave sensors. Ultrasonic sensors detect a change in a transmitted pattern of acoustic energy. While very effective indoors, their use outside is questionable. Microwave sensors operate in essentially the same manner, however, radio waves are transmitted rather than acoustic energy. Any change in the frequency of the radio waves reflected back to the receiver initiates an alarm. Their use in a maximum-security environment can be quite effective also. Their principle disadvantage is that radio waves are not easily confined and may penetrate beyond the confines of the area to be protected, thus resulting in inadvertant activation, that is, false alarms.

Detecting capacitance change in an electrostatic field can be quite effective in addition to other principles of detection. A "capacitance or electrostatic intrusion-detection system can be installed on a safe, wall, and/or openings therein in an effort to establish an electrostatic field around the object to be protected. This field is tuned by a balance between the electrical capacitance and the electrical inductance. The body capacitance of any intruder who enters the field unbalances the electrostatic energy of the field. This unbalancing activates the alarm system."[16]

This type of system is extremely flexible and can be used to guard any ungrounded metallic object within the maximum tuning range.[17] One primary disadvantage, already stated, is that objects must not be grounded. Additionally, the system's use in high-traffic areas could result in a high rate of false alarms.

Detecting heat is the principle employed by passive infrared intrusion devices. These detectors are used quite effectively in the maximum-security setting due primarily to their resistance to false alarms when properly installed. A passive infrared detector is a line-of-sight device and should not be installed so that it is "looking" at open flames, neon signs, or anything that emits heat while in motion. This type of device detects changes in the radiation of heat from the area being protected. An intruder's body heat, emitted while he is in motion, will be detected.

ALARM SYSTEMS AND COMPONENTS

There are several products that may have maximum-security application, depending on installation, purpose, and use.

Exterior Systems

Certain types of alarm systems employ microwave energy to generate a signal that when interrupted, triggers an alarm. Microwave energy is invisible, soundless, has no smell or taste, and is virtually undetectable by anyone who is unaware of the presence of such a system. To understand this principle, it helps to think of the invisible microwave energy as a beam of visible light.

In general outdoor use where such a system would provide penetration detection coverage along an established perimeter, the apparatus most commonly found uses a transmitter at one end of the perimeter "leg" and a receiver at the other. Because the equipment depends on line-of-sight transmission of the beam, long stretches may be covered adequately as long as there is nothing in the beam's path that interferes with signal reception. Items that could cause the system to generate false alarms or worse still, fail to recognize a genuine breach, could include tall grass, bushes, ditches, hillocks, large pieces of machinery or vehicles left in the detection zone, debris scattered by the wind, animals, and large birds. Fortunately, this problem can be easily overcome by keeping the perimeter graded to eliminate low spots through which an adversary could crawl below the microwave beam; and keeping all grass, bushes, shrubs, and other natural growth cut back or mowed periodically to prevent their swaying in a breeze and causing an alarm. Large pieces of machinery or vehicles that may be left in the detection zone could present a two-pronged problem—they could be used as a means of breaching the perimeter fence and, depending on the manner in which they are located, to mask someone's passage through the detection zone. It is not unusual at many large facilities occasionally to find debris scattered by the wind. In addition to the housekeeping problem thus presented, debris is often blown into perimeter zones where the microwave detector notes its presence and reports it by generating an alarm signal. All of this can be controlled. Animals, however, especially wild animals and birds (primarily large ones) do pretty much as they please without regard to the elaborate procedures and requirements man sets down. Where animal-caused false alarms are a problem, the solution is often to decrease the sensitivity of the signal, but not to the point where it occasionally fails to detect a human's passage during testing.

In general, most microwave alarm systems exhibit the same characteristics—they can be used to protect large indoor areas as well as long outdoor spans; special circuitry allows the apparatus to "recognize" certain obstacles or inanimate objects in the detection zone; and the beam is projected under, over, and around the object. Because modern transistors and microcircuits have reduced the bulk and weight of components (while enhancing dependability), the units are now relatively lightweight and easily mounted. They are protected in their housing by tamper switches and these housings are generally constructed to withstand the elements. The usual power supply is hard-wired 110-volt alternating current, which is run through a step-down transformer that converts it to 12 volts AC. For dependability, most manufacturers also offer an optional rechargeable standby battery system.

Interior Systems

One method of alarm generation consists of a switch (available in a variety of configurations) that is physically activated by an individual or piece of rolling stock stepping on or passing over the switch gear. This system is nondiscriminatory—anyone or anything will cause a signal to be generated. When properly used, such an alarm may have maximum-security applicability, not so much as a vital link in the security envelope as an adjunct to established systems.

Door Contacts

In the maximum-security environment, doors are usually protected by contacts whereby opening a door breaks or initiates an electric circuit and signals an alarm. The minimum type of door contact suitable for such use is a balanced magnetic switch. This differs from a magnetic switch in that it uses a balanced magnetic field in such a way that it resists defeat by someone using an external magnet. A balanced magnetic switch will detect a change in magnetic field strength and initiate an alarm.

It is expected that the maximum-security practitioner will evaluate his specific needs, consider those principles of alarm application offered, and make a decision regarding the best site-specific systems. It is hoped that an imaginative security director can devise ways to make his systems more effective. For example, in some environments it may be appropriate to connect detectors to a fail-safe electromechanical locking system whereby generation of an alarm signal would cause all doors in the affected area to fail in a closed and locked position, thereby trapping an intruder (safety considerations notwithstanding). Where it comes to alarm devices, a practitioner is limited only by his imagination and the principles expressed here.

ALARM MONITORING

As previously discussed, detection devices plus alarm controls equal alarm signaling. It does little good for a sophisticated maximum-security alarm to detect an intrusion and signal it if there is no one to be alerted. Alarms must be monitored for the intrusion to be detected. Monitoring can be performed off site or on site.

Off-Site Monitoring

Off-site monitoring, as the term implies, is accomplished away from the area being protected. Many alarm systems terminate in a central station. Monitoring capability at this location is often provided by the company installing the alarms (including such reputable firms as ADT and Sonitrol). Operators watch the alarms and, if an unauthorized intrusion occurs, notify authorities, which could include the local police department, patrolling security force, and the person whose responsibility it is to respond to the facility in the event of an alarm (usually referred to as the keyholder).

Central stations monitor a facility's alarms at the direction of the client, for example, during specified hours. A representative of the client usually sets up or secures the facility by activating the alarm system just prior to leaving after the close of business; or the central station can do this at pre-determined times. If access is required after the system has been activated, a system of codes is used to verify the identity and authority of the person requesting access. There are many modifications, but the process is basically the same for them all.

A great many alarm systems terminate at the local police department, and when an alarm is received it is responded to by police officers. Usually, the keyholder is notified and requested to respond or provide alternative instructions.

There are cases where a system will terminate at the keyholder's home. When an alarm is recieved, the keyholder determines the course of action, which could include personal response or notification of local law enforcement authorities.

Signal Transmission to Off-Site Monitors

There are several methods by which an alarm signal is transmitted to an off-site monitoring location: digital and tape dialers using commercial phone lines, dedicated or leased phone lines, radio-frequency transmission to an off-site receiver, and in some cases, microwave transmission to an off-site receiver. The use of off-site monitoring is never appropriate in a maximum-security setting because response to an intrusion takes more time than it does for an on-site security force. Some less-than-minimum-security facilities do rely to varying degrees, however, on an alarm system that is monitored off site. For these facilities, the following guidance is offered:

1.   Tape dialers and digital dialers usually depend on commercial telephone lines to transmit their message. With tape dialers, a problem could

occur if the number electromechanically dialed is busy or there is no answer. A digital dialer relies on electronics to check the commercial phone line at intervals to ensure that it has not been compromised. This is sometimes referred to as an interrogation and reply scheme. The problem is that these intervals can be up to 30 minutes apart, and a good thief hardly needs that long to commit a crime. Yet another problem occurs when commercial phone service is disrupted, for example, by an accidentally downed telephone pole. Whenever any part of an alarm system is disabled—sensor, control, or signaling device—the entire system is disabled. If phone lines are cut, a tape dialer cannot work and, in its basic design, will not sense the interruption. A digital dialer can be made to sense an interruption but not continuously. In other words, if an interruption in service occurs shortly after the line is checked by the dialer, it will not be detected until the next time a check is made of the line. Obviously, this could be costly.

2.   A better although more expensive proposition is the use of dedicated or leased telephone lines. With this method, a private telephone line is leased and used to carry nothing but alarm signals from the area being protected to the off-site monitoring station wherever it is located. A dedicated line has the added advantage of being easily supervised, that is, electronically protected against tampering or interruption. If a line is damaged accidentally or by design an alarm is generated, which should elicit the required response. Because the phone line is reserved exclusively for alarm signal transmissions, there is no need for automatic or digital dialers.

3.   Yet another type of system relies on radio signals to transmit an alarm to an offsite monitoring station known by the U.S. Army as FIDS (facility intrusion detection system). It is certified for use in areas such as those that store sensitive weapons, nuclear fuel, and chemical weapons. In its advanced configuration, FIDS can use radio frequency as a data-transmission link. To preclude compromise, radio signals should be encrypted prior to being sent to a monitoring receiver or processor. The Army requires its radio relays to "have an RF [radio frequency] output capable of extending each transmission link 15 km [on a line-of-sight basis]. . . . "Airborne relays must have a line-of-sight range of 100 km."[18] Therein lies the basic problem for commercial use of radio frequency as a data-transmission link. Radio frequency has limited applications in the commercial sense, at this time, in that its range is limited and it is susceptible to malfunction due to the limited number of frequencies available and the maximum use of radio communications. It is also affected by terrain.

As with any type of monitoring system, on site or off site, the most essential element is dependability of components and transmission lines. Any malfunction of the system must generate an alarm of some sort so that personnel can be alerted to the fact and effect repairs or initiate compensatory measures. Any intrusion or trouble alarm should be responded to in an appropriate manner and thoroughly investigated. Responding personnel should also be aware of the possibility of a diversion on receipt of a trouble alarm (see Chapter 9).

On-Site Monitoring

In a maximum-security environment, all alarm monitoring should be done on site. Alarms should annunciate in a continuously manned alarm station referred to as a central alarm station, or CAS, located on site. The CAS should be situated such that it cannot be seen from the facility's perimeter—inside an existing building, for example. The CAS should have primary and secondary means of auxilliary power—emergency generator and battery backup. Each should be capable of automatically and instantaneously supplying power in the event of a commercial power failure.

Constructing the CAS

The CAS should be as impregnable as possible. It must be constructed of bullet-resistant material, including glass and/or vision blocks. Construction methods such as those outlined in Chapter 2 would be appropriate. Entrances and exits should be kept to a minimum and should be of the same integrity as the CAS itself. It should be heated, air conditioned, and gun ports should be installed. It should be well ventilated (ducts should be screened so as to preclude attack through them).

Outfitting the CAS

The CAS should be outfitted with certain basic equipment:

1.   The primary purpose of the CAS is to provide a safe and secure haven for those charged with on-site monitoring of alarm and other security systems. Alarms must terminate and annunciate in the CAS. Depending on the type of system used, the annunciator could consist of nothing more than a simple bell or horn and/or light to indicate an alarm condition, or it could be sophisticated, complete with a cathode-ray terminal (CRT) that will indicate and analyze an alarm condition.

     A printer of some sort, preferably a high-speed one, is desirable so that alarms and/or routine changes in status are automatically recorded on paper and can serve as a permanent record.

     It is possible to synchronize an alarm signal with various appropriate assessment capabilities such as closed-circuit television (CCTV) and remote audio coverage of the affected area. Additional capabilities that can be added to an alarm system to enhance its existing capabilities are always appropriate in a maximum-security setting. It must be remembered, however, that the more complicated an overall system, the more prone it may be to malfunctions or failures. No maximum-security alarm system should be designed so that the failure of a component causes a failure of the total system. Again, the principle of diversity and redundancy applies.

2. In a maximum-security environment, CCTV is widely used as a surveillance and assessment tool. Monitors and remote controls for such features as tilt and pan, zoom lenses, focusing, and iris settings should be located within the CAS.

3. Other remote controls and devices such as electric strike door releases, CRTs, and access-control subsystems must be located within the CAS.

4. If and where possible, the CAS should be equipped with dedicated telephones or hot lines to local law enforcement, firefighting, and other support agencies. Hot lines should be of the type that uncradling the handset initiates the call at either end. Transmission lines should indicate when they have been tampered with or have other malfunctions. These problems should be corrected immediately or, if this is impossible, equivalent compensatory measures instituted until repairs can be effected.

5. The CAS should have at least one, and preferably two or more, commercial telephones for handling routine calls and as an additional means of summoning assistance should it become necessary.

6. The facility's radio base station should, if possible, be located within the CAS. If this is impractical, other measures, more fully described in Chapter 6, must be taken to provide adequate security for the base station. The CAS must have the capability of communicating by radio with all members of the security force. If possible, two-way (or at the very least, one-way) communications should be established with local law enforcement authorities.

7. It is a good idea to equip the CAS with a citizens band base station as yet another means of summoning off-site assistance.

8. An intercom system base station should be located in the CAS.

9. The CAS should have inherent fire-fighting capability so as to preclude attack by this method.

10. A well-stocked first-aid kit should be maintained in the CAS.

Certain additional equipment, supplies, and resources could be located within the CAS so as to increase its capabilities (not listed in any particular priority or order of necessity):

1. Protective masks (gas masks) should be available for every person normally assigned to the CAS, plus at least two spares.

2. A Scott Air-Pak or other self-contained oxygen supply should be available for every person normally assigned to the CAS, plus at least two spares.

3.   A system for ejecting smoke or gas should be considered when designing or retro-fitting the area.
4.   A remotely controlled (by the CAS operator) system for dispensing noxious gas to areas around the CAS should be considered where feasible. Gas jets could be situated near the doors or other openings.
5.   A supply of drinking water and food, perhaps C-rations, should be kept on hand.
6.   If possible, installed or portable toilet facilities could be incorporated into the station.
7.   CCTV monitors should be connected through a switching device to a video tape recorder (VTR) that can be controlled by the CAS operator. The VTR should have time/date-generating capability.
8.   All conversations by telephone or two-way radio should be tape-recorded. The recorder should be wired directly into the communications system and could be voice-activated.
9.   The CAS operator should have the capability to observe in all directions. Periscopes, vision blocks, fiberoptics, or other secure method could be used.
10.   Bullet-resistant, remote-controlled (by the CAS operator) shutters or louvers could be used over exterior glassed areas of the CAS.
11.   Some system of emergency lighting should be part of the station. Power could come from an emergency generator or batteries. Additionally, there should be a supply of flashlights and other battery-powered lighting devices available.
12.   In addition to any emergency generator, all electric and electronic systems should be equipped with batteries that will sustain the CAS operation for at least eight hours. This includes, at a minimum, alarm system, telephone, and two-way radio.
13.   All personnel should be equipped with or have available in the station bullet-resistant vests or flak jackets, helmets, etc.
14.   There should be at least two shotguns stored in the CAS and at least 50 rounds of 00 buckshot for each.
15.   A tool kit, including a fire axe and bolt-cutters, should be maintained.

In other words, the CAS should be capable of completely independent operation and be completely self-sufficient for up to eight hours at least, in case it is cut off. During that eight-hour period, the station must retain some way of summoning off-site assistance.

Secondary Alarm Station

All maximum security-facilities should have an alternate control center. Usually referred to at nuclear sites as SAS, or secondary alarm station, it should duplicate the CAS in construction, equipment, and capabilities, and be capable of replacing the CAS as the primary security-control center. The SAS should never be "slaved" off the CAS, that is, all alarms should terminate in both stations so as to allow the SAS to function independently in the event the CAS is immobilized or rendered inoperative.

Additionally, two stations should monitor each other to preclude compromise of either facility or the security functions they control. Neither the SAS nor the CAS should be able to allow access to any sensitive areas without the knowledge of the other.

Monitoring alarms in the maximum-security environment must be done constantly by personnel dedicated to that purpose. These people should have no other duties or assignments that would preclude their alert and careful monitoring and, when necessary, initiating the proper response to an unscheduled alarm.

When alarm signal recording is done manually, each alarm station operator should independently record the information in the format required by security management. To evaluate the performance and accuracy of the operators, a comparison should be made between station logs to point up discrepancies.

When the establishment of primary and secondary alarm stations is not feasible, one method whereby the possibility of operater-caused security lapses may be minimized is to establish a two-man rule in the station. This rule requires that there always be two fully qualified operators on duty. In this way, one operator is always checking to ensure the other is performing properly. At some locations, the volume of alarms received or other tasks for which the operators are responsible may be such that two men may not be enough to staff the post adequately. In this case, it may be necessary to assign a supervisor under whose direction and supervision the operators function. In this case, it becomes a three-man rule. In some larger facilities, it is not unheard of for the alarm station supervisor to have three or more individuals under his control.

ALARM RECORDS AND DOCUMENTATION

Many of the alarm systems described provide for a permanent record of alarms though the incorporation of a printer. Often, however, these printers are options that increase the systems costs, sometimes by considerable amounts. This additional cost may result in a system that will not provide the service necessary, but which includes a printer at a price that is within budget. Before this action is taken, however, consideration should be given to the number of alarms that are, or can be expected to be, received during a regular work day. If the number of received alarms is less than one every 30 seconds during limited duration peak or emergency periods, consideration should be given to establishing and maintaining a manual alarm log (Figure 4-2).

ALARM LOG

No. _____   Date: _____

Time received	Point/ sensor	Type alarm	Alarm cause	Responding guard	Time reset	Operator's initials

Page ____ of ____ Pages

Figure 4-2   Manual alarm log.

This is prepared on a daily basis and records the time of the alarm, the point sensor from which it originated, what type of alarm it was (door contact, perimeter intrusion, motion detector, etc.), its cause as determined by the guard who was dispatched to the alarm scene by the station operator, time of alarm reset, and the operator's initials. When the operator accesses (takes out of operation) an alarm point, this is also recorded on the log, leaving the time of reset blank and entering this information as soon as the alarm point is placed back into operation, provided it is on the same date. If the alarm point remains in the access mode at the start of the next day, this information should be transferred or carried forward to the next log. It is recommended that these individual alarm log sheets be serially numbered to avoid falsification of records. If the sheets are professionally prepared, a print shop can accomplish this. If they are reproduced on site, a numbering machine could be used.

These log sheets should be forwarded to the site security manager or his designee daily along with all security paperwork generated during that 24-hour period. The individual receiving the alarm logs should check them over carefully to ensure that all entries have been properly made and that the response actions initiated were correct. Other areas to check include long unexplained intervals between the time an alarm is received and the time it is reset; and point or senor location not agreeing with the type of alarm (the individual checking the paperwork must be thoroughly familiar with the site alarm system to be able to recognize such faux pas). Completed alarm logs may then be filed for whatever period of time is required by regulation or as may be determined by the site security manager. When an alarm system is equipped with an integral printer, it should be tested periodically for accuracy and dependability. A member of the security force can cause an alarm at every alarm system point or sensor to determine that the printer is recording the information correctly. In addition, preventive maintenance programs should include this unit for periodic checks.

Unscheduled Alarm Reports

Whenever an unscheduled alarm is received at the continuously manned station, in addition to the dispatch of one or more security officers to assess and evaluate the situation at the scene of annunciation, the console operator or station supervisor should generate reports. These may be simply on-going records prepared in a format specified by the security department. To ensure consistency, a printed form that requires only the addition of relevant bits of information to complete would be the best choice for most sites. In certain situations, especially when an unscheduled alarm develops into a serious incident, a narrative summary would be of use to security management. This type of report should contain all the information to be found on the printed form, but include all events that transpired subsequent to the alarm receipt, showing times, personnel involved, and actions taken. As with all security record keeping, accuracy must be maintained at all times.

OTHER CONSIDERATIONS

At facilities with large outdoor expanses that must be kept under surveillance, there are really only three practical methods of accomplishing the task. The first is to establish roving patrols. These may be walking or vehicle patrols and at some locales where neither is practical, horses can be used to cover difficult terrain. The second alternative involves the installation of CCTV cameras to provide coverage of the grounds. The last alternative involves the installation and use of guard towers.

Guard Towers

Guard towers are certainly nothing new in high-security settings, having been used for centuries to maintain surveillance over wide expanses, principally by military and penal authorities. Only recently has the use of guard towers become acceptable in nonmilitary security installations or in those that have no connection with correctional facilities. From the technological standpoint, prefabricated guard towers are available that provide a comfortable environment. In addition, they have all the equipment needed for one or more security officers to provide a high degree of visual coverage over considerable areas of open land or outdoor storage yards. At some maximum-security facilities, these guard towers are hardened to withstand small-arms fire; are provided with redundant means of communications; and have remotely controlled area spot or flood lights, gun ports, and the like. When such an installation is contemplated, the first consideration should be whether or not one or more guard towers will substantially improve security coverage of the facility by the on-site guard force. The next point to address must, of course, be whether such installation would be economically feasible, both in short-term and long-term benefits. Other considerations include whether or not future construction might require relocation of the towers or make their use unnecessary; and the existence of weather or environmental conditions unique to the area that could make use of the towers unsafe or impractical.

Once the decision is made to install guard towers, planning should proceed to site them in locations that allow full and unobstructed view not just of the area inside the perimeter fence, but of approaches to the site and along the isolation zone outside the perimeter fence. If the facility may be subject to an armed attack, one should plan on hardening the towers and providing them with gun ports. Glare lighting, which could be used to blind anyone attempting to use a weapon against a tower, should also be considered. This lighting will also prove to be a deterrent to anyone contemplating breaching the perimeter fence. If possible, the stairway or ladder leading to the tower house should also be provided with some shielding and an emergency means of exit such as a fireman's pole.

Other Alarms

Other alarms that may be part of the system monitored by the on-site security force could include metal detectors, special nuclear material (SNM) alarms, toxic substance alarms, water pressure alarms, fire alarms, sprinkler valve alarms, boiler alarms, explosives detectors, and duress alarms.

Metal Detectors

Metal detectors could be large, walk-through or simple hand-held battery operated devices. They would be used to scan personnel and hand-carried objects entering or leaving a controlled area. On entry, they would be used to detect the attempted introduction of unauthorized items such as weapons or cameras. On exit, detectors could be used to scan for company property such as tools and equipment, parts, or the company product. Within a security-controlled facility, metal detectors may also be used to maintain control over unauthorized movement of items from one part of the plant to another. Metal-detecting alarm systems are covered in Chapter 8.

SNM Detectors

At facilities that process or use quantities of special nuclear material (SNM), detectors are used to ensure that none of this material is surreptitiously carried off site. These detectors are often portal monitors set up in areas of controlled traffic flow so that everyone passing a specific point is forced to pass through the detector. Hand-held scanners may also be used to conduct checks of suspected material or individuals when a portal monitor is not conveniently located. While slower in use, the hand scanner (also known as a scintillator) is extremely effective. When a walk-through metal detector is used in tandem with a radiation portal monitor, the possibilities for the undetected removal of any quantity of SNM become very remote. If the SNM has been placed within a metal shielding container, it may get past the radiation monitor, but the metal detector will alarm on the container mass.

Toxic Gas Alarms

Toxic gas alarms are usually continuous-action air samplers that are capable of detecting quantities of toxic substances in the surrounding atmosphere before they become threatening to human life. Another type of air sampler monitors the amount of oxygen available. These are often found in mine shafts or in other environments where oxygen may become depleted through use or through displacement by carbon monoxide.

Water Pressure Alarms

Water pressure alarms are installed on equipment that requires a constant flow of water to cool a vital process. These alarms may be found in nuclear power reactors where a sudden loss of cooling-system water pressure immediately triggers a complicated process for shutting down the reactor before damage to the physical plant occurs or before radiological release can take place. These alarms can also be installed in high-pressure feed lines for viscous fluid, where the loss of pressure could result in costly damage to pumps and other equipment. A pressure alarm would also be desirable in a fuel line feeding a vital piece of equipment such as a generator.

Fire Alarms

The importance of fire alarms is obvious. Detection may be through the use of heat or smoke sensors that would automatically trigger local as well as remotely monitored alarms. Important components of a fire detection system are its personnel. When a person detects a fire, the alarm system should have the means available for him immediately to alert all personnel in the area of the danger and broadcast the fact to the on-site alarm station. Building codes and local fire regulations are almost unanimous in their requirements for a plant or building employing over a certain minimum number of personnel, or which provides an opportunity for a fire greater than would otherwise be expected because of the materials and processes used or products manufactured. These sites must have fire alarm pull boxes and locally annunciated alarms in addition to escape doors and possibly other devices such as automatic sprinkler systems.

Sprinkler Alarms

When an automatic sprinkler is installed, consideration should be given to equipping the system with alarms. If the sprinkler malfunctions and goes off when there is no fire, considerable water damage could be incurred by machinery and materials in the area. With an alarm system, responding on-site personnel could quickly secure the water supply and thus minimize such damage. A secondary benefit of a sprinkler alarm would be in alerting personnel to a possible fire in the event the automatic alarm system failed.

Explosives Detectors

Explosives detectors would be another desirable addition to the security equipment array on site. These would be used at security-controlled personnel access points to screen for the introduction of incendiaries or explosives. The newer explosive detectors are automatic and are constructed to be used as walk-through portal monitors. Entry and exit are controlled by a red/green traffic light built into the unit, and actual testing is accomplished by the machine sampling air drawn into it past the subject who is held stationary before the sampling port by the red light. If the air sampling detects no explosive vapor present, the red signal changes to green and the subject proceeds. Hand-held explosives detectors have also been manufactured that could be used in a mail check or in a field inspection. Explosives detectors are more fully covered in Chapter 8.

Duress Alarms

Duress alarms are not generally used at many high-security facilities, although here perhaps more than at any other type of installation their use seems desirable. Duress alarms are not necessarily alarms in the traditional wire-switch-bell sense. They could include radio transmissions by the use of a belt-type battery-operated radio signal generator that can be activated by touch or when reoriented to 45 degrees from the vertical angle, as would be the case if the individual were knocked to the ground or forced to lie flat. Other duress alarms include verbally transmitted codes, hand signals, or a challenge-and-reply system with a new code word every day. They are almost useless, however, unless the personnel using them are completely familiar with their use and the manner in which each such alarm received is to be handled. To ensure the proper actions by all concerned with a duress alarm, the system should be periodically tested, with personnel performance being evaluated for corrective action.

NOTES

1. "Exploring the Micro World" *Newsweek*, October 26, 1981, 85.
2. *The Code of Federal Regulations* (Washington, D.C.: 1981), title 10, part 73.20(b)(2).
3. Ibid, part 74.45(g)(5).
4. Robert P. Lee, "Business and Residential Security." Address presented to the Chamber of Commerce and The American Society for Industrial Security, Warwick, R.I., October 27, 1981.
5. Ibid.
6. Ibid.
7. Ibid.
8. Robert L. Barnard, *Intrusion Detection Systems* (Woburn, Mass.: Butterworth's, 1981).
9. Ibid.
10. Ibid.
11. Nuclear Regulatory Commission, *Regulatory Guide* 5.44. REV. 2 (Washington, D.C.: The Commission, 1980).
12. Ibid.
13. Pierce, R. Brooks, *Officer Down, Code Three* (Schiller Park, Ill.: Motorola Teleprograms, Inc., 1975), p. 6.
14. *The Code of Federal Regulations*, title 10, part 73.46(g).
15. *Physical Security, U.S. Army Field Manual 19–30* (Washington, D.C.: Department of the Army, 1979), p. 94.
16. Ibid., p. 99.
17. Ibid.
18. Ibid, p. 130.

CHAPTER 5

The Use of Light to Enhance Physical Security

Man has always feared the dark and the many dangers it threatens. In primeval times he was often forced to spend nights in trees rather than on the ground because he was no physical match for prowling carnivores. The discovery of fire of course, changed this forever. The light and heat given off were usually enough of a deterrent to make the meanest cave bear or saber-toothed tiger decide to look elsewhere for food or shelter rather than risk the pain and suffering of a scorched hide. Once man decided that travel after dark could be made safer by a portable fire, it wasn't long before torches came into being.

Ancient armies used light to confuse their enemies. Instances of an army setting up a large encampment complete with a large number of cooking fires and illumination torches well within visual range of the enemy force and leaving this camp under the care of a small force of personnel who maintained the fires while the main body of soldiers slipped away under cover of darkness to circle and hit the opposing force from an unexpected quarter, are not unknown. In these instances, the light of the cooking fires and torches provided physical security by making the opposing army believe the invaders had bivouaced and settled down for the night when in fact, they were mounting an attack under cover of the ruse.

The safety and security provided by a walled city with controlled access points was enhanced by the torches or illumination fires that were maintained at each manned gate into the city. These fires or torches provided light by which the gate sentries could identify personnel entering to ensure that only authorized individuals gained access. The same procedures were used when feudal lords built their castles.

With the coming of candles and the fabrication of practical devices that would allow the candle to be used outdoors in all types of weather, the use of inefficient torches began to decline. In the East however, while the necessity for a dependable source of light was early recognized, the development of a source for this centered on liquid-fueled lamps. The typical artist's rendering of Alladin's Lamp is a good representation of the type of lamp utilized in this area of the world for centuries.

Candles, torches, and oil lamps were the best sources of artificial light available for a very long time, but in the nineteenth century it was discovered that the controlled burning of coal gave off a combustible gas. Soon most major cities boasted gas street lamps and even gas lights in the home.

This was a rowdy period in some of our major metropolitan areas. The Civil War had been over for a few years and the nation was really beginning to grow - Chicago was starting to establish itself as a major commercial center; New York was continuing its own almost frenetic growth with more and more immigrants arriving daily - those who didn't settle in New York scattered to other areas - St. Louis - Boston - New Orleans - Philadelphia - the farmlands of the Mid-west - around the Horn to California and everywhere in between. Most major cities during this period, experienced a great deal of lawlessness in certain quarters. Hold-up men prowled the streets - burglars, "cut-purses" (muggers) and "grifters" (con-men)made the darkness their ally - "press-gangs" (kidnappers) worked the waterfront saloons and "flop houses" (and occasionally were known to cross the tracks into the respectable side of town) in search of able bodied men to fill out the crew lists of vessels leaving on long commercial voyages. No crime or immoral act was unheard of in the cities. The advent of the gas lamp as a cheap and dependable method for lighting the streets was probably the first step (and certainly the one showing the most immediate results) in what was to become the beginning of the war on crime in the streets in this country.

While these were better than anything that had ever come before, they had drawbacks. They cast a relatively weak light that had a limited area of coverage; they required the services of an individual to ignite the flame manually every evening and extinguish it each dawn. When used as a source of home lighting, gas from a defective fixture would sometimes lead to death by asphyxiation, fire, or explosion. The discovery of petroleum in Pennsylvania led to distillation of crude oil. This distillate known as coal oil (later renamed kerosene) was intended for use in lamps and lanterns and eventually became the energy source for kitchen stoves and home heating systems. Attempts were made to use kerosene-fueled apparatus for public service, but the drawbacks outweighed the advantages. For private security use, however, kerosene lamps and lanterns served admirably, particularly in areas where commercial gas service was not available.

The invention of a practical electrical generator was initially regarded as an interesting phenomenon, but with little practical application. At last, Thomas Alva Edison unlocked the secrets of producing a dependable source of light powered by electrical energy. From Edison's first successful experiment, we have seen the types of lights grow from simple incandescent bulbs of very low wattage, to today's bewildering assortment of high-wattage incandescent, flourescent, carbon arc, sodium vapor, quartz halogen, and mercury fixtures.

Far-sighted individuals also realized that electrical lighting could deter criminals by using it to illuminate the outsides of buildings. The criminal element was now deprived of its most important advantage—darkness. When other merchants and manufacturers began to realize that their darkened factories and warehouses were being broken into much more often then those which used the new-fangled electric lights to illuminate the outside, it wasn't long before the idea began to really catch on. While the incandescent lamp was for many years the most efficient method of providing light, it still had its limits, primarily in the amount of light it could generate over a given area. Its effectiveness could be increased by use of efficient reflectors. In some applications such as military searchlights, a compact but very bright lamp was coupled with large motor-driven reflectors to produce powerful beams capable of illuminating objects hundreds or even thousands of feet away.

Flood lamps use fixed focus reflectors integral with the lamps to produce a bright but diffused light over a wide area. These are the types most often found in outdoor security applications. They may be of the incandescent type mounted in an approved outdoor receptacle, an arrangement of several in the same mounting that are angled to provide illumination over a wide area, or the newer type of that use the searchlight principle of a small but intense light source in conjunction with a concave reflector. This type is most often used in glare lighting or in an application where one glare lighting fixture would be mounted so that it would serve the same purpose as several of the smaller sealed-beam flood lamps mounted in weatherproof holders.

Another source of artificial light that is not usually considered as such is infrared. Infrared light waves travel in a color spectrum that is generally invisible to the naked eye. It is only with the aid of special viewing devices that we are able to see objects illuminated with infrared light. While some infrared night-viewing equipment was used in World War II, one of its greatest applications at the present time is in alarm systems, and it can thus be considered a use of light in the enhancement of physical security.

In this chapter we discuss lighting in the maximum-security environment, describe various types of lighting devices available, and indicate some methods in which they may be used to enhance physical protection.

MAXIMUM-SECURITY LIGHTING REQUIREMENTS

In some cases, protective lighting is the predominant, if not the sole, element of the security system. Whether it is applied to maximum or a lesser degree of security, to be effective, lighting must accomplish some basic things or its value is dubious.

Basically, lighting should allow the property's protectors to observe goings on without being observed themselves, "make detection likely," and discourage attempts to penetrate the system.[1] A National Bureau of Standards publication states that the design of protective lighting systems should optimize "conditions for intruder: (a) psychological deterrence, (b) visual detection and identification, and (c) visual incapacitation."[2]

Psychological deterrence is perhaps the optimum condition loss prevention people hope for. It is obviously much easier all around if a potential intruder is deterred from attempting a penetration. Unfortunately, deterrence cannot be measured in a qualitative way; what may deter one may not deter another. Lighting has been afforded a high priority when it comes to designing an overall security system. This is due to the obvious (and correct) presumption that the kind and amount of lighting is the first observation of a facility an adversary will make after the hours of darkness. As stated earlier, desire and opportunity must exist for a crime to be committed. Lighting is a means of eliminating or alleviating a criminal's desire—in other words, it is a deterrent. Criminals fear detection much less than they fear identification: "Optimization of intruder visual identification probabilities serves a dual purpose: (a) it may serve as a deterrent against potential intrusion attempts, and (b) it may increase the likelihood of an intruder being apprehended once an intrusion has commenced."[3] It should be quite obvious that any criminal makes an estimate, consciously or unconsciously, of the odds against getting caught. If he feels he can get away with it, he will try. If not, he will pursue other options. Various factors contribute to this decision, among them, lighting, in conjunction with security response forces (or police). "The deterrence value of a security lighting system is associated not only with a potential intruder's cognitive estimates of apprehension probabilities, but also with the subjective impression or 'mood' which the lighting system induces. The more 'foreboding' and 'hostile' a [site] is made to appear through special lighting effects, the less inclined a potential intruder should be to initiate a break-in attempt."[4] Security lighting, therefore, involves both objective and subjective evaluations on the part of a potential adversary. In a maximum-security environment, this phenomenon should be exploited.

There are certain other basic requirements that are so obvious that they may sometimes be overlooked. As obvious as they may be, they are often considered important enough to be included in security lighting planning documents. For example[5]:

Protective lighting systems will be operated continuously during hours of darkness.

Lighting . . . must be [under] . . . the control of the security force.

Protective lights should be employed so that failure of one or more lights will not affect the operation of remaining lights.

However obvious these points may be, they are valid and must not be overlooked.

Effectiveness

There are certain objectives associated with security lighting, realization of which will certainly increase the effectiveness of the lighting system[6]:

1. Provide deterrence to criminal acts
2. Increase the likelihood of identifying intruders
3. Capitalize on glare lighting to the advantage of security forces
4. Be completely reliable with minimum maintenance
5. Provide enough light, primary and auxillary, to achieve its intended purpose and enough additional light at likely penetration points
6. Be located within the facility's perimeter where damage potential can be minimized

A most complete statement of goals for effective security lighting are specified by the Nuclear Regulatory Commission (NRC). "The goals of an effective security of lighting system are:

1. Discourage or deter entry attempts by intruders.
2. Maximize the probability of intruder detection should entry be attempted.
3. Provide glare effective in handicapping the intruder and avoid glare which handicaps guards or other personnel authorized to be in the immediate area of the security lighting system.
4. Provide additional illumination for areas most susceptible to intrusion.
5. Provide adequate illumination levels for intruder detection.
6. Provide adequate illumination levels and suitable light-to-dark ratios for the determination of false alarm causes on existing or planned perimeter intrusion-detection systems.
7. Provide convenient switch and control access.
8. Provide supplementary, portable lighting or searchlights to permit exploration inside and outside the protected area, and to backup fixed lighting systems during emergencies.
9. Provide protection for luminaires, supports, distribution systems and auxillary equipment by locating them within the protected area where they are not readily accessible.
10. Provide an adequate maintenance program to assure lighting reliability.
11. Provide an adequate testing program to assure lighting capability and performance to specifications.
12. Provide for operating procedures for use during normal and emergency situations."[7]

While the NRC document lists these points as goals, they can rightfully be considered by the security practitioner as requirements for maximum-security lighting.

Lighting Levels

Much has been written and said about the intensity of security lighting. The *Code of Federal Regulations* specifies that outside areas within the protected

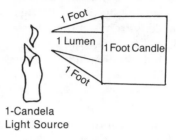

1 Square Foot

1 Foot

1 Lumen   1 Foot Candle

1 Foot

1-Candela
Light Source

Figure 5-1 One footcandle. (Courtesy of Security World.)

area must be lighted to a level of at least 0.2 footcandles.[8] The Army has varying standards of lighting intensity. Open yards, for example, should have at least 0.2 footcandles at any point; docks or open piers should have at least 1 footcandle; and water approaches at least 0.5 footcandles[9] (a footcandle is a unit for measuring the intensity of illumination; it is equal to one lumen per square foot) (Figure 5–1).

Recommended light levels usually range from 1 to 0.2 footcandles measured horizontally at ground level. "These are maintained levels and should still be attained when the lamp lumen depreciation is greatest and the luminaires the dirtiest, a point usually reached at the end of lamp life or about the time of group relamping."[10]

William A. Weibel[11] suggests four zones of security lighting concern:

Zone I: Building exterior surfaces—entrances, walls, and roofs
Zone II: Exterior areas near buildings—parking lots, roadways, and walkways
Zone III: Exterior intermediate areas, between buildings and the area perimeter—storage areas, parking lots, roadways, walkways, and open areas
Zone IV: Exterior perimeter areas—fence lines, water approaches, rail entrances, roadway entrances, pedestrian entrances, and open areas

He further suggests minimum levels of illumination for each, with the recommendation that levels (in footcandles) should be doubled for critical areas[12]:

Zone I: 2.0 for building entrances and exterior walls, to a minimum height of eight feet, for vital locations or structures 1.0 for roof surfaces requiring surveillance
Zone II: 1.0 for parking lots
            0.4 for roadways
      0.2 for storage areas
      0.2 for walkways

Zone III: 1.0 for parking lots
              0.4 for roadways
          0.2 for walkways
          0.1 for storage areas
          0.05 for open areas
Zone IV: 2.0 for pedestrian entrances
              1.0 for roadway entrances
          1.0 for rail entrances
          0.2 on vertical plane at points three feet above the ground plane for glare barrier
          0.1 for fence line (nonisolated)
          0.1 for water approaches
          0.05 for open areas
          0.05 for boundary lines (isolated fence or no fence)

It is, of course, up to a facility's security director to determine his own needs and system applications. These recommendations for maximum-security lighting are suggestions for minimum standards. Anything more may enhance lighting security (as will be seen in the following section).

DESIGNING A LIGHTING SYSTEM

In designing a lighting system, particular care must be paid to its power demands. Weibel makes the point that "an electrical system designed for incandescent lamps exclusively will require a higher current-carrying capacity (voltage and light output being the same) than a system of fluorescent, HID, or LPS lamps, because of the low efficiency of incandescent lamps. . . . At one time many outdoor systems for roadways and area lighting were of the series-circuit variety, but today the multiple-circuit type is preferred."[13] He further mentions that while 120-volt multiple-circuit voltage is still popular, other voltages are used, particularly in large systems. This use of higher voltages is indicative of the increased awareness by security managers and lighting designers of the necessity for providing an adequate power supply and distribution system. Not only must dependable service be provided under all existing conditions, it must be capable of being expanded or upgraded at a later time through the addition of more luminaires, or possibly, installation of luminaires that achieve peak efficiency at the higher voltages.

Amount of Lighting

Another important planning consideration is the amount of light desired. It has been recommended that approximately 2 footcandles be provided for major expressways, bikeways, and pedestrian ways. It should be kept in mind that the measurement of two footcandles on horizontal surfaces is subject to a great many variables such as differences in materials that affect reflectivity, seasonal changes in vegetation that affect light patterns, and weather conditions that may reduce the available light to below minimum acceptable levels. When planning placement of light poles or standards, these and other site-peculiar problems must be taken into consideration to ensure that the light level will be adequate under even the most adverse conditions. This will probably require a system that provides an overabundance of light under ideal conditions in order to meet the minimum requirements under less than ideal conditions, a method of controlling the intensity of light provided, or auxiliary lighting that may be activated to supplement the primary system when environmental conditions deteriorate.

Naturally, a system that provides an overabundance of light under ideal conditions does so at the cost of increased energy use. Incorporation of a dimming device into the perimeter control circuit will provide only the necessary light under conditions existing at that point. This device should have positive stops to ensure uniformity of light levels, rather than being the rotary type, which may be found in many homes and which provides for an infinite number of levels. The power demand of a reduced light level should result in savings in the amount of electrical energy consumed and in increased bulb or luminaire life.

From a practical standpoint, the best choice would appear to be a system designed to provide adequate light under the most adverse conditions, yet, through the use of a dimming control, provides only that amount necessary under all other environmental conditions. In such a system, failure of or damage to one or more luminaires or standards could leave large gaps in the light curtain. A more dependable albeit more expensive system consists of luminaires that provide adequate light levels under normal operating conditions. This is backed up by a second system of incandescent or other rapid-start auxiliary lights that are independently circuited and manually controlled from the on-site alarm station. It would provide the necessary additional light when weather or other adverse conditions reduce the main system's output. In addition, if parts of the primary system were damaged or if it could not function for other reasons, the auxiliary (or secondary) system could provide at least minimum lighting.

Other Factors

While planning where lights or standards should be placed, several factors should be considered: can the lights be mounted on existing structures (buildings, utility poles, water towers, etc.)? Is the isolation zone inside the protected area fence wide enough (or possibly too wide) to provide a reasonable degree of detection probability under the conditions planned? Are there anticipated construction plans that could be taken into consideration so that installation of necessary lighting could be accomplished in one master operation rather than in several piecemeal stages? Will poles or standards be so tall as to require aircraft warning lights? Coordination among departments at all stages of planning for perimeter security lighting should cover antici- pated plans for new construction, relocation of facilities within the protected area, and/or anticipated problems from a maintenance standpoint. If the fa- cility is located in an area where low-flying aircraft may be operating or if the light standards are extraordinarily tall and not in use during all hours of darkness, aircraft warning lights may be a requirement. The selection of a standard from which the chosen light source will be hung could depend on not only cost, but on such factors as soil conditions, the amount of routine seismic activity occurring in the area, the amount of rain and/or snow nor- mally received, temperature extremes, and wind velocities experienced at the site.

Site Survey

The next step consists of a detailed site survey to determine not only where the perimeter lights will be located, but what types of support poles or stan- dards to use; what modifications to existing structures, fences, or terrain may be necessary to optimize the planned lighting; whether the planned lighting could prove a liability to security officers; and so on.

Determination must then be made as to what type of luminaire will provide the desired light pattern; level of illumination; service life; ease of maintenance, ruggedness, and ability to remain functional in harsh climatic conditions; restart time in the event of power interruption; and the like. Care must be taken to ensure that light from the luminaires does not "splash" back onto guards who may be patrolling in the shadows.

A construction engineer or other individual experienced in installation of outdoor light standards should be part of the survey team. After exami- nation of the site, he can determine what type would be best for each location, and the best manner for their installation. A qualified electrician should also assist in the survey and, of course, should always effect installations. There is a wide variety available in many sizes, to suit every requirement. Probably the most common would be the wooden telephone pole type, which is avail- able pressure-treated with an insect-resistant wood preservative. It comes in lengths to meet most site requirements. It requires burial and is generally suitable in almost any soil condition. A disadvantage is that the power supply line from the buried circuit cable must be run up the side of the pole where it is exposed and vulnerable to attack. By attaching this cable to the side of the pole facing into the protected area, its exposure to attack from outside the fence is minimized.

Another wooden standard consisting of wood laminated and bonded with weather-resistant adhesive is available for installation where esthetics are a concern. This type of standard is generally not available in lengths over

20 to 25 feet (above ground when installed). Because this wood is usually only surface-treated with a wood preservative rather than pressure-impregnated, its service life will be shorter than the telephone pole type.

In areas where grass or brush fires may be a seasonal problem, it must be kept in mind that the pressure-treated wooden standards are particularly susceptible to burning, and any fire-retardant coatings now available need periodic renewal.

Standards constructed of metal possess inherent deterioration-resistant properties. They are very popular for several reasons such as functional attractiveness, ease of installation, low maintenance, easy replacement, and the wide variety of sizes available. Metal standards are available of aluminum, steel, and stainless steel. Aluminum, because of its relatively light weight, flexibility, and strength is the most popular for standards up to approximately 50 feet. When exceptionally tall standards are required, steel is the best choice, because of its superior strength and rigidity in these extreme lengths. In areas where steel or aluminum are not capable of coping satisfactorily with environmental conditions, stainless steel may be the best choice.

Standards made of concrete are also available. These are reinforced internally and are available in lengths up to 40 feet with finish coats such as polished terrazo or a rough pebble. They are esthetically pleasing, although they offer no functional advantage over other types. Therefore, because of their higher costs, their use would be questionable in a maximum-security facility where function and utility are the primary concerns. Obviously, if the site is strictly utilitarian, esthetics are of little concern and a wooden light pole will suffice.

In some extreme situations, such as areas that are swampy, soil conditions will not support a pole-type standard. It may be necessary to construct a steel or wooden tower that distributes the static load over a greater area, and from which luminaires may be hung.

Another consideration when choosing standards is whether or not CCTV cameras can be added with little or no additional expense or effort. Weibel recommends, "Cameras to be used for surveillance during daylight hours only can usually be of lower sensitivity, and generally of lower cost, than those to be used at very low levels of light. A camera for 24-hour use needs to be designed so as not to experience 'washout' of image as the light level increases. . . .The light available, or to be provided, will need to be matched to the requirements of available cameras or those to be supplied. In some cases, an economic compromise might be to supply somewhat more than the recommended minimum level of light in an area in order to utilize cameras of less than full sensitivity and of lower cost."[14] John P. Frier states, ". . . luminaires should be mounted so they are above the lines of sight of the camera. If a camera pans through a light source, the picture will be obscured momentarily. A good position for luminaires would be slightly above and behind the TV cameras, or on a tall pole within the area"[15] (Figure 5–2). Additional points made by Frier include that, while high-mast poles of

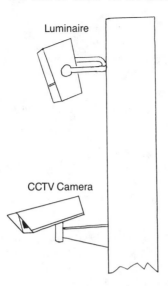

Luminaire

CCTV Camera

Figure 5-2 Light mounted above and behind CCTV camera.

any height may be used for CCTV surveillance systems, these poles should not be taller than one-fourth the distance across the lighted area, and that "the taller the pole, the fewer problems will be with shadows. . . higher poles also make it possible to cover more area from one location, thus cutting down on pole costs. . . . A guard watching a TV monitor . . . needs good illumination to see everything in his field of view. The intruder should appear as an actor, seen by the guard, but unable to see past the floodlights."[16]

Reflected Light

Lighting can be enhanced or maximized through reflection from building walls that are painted white or almost any light pastel color. When high-intensity light is not necessary in a large area, but lighting adequate for reliable detection of unauthorized activity is required, a large blank wall painted with white enamel, an aluminized paint, or even a reflective paint can be very effectively used to "bounce" and spread the light emission from two or three well positioned high-intensity lights over a large area. Conversely, because flat, dark colors absorb light and could cause confusion in a monitored area by providing cover for intruders, their use in a maximum-security environment must be carefully weighed.

A paved perimeter or yard area can also be used to reflect light by painting it white. Where this is not desired, a reflective temporary surface may be applied in emergency situations or for a security contingency by spreading lime in those areas in which reflected illumination is wanted. An

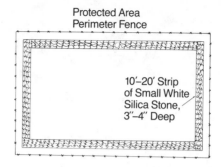

Figure 5-3   Perimeter coverage and reflected light.

unpaved perimeter or yard area that is covered by pole or roof-mounted lights may have its reflectivity (and general appearance) improved by the addition of a covering, several inches deep, of white silica stone. For a perimeter, this coverage should be a band at least 10 to 20 feet wide (Figure 5–3). In addition to the light reflected by this covering, other benefits provided would be the sound produced by anyone crossing it. This could be picked up on open microphones or intercoms along the perimeter, which are monitored in the manned on-site alarm stations; the slight delay in crossing the band of stones because of their tendency to shift under a person's weight; and their ability to choke off most weeds and grasses that sprout quickly in generally un-traveled perimeter or isolation zones.

In indoor areas, light-colored walls and ceilings also help to spread light. If the space is not exceptionally large and if there are no obstructions such as columns, machinery, piping, boxes, or crates to restrict the reflected light, CCTV monitoring capabilities should not be adversely affected. In areas where there are obstructions that restrict the light pattern, the installation of angled mirrors to reflect available lighting into restricted areas or behind an obstruction may be more economically feasible than the installation of ad-ditional lighting.

Table 5–1 is a general guide for use in computing light necessary to illuminate a scene sufficiently to enable satisfactory CCTV surveillance. It shows the approximate percentage of relative reflectance from different build-ing materials or areas common to most protected facilities. The table assumes that the illumination will be flat rather than a point source, and thus would eliminate the variables that would otherwise be provided by the angles of incidence and reflection. It illustrates how a facility may be losing effectiveness in lighting simply because the reflectance surfaces available are not efficient in that area. For example, many older buildings are constructed of red brick for which the reflectance value is 35 percent. If these red-brick walls were provided with a glossy white painted or aluminized surface, it should boost the reflectance value into the area of 65 percent, or approximately that of a smooth-surface aluminum building.

Table 5-1   Reflected Light = (Scene Illumination) × (% of Reflectance)

Scene Being Televised	% of Reflectance
Empty asphalt parking lot	5
Parkland area, trees, and grass	20
Red brick building	35
Unpainted concrete building	40
Parking lot with automobiles	40
Smooth-surface aluminum building	65
Glass windows and walls	70
Snowy field with chain link fence	85

Source: Video Applications Co., Inc.

After the decision has been made on what kind of standards to use and where to place them, consideration should be given to elimination or relocation of unnecessary exterior building or facility lights that are behind the perimeter lighting curtain. This will avoid back-lighting security patrol or response force personnel, and prevent an attack against a sensitive or critical facility within the protected area from outside the perimeter fence by keeping this location cloaked in darkness. "Critical structures or areas classified as vulnerable from a distance should be kept dark (standby lighting available) and those that can be damaged close at hand should be well lighted. The surroundings should be well lighted to force an intruder to cross a lighted area, and any walls should be lighted to a height of 8 feet to facilitate silhouette vision."[17] Care should also be taken that restricted access paths used for patrolling or by response force personnel are not unnecessarily illuminated either by direct light or "splash."

Emplacement

Figure 5–4 shows various methods by which wooden or metal poles are generally embedded. These methods are used to overcome instabilities that may be caused by sandy soil, soils with a high water content, clay, and so on.

Where periodic flooding or washouts are experienced or where extremely high winds are prevalent, the installation of guy wires and buried anchors should be considered. They will ensure stability of the standard under even the most adverse environmental conditions. Whenever possible, mounting of the luminaire on an existing structure is recommended. This saves the cost of not only purchasing a light standard, but that associated with its installation, maintenance, and if damaged, its replacement. Standard brackets available from most light-fixture manufacturers allow the mounting of their products on buildings, towers, and so on.

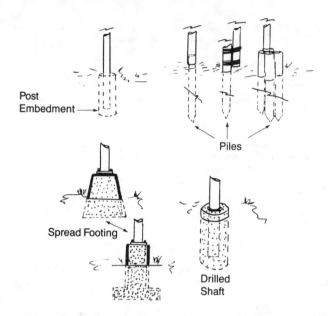

Figure 5-4   Methods of embedding light pulses. (U.S. Nuclear Regulatory Commission.)

In some installations, floodlights are mounted at ground level and aimed at a building or wall that will act as a reflector. These serve as deterrents, because the shadow of anyone who passes in front of them will be cast onto this building or wall in greatly exaggerated size, thereby increasing the chance of detection (Figure 5–5).

Limited-access areas that are under CCTV observation or require regular checks by a patrolling sentry should be adequately illuminated to ensure that any unauthorized individual or activity in that area will be detected. As with

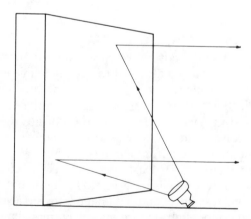

Figure 5-5   Floodlight mounted at ground level aimed at wall that acts as a reflector.

the perimeters, lighting should not glare into the eyes of a security officer who may be checking the area from outside, nor should it back-light patrolling or responding guards. If the limited-access area is constantly manned rather than periodically checked or monitored, consideration may be given to providing glare lighting at a height that will ensure that someone approaching the area cannot detect anyone behind the light curtain. Glare lighting should not extend outward to the perimeter; if it does, some sort of screening should be placed between the light and the perimeter to maintain an area of darkness from which patrols may operate.

Protected areas within a properly lighted perimeter should be provided with total-area lighting as well. This should be adequate to enable visual detection by CCTV or patrolling security officers. It should not place the officers at a disadvantage by forcing them to travel through areas in which they may be highly illuminated and clearly visible to an observer outside the perimeter fence.

Vital sensitive or controlled-access areas should be located only within a protected area, which in turn is located within a properly fenced, lighted, and alarmed perimeter. Because it is provided with total-area lighting, no additional lighting requirements would be necessary for the vital areas under normal operating conditions. It is recommended, however, that additional high-intensity lights be installed to illuminate these areas totally (or if they are located within a larger building, to illuminate all approaches and entrances). This additional lighting should be on a separate circuit from all other perimeter or protected area lights and controlled by a manual switch located in the continuously manned on-site alarm station. When a confirmed intrusion occurs, the officer in the alarm station can activate these lights to illuminate the areas, thereby creating a psychological deterrent for the intruders. More important it allows response force personnel an exceptionally clear view of those attempting to gain entry.

Controls

There are several different systems for controlling the activation of a security lighting system. In addition to manual switches, it may be operated by a photocell or a time clock. Weibel notes, "The usual photocell control is designed and built on the fail-safe principle, so that in the event of a malfunction of the cell the lighting circuit will become energized."[18]

An article in *National Safety News* stated, "New time clocks have a variety of features such as the astronomic feature that causes the control to adjust automatically for changing hours of light and darkness during the year. Programmable time clocks permit the user to schedule lighting for a week at a time. Time clocks also can be applied indoors so that all lighting (except emergency lighting) is turned off and on at preset times. Local switches can act as overrides. Photocell controls activate and deactivate lighting depending on the amount of ambient lighting that exists, be it from the sun or some other source. When the amount of ambient lighting falls to a certain level, lighting is automatically turned on. When ambient lighting rises to a certain level the electric illumination is automatically turned off."[19]

For indoor control of four-lamp fluorescent light fixtures in a large space, a significant savings in energy consumption may be achieved by having a qualified electrician rewire the fixtures so that a single switch controls the two outboard fluorescent tubes in each fixture, while a separate switch controls the two inboard tubes. For normal operations, both circuits may be energized to provide an ample supply of light. For those periods when the space is unoccupied but a light level necessary for monitoring by CCTV or patrolling officer is required, only one circuit need be energized. If this reduced light level is more than required to allow proper monitoring, the light system could be wired with a third or even fourth circuit to control the on (or off) lights by entire fixture as one of three or four, two of three or four, three of three or four, and so on. This will reduce the energy consumption rate even further.

Of course, before any changes are made to a presently installed system in an effort to reduce operating costs, one might consider the following comments: ". . . if lamps are removed or fixtures disconnected to save energy . . . it may be the wrong thing. . . . it may actually cause consumption of more energy rather than less. . . . To get the most from lighting system changes, it's best to develop a plan that indicates what will be done, when it will be done, how much it will cost to make a change, how much energy will be saved, and how much the energy saving will be worth. To develop such a plan you have to start by. . . . conducting a lighting energy audit. Remember, saving money is saving KWH, not just reducing watts."[20]

Power

When planning power distribution for a security lighting system, there are really only two choices available: lines that are strung overhead or that are buried. While overhead lines will be slightly less costly, their use in a maximum-security environment is not recommended. They are susceptible because of their exposure to damage by natural events or willful intent. At certain large installations, it may be possible to bring the power feeder cable into the protected area in an underground installation that terminates at a transformer substation, from which it is routed through overhead lines. This may be acceptable if the substation is shielded from the view of anyone outside the protected area and if the overhead lines are not routed near the perimeter where they would be vulnerable to attack. Wherever possible, however, buried lines are recommended because they are more secure, although the additional time and cost involved in trenching and back-filling will increase installation costs.

In addition to commercial power, a maximum-security installation will require a dependable backup emergency power supply. Most alarm systems are or can be easily equipped with battery backup power that can sustain them for quite a few hours. A security lighting system, however, requires a great deal more energy to keep in operation; therefore the only practical backup would be a gasoline- or diesel-powered generator. This generator should be capable of continuous operation and rated at a *minimum* of 150 percent of the total security alarm, assessment, and lighting systems wattage. It should be housed in an independent structure that is exclusively under the control of the security department and is located well inside the protected area. The generator should be designed to start immediately on the loss of commercial power and to pick up the security equipment load without delay. Its fuel supply should be buried with the filler pipe located within the independent generator structure that is under exclusive security control or, if in an area accessible to anyone inside the protected area, should be capable of being locked to prevent tampering. This emergency generating equipment should be tested for operability on a monthly basis. Quarterly or semiannually, the machinery should be exercised under full load for several hours. A routine off-hours program should be set up for this equipment, and the fuel supply should never be allowed to fall below two-thirds of maximum capacity.

Next to the power supply cables, the most likely target for willful or mischievous damage to a lighting system would be the luminaire itself. An article in *Security World* magazine stated, "Development of vandalproof light fixtures to protect the light-emitting source (lamp or bulb) and permit it to illuminate a desired area has reduced the costly breakage maintenance problem, primarily caused by exuberant youths and the determined onslaught of the 'strong-arm' burglar. There are four basic design characteristics for a vandalproof light: unbreakable exterior, secure anchoring to mounting surface, vibration-free lamp mounting to prevent premature lamp failure, and tamperproof hardware. Until the fifties, glass was the common material for lighting fixtures—easy targets for local rock throwers or would-be-thieves. Then came thermoplastics (molded by heat), which provided low-cost parts and provided impact resistance and good light transmission. Polycarbonate has become the logical candidate where breakage is the main consideration. It is more impact-resistant than glass, acrylic, butyrate, etc. . . . injection-molded polycarbonate has permitted various shapes of lighting fixtures with structural strength approaching that of steel and an improved appearance over polycarbonate lenses. Further developments include special additives to the polycarbonate to minimize the browning caused by the ultraviolet in some light sources. Fluorescent, mercury vapor, and high-pressure sodium 'vandalproof' lights have become available for energy-conscious users."[21] When current luminaires do not meet current standards for resistance to such attack, the installation of locally fabricated wire mesh screens or baskets over the breakable light could provide the necessary protection with minimal adverse effect on the level of light.

Planning should not stop with the routing of power cables and the selection of damage-resistant luminaires. The Nuclear Regulatory Commission recommends, "Caution should be utilized to assure that each luminaire is independent from others. Damage to one pole should not affect other poles nor cause large segments of the security lighting system circuit to open. Separate pole fusing will prevent this in case of luminaire malfunction or pole/luminaire damage."[22] Additional considerations include planning lighting circuits to avoid overloading that will cause fuses to blow and/or breakers to trip. This results in a degradation of the lighting system. Also, "Separate lighting systems for portals (vehicle and personnel), protected area outdoor lighting, material access areas, vital areas, and security alarm stations are recommended."[23]

The National Lighting Bureau writes on planning a preventive maintenance program for a system already in operation. It recommends, "Look into the type of lighting maintenance being performed. In many cases it amounts to little more than changing lamps after they burn out, a practice that is wasteful. The amount of light produced by most types of lamps steadily diminishes with use; the amount of energy they consume does not. This causes the per-footcandle cost of lighting to increase. It becomes so high that eventually it is cost effective to replace a lamp even though it still is serviceable."[24] "When there are substantial numbers of lamps and luminaires in a system, it often is best to rely on group relamping, that is, replacing all lamps at the same time instead of one at a time (spot relamping) as they burn out. Time and motion studies show that it takes about 30 minutes to change a lamp on a spot-relamping basis. When lamps, ladders, and labor are assembled to change all lamps at once, it takes only about three minutes per lamp."[25] In relamping, "It is advisable to check very carefully before considering an interchange of lamps other than those selected in the original design of the system. . . . Lamps should be marked and records kept so that they will be replaced as required by the LLD, (Lamp lumen depreciation) lamp life, and the economics of the situation."[26] All electrical work should be accomplished by qualified electricians.

In a good maintenance program, the individuals directly involved in routine relamping will also take the time to ensure that all luminaires are clean and that they give light coverage in the area required. The program should also require that relays on emergency lines that are held open when power is being received from commercial sources are frequently cleaned to prevent dust from collecting on their contact points, thereby possibly preventing their operation when closed.[27]

Another good point is made by Weibel, who states, "All elements of the electrical system should be suspect in that at one time or another, they could fail without warning. A segregated, secure, inventoried stock of switches, circuit breakers, lamps, etc. should be set up to be used only for the security lighting system."[28]

COORDINATING SELECTION WITH DESIGN

Once the planning is completed and on-site requirements are determined, it becomes necessary to direct attention to the selection of hardware to use in achieving site-specific objectives. Prior to active selection of hardware, however, some considerations should be given to how to meet the established objectives. There are certain principles or methods of application that can be incorporated into a lighting system that will serve to increase its effectiveness. The security practitioner who designs his system with psychological deterrence as its exclusive objective fails to capitalize on other principles that could be used to advantage. Certain basic guidelines are usually followed by, or at the very least are known to most security practitioners. They include such things as ways to prevent glare and avoid silhouetting.

"While security lighting is accepted as an integral part of a security system for controlled-access facilities, most requirements are based solely upon illumination level with little consideration of the impact of various lighting techniques upon intruder and response force behavior and operational efficiency."[29]

Spotlighting and Surface Grazing

Two effective techniques are spotlighting and surface grazing. Spotlighting is just as the term implies, directing additional high-intensity light at an already detected intruder and then tracking or hindering his progress. Surface grazing, also referred to as shadowing, occurs when high-intensity illumination is directed at the surface around an intruder to produce exaggerated shadows[30] (Figures 5–6 and 5–7).

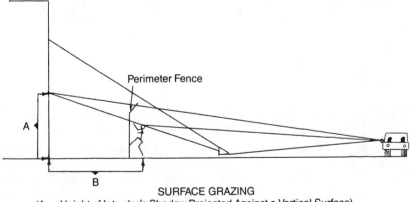

SURFACE GRAZING
(A = Height of Intruder's Shadow Projected Against a Vertical Surface)
(B = Length of Intruder's Shadow Projected Against a Horizontal Surface)

Figure 5-6 Surface grazing. (National Bureau of Standards.)

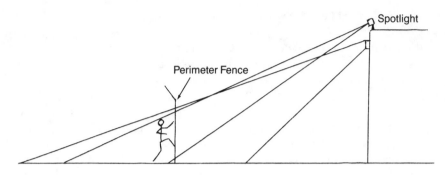

Figure 5-7   Spotlighting. (National Bureau of Standards.)

Adequacy of Illumination

When it comes to coordinating hardware selection with system design, it is important to obtain adequate illumination. Several factors affect adequacy and should be mentioned. The Army believes that "good protective lighting is achieved by adequate, even light upon bordering areas, glaring lights in the eyes of the intruder and relatively little light in security patrol routes. All of these abilities are improved by higher levels of brightness [as is] the ability of the observer to distinguish poor contrasts."[31] While light should be adequate to meet the objectives of the system, too much light, especially if used and/or located improperly, can result in shadows that could conceal an intruder. Attempting to increase the system's efficiency could result in problems if components are modified.

"Altering the position of any elements of the optical system with respect to the design position and light center of the intended lamp(s) could result in a distinctly different light distribution of the luminaire and the entire lighting system."[32]

Contrast

An area frequently overlooked when coordinating selection with design is contrast. Contrast can and should be used to advantage by the maximum-security practitioner. Many people think that more light is better all of the time. This is not necessarily true all of the time.

"A form of indirect glare known as a veiling reflection typically occurs when a lighting fixture is in the offending zone directly above and in front of the viewer. Light from the fixture bounces off the task surface and into the viewer's eyes. This reduces contrast rendition, that is, the contrast between the foreground and background of a task surface, such as the type on this page (foreground) and the color of the paper (background). When contrast rendition is reduced, it becomes more difficult to distinguish what is on the task surface. Because an insufficient amount of light also makes it more difficult to distinguish what is on the task surface, lower quality can have the same effect as lower quantity. The difference is that lower quantity results in less energy consumption; lower quality does not."[33]

"The visibility of a target is far less dependent on the total amount of illumination falling on the target and its background than it is on the relative luminance differences (i.e., contrast) between the target and its background (Figure 5–8). Thus extremely high levels of illumination may not succeed in making a low-contrast target visible, while extremely low illumination levels may succeed in making a high-contrast target visible." Intruder-detection capability can be increased if the lighting system "maximizes intruder to background contrast and observer contrast threshold sensitivity."[34]

The implications are that lighting systems should be designed to maximize intruder/background contrast by increasing illumination of the intruder or the background while decreasing illumination of the other. A further implication can be made that "visual threshold contrast sensitivity should be a criteria for guard force selection."[35] Whatever the implications, it is a good idea to maximize contrast whenever and wherever possible as an aid to intruder detection.

"When the intruder is darker than his background, the observer sees primarily the outline or silhouette. Intruders who depend on dark clothing and even darkened face and hands may be foiled by using light finishes on

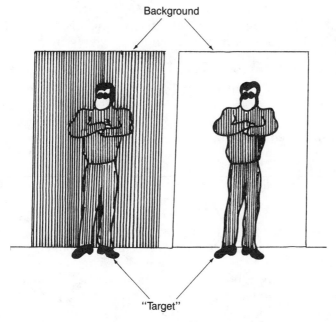

Figure 5-8   Sketch of contrast between "target" and background.

the lower parts of buildings and structures. Stripes on walls have also been used effectively, as they provide recognizable breaks in outlines or silhouettes. Good observation conditions can also be created by providing broad lighting areas around and within the installation, against which intruders can be seen."[36]

Contrast plays an important role in CCTV surveillance and observation. Certain cameras require fairly high levels of illumination in the area the camera is watching. Other, usually more expensive, low-light cameras can operate with less than one footcandle of light. The choice of illuminating the scene or using low-light cameras belongs to the facility's security officer and basically depends on site-specific needs and objectives. Areas of consideration include purchase price, energy consumption, and maintenance.[37]

Glare Lighting

Glare lighting can be used to distinct advantage by the security force provided it is directed against potential adversaries and not friendly personnel. The placement of glare lighting devices is very important. Frequently, not enough thought is given to their location, with the result that glare is projected toward adversary routes and also silhouettes or incapacitates security personnel when they are on patrol. The primary technique is to ensure that security personnel remain behind the glare projection devices while observing an area. The Army sometimes prefers "floodlights that provide a band of light with great horizontal angular dispersal and which directs the glare at a possible intruder."[38]

There are two recognized forms of glare lighting; disability and discomfort glare. Disability glare occurs when peripheral light is much brighter than that on which the eye is focused. The eye's target is "veiled" or "masked," and this effect is induced by both the intensity and emplacement of the glare source. Discomfort glare manifests itself in physical or "subjective" discomfort to the affected person. It can cause impairment of visual performance. "The most common forms of physiological stress produced by intense glare illumination are repeated blocking of the eyes, abnormal extraocular muscle tonus and excessive tearing."[39] Discomfort glare could result in aching eyes and head, which may be the result of visual fatigue.[40]

An NBS publication provides some guidance for employing glare lighting[41]:

1. High-intensity light sources and highly reflective objects should be removed whenever they interfere with security personnel observation capabilities.
2. Where this is impossible, light sources should be shielded and reflective objects painted.
3. Glare lighting should be directed toward likely areas of adversary approach.

4.   Glare lighting should be highly intense and directed in the line-of-sight of intruders.

Other Techniques

Certain other techniques may prove beneficial in the maximum-security environment, including the effects of flash blindness, stroboscopics and phototropy. Flash blindness can be induced by an extremely intense burst of illumination in the eyes of an intruder, which results in a period of visual incapacitation. Stroboscopic illumination can have physical and psychological effects on certain people, as rapidly flickering illumination can cause feelings of confusion and anxiety and result in disorientation. Phototropic effects result from a natural tendency for the eyes to orient themselves toward light. This phenomenon can be used as a discreet "means of directing potential intruders into an area where incapacitation by other means . . . is possible."[42]

TYPES OF PROTECTIVE LIGHTING

Several types of protective lighting are outlined by the Army, such as continuous, standby, moveable, and emergency lighting.[43] Hand-held lighting is yet another type. Continuous lighting is further broken down into two types—glare and controlled. Glare lighting has been previously discussed. Controlled lighting, as the term implies, is flexible and can be applied in a variety of ways. It is not fixed and can be adjusted to meet specific requirements.

Standby lighting is much the same as continuous lighting but with the major difference that luminaires do not remain lighted. They are controlled, turned on and off, manually at the discretion of security personnel. Movable lighting is flexible and used primarily to supplement existing lighting on an as-needed basis. Searchlights and portable spotlights are examples.

Emergency lighting is used as a backup for other systems in the event of failure, compromise, or malfunction. It is any system that can be used to duplicate the effects of permanent lighting.[44]

Hand-held lighting consists of flashlights, spotlights, and searchlights. In addition to these more common forms, other systems such as blinding flares, emergency flares, and photographic strobes are available. These are used primarily to incapacitate intruders rather than illuminate by capitalizing on the phenomena already described, particularly the effects of flash blindness.

Special-purpose units for contingency or emergency operations can be fabricated by a licensed electrican and stockpiled. These would consist of a galvinized steel pole, approximately 2 to 3 inches in diameter and 12 to 16 feet long (which has been capped to prevent moisture from causing premature deterioration) on which is mounted at the top a weatherproof outdoor elec-

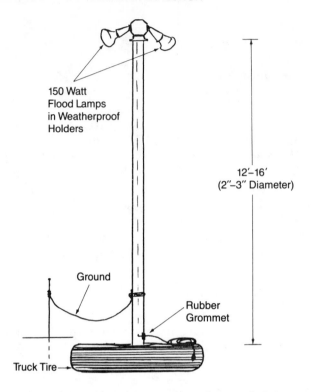

Figure 5-9 Locally fabricated special-purpose emergency lighting.

trical box with two or more 150-watt outdoor floodlamps in weatherproof lampholders that are angled for proper area illumination. This post is embedded in a base made by filling an old 16- to 20-inch diameter truck tire with concrete. This unit would be prewired so that it need only be moved (by forklift, hand truck, or pickup, or even wheeled on edge) to the location where needed, then plugged into a grounded weatherproof electrical power supply. The steel pole should have a long pigtail attached, which after set-up is attached to a ground rod. An additional advantage offered by such a portable system is in its ability to be moved quickly to remote sites and connected to a portable gasoline generator (Figure 5–9). The heavily weighted base and relatively low wind resistance offered by the pole and standard outdoor fixtures should provide a unit that gives dependable service over a wide variety of operating conditions. If there is concern that extremely high winds could topple the unit, the base may be buried to a depth of six inches over its top to provide an added measure of stability.

TYPES OF LIGHTING

"Tests run by the National Bureau of Standards indicate that a person can penetrate a perimeter chain-link fence in 6-47 seconds. Intruders in a running mode can cover 15-25 feet per second. This would indicate that a 60-foot isolation and fence zone at a protected area perimeter could be penetrated and cleared in from 8.4 to 51 seconds. If the intruder continues to run into the protected area, penetration of up to 135 to 1,290 feet could be accomplished within one minute. If the intruder initiates the power outage, access to the proximity of vital or material access areas could readily be accomplished for the purpose of sabotage or threatened sabotage. Using this rationale, it is recommended that lighting systems for the isolation zone provide for a maximum of 10 seconds outage. The backup power supply should be of an uninterruptible type or a generator type with luminaires which will reliably restrike within 10 seconds."[45]

Incandescent

Table 5–2 shows the types of luminaire lamps that may be found in a maximum-security environment. As can be seen, each has its advantages and disadvantages. While the incandescent lamp has some definite application, it should be reserved for emergency lights, spotlights, or augmentation. Because of its instant restrike/restart capabilities but rather limited watt output and service life, confining outdoor incandescent lighting to a backup or emergency role is recommended.

Fluorescent

"Fluorescent lights—are mercury vapor lamps that produce large quantities of ultraviolet radiation, and have a thin coating of phosphor on the inside of the tube that fluoresces and gives off visible light. The efficiency of these lamps is approximately 62 lumens per watt. Fluorescent lamps are sensitive to surrounding air temperatures with an ideal at 70 degrees to 80 degrees F.—making them primarily an indoor lighting source in many climates."[47] While fluorescent lamps offer more wattage output and a longer life than incandescent, they are subject to a condition that results in flicker effect. Depending on its rate of flicker and other conditions present, this can cause disorientation among some individuals, and the electromagnetic radiation given off by a fluorescent fixture can cause interference with some electronic equipment. This can be often noted when attempting to operate a transistorized AM radio in a room with fluorescent light fixtures in operation.

Metal Halide

Metal halide lamps, when combined with the proper ballast, are very tolerant of power dips or brown-outs. They are an excellent source of light with a

Table 5-2 Types of Luminaire Lamps Found in a Maximum Security Environment

Lamp Type	Mean Lumens per Watt	Start	Restrike	Nominal Life of Lamp (hrs.)	% Lumen Maintenance at Rated Life	Color Discrimination
Incandescent	4 (21) 22*	Instant	Instant	750–1,000	85–90	Excellent
Fluorescent	35 (62) 100	Rapid	Rapid/Instant†	7500–10,000	70–90	Excellent
Metal halide	68 (80) 100	3–5 min.	10–20 min	10,000–15,000	65–75	Excellent
Mercury vapor	20 (48) 63	3–7 min.	3–6 min.	16,000–24,000	50–75	Good
High-pressure sodium	95 (127) 140	4–7 min.	Instant‡	16,000–24,000	75–85	Fair
Low-pressure sodium	131 (183) 183	8–10 min.	Instant‡	16,000–24,000	Basically constant§	Poor
Xenon ARC	‖	Rapid/Instant	Instant	1500	—	Excellent

* 4 (21) 22 (4) = minimum mean; (21) = nominal rating for most protective lighting applications; 22 = maximum mean.
† Low-temperature ballast must be considered.
‡ Instant for most lamps if less than one minute of power interruption but at a reduced lumen output.
§ Current increases until end of lamp life to keep lumen output consistent.
‖ Use for searchlights only.

service life almost 20 times greater than that of incandescent lamps. Their chief disadvantage is in the amount of time required to restrike/restart them after a loss of power. A loss of power of only one-twentieth of a second is enough to knock a metal halide lamp off line.[48]

Mercury Vapor

Mercury vapor lamps give good light and have an excellent service life. When combined with the proper ballast they are capable of continued operation even with power dips of 40 to 50 percent.[49] As with metal halide lamps, a power loss of only one-twentieth of a second could be enough to cause the lamp to extinguish because of a power interruption; restrike time, as shown in Table 5–2 can be excessive. Still, mercury vapor lamps have experienced a high level of use in security applications.[50]

"While mercury vapor lighting still tends to have a greenish-bluish hue, sodium vapor light has an amber quality. This amber color is common to both high-pressure (HPS) and low-pressure (LPS) sodium lighting, but the similarities seem to end there."[51]

High-Pressure and Low-Pressure Sodium

High-pressure sodium lamps have an excellent service life, and like the metal halide and mercury vapor lamps, when combined with the proper ballast they tolerate 40 to 50 percent dips in power. A power interruption of only one-twentieth of a second may be enough to cause this type lamp to extinguish and begin its restrike sequence. This restrike is rated as instant; however, the lamp will not be at its fully rated output until it has returned to its normal operating temperature.[52]

"High-pressure sodium luminaires are an excellent choice for lighting systems to be used in conjunction with TV surveillance systems, both indoors and outdoors. They provide high efficacy (lumens per watt), good uniformity, and a short restrike."[53] A possible disadvantage of high-pressure sodium is electromagnetic radiation, which could cause interference with electronic equipment or systems, including alarms. "The designer of a lighting system, noting the long life of this lamp, its high efficiency, and the larger number of lumens available from a lamp of given wattage, and recognizing the high first cost of lamp and luminaire, will conclude that the HPS lamp offers advantages over the other lamps."[54]

Low-pressure sodium lamps also have excellent service life and are considered very reliable starters, although they require approximately 8 to 10 minutes to reach full lumen output. This long initial warm-up poses no special problem, however, if the lamps are controlled by a photoelectric switch. If the proper type of switch is used, this lamp will have reached its full rated output prior to a point at which an observer's view would be seriously hampered by diminished natural light. It is indicated by manufacturers that 90 percent of these lamps will reliably restrike after power interruptions of up to five minutes, while the remaining 10 percent will restrike in less than one minute. The only disadvantage of low-pressure sodium lamps appears to be their highly monochromatic yellow light, which offers poor color discrimination. This yellow light, however, has advantages in that it provides better contrast on uneven surfaces than a white light. (Anyone who has ever used a pair of yellow shooter's glasses is aware of the tremendous increase in clarity and image sharpness when available light reaching the eye is shifted into the yellow spectrum.) This contrast and perceived image enhancement works extremely well with a black-and-white CCTV system and records well on film. Because these lamps are very efficient, smaller cables and lower power requirement distribution systems can be used, but since a higher operating current is required at the end of their life, the system should be sized for this end-of-life cycle.[55]

Thorsen sums up the issue when he states, "The majority of security applications would be found in the high-intensity discharge (HID) class of lighting, which *does not* include the incandescent lamp. The principle in all of vapor lighting is the same: an inert gas is contained within the tube to initiate the ignition— the inert gas carries the current from one electrode to another—the current then develops the heat, which vaporizes the metal solid or metallic oxide inside the tube—and the light is discharged from the vaporized substance through the surface of the discharge tube and beyond the outside envelope tube into the area to be lighted. The ultimate question for security lighting comes down to effective visibility vs cost."[56]

CONCLUSION

It should be remembered that lighting that has been designed, selected, and installed specifically for security purposes provides a threefold service. First, it serves as a deterrent—anyone entering a well-lit area cannot help feeling exposed to unseen eyes in the shadows beyond. This is not merely a psychological ploy; patrolling officers in the shadows could very well apprehend someone who has penetrated the perimeter fence when he is exposed in this lighted area. This possibility is certainly not lost on the average burglar, and when faced with a situation like this, he will usually seek easier pickings elsewhere. The second advantage has already been mentioned—detection. The highest and strongest fences and most sophisticated perimeter alarms are useless if the security officers responding to the scene of an intrusion cannot see their adversaries. A properly designed and installed lighting system will allow the officers to detect the intruders before they have reached any vital areas within the protected area. This allows the response force to engage the adversary in a neutral zone where he is at a definite disadvantage.

The third attribute of a good security lighting system is incapacitation. Flood-lights or high-intensity strobe units can be placed along the inner edge of the light curtain at about eye level, so that the projected light path is directed only toward the perimeter fence and activated in the event of an intrusion. This would serve to cause disorientation and confusion among most adversaries, and thus make their eventual neutralization easier.

In designing an incapacitating light system, thought should be given to eliminating all unnecessary objects in the lighted zone that could create shadows or cause confusion to the site defenders. Ideally, this area should be flat, with a smooth, light surface to increase reflectance. When buildings or walls are in the lighted area, they should be painted with a white or very light pastel, with floodlights installed at ground level to bounce light off their surfaces. Not only will this maximize the amount of light in the area, but through proper design, any intruders could be channeled between the flood-lights and the walls so that their shadows are projected thereon, thereby increasing detection probability.

In a maximum-security setting, a dependable alternate or backup power supply is a necessity and should be considered vital equipment. This must be uninterruptible, sited inside the protected area, and should, whenever possible, be dedicated to the exclusive operation of security equipment necessary for the continuation of required services. The most dependable source for this backup system is a stationary diesel-powered generator of sufficient capacity to handle all the power requirements for essential equipment plus special requirements. The emergency generating and power distribution panel should be housed in an enclosed and alarmed structure that is under exclusive control of the security department. The fuel tank should be of sufficient capacity to allow continuous operation of the generator for a minimum of 240 hours (10 days). The tank should be buried and the fuel filler cap should be capable of being securely locked.

The selection of luminaires, lamps, standards, voltages. secondary lighting systems, glare lighting, and the like boils down to a process of elimination, with cost ideally not being one of the factors. The information provided on preceding pages is intended to provide the pros and cons of each type of lighting system to make this process easier and less time consuming, and to generate a basic understanding of the important role lighting can play in the maximum security environment.

NOTES

1. *Physical Security, U.S. Army Field Manual 19-30* (Washington, D.C.: Department of the Army, 1979), pp. 85–86.
2. National Bureau of Standards, *Security Lighting for Nuclear Weapons Storage Sites: A Literature Review and Bibliography* (Washington, D.C.: Department of Commerce, 1977), p. 3.

3. Ibid., p. 7.
4. Ibid., p. 5.
5. *Physical Security*, p. 84.
6. National Bureau of Standards, *Security Lighting*, p. 4.
7. Nuclear Regulatory Commission, *Security Lighting Planning for Nuclear Fixed Sites Facilities* (Washington, D.C.: The Commission, 1980), p. 3.
8. *The Code of Federal Regulations* (Washington, D.C.: 1981), title 10, part 73.46(c)(4).
9. *Physical Security*, p. 89.
10. John P. Frier, "How Much Light for the Shipping Dock?" *Security World* (November 1978):26.
11. William A. Weibel, "Lighting," in *Handbook of Building Security Planning and Design*, ed. Peter S. Hopf (New York: McGraw-Hill Book Company, 1979), p. 14-1. Material used with permission.
12. Ibid., p. 14-2.
13. Ibid., p. 14-18.
14. Weibel, "Lighting," p. 14-16.
15. Frier, "How Much Light for the Shipping Dock?" p. 43.
16. Ibid., p. 26.
17. *Physical Security*, p. 90.
18. Weibel, "Lighting," p. 14–19.
19. "Conducting a Lighting Energy Audit", *National Safety News* (February 1982), 24. Adapted by permission from *Lighting Energy Audit Workbook*.
20. *Ibid., p. 19.*
21. *"Security Idea File: Three Protection Innovations," Security World* (April 1979).
22. Nuclear Regulatory Commission, *Security Lighting*, p. 58.
23. Ibid.
24. "Conducting a Lighting Energy Audit," p. 22.
25. *Physical Security*, p. 22.
26. Weibel, "Lighting," p. 14-3.
27. *Physical Security*, pp. 6–9.
28. Weibel, "Lighting," p. 14-21.
29. National Bureau of Standards, *Security Lighting*, p. 1.
30. Ibid., p. 17.
31. *Physical Security*, p. 85.
32. Weibel, "Lighting," p. 14-9.
33. "Conducting a Lighting Energy Audit", p. 22.
34. National Bureau of Standards, *Security Lighting*, pp. 9–12.
35. Ibid.
36. *Physical Security*, p. 86.
37. Frier, "How Much Light for the Shipping Dock?" p. 26.
38. *Physical Security*, p. 86.
39. National Bureau of Standards, *Security Lighting*, p. 16.
40. Ibid.
41. Ibid.
42. Ibid., pp. 23–24.
43. *Physical Security*, pp. 86–88.
44. Ibid.
45. Nuclear Regulatory Commission, *Security Lighting*, p. 62.
46. Ibid.

47. J. E. Thorsen, "Considering the Sources," *Security World* (May 1978):44.
48. Nuclear Regulatory Commission, *Security Lighting*, p. 31.
49. Ibid., p. 30.
50. Thorsen, "Considering the Sources," p. 44.
51. Ibid., p. 30.
52. Nuclear Regulatory Commission, *Security Lighting*, p. 32.
53. Frier, "How Much Light for the Shipping Dock?" p. 43.
54. Weibel, "Lighting," p. 14-8.
55. Thorsen, "Considering the Sources," p. 33.
56. Ibid., p. 50.

CHAPTER 6

Communications

A baby's cry, a distress flare, a string of signal flags flying from the mast of a naval vessel, a traffic light are methods of communication with which we are probably familiar but about which we seldom think.

Communications are generally thought of only in the modern sense—television, radio, newspapers, telephone—but their roots go back farther than the beginning of recorded time. Communication in its primal form was used between animals to warn, threaten, or paralyze with fear prior to an attack, and this holds true today. Primitive man, until some rudimentary langauge was developed, communicated in much the same way as animals, with grunts, growls, gestures and screams. Man also developed the ability to communicate simple and basic wants or needs through gestures and direct action. While his methods were somewhat more sophisticated than those of the animals that shared his world, his capacity for transmitting or receiving anything other than elemental signals was many centuries in the future.

As he evolved, man first standardized common vocal sounds to put forth simple basic thoughts. Over the course of centuries these sounds evolved into speech and a language, which, because of the often insurmountable difficulties and dangers encountered in traveling great distances, seldom bore commonality with those of other similarly isolated communities. Despite these travel difficulties, isolated and infrequent contact did occur and this helped spur the parallel development of verbal communications among those of our forbearers who were ready to progress up the evolutionary ladder.

As tribes banded together for mutual protection or were subjugated through force their language was expanded and enriched through the addition of new or more efficient words. With a common language, common customs, and a system of rudimentary government, the first seeds of group identity were planted.

As these communities grew, developed and became more civilized, the infrequent traveler or adventurer passing through was usually welcomed for the news he carried. The stories told by these wanderers were often of kingdoms and lands filled with strange peoples and customs, and they encouraged the adventurous to travel to far-away places. These trading expeditions often served to establish formal links between widely separated communities, and the traders more often than not were forced to act as ambassadors, which of necessity included learning new languages.

This led to these early traders bringing back new words, thoughts, and ideas in addition to goods. Eventually, more and larger trading expeditions were mounted, traveling far and carrying not just trade goods representative of their own culture and civilization, but often led by some of the best trained and most articulate individuals available, whose communications skills and abilities were known and had been proved in previous expeditions. Their ability to handle complicated transactions in a foreign tongue was crucial to the success or failure of a mission. The fact that more and more trading routes were established and that trade flourished is testimony to the communications skills of these persons.

With the establishment of trade among communities, written records became a necessity. Early sign language was adapted to a permanent record through the use of pictures and this kind of business record was successful for many years. In the often complex communications that were developing, reliance on pictographs or memorizing messages was not enough. History records the many written languages developed to fill this void. Some became dead and lost for centuries, such as Sanskrit and the writing on the Dead Sea Scrolls. Others developed and grew, such as Phoenician into Syrian and Lebanese, or begat derivatives such as the languages of the Orient. Still others remain with us today in only moderately altered form such as Italian, Spanish, and Portuguese, which trace their derivative roots directly back to the Latin of the ancient Roman Empire.

With the invention of the Gutenberg press in Germany about 1450, mass production of printed material became possible. Heretofore, each page of a book or manuscript had to be laboriously hand-copied, taking months and even years for the reproduction of a single volume. This made the cost of printed material prohibitively expensive and severely limited its subject matter, usually to Bibles or other religious tracts. The Gutenberg press now ensured quick, easy, and cheap reproduction of any printed matter. Although printing now allowed wide dissemination of the same information, this was still dependent on the transportation system available. It still took many days, weeks, and even months for material to be transported from its point of origin to its ultimate destination. The advantages, however, were that on arrival, the information was accurate, not having been passed by word of mouth through several travelers. Also, it was in a format that could be referred to by many individuals over a long period of time.

In the interests of improving the rapid transmission of information, the use of such novel techniques as semaphore flags, signal lanterns and heliograph were all used and eventually discarded as newer and more practical methods were developed.

The invention of the telegraph and development of Morse code probably did more to link together the scattered outposts of civilization with the great commercial and cultural centers than all previous means of communication combined. With the successful laying of the first transoceanic telegraph cable, communications between Europe and the United States was now only a matter of minutes or hours rather than days or weeks. The forerunner of radio communications was a derivative of the telegraph, known as "wireless". It was through the transmission of a wireless message than a tense world first learned of the torpedo attack and the sinking of the British passenger liner Lusitania in May 1915, an event which served to further turn the tide of American sentiment against Germany which had been at war with Britain and France since August 4, 1914.

The initial great battles of this War were fought, primarily, with weapons, tactics and equipment that had remained virtually unchanged for decades. However, modern technology soon introduced such items as combat aircraft, transport vehicles dependent upon internal combustion engines for power rather than horses or mules, large scale chemical warfare, tanks, concentrated use of fully automatic weapons and "modern" communications.

During World War I operational commanders no longer had to rely solely on carrier pigeon or messenger, but had available wireless sets or, if in a relatively stable area, telephones over which their orders could be passed or received. The postwar period saw great technological leaps. Wireless sets were introduced into aircraft but voice radio communications soon made these systems obsolete except for such special purposes as transmission of encoded messages over great distances. Sophisticated radio navigation devices, portable radios, and so on were all the result of wartime efforts to upgrade military hardware. These plus many other items were further developed and refined for peaceful purposes such as carrying mail and making the average citizen much more aware of newsworthy events all over the world. Today it is commonplace for communications to be routed through an orbiting space satellite rather than over the old hard wire cables. In this chapter we detail some of the methods of communications available and suitable for use in a maximum-security environment. Some are old, some are new, all are effective when properly used.

VISUAL MEANS OF COMMUNICATION

Hand Signals

The use of hand signals was probably man's first attempt to convey a message to another human being. Hand signals have been and continue to be useful means of communicating certain elemental and even complex thoughts or directions. When two strangers meet who are unable to understand each other's language, hand signals soon come into play. When used in certain combinations, they can convey some reasonably sophisticated thoughts. They are still in use by the military and certain police units, which require the ability for silent communications in highly dangerous and sensitive operations such as scouting missions behind enemy lines, communications between ground personnel and aircraft, or between ground personnel and vehicles.

The universal sign language that has been developed by use by individuals who are mute and/or deaf is the most advanced form of hand signals, and one that many persons with no physical impairment have been able to master with reasonable ease.

Light Signals

Light signals are thought of as being used primarily in military applications, however, they are around us every day. Traffic lights, brake lights, police cruiser, fire engine, ambulance lights, turn signals, construction barricade warning flashers, on/off switches, and alarm panels are just a few examples. These have become so accepted that they are seldom even thought of, yet they are all true light signals. They warn or advise us of an action that is about to occur or has already taken place, and call our attention to a possibly dangerous situation or one in which increased alertness is necessary.

Military signal lights are used to transmit semaphore signals (this is actually the morse code alphabet, which transmits the dots and dashes by light beam rather than over a hard wire). In a maximum-security setting; there would appear to be little need for the transmission of complex messages by such a system. In contingency situations, however, simple signals may be broadcast by means of existing external building lights controlled from a central alarm station. This could eliminate the necessity of resorting to radio communications that may be knocked out of operation, electronically jammed, or be monitored by an adversary force.

Flares

Another military system of light signal that may be commonly found in a maximum-security facility is the signal flare. It is available in a variety of colors. The projectors range from the relatively inexpensive single-shot, pen-type that are largely made of aluminum, to single-shot pistols fabricated from high-impact plastics, aluminum, brass, and steel, or the highly engineered repeater-type. This last does not resemble the traditional flare gun, but it functions in a manner similar to a semiautomatic pistol and is manufactured by one of Europe's largest manufacturers of military rifles and pistols. (Some flare projectors are illegal to possess. For further information, contact the Bureau of Alcohol, Tobacco, and Firearms of the U.S. Treasury Department.)

Flares can be used to signal certain messages simply by color. Their use is not without some danger, for when a flare is projected, the point of origin can be attacked; and if any portion of the burning projectile touches or lands on anything flammable, a serious fire can result.

Probably the most useful in maximum-security application are parachute flares. These may be launched from a mortarlike tube, and a hand-held model is available that is totally self-contained. It is about the size of the cardboard tube in the center of a roll of kitchen paper towels, and when hand-fired, it sends its projectile approximately 200 feet into the air, where the parachute opens and the flare begins burning, brightly lighting the area below. Because the parachute slows its descent, the light lasts for a considerable period of time.

A supply of this type of flare should be a part of every emergency response locker or security patrol vehicle. They are not inexpensive, but when an emergency makes their use necessary, their cost quickly becomes inconsequential in comparison to their benefits.

Signal Flags

Signal flags, while not commonplace in security use, may have some application at larger facilities where the conditions of certain processes or spaces can be communicated over considerable distances. An example of this is a fuel depot where the flying of a solid red flag indicates that flammable fuel is being transferred and that a dangerous condition exists.

AUDIBLE MEANS OF COMMUNICATION

Voice

The basic form of audible communication is the human voice, which can be amplified and transmitted over long distances. While most present-day voice communication uses amplification, this is by no means always necessary—a simple shout will transmit a message provided the recipient is within earshot. For those cases where the use of unaided voice transmission is not feasible, alternative means must be used. Most people are familiar with chimes used for signaling (more so in the past than at present). Whistles, sirens, and other such devices can be used to good advantage, even though their sound is more limited in application than are visual signals.[1] Klaxons are also used to communicate messages, the most familiar being the submarine's signal to dive.

"The principal advantages of visual and sound communications are that they can be used to circumvent language problems and that they require only simple, lightweight devices for execution. [They are] . . . easily misunderstood and their use is restricted during periods of poor visibility or when line-of-sight locations are not available. In addition, security of both visual and sound signals is extremely difficult to maintain and [adversaries] can employ either with relative ease to mislead or confuse friendly [forces]."[2]

Amplified Voice

Amplifying the human voice by mechanical or electronic means, for example, megaphone or public address system, extends its range. Amplified voice and/or sound-producing devices can overcome unique situations for example, a need to communicate with someone wearing protective ear coverings. By situating loudspeakers effectively, a basic amplified voice communication system results that can be useful for one-way communications. It has even been suggested that speakers be placed in elevators to advise occupants of an emergency situation.[3]

Another form of amplification is found in electronic sirens. By transmitting a radio signal, a beeper or pager can be activated. Present-day pagers come with a variety of useful features that include different tones to signal different responses, and digital message readouts.

Intercom

When amplified voice is transmitted over hard wire or hardware and is used for two-way communication, it becomes the basis for an intercom (intercommunication system). In a maximum-security environment, intercoms can and should be used fully to limit extraneous radio and telephone transmissions. Depending on the type of system, an intercom can be used to monitor areas of the perimeter or facility for strange sounds, voices, or other indications of suspicious activity. It can also monitor the safety and well-being of security officers on patrol.

As a means of communication with persons, other than security personnel, during an emergency situation, for example, a high-rise building fire, the more sophisticated versions of intercom systems are exceptional.

Telephone

The most common means of two-way communication is the telephone. It is an extremely easy instrument to operate and it is widely used. In a maximum-security environment, it becomes the primary means for administrative communications. It also carries a heavy load of logistical communications within the security force. In spite of their obvious shortcomings, telephone systems are more secure than radio systems.[4] The Army suggests, "One or more of the following means of communications should be included in the protective system:

a.   Facilities for local exchange and commercial telephone service.
b.   Interplant, intraplant, and interoffice telephone systems using either government-owned or rented circuits and equipment; but not interconnected with facilities for commercial exchange or toll telephone service"[5]

Telephone lines are always subject to attack and sabotage. For these reasons, they should be buried starting from the farthest possible point away from the maximum-security facility. Whenever lines are installed where sabotage is a possibility, they "should be routed to facilitate observation and inspection."[6] Inspection of all means of communications, including antennas and transmission lines should be routinely made during every security shift at a maximum-security facility.

Some of the more sophisticated telephone systems on today's market offer a varied, interesting, and exciting array of features, including intercom capability, automatic dialing, call forwarding, and automatic call back. Properly used, a sophisticated telephone system can increase communications efficiency and save time and money.

The McCain Correctional Center in McCain, North Carolina uses a ProtoCall TM PBX System. It has several useful features that have managed to save several hours of working time per week while enhancing efficiency and security: the ability to handle multiple conversations simultaneously; automatic call back; call forwarding; and speed calling (frequently called numbers can be reached by dialing only two digits). The system can be adjusted and expanded to accommodate new communication needs.[7]

Any telephone system in a maximum-security environment should have an interoffice/intercom capability and unrestricted commercial use for security personnel. If need be, separate telephones should be used to provide these capabilities. Hot lines, that is, telephones dedicated to an exclusive use, should be maintained. At least one hot line should connect maximum-security personnel to local law enforcement authorities simply by picking up the handset; no dialing should be required. This line should be supervised and tamper-indicating. Trouble on the line or interruption of capability should generate an alarm and a response. Malfunctions should be corrected as soon as possible. Until repairs can be effected, compensatory measures must be initiated and maintained, for example, a portable radio tuned to the security frequencies could be temporarily situated at law enforcement headquarters, or an open commercial telephone line could be established to an off-site location, perhaps the local police department or an off-duty guard force member. At the very minimum, periodic status checks should be initiated and maintained whenever hot lines are malfunctioning. These checks should be scheduled, and personnel at both ends must be aware of normal testing procedures.

Other direct lines to all or some of the facility's security management personnel should also be considered. Other areas for consideration should be hot lines to fire fighting and medical service resource agencies.

Radio

Because of its mobility and flexibility, two-way radio communications have become the backbone of police, security, and military communications systems. Many interesting capabilities have developed since the days of the wireless, and have been fully capitalized on by protective firms worldwide. The same is no less true in a maximum-security environment—two-way radio communications constitute the bulk of the maximum security communications capability.

Most two-way radios are FM (frequency modulation). Basically, FM is a line-of-sight transmission of radio signals. While the range is less than AM radios (amplitude modulation), the quality of the transmission is superior. During many routine and most tactical situations, radio will be the primary method of security force communications.[8]

The advantages and disadvantages of radio communications are summed up quite accurately by the Army. "The principal advantage of radio as a means of communications is the speed of installation. Portable and vehicular-mounted radios may be made operational in a matter of seconds. Radio is a flexible means of communication. No fixed circuits are required to be constructed, extended, or maintained. Stations may be added to or deleted from a radio net as required. Communications by radio can be maintained while troops are mobile. It may be integrated with wire, used from ground to air, or air to air. It provides communications across terrain over which it may be impractical or impossible to install wire.

Disadvantages of Radio

Radio is the least secure means of communications. It must be assumed that interception takes place every time a message is transmitted. Radio communication is less open to enemy fire than wire, but it is subject to interference from static, jamming, and other radio stations."[9]

Alan B. Abramson agrees that a radio communication system is essential to security communications. "It enables security personnel to be mobile and minimize response time to an emergency situation. Because all radio communications are licensed by the Federal Communications Commission, a thorough knowledge of their rules and regulations is required to design a system. In general, radio systems provide communication in the form of voice or signaling between a fixed location (the base station) and mobile units. These mobile units may include personal portable two-way radios, vehicular radios, pagers, or signaling devices. In most systems mobile-to-mobile communication is required, as well as base-to-mobile communication. When the base station is configured so that it automatically rebroadcasts weak mobile signals to other mobiles, it is called a repeater-type operation. Portable radios and vehicular radios are generally used for two-way voice communications. Paging and signaling systems are generally used for selective calling by use of a modulated tone. Pagers receive coded signals transmitted from a base station, while signaling systems transmit coded signals to a base station. All paging, signaling, and repeater systems require a base station. Two-way voice communication requires a base station only if the transmitted power of the mobile is not sufficient for coverage of the desired area."[10]

Base Radios

In a maximum-security setting, the basic radio communication system should consist of at least two base radios, one of which can be of lesser wattage than the other. The primary base radio (and any remote units connected thereto) must be secured in the central alarm station (CAS). The other unit, used primarily as a backup to the first, should be afforded equal protection and, if the facility is so designed, located in the secondary alarm station (SAS). It is desirable that yet a third base radio be located in the CAS or SAS as a dedicated backup. At no time should the primary and only backup base radios be located together. If such were the case, a single adversary action could destroy the facility's capability for off-site radio communications.

Base radios must have the necessary power to reach any intended off-site location, the local police department, for example. If the facility is located so far away that radio transmission to off-site assistance agencies is undependable, regardless of the base station's power output, consideration must be given to using a repeater system. Establishing and maintaining an off-site two-way radio communication link with at least one support agency is a definite maximum-security requirement.

Portable Radio

One basic component of the radio system is the portable or hand-held unit. At the minimum, every security officer should be equipped with a portable radio unless he is assigned to an internal fixed post that has an alternate and reliable means of communication. It is preferable to ensure that every on-duty security officer is equipped with a portable radio. Minimum power output should be five watts.

Pagers

In some facilities, the nature of the work being performed sometimes precludes the use of portable radios. Sensitive electronic equipment could be affected by nearby radio transmissions, especially if it is not properly shielded. In cases such as these, tone or voice pagers can provide at least one-way radio communication to patrolling officers. Use of one-way radio as the primary means of communication should, however, be avoided. As an alerting system, pagers can be quite effective. Newer models feature tone and/or voice transmission capability as well as digital readouts. Some can even "tickle" the wearer, thus providing a silent alert.

Mobile Units

If vehicles are used, each should be equipped with a mobile communications unit. If possible, wattage should be sufficient to allow communication with off-site response forces. If circumstances permit, a mobile unit could be used as a backup to the base station.

It is desirable that the various units used in a radio communications system have at least some degree of component interchangeability. For example, if a base radio were to malfunction due to component failure, it would not disable that initial unit if the same component from a portable or mobil unit could be used in the base radio, thus putting it back on line. In this regard, it is unacceptable for a radio repair service, whether in-house or contracted, to allow excessive turnaround time when it comes to maximum-security radio repair. Sufficient spare units and/or parts should be stocked so that repairs can be effected as soon as possible.

Mobile Telephones

Another component of maximum-security communication is a mobile telephone. It is effective when key security decision makers must maintain a communication capability no matter where they might be. Pagers that can be activated just about anywhere in a state can be obtained by subscribing to an appropriate service. Their principal disadvantage is their one-way capability. A mobile phone provides two-way capability and some models are surprisingly inexpensive. The prime requisite for service is the availability of operators or stations. Commercial telephone companies offer mobile phone service but their capability may be limited by geographical location, and service may not be available. An alternative is RCC service (radio common carrier). There is a network of RCC stations throughout the country and RCC is offered in many areas where commercial service is unavailable.

CB Radio

Although the CB fad has passed, citizens band radio can still play an important part in a communications system. Because of the interest generated by CB radio a few years ago, there are many serious users who are additional sources of off-site communications capability. Many police agencies continue to monitor CB channel 9 for emergency communications. A high-quality CB base station can be installed and serve as yet another backup radio system in the event all others fail.

Scanners

Radio-frequency scanners can be effectively used whenever it is impossible to establish an off-site two-way radio link to law enforcement or other response agencies. Scanners can be used by the security force to monitor police frequencies and vice versa, thus establishing two-way radio communication, albeit on different channels. Additional frequencies can also be monitored as necessary to enhance the security function. In the event of a contingency situation, security personnel can use a scanner to monitor transmissions so as to provide better coordination and cooperation. Scanners are available that can be programmed by the user. Additionally, other important information usually transmitted by radio such as weather alerts and broadcasts can be obtained by using a scanner.

Radio Duress Alarms

Radio has increasingly been used as a personal or duress alarm system (Figure 6–1). There are several products on the market today that signal for assistance in the event that an officer requires it. Such units are basically one-way transmitters with a range within a mile, depending on wattage. If the transmission must travel a greater distance, a repeater, located in the officer's patrol vehicle, can be used to achieve the extra range. Many of the units can be manually activated or, in the event the officer is attacked, automatically activated by a mercury-type switch that initiates the alarm when the officer's body assumes a position a number of degrees from normal, for example, supine.

It is also possible to provide for a personal duress alarm by modifying an officer's portable radio so as to transmit an alarm signal or tone on activation by the officer. Such modification usually includes the installation of a tone generator and manual activating switch, and costs anywhere from $100 to $500, depending on the degree of sophistication required.

A method of conveying a duress alarm that is as old as two-way radio itself is using the radio to ask for assistance. Normal and contingency welfare

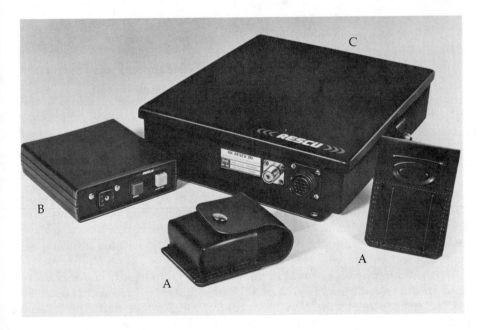

Figure 6-1 Emergency location alerting system A Remote actuator, B control and interface unit, C voice storage/logic unit. (The Antenna Specialists Co.)

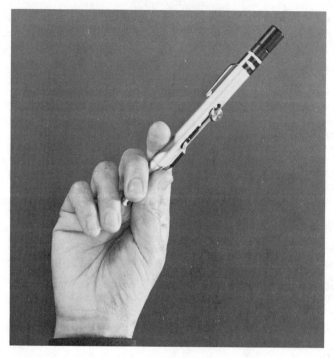

Figure 6-2 SCAN—silent communications alarm network. (Sentry Products, Inc.)

checks should be made, however, through the use of innocuous codes. (This is covered more fully later in this chapter.)

It does little good to have the most elaborate duress alarm system if the officer's location is unknown. Some sophisticated systems use a series of transponders electronically to locate an officer under duress, but these are quite expensive and are not in widespread use. It is *always* a good idea for the security organization to know the whereabouts of individual officers at all times. Depending on an officer's assignment, this may be a fairly simple task, for example, he may be assigned to a limited area. For an officer assigned to a large area, the security control center should have a method whereby his location is reasonably known whenever he investigates anything out of the ordinary. He should advise the security control center of his location, if this is practical. Under no circumstances should an officer be allowed to leave his assigned area without appropriate permission and without advising security control personnel.

A unique duress alarm system, while not radio-based, is designed to send an ultrasonic signal from a penlike transmitter to a receiver (Figure 6–2). The receiver relays the signal to a control console that alerts the console operator and displays the location of the signal. Its application in a maximum-security environment is obvious.

New Developments

A new development that shows promise for security personnel is a voice-activated, hands-free radio communication systems (Figure 6–3). This unit is inexpensive, lightweight, and easily carried by a security officer. It allows hands-free operation thanks to a headset consisting of an earphone and a voice-activated microphone. While its range is limited, its design can make its use desirable. These units are AM rather than FM, and this, coupled with the few channels available, restricts their use to other than sensitive communications.

Yet another interesting development permits interconnection of telephones with radio transceivers. In effect, a telephone can become part of the communications network.

"By dialing a standard seven-digit telephone number, a microprocessor computer activates the transmitter, automatically broadcasting the call to a . . . walkie-talkie. The result is instant, two-way voice contact. A telephone touch pad dialer on the walkie-talkie enables the user to make calls as he would on a regular telephone."[11]

Computer-Based Systems

With the advent of computer-based communications systems, many new applications for high security are emerging. Messages electronically sent in digital form provide for more efficient use of the frequency spectrum as well as a more confidential and secure method of data transmission. There are basically three types of digital messages that can be transmitted to a mobile unit: canned, composed, and automatic. Canned messages are sent by pushing a

Figure 6-3 Talkman voice-actuated (hands-free) communications system. (Standard Communications.)

button and consist of routine messages used repeatedly, such as in-service, out-of-service, and so on. Composed messages are made up as necessary and transmitted in total while automatic messages are transmitted at present intervals.

Because mobile units in such a system require sophisticated and expensive equipment such as cathode ray terminals (CRTs) and hard-copy printers, their use is not widespread.[12]

Frequencies

One area of radio communication sometimes overlooked is the frequency or frequencies used by the security force. In a maximum-security environment radio frequencies should never be shared. Security radio communication must be conducted on at least one channel or frequency dedicated exclusively to that use. Communications, especially during crisis situations, allows all those directly involved to receive the appropriate information without the interference of a shared frequency.[13]

A maximum-security radio communications net should have at least one dedicated channel for routine communications. Regular transmission will use this routine frequency and will make up the bulk of all radio transmissions. Because of the fact that well over 40,000 law enforcement and security agencies in this country use one or more radio frequencies, it has become necessary to limit the power output of radio transmitters. Generally, power output limitations restrict effective voice communications to a radius of less than 100 miles.[14] Thus there is likely to be more than one agency on the same frequency, and atmospheric and climatic conditions can result in agencies outside of a 100-mile radius being able to receive each other's transmissions. Therefore it becomes necessary to incorporate a feature into the radio system that will block out unwanted transmissions. This feature is called tone-coded squelch or channel guarding. Each radio is equipped with a device that, on activating the transmitter, produces a coded tone that opens the receivers of all other radios suitably equipped. Thus two users sharing the same frequency cannot hear each other when transmitting. A radio system should always be equipped with channel guarding and this feature should always be routinely used.

The maximum-security force should also have at least one nonroutine or contingency frequency at its disposal. During crisis operations, all radio communications directing the situation should use this second channel, thus leaving the first, or routine, channel free for normal radio traffic.

In addition to those used for routine and contingency communications, it may be desirable to monitor other channels and frequencies of interest, such as local and state police, other response organizations, and weather broadcasts. If monitoring more than one frequency, however, there should be a capability on the part of the radio operator to "kill" the other frequencies in an emergency situation so that extraneous radio traffic does not interfere.

The radio operator should never let interesting happenings on one frequency detract from his ability to monitor other frequencies.

Some advanced maximum-security installations use fairly sophisticated radio systems. At the Idaho National Engineering Laboratory, "Those responsible for site actions during severe weather, fire, flood, radiological or industrial incidents, civil disturbance or national defense emergency report to [an] emergency center to assume control. The center monitors and controls 19 radio nets and can 'tie' any or all together as necessary. They have state police, city police, State Highway Department, National Warning System (NAWAS), and Radio Amateur Civil Emergency Services (RACES) monitoring the radio capabilities and all communications to the center can be recorded."[15]

Telegraph or Telecopier

The use of telegraph service in a maximum-security facility is possible, although much better methods of communication are available. Teletype and telecopier service over commercial or private telephone lines provide means for the rapid transmission of lengthy communiques. When a facsimile of particular document is necessary, it can be sent or received between properly equipped stations. When suitable codes are employed, teletype or telecopier transmission of restricted information would be possible between facilities. Anything transmitted by this method, however, must be such that its interception and deciphering pose no significant threat to the site, its personnel, or any proprietary information, process, or product.

Most teletype and telecopier installations are of the conventional type, depending on the transmission of bits of electrical energy over a wire to a receiving apparatus. Lately, however, the technology in this field has made great progress with hybrid designs using radio signals bounced from orbiting space satellites to transmit information to teletypes designed to translate these electronic signals into readable copy.

MESSENGER OR COURIER

The use of messengers or couriers, the oldest, most secure means of signal communication, in a maximum-security setting would be appropriate when:

1. The site is involved in an emergency operation when an adversary force is suspected of monitoring radio communications or intercepting telephone transmissions
2. The sensitivity of the information being transmitted is such that a continuous chain of custody must be established, or assurance that this material has been delivered into the custody of a specific individual is paramount
3. When all other means of communication have been rendered inoperable

COMMUNICATIONS SECURITY

Security of information transmitted by way of electronic communications systems is of utmost concern. With the increasing availability of programmable radio-frequency scanners, anyone can listen in on radio transmission. Fairly sophisticated and inexpensive devices are available to monitor telephone conversations and verbal communications conducted "in private."

Because of the advent of inexpensive devices coupled with great advancements in electronics, the threat of eavesdropping by anyone—spy, terrorist, or average criminal—has significantly increased. Those charged with providing maximum security should be aware of the threat and incorporate security into their overall communications doctrine.

The basic effort along these lines must of necessity create and maintain awareness on the part of those using communications at sensitive locations. It must be stressed that if a maximum-security system is safeguarding a particular commodity, that commodity is always at risk and the security force is always vulnerable to whatever means may be directed against it, including illicit gathering of information.

Of the basic methods of communication—messenger, mail, hard wire, and radio—messenger is the most secure. For highly critical communications, this method should be employed whenever possible and feasible. Telephones and radios, aside from their shortcomings in terms of security, are used to expedite control and coordination, and must, of course, be used in maximum-security environments. Risks to the security of communications can and should, however, be minimized.

Physical Security of Equipment

It should be obvious that security of equipment is always necessary. Base radios (and remote units) and portable and mobile units should be physically secured or attended to preclude damage, intentional or otherwise. There is a tendency at times to place communications equipment away from security records or information sources. This makes it extremely difficult for the security dispatcher to look up information when necessary and at the same time maintain the required degree of communications integrity. To facilitate the often dual functions of the operator, the communication point should be established in two places: (1) at a remote dispatching point, close to records; and (2) at the site of the actual communications equipment, which may be located away from the operator.[16] Both locations must be protected and restricted to prevent unauthorized access to equipment, espionage, sabotage, damage, and theft.[17,18]

Security of Circuits

Whenever possible, communication lines should be on separate poles or in dedicated conduits. Tamper-indicating devices and supervised circuits are essential. All circuits and each individual piece of communications equipment should be tested at least once per shift, preferably at the beginning of a shift. If equipment has self-testing features, it should be checked at the beginning and periodically during the course of each shift. Equipment should also be periodically checked by maintenance personnel, in the presence of a security officer, for potential problems.[19] Immediately after repairs are effected, the equipment should be tested by security personnel.

Telephone Security

Many devices are now marketed commercially that legitimately or otherwise allow very efficient (and surreptitious) monitoring of telephone conversations. Some devices are so sophisticated that they can monitor telephone lines by induction, without being attached to them. There are also effective equipment and measures that can counter such eavesdropping.

Rather than go into a complete narration regarding each device and method, suffice to say that communications security, telephones included, starts with a sense of awareness. There are some methods and devices that can minimize susceptibility of clandestine eavesdropping, but the general rule of thumb is simply: if you don't have to discuss sensitive information over the phone, don't.

In a maximum-security environment the telephone may be used for all routine communications. It should never be used to discuss or relay sensitive information unless the requirement for expediency outweighs the potential damage associated with interception. This usually occurs on a case-by-case basis and the decision is made on the spot. One example would be a telephone call to local law enforcement authorities requesting their immediate assistance to counter a threat or potential threat to the facility. The decision has to be made, therefore, on the basis that, if the conversation is overheard by unauthorized persons, the resultant disadvantage is offset by a quick response.

The best possible first step toward telephone (and radio) security is transmission discipline. "It is very important for telephone subscribers to understand the relative security inherent in different types of circuits. In many cases, users are seldom aware that circuits are routed over a combination of wire and radio means. Portions of the system establishing the circuit may be equipped with security devices; however, this does not necessarily provide a secure circuit from terminal to terminal. Both wire and radio systems are susceptible to enemy intercept or monitoring. In addition, most telephone circuits are wired through one or more telephone switchboards or other communications facilities where they may be monitored by operating or supervisory personnel who are not necessarily cleared for the higher security classifications. A false feeling of security may exist on the part of many telephone users who may assume that the telephone is inherently more secure than the radio. A high degree of transmission discipline must be achieved to avoid this hazard."[20]

The following rules should provide basic telephone transmission discipline:

1. Always know who you are talking to. If there is any doubt, call the party back. Do not accept a caller's telephone number; instead, obtain a name, address, and affiliation and look the number up yourself.
2. Do not discuss anything relative to the safeguards employed at your facility, including, but not limited to security force strength and deployment, alarm systems, patrol routes, etc.
3. Do not discuss employees, especially key management personnel, over the phone.
4. Do not give home phone numbers to anyone over the telephone. Obtain the caller's number and advise him that you will contact the person he wishes to speak with and have him return the call.
5. Do not give out names of security personnel on duty.
6. Be alert to seemingly innocuous attempts to elicit sensitive information. Document all such calls and any others that arouse your suspicion.
7. Do not maintain lengthy telephone conversations with anyone if you are operating the communications control center. Long, seemingly pointless conversations could be a ploy to divert your attention from your duties. The only exception could be a bomb or other threat directed against the facility. In these cases, contact with the caller should be maintained and you should immediately advise your supervisor.
8. Confirm any orders given by law enforcement authorities over the telephone. Advise your supervisor.
9. If possible, tape-record all phone conversations received at the communication control center.
10. Consider every telephone to be tapped and conduct your conversations accordingly.

These guidelines also apply to other than security personnel, such as key management. No executive should have a listed telephone number. Travel information should never be discussed over the phone unless absolutely necessary and such conversations should be most discreet.[21]

While not directly related to security, telephone techniques are important nonetheless. The following techniques should ensure a professional and efficient response[22]:

1. Answer each call promptly, within three rings, if possible. Treat each call as an emergency.
2. Identify yourself and your unit. This ensures that the caller has placed his call properly and reassures him if he requires assistance.
3. Speak directly into the mouthpiece so that you will be properly understood and will not waste time repeating information. Speak clearly so you will be sure each word is understood.
4. Observe telephone courtesy. A calm, competent, decisive voice that is courteous will not antagonize the caller.

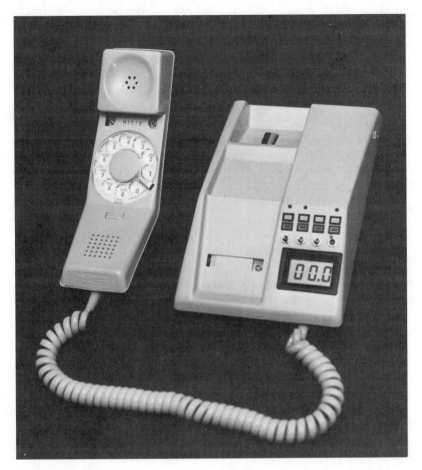

Figure 6-4 "The Controller" privacy telephone. (Viking International.)

5. Take charge of the conversation. After the initial exchange, when you understand the need of the calling party, ask questions to cover the who, what, where, when. Be courteous but firm.
6. Take all information down in writing. Never leave anything to memory. Always write down the name of the caller.
7. Explain why it will take time to check for information, and that you will call back.
8. Avoid jargon, slang, or unfamiliar abbreviations. Use good English.
9. Show interest. The person calling has or needs information and to him the call is important.
10. Use caller's name when possible, to make the individual feel you have a personal interest in the call.

Telephone scramblers, privacy devices, and masking devices (Figure 6–4) are available and may be considered. Careful research and evaluation should precede purchase of such devices. A. M. McCalmont[23] offers the following guidelines for communications security system selection:

I.   Level of security
   A.   Determine level of security needed
   B.   Evaluate channel and system constraints
   C.   Evaluate scrambling technique used in equipment and associated parameters
      1.   Security device technique, static and dynamic
         a.   Frequency inversion
         b.   Frequency hopping inversion/displacement
         c.   Band-splitting, static/dynamic
         d.   Time division coding
         e.   Time/frequency division coding
         f.   "M"ary Dynamic Rolling Code (MRCT/F) coding
         g.   Digital coding
      2.   Key elements to consider in evaluation
         a.   Degree of time and/or frequency segmentation
         b.   Regular or irregular segments
         c.   Rate or frequency of change
         d.   Sophistication of control codes/coding
         e.   Code depth
II.   Operational factors
   A.   Ease of use and operation
   B.   Clear voice override
   C.   Dual synchronization
   D.   Ease of installation
   E.   Field maintenance and service
   F.   Recovered voice quality
   G.   Half duplex vs full duplex
III.   Systems considerations
   A.   Channel modulation (AM, FM, SSB)
   B.   Band width and frequency response
   C.   Distortion
   D.   Frequency drift and offset
   E.   Electrical noise
   F.   Signal: noise ratio
   G.   Electrical noise
   H.   Radio Frequency Interference (RFI)
   I.   Prime power
   J.   Supervisory signals
IV.   Installation
   A.   Impedance and level matching
   B.   Physical location
   C.   Remote control
   D.   Interconnection and connectors

V.   Selection
     A.   Security trade-offs
     B.   Cost/performance evaluation

As can be seen, the principles involved in communications security devices are sophisticated and beyond the capabilities of many persons charged with providing such security. The best advice when it comes to acquiring and using this equipment is to discuss the situation with a reputable consultant or vendor and be guided accordingly.

Radio Security

Two-way radio systems are essential to any maximum-security program to facilitate and expedite command and control of the security force. Radio transmissions may occur occasionally or quite frequently. In either case, and everywhere in between, security of radio communications must be a major concern. The increasing sophistication of the equipment has resulted in the ability of anyone to listen into radio conversations by use of frequency-programmable radio scanners.

Much of the advice given under "Telephone Security" is applicable to radio security. Radio transmission security can be improved by following certain guidelines:

1.   Keep the number and length of transmission to a minimum.
2.   Use radios whose transmission power meets your needs but does not extend beyond your range of operations.
3.   Strictly adhere to established radio transmission procedures.
4.   Be alert for attempts to enter your radio net by unauthorized persons (imitative deception).
5.   Guard against radio traffic analysis.
6.   Require authorization of all messages.
7.   Ensure that every person using a two-way radio has been familiarized with the fundamentals of radio transmission security.

Radio operators must be trained to recognize and avoid improper practices that could compromise transmission security[24].

1.   Violating radio silence
2.   Unofficial and/or unauthorized transmissions
3.   Unauthorized use of unit identifiers and/or codes and exercise repetition
4.   Use of plain language instead of codes or signals
5.   Transmitting at a pace beyond the receiving operator's capability
6.   Using excessive transmitter power

7.   Taking too much time in testing, tuning, or adjusting equipment
8.   Unnecessarily lengthy transmission

Scramblers, special frequencies, and other such devices for sensitive radio communication are usually found in the military and certain large police departments.[25] They are not in widespread use among smaller police departments and most security operations. While it is a good idea to employ such safeguards in a maximum-security environment, cost often precludes their use. The communications security devices guidelines offered earlier can be valuable to the security director contemplating integration of these safeguards into his radio communications system.

For the high-security operation, radio transmission security demands definite procedures and adherence thereto. The Army offers the following guidance regarding radio techniques.[26]

"Base Station Techniques. The foundation of a good radio operator is reliability and promptness. Reliability should never be sacrificed for speed, yet speed is of equal importance. Learning and applying the following techniques will help to equalize speed and reliability:

"1.   The radio operator should be familiar with the call signs of all stations monitored and the call signs of mobile units.
"2.   Do not make adjustments to the radio equipment except as provided in the nature of control knobs.
"3.   Listen before keying the transmitter in order not to cause interference. Never transmit while another station or unit is transmitting.
"4.   Courtesy can be more aptly expressed by the tone of voice and manner of presentation than by words.
"5.   Eliminate all unnecessary talking. Be absolutely impersonal while on the air.
"6.   If, after calling a station or car twice, no reply is received, call another car and attempt a relay or instruct the second car to check on the first. Do not fill the air with continual and useless calls and do not neglect to send assistance when a car cannot be reached.
"7.   When you receive a request for information which is not immediately available, transmit, "WAIT, OUT," look up the information and call the unit back. Don't tie up the air while you look for something.
"8.   Under no circumstances allow a calling unit to go unheeded. Give a "WAIT" if necessary, but at least answer the call. If you have asked a unit to wait, call him as soon as possible.
"9.   Always identify the station when transmitting.
"10. Definite date and time should be specified; for example: 15 November instead of today, yesterday, or tomorrow; definite hour and minute time should be used and not "a few minutes ago."
"11. Avoid phrases and words that are difficult to copy or understand. Some examples of poor and preferred words are:

Poor	Preferred
Want	Desire
Can't	Unable
Buy	Purchase
Get	Obtain
Send	Forward
Do you want	Advise if
Find out	Inquire
Call and see	Check

"12. Remember the word CYMBALS when describing motor vehicles. Start at the top and move down according to the following:

Color

Year

Make

Body style

And

License

Serial number

"Mobile Unit Techniques.   The mobile unit is the second half of the radio system. It provides for command and control over great distances and in highly dispersed situations. It also enables patrols to request assistance and information, and keep the base station aware of their location. The following techniques will assist you in operating a mobile unit and in adding to the overall efficiency of the radio system.

"1.   Keep the base station advised of your status. If you go off the air, notify the base stations; when stopping a vehicle notify the base station of the color, year, make, body style, license number, and number of occupants. When you come back on the air, advise the base station of that fact. Always request permission of the base station to go off the air.

"2.   In most radio systems all transmissions pass through the base station. Normally, you will not talk to another mobile unit without first requesting permission from the base station.

"3.   Hold commercial-type microphones approximately one inch from your lips, press the microphone button down firmly, and then speak slowly and clearly across the mouthpiece in a normal to loud voice. Do not hold the microphone directly in front of your mouth, but slightly to the side, and at an angle of about 45 degrees, so that you talk across the face of the microphone instead of "blowing" into it.

"4.   Shouting or yelling into the microphone will cause an extremely distorted signal and must be avoided.

"5.   Think before you transmit. Know what you want to say. Say it and get off the air. Speak distinctly, be brief and concise; and do not mumble.

"6.   Always identify your unit when transmitting."

Codes

An essential part of radio transmission procedure is the use of codes or signals. They typically serve two basic functions: they decrease transmission time and ensure security of messages. The use of codes can greatly reduce the length of a radio transmission and can make it extremely difficult for an eavesdropper to decipher the message, especially if the codes are changed frequently.

The police service has used codes for many years. The basic system uses a series of ten-codes or signals to denote certain activities and responses to them. The main problem for agencies using this or any other series is that the codes are seldom if ever changed. Therefore it requires little effort on the part of an eavesdropper to decipher their meaning quickly and use the information for his own purposes. To be effective, then, codes should be periodically changed; the more frequent the change, the greater the security.

At a minimum, the following information should be encoded:

1.   Locations (zones, buildings, rooms, doors, parking lots, etc.)
2.   Operating units (patrols, fixed posts, etc.)
3.   Personnel (those associated with security and key management)
4.   General areas within and around a facility
5.   Activities (alarms, intrusions, etc.)
6.   Responses to activities (proceeding to area, securing door, etc.)
7.   Routine health and welfare checks of personnel
8.   Requests for assistance (backups, etc.)
9.   Officer under duress (to summon immediate assistance)

A typical code system could include numeric and alpha identifiers and a series of colors, for example:

Base to roving security patrol. We have an alarm at the south door to shipping. Proceed with caution. An intruder has been sighted on CCTV—204, red 22, 10-2 delta, 10-10.

Message	Code	Code Meaning
Base to roving security patrol.	204	204 is the call sign for roving security patrol.
We have an alarm at the south door to shipping.	Red 22	Red means an unscheduled alarm; 22 is the south door to shipping.

Proceed with caution.	10-2 Delta	10-2 means to check the area; delta means to use caution.
We have an intruder sighted on CCTV.	10-10	10-10 means the confirmed presence of an intruder.
A typical response might be: 204, 10-4, 10-2, 10-14, 10-15	—	Roving security patrol responding, message acknowledged. Proceeding to check it out. Request a backup. Also request you notify local law enforcement authorities.
Roving security patrol responding.	204	By repeating 204, the roving security patrol identifies himself and assures that he heard the call from base.
Message acknowledged.	10-4	Roving security patrol acknowledges receipt of the message.
Proceeding to check it out.	10-2	10-2, as a response, means area will be checked.
Request backup.	10-14	10-14 is a request for a backup security officer.
Also request you notify local law enforcement authorities.	10-15	10-15 is a request to notify the local law enforcement authorities.

As can be seen, the use of codes greatly expedites the transmission process. Unless the codes are known to the intruder (who may be equipped with a scanner), he remains unaware that an alarm was received and a response generated, thus making the security patrol's response somewhat safer.

The military uses a very complicated series of codes, signs, countersigns, and authenticators. *Signal Orders Records and Reports, U.S. Army Field Manual 24-16* describes the whole process in detail.

A system of codes should be used for key management personnel and others susceptible to a kidnapping or hostage or extortion threat. If these persons call in after hours, they should be able to identify themselves not only by name but by a code number or word. If they are under duress, they should be able to convey that message by using a different code or modifying the first.

For security personnel, some sort of health and welfare check should be made in the following circumstances, for example: whenever an officer investigates anything out of the ordinary; if he has not been heard from for 15 minutes during routine activity; or whenever he is on a special assignment, which by its nature could present a hazard (a special observation post on top of a multistory building, for example).

Protecting Communications Information

Information pertaining to communication that is considered to be sensitive should be protected, as would be any other classified information (this subject is covered in Chapter 15). Communications frequencies, codes, logs, signals, and other such information, including the frequency of code changes, should be known only to those persons who have a need to know it. All others should be excluded from access to such information. Written procedures, codes, and signals should be secured in the same manner as government classified information.

Whenever a person who has had access to such information terminates employment or is reassigned to a position where access is no longer necessary, all codes, signals, and lock combinations or keys used to secure such information must immediately be changed. Procedures may have to be modified accordingly.

While it is not as secure as a completely new code system, one method is to develop several (at least six) sets of codes and use them whenever random and/or periodic code changes are necessary. This enables personnel to learn all code sets and minimizes confusion when a new code must be used. Codes should be changed frequently in the maximum-security environment.

COMMUNICATIONS METHODOLOGY

Why are off-site security communications necessary? The answer, obviously, is to summon aid, for example, police, fire department, or emergency medical assistance. The federal government insists that licensees of nuclear materials maintain one or more methods of summoning off-site assistance in the event of a contingency that plant or site protection personnel are not capable or equipped to handle. While traditional means of summoning such aid are usually thought of (telephone, commercial and/or dedicated hot line, and radio), older systems may still be effective. For example, if a natural or man-made disaster disrupted all power sources including battery backup systems, the use of a messenger would be the next logical step. If time, distance, terrain, or other obstacles precluded the use of a human messenger, the use of a carrier pidgeon could be feasible. The emergency planner should not allow himself to be locked into a limited range of options in this or any area.

When commercial telephone transmission lines can be afforded a reasonable degree of protection, such as when they are buried or there is microwave transmission, several of them should be available to security personnel. In addition, a dedicated hot line should link the primary and secondary alarm stations and local law enforcement authorities. These lines, both commercial and dedicated, should be tested daily at the beginning of each security shift, and the results of such tests fully documented.

In addition to maintaining contact with every security officer on duty, radio communications systems should provide two-way communications with local law enforcement authorities (LLEA). Subjecting these personnel to listening to routine communications would eventually result in the volume on their receiver being turned down to an inaudible level or completely off. To avoid this, the link should be equipped with an encoder at the site, which, when activated, sends a signal to the decoder on the LLEA receiver and opens the channel, enabling them to hear the broadcast. One or more security vehicles should be equipped with powerful transmitter/receiver units to enable them to be pressed into service as self-contained emergency base units.

The dependability of any item of security equipment is only as good as the care and maintenance it receives. Security radios that are carelessly used will have poor service life and their downtime and repair cost will quickly become prohibitive. One of the most common causes for portable radio breakage is failure by the officer to carry the units in proper cases. All too often, officers will simply stick a unit into a pants or jacket pocket, only to have it fall out later, with resultant damage to the case, battery, and fragile internal mechanisms, or all three. When in-house technicians are not available to provide the necessary repair and/or preventive maintenance services, a maintenance contract should be arranged with a reputable local dealer. If the services of the manufacturer's local representative fail to meet requirements, the manufacturer should be contacted with documented complaints regarding poor service.

A maintenance record should be set up on each piece of equipment. Periodic review of these records will show which ones are requiring more than normal repair service, and could lead to retirement of units that cost more to keep in operation than they are worth.

Before an individual is allowed to operate any item of security communications equipment, he must be thoroughly trained in such use. This training must be formal, with periodic testing to ascertain the trainee's comprehension of the material. Only after an individual has successfully proved his abilities should he be allowed to use the equipment.

CONCLUSION

Communication in a maximum-security environment is an essential ingredient in the overall safeguards system. It is the single most important element of coordination and control. As such, communication has long been recognized as being vulnerable to attack in an adversary situation.

Just as with any other maximum-security hardware, communications systems must be top quality and reliable. "The improper or imprudent use of gadgets as they come along results in inconsistent and unrelated systems. This may produce an operation which gives the appearance of being modern and consists of many individual pieces of equipment but which contributes virtually nothing to the accomplishment of . . . goals. In addition, a tremendous amount of money is improperly spent."[27]

The security director should avoid a fragmented system and, when designing or upgrading communications, should adapt a master plan approach and implement it accordingly.[28]

The *Handbook of Building Security Planning and Design* offers certain basic guidelines regarding communications. While they pertain to cargo storage they are valuable as a basic communications checklist.[29]

"I.   Is the security communications system adequate?
II.   What means of communications are used?
    A.   Telephone
        1.   Is it a commercial switchboard system? Independent switchboard?
        2.   Is it restricted for guard use only?
        3.   Are switchboards adequately guarded?
        4.   Are there enough call boxes, and are they conveniently located?
        5.   Are open wires, terminal boxes, and cables frequently inspected for damage, wear, sabotage, and wiretapping?
        6.   Are personnel cautioned about discussing cargo movements over the telephone?
    B.   Radio
        1.   Is proper radio procedure practiced?
        2.   Is an effective routine code being used?
        3.   Is proper authentication required?
        4.   Is the equipment maintained properly?
    C.   Messenger
        1.   Is the messenger always available?
    D.   Teletype
        1.   Is an operator available at all times?
    E.   Public address
        1.   Does it work?
        2.   Can it be heard?
    F.   Visual signals
        1.   Do all guards know the signals?
        2.   Can they be seen?
III.   Is security communications equipment in use capable of transmitting instructions to all key posts simultaneously?
IV.   Does the equipment in use allow a security officer to communicate to security headquarters with minimum delay?
V.   Is there more than one system of security communications available for exclusive use of security personnel?

VI.   Does one of these systems have an alternate or independent source of power?

VII.   Has the communications center been provided with adequate physical security safeguards?"

In the maximum security environment it is always essential that communications can be conducted by more than one, preferably several, means—the principle of diversity and redundancy is compelling in the area of maximum-security communications. All communications should, if possible and feasible, be tape-recorded and preserved for at least six weeks. Additionally, backup systems are necessary should the primary system fail by chance or design. All communications systems in the maximum security environment should have backup power sources that can take over automatically in the event of a purchased power failure. Any power failure or condition affecting the site's communications capability should immediately be suspect and a contingency communication system or plan activated.

NOTES

1.   *Tactical Communications Doctrine, U.S. Army Field Manual 24-1* (Washington, D.C.: Department of the Army, 1968, p. 72.

2.   Ibid.

3.   Charles E. Gaylord and Jerry W. Hicklin, "High-Rise Office Buildings," in *Handbook of Building Security Planning and Design*, ed. Peter S. Hopf (New York: McGraw-Hill Book Company, 1979), p. 26-9. Material used with permission.

4.   *The Military Police Handbook, U.S. Army Field Manual 19-5* (Washington, D.C.: Department of the Army, 1975), p. 11-15.

5.   *Physical Security, U.S. Army Field Manual 19-30* (Washington, D.C.: Department of the Army, 1979), p. 110.

6.   *Tactical Communications Doctrine*, p. 70.

7.   Correctional Communications," *Security Industry and Product News* (April 1982):24–28.

8.   *The Military Police Handbook*, p. 11-16.

9.   Ibid., p. 11-17.

10.   Alan B. Abramson, "Electronic Security Systems," in *Handbook of Building Security Planning and Design*, ed. Peter S. Hopf (New York: McGraw-Hill Book Company, 1979), p. 11-13. Material used with permission.

11.   "Homeowner in Distress," *Security Industry and Product News* (August 1982):24.

12.   William J. Bopp, *Police Administration: Selected Readings* (Boston: Holbrook Press, Inc., 1975), pp. 282–284.

13.   Robert H. Kupperman and Darrel Trent, *Terrorism* (Stanford: Hoover Institution Press, 1979), P. 397.

14.   Harry Caldwell, *Basic Law Enforcement* (Pacific Palisades: Goodyear Publishing Company, Inc., 1972), p. 72.

15.   Harold J. Argyle, "Nuclear Security in a Sagebrush Environment," *FBI Law Enforcement Bulletin* (September 1982):6.

16. O.W. Wilson and R. C. McLaren, *Police Administration* (New York: McGraw-Hill Book Company, 1972), p. 480. Material used with permission.
17. *Tactical Communications Doctrine*, p. 74.
18. *Tactical Communications Center Operation, U.S. Army Field Manual 24-17* (Washington, D.C.: Department of the Army, 1967), p. 10.
19. *Physical Security*, p. 111.
20. *Tactical Communications Doctrine*, p. 77.
21. *Countering Terrorism* (Washington, D.C.: Department of State, 1977).
22. *The Military Police Handbook*, pp. 11-3–11-4.
23. A. M. McCalmont, "Communications Security Devices," *Security Industry and Product News* (March 1980):19.
24. *Tactical Communications Doctrine*, pp. 75, 77.
25. R. E. Anderson, *Bank Security* (Boston: Butterworth Publishers, 1981), p. 158.
26. *The Military Police Handbook*, pp. 11-6–11-8.
27. Bopp, *Police Administration*, p. 280.
28. Ibid.
29. "Cargo Storage," Adapted from "Guidelines for the Physical Security of Cargo," Dept. of Transportation, Office of the Secretary, Washington, D.C., May 1972, in *Handbook of Building Security Planning and Design*, ed. Peter S. Hopf (New York, McGraw-Hill Book Company, 1979), pp. 22-13–22-14. Material used with permission.

CHAPTER 7

Closed-Circuit Television

Only with the relatively recent introduction of CCTV (closed-circuit television), has the security practitioner finally been able to achieve true economy of manpower. Where he was once forced to have a number of individuals scattered about the facility in fixed posts or roving patrols, he is now able to monitor all critical or vulnerable areas electronically from a central location faster, more effectively, and more efficiently than ever before. This ability to instantly assess and evaluate the cause for alarms or to identify individuals or actions within the monitored area has allowed the size of the on-site guard contingent to be down-scaled to a smaller, more efficient, better trained, and more easily managed force.

Because of technological breakthroughs that occur seemingly overnight in the electronics field, the maximum-security practitioner contemplating the use of CCTV should prepare himself by obtaining at least a basic understanding of what it is, what it can and cannot do, and how best to use it to enhance the site protection.

A CCTV system can be used whenever observation is needed and where direct viewing is impossible, undesirable, or inconvenient. It not only can provide a better vantage point for observation but also can augment the sensitivity, contrast discrimination, and spectral range of the human eye. TV cameras can be placed in all types of environments from vault-type rooms under constant lighting conditions to outdoor environments where the lighting can vary from bright sunlight to overcast night conditions and temperatures can vary from −40 degrees to 125 degrees F. The first step in deciding what type of CCTV system is needed is determining the location and use of the CCTV system. For some operations, CCTV is helpful (1) in providing protection to operating personnel by making it possible to increase the distance between control personnel and a dangerous operation, (2) in monitoring operations occurring in an extreme or uncomfortable environment, (3) in coordinating a number of different operations, (4) in preparing educational videotapes, (5) in inspecting machinery, control equipment, and production lines, and (6) in various security applications such as observing sensitive areas, remotely assessing alarms, or identifying personnel desiring entrance into sensitive areas.[1]

CCTV COMPONENTS

To the uninitiated, the CCTV field offers a bewildering assortment of cameras, monitors, lenses, housings, brackets, transmission systems, and recorders ad

Figure 7-1   Covert CCTV cameras. (Visual Methods Incorporated.)

Figure 7-1   (*Continued*)

infinitum. The features offered by the various manufacturers are innovative in many cases and can even be custom-packaged to suit a particular need or specification. Every system, however, is composed of certain basic elements.

Cameras

The latest state-of-the-art cameras are of solid-state electronic fabrication, which means they are very compact, but highly reliable and capable of offering dependable service through a range of environmental conditions. The ever decreasing sizes available have led to innovations in their security application wherever undetected monitoring is desired. They have been built into such innocuous items as a standard exit sign, a department store mannequin, a 5″ × 8″ card file, and a popular brand AM/FM table radio (Figure 7–1). The list of objects that may be used to hide a surveillance camera is governed only by the space available. For most security applications, the use of monochrome (black-and-white) cameras is recommended. These give satisfactory picture resolution and are far less expensive than color cameras.

Lenses

No matter how good or expensive a camera may be, it is useless (or nearly so) without the proper lens. For most applications a fixed-focus lens is adequate. It should be matched to the camera and designed for the purpose, such as ability to function in ambient light conditions, clarity of images at the focal distance specified, field of view at the desired viewing distance, and so on. In applications where the camera's position can be changed through remote control, the most versatile lens has zoom capabilities. Again, it should be matched to provide image clarity through the entire zoom range and desired field of view, under ambient light conditions.

Because the CCTV industry, like any other highly competitive technological field, has developed a set of manufacturing standards, the lenses offered by most manufacturers are often usable with a competitor's product. This allows greater flexibility in designing a specialized system and assures that several makes of camera may be intermixed in the same system without the necessity for stocking separate lenses for each brand.

Signal Transmission

"Selecting the proper video distribution and control system may prove to be the most demanding and expensive decision in the selection of CCTV systems. The decision must involve not only the transmission of the video signals to the monitor, but also, in some configurations, the transmission of control signals from the central station to the camera, pan/tilt units, lights, or camera environmental housing."[2]

Video signal transmission systems include coaxial cables and infrared optical signal. In most installations the system will be coaxial cable, since it permits the highest picture resolution receivable at the monitor. To assure minimum interference and signal loss, it should be designed and installed by a qualified professional with experience in this field, rather than assigned to a maintenance department in hopes of saving on installation costs. Microwave optical systems such as General Electric's GemLink® (Figure 7–2) offer the flexibility of a video signal transmission across line-of-sight spaces where it would be impossible or impractical to string coaxial cable.

A third system uses optical fibers to transmit the signal from camera to monitor. Because such a system contains no metal in the transmission lines,

Figure 7-2 GemLink®. (General Electric.)

it offers several distinct advantages over conventional coaxial cable. Coaxial cables use copper wire with a metallic sheath to prevent signal loss or interference. Absence of these metals makes an optical fiber system less vulnerable to detection (and therefore tampering or attack) by metal-detecting devices. Because the signal passes through the optical fiber as light, the transmission of an electrical impulse is eliminated. This makes such a system impervious to normal interference-producing pieces of equipment and allows the transmission line to be routed through spaces or areas where this was not previously possible. This versatility in installation, coupled with its abilities to transmit a great many signals over a very few glass strands, its light weight, and low cost (relative to multistranded metal cable) offer the individual or company contemplating a complex and widespread CCTV system a very attractive alternative to conventional means of signal transmission.

Another transmission system offers interesting possibilities by converting the video signal into an audio signal, then sending it anywhere in the world by telephone. The manufacturer claims that visual data can be transmitted almost instantaneously to any place that can be reached by telephone, and with few exceptions, anything that can be televised with CCTV can be televised with this system. There is no special training required to operate this system, and in fact it has been designed for simplicity of operation so that anyone can do it.

Housings

Cameras installed outdoors, even in protected areas, must provide dependable service regardless of the prevailing weather and environmental conditions. Thus they must have housings that not only protect the camera against dust and moisture, but ensure that service continues with no interruption through the incorporation of accessories such as heaters, lens-cover wipers, hoods, and the like.

Monitors

Afters assuring the site CCTV cameras and lenses are matched and protected from the elements by an adequate housing, and that the video signal is being transmitted by the most efficient method, the next consideration should be the monitor on which the signal will become a comprehensible picture. There are numerous monitors available that have been designed and built to provide dependable 24-hour continuous service. The clarity and quality of its picture are the result of the resolution capabilities inherent in the camera, lens and transmission mode over which the video signal is sent. The monitor, however, must be capable of reassembling these electronic signals onto a display screen made up of a number of very fine, closely spaced lines. These, in turn, must be capable of reproducing all 10 shades of gray on the Electronic Industries Association resolution test chart.[3] The more lines available on the viewing screen, the better the picture. The industry standard viewing screen had provided about 525-line resolution, but as technology and manufacturing methods improve, this figure has increased to 600, 700, and even over 800 lines.

Monitors are available with screens of 5, 6, 9, 12, 14, 17, 19 and 23 inches. In general, the smallest screen that should be considered is the 9 inch, unless the scene being monitored is a small space where positive identification of an individual is not necessary, or the camera has been placed close to the object being viewed, such as gauges on a piece of equipment that requires remote monitoring. In specialized cases such as this, the smaller monitors may be acceptable. In a multimonitor alarm station, the 9 inch monitors are adequate for fixed monitoring. One or more 17 inch units are recommended where sequential switchers pass the scenes being displayed on the banked individual monitors before the guards at that post. The larger monitor allows for easier and quicker identification of personnel and activities.

Video Recorders

While video tape-records have been in existence for a number of years in the television broadcast industry, it was only with the introduction of down-sized and more affordable recorders aimed at the home or small-consumer market that this equipment began to receive serious consideration by security practitioners. Like the sound tape recorder after which it appears to be modeled, the video version uses a magnetic tape on which the images to be recorded are placed. This tape requires no special processing and is ready for viewing merely by rewinding for playback. Recorders generally found in security use are of two types, one that is designed for permanent or semipermanent installation in the alarm station where it is instantly available to record any unusual event; and a compact portable, which when coupled with a suitable camera and power pack, enables the security department to go to the scene of any contingency and provide a complete visual record of the event (Figure 7–3). This package is also a valuable training tool. At the scene of a riot, demonstration, or strike, the portable system can be an especially valuable security tool.

Additional advantages of a video recorder over a conventional photographic film camera include the fact that, like a sound recorder, it is used to play back the recorded tape. Depending on the existing requirements, sound may be recorded on the video tape at the time it is recorded, or it may be added later to an already recorded tape. The similarities between sound and video tape recorders continues, as both can be edited, erased, and reused.

The video tape recorders most commonly used in a security environment use either a half-inch, three-quarter-inch, or one-inch recording tape. While all are capable of providing adequate service, the one-inch models have the best reproduction capabilities.

Features offered by commercially available video recorders include multiple playback modes (slow motion, quick motion, freeze frame); full remote-control capability; timer switch (for time-controlled unit start and stop); tape

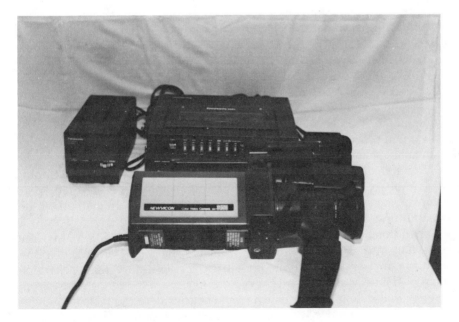

Figure 7-3 Portable CCTV unit. (S. Messemer.)

counter with memory; auto rewind at end of tape; meter to show accumulated hours of operation; internal power backup; external battery connections; direct-drive capstan motor; automatic alarm search (locates all recorded alarms); built-in time/date generator; electronic security lockout (secures recorder from unauthorized tampering); time lapse recording; ability to be coupled to alarm sensors to start video recording at a normal speed from a time-lapse mode; audio dub feature; and tape reels or cassettes.

Accessories

Included in this category are such items as pan/tilt units, scanners, video switchers, mounting brackets, controls, video signal equipment, consoles, and miscellaneous other items.

Sequential switchers are control units that among other things, provide a visible signal to the alarm station operator for which camera is being viewed on the monitor screen. Depending on the manner in which it is programmed, automatic switching from one camera to the next in a routine sequence may be altered by the operator either to speed up or slow down the sequencing. This allows longer periods for detailed viewing of each area under CCTV surveillance or rapid assessment of each area to detect major changes in the scene. The sequential switcher also provides the capability for locking one camera out of rotation and onto a separate monitor screen for unbroken surveillance.

When a video record of a security contingency will be needed as evidence in civil or criminal court proceedings, the use of a time/date generator appears warranted. If the recorder being used does not have this as a built-in capability, an accessory generator is available. It is connected in-line between the camera output and the monitor, and superimposes a continuous display consisting of the month, day, and year, plus time of day in hour, minutes, and seconds. This information is placed on the scene being recorded on video tape, and becomes a visual record to show a judge and jury or site management officials the second-by-second course of events that constituted an unusual event or emergency.

There are large numbers of mounting brackets available, which through an evolutionary process, have become basically similar in design. The products of various manufacturers differ somewhat, however, in methods of surface mounting, product finish, construction material, and so on. Because of the varied positions selected for camera mounting and the different weights the bracket must support, units are available that allow an indoor ceiling mount; an indoor wall mount (both basically light-duty units where the weight of the camera is not excessive and no camera motion is necessary); a universal wall/ceiling mount, which would be considered suitable for medium duty; heavy-duty indoor wall mount and outdoor mount; pedestal mounts;

heavy-duty scanner mounts for building corners; combination mounting bracket and automatic scanning device; and pole mounts.

Some CCTV camera enclosures differ from housings in that they protect equipment that is subjected to stresses on the pan/tilt or scanner drive mechanism caused by heavy winds and snow or ice buildup in addition to the weight of the camera and housing. These extra stresses can lead to early mechanism failure. A camera inside an enclosure is free to move with no external influence by wind or snow or ice load.

The enclosure is basically a sphere that is available with a clear lower half where there is no desire to hide the fact that an area is under CCTV surveillance. In areas where discreet surveillance is necessary, such as furriers, gem merchants, and museums, the lower enclosure may have tinted or reflective mirror finish to hide the camera inside. The tint or coating does not affect the camera's ability to provide clear and distortion-free surveillance. Another spherical enclosure has a number of projections that appear to be camera lenses, however, only one actually is a lens (Figure 7–4). Its deterrent value is in an adversary not knowing that only one is real or which one that is. Another enclosure consists of a rail or track (which may be up to 100 feet long) within a translucent covering that does not allow anyone to locate the camera position(s). Another system uses compressed air for noiseless movement of the camera along a track up to 150 feet long. It is suitable for covering large areas such as building exteriors, bonded warehouses, and correctional facilities.

A scanner is a motor-driven device on which a CCTV camera is mounted. Once it has been adjusted, it allows the camera to traverse or "pan" through an arc of up to 355 degrees. A pan/tilt unit is also a powered device on which a camera is mounted, however, unlike the scanner, it can be remotely operated through its arc with stops at any point. The camera can also traverse in a vertical direction up to 90 degrees for a better look at a subject. These units are usually available in indoor and outdoor models. One manufacturer even has models suitable for service in an explosive atmosphere.

Installation of CCTV cameras around a site perimeter would require adequate light or use of cameras designed for operation in low light. The cameras would require protection from the elements; depending on the prevailing climate, housings and enclosures, mounting brackets, scanners, pan/tilt units, and the like should not necessarily be chosen on a dollars-and-cents basis. Keeping the costs down by accepting a lower-quality item, or overextending equipment by attempting to use an item designed for indoor or light duty in an outdoor or heavy duty application, will probably result in unsatisfactory service because of breakdowns and necessary replacement of prematurely worn or broken parts. Cameras should be installed high enough to provide an unobstructed view and prevent surreptitious tampering or redirection. They should, whenever possible, be placed below sources of area light to prevent their inadvertent pan through a bright light and the resultant

Figure 7-4   Multiple-lens CCTV enclosure. (Executive Video International Corp.)

"bloom" that will temporarily blind them. All such perimeter cameras should be equipped with pan/tilt capabilities and zoom lenses. At facilities where the perimeter is an isolation zone wherein no authorized movement will be taking place, the use of a video motion-detector system such as that by Video-Tek described in Chapter 4, or one available from RCA, Javelin Electronics, or Visual Communications Specialists appears to offer excellent backup to a perimeter microwave intrusion-detection system.

At facilities that require visitors to sign in and be searched prior to authorized entry, CCTV monitoring of the officer on duty at the entry control post and the individual being processed assures a measure of protection for the officer. Aggressive actions by the person or persons attempting to gain entry would result in the immediate closure of that access point and the dispatch of assistance forces.

Where the facility has security-controlled remotely operated doors, CCTV cameras positioned at that point allow the identification of individuals to determine their access authorization. Where the door is an entry or exit point to a controlled area that prohibits the introduction or removal of certain items, a CCTV installation enables the security officer to observe the individual to ensure this prohibition is being observed prior to activating the door-release mechanism. Used in this manner, CCTV is part of the site access-control system.

The use of CCTV would be of great benefit in facilities where precious metals or minerals are mined, refined, or processed; used in the manufacture of a product; stored as raw stock or as a completed product awaiting shipment; or displayed for sale or as art objects. Because of the high dollar value of a relatively small amount of precious metal and certain rare or strategic minerals, the unauthorized diversion of any quantity would result in a monetary or other unacceptable loss to the owner. Where the potential for such diversion exists or where losses are already being experienced, the installation of a quality CCTV surveillance system that offers total coverage of all areas is highly recommended. (This would preferably be in conjunction with the institution of a system of access controls, personnel and package searches, and other procedures to curtail such diversion.) The cameras should be equipped with pan/tilt features as well as zoom lenses. Where the spaces being monitored contain machinery or material that obstructs the camera view, consideration should be given to:

1. Removing the obstructions to allow a clear field of vision
2. Rearrange the items in the space to allow a clear field of vision
3. Use of more cameras so that no area within the monitored space(s) could hide a human or provide cover for an unauthorized act
4. Use of a tracked system that allows more flexibility in camera position
   Note: While such an installation appears the best alternative observation of the camera by an adversary would allow the commission of a misdeed after the camera has passed his position.)

In reality, a combination of these features would be the best solution. The use of translucent domes for all cameras is recommended so that personnel in the monitored spaces cannot see in which direction the camera may be pointing and therefore do not know if they are under observation. All cameras should be monitored in an on-site central alarm station that is continuously manned. Depending on the amount of station activity, it may be necessary to assign one security officer exclusively to monitoring the CCTV surveillance system. The console should be equipped with a bank of dedicated monitors, one for each of the cameras; at facilities with a great many cameras, two or three may share the same dedicated monitor through the use of a sequential switcher. Immediately in front of the operator there should be a single larger monitor on which all cameras are monitored through another sequential switcher. The system must allow the operator instantly to switch the scene from any camera onto the main screen and begin video recording of the scene displayed. (The video recorder should be equipped with a built-in or in-line time/date generator.) Some facilities use fake CCTV cameras to give the illusion of surveillance, however, this seldom fools in-house personnel for long. Other facilities opt for a mix of real and fake cameras, but this system also only buys a little time before site personnel learn which are real and which are not.

Where a facility has two or more alarm stations capable of independent operation, each should have a CCTV camera viewing all activities within the space but monitored at the other station. This dual monitoring enables either station to observe any unauthorized activity in the other, so that corrective or compensatory action may be initiated. In addition, both of these scenes could be monitored in the security supervisor's office or in some other protected on-site location that has the capability to freeze doors and summon on or off-site assistance.

For a facility with a number of remote or isolated guard posts on access roads, CCTV surveillance of the approaches would be a psychological boost to the officers assigned there, plus afford an extra measure of protection for the site by early warning of an unauthorized or forced entry.

At facilities where highly volatile or explosive materials are stored in outdoor or remote areas, CCTV surveillance within the storage perimeter and even among the material would eliminate the necessity for an officer patrol to conduct periodic checks. This has the added safety feature in that the officer could accidentally be the cause of a major catastrophic loss, whereas the camera system could not.

Medical research facilities or pharmaceutical laboratories are often engaged in the development of new drugs or in disease research involving the use of live viruses, some of which are extremely virulent. They frequently use CCTV to observe experiments and, at certain facilities, test animals to monitor the development of a disease and the results of experimental immunizations. Because the bacteria and viruses are sometimes deadly CCTV surveillance and positive control of all personnel entering, working in, and leaving such a facility is a necessity.

In the area of training, CCTV should prove itself extremely versatile. For example, a facility that trains its security officers in the use of firearms can use video tape to record the progress of students through each phase of range firing. Students can then view their performance and most will be able instantly to recognize their mistakes. The instructor can go over the video record, showing students point by point where they could make corrections or adjustments. Another use of CCTV for training is in recorded indoctrination or welcoming addresses, taping of site drills or training exercises for later critique, and even play-acting scenarios where "aggressors" are detected on-site committing any of a variety of unauthorized deeds. Each officer to be tested is suddenly confronted with the evidence and required to act quickly and decisively. His actions are then evaluated by the instructor and other officers present to decide if they were proper and timely.

At sites or facilities that may be the scenes of a riot, strike violence, or protest demonstration, CCTV video recording is highly recommended. The recorder should have a time/date generator to validate the recorded information. The camera operator should be positioned behind potential violent action and high enough to have an unobstructed field of view. He should attempt to get clear shots of all such acts as well as of all rear area agitators and vehicles (including license plates) involved in violent acts or that appear to be adversary command centers. The operator must ensure that he does not allow himself to become enveloped by violent action. If he is not already in a position of safety, he should always have an avenue of safe escape available or be protected by security personnel.

When alarm console operators monitor only fixed cameras, they must be alert for attempts to defeat the system by placement of a photo of the area being viewed, taken from the same angle at which the camera is mounted, before the camera. To the security officer monitoring the CCTV console, this photo could make it appear that all was well within this space when, in fact, it was effectively blocking his view of the area. Other ways in which the system may be circumvented include repositioning cameras so that they do not provide total area surveillance or breaking the signal transmission line between camera and monitor.

At facilities with no response force, or where the officer on duty at the monitoring station is not familiar with the areas being monitored, such simple ploys have a chance for success. Where response force personnel are available, however, they should be immediately dispatched to the scene of any alarm or assessment system component failure or malfunction to check on the cause. In cases where camera repositioning only is required and the response force is able, they should be directed to do this. When a space being monitored is not protected by an alarm system, a security patrol should check it frequently or a security officer can be posted there as a compensatory measure in the event of camera or monitor failure.

Where monitoring of personnel is necessary such as in a penal or mental institution, CCTV can provide comprehensive coverage with minimum personnel. Again, some method is required of assuring that problems of situations observed are promptly responded to by qualified persons.

MAINTENANCE

While most items of CCTV equipment have been designed and engineered for long and dependable service life, there eventually comes time when something will wear out or break. At large facilities with extensive and sophisticated electronic security systems, addition to the staff of a qualified technician should be seriously considered. Such an individual would thus be readily available to perform necessary repair service and maintain a timely preventive maintenance program to ensure equipment failure is kept at the minimum. The establishment of such a position would necessitate setting aside appropriate shop space and the purchase of tools, test equipment, spare parts, and replacement equipment; specialized equipment training might be warranted for the technician. The monetary cost of establishing such a position (which would include intangibles such as time spent in waiting for an off-site independent contractor to respond to a service call, time awaiting receipt of special-order parts, availability of emergency service, etc.) would determine whether it would be beneficial and cost effective. Systems should always be checked, after maintenance, by a security officer.

SPECIALIZED EQUIPMENT

For specialized operations, CCTV equipment is available that is built into an attache case and contains an independent power supply. Where the undetectable monitoring of a space is desired but the physical layout or contents preclude the use of conventional CCTV cameras, a pinhole lense, conventional, angled, with auto iris, and so forth, or attached to the camera by a fiber optic transmission line may be used. This would allow the camera to be completely hidden, as in a false ceiling. Lenses are also available that allow a two- or three-way split image on the same monitor of the same scene at different magnifications.

NOTES

1. Nuclear Regulatory Commission, *Basic Considerations for Assembling A Closed-Circuit Television System* (Washington, D.C.: The Commission, 1977), p. 1.
2. Ibid., p. 12.
3. Ibid., p. 16.

CHAPTER 8

Access Controls

Whenever there exists a facility that is provided with the maximum in safeguard measures, there also exists a need for authorized personnel to have access to and within that facility. The term "authorized personnel" can refer to anyone who has a need to be in a facility and/or to have access to its contents. They can be workmen, managers, scientists, material handlers, and just about any other occupation depending on the nature of the facility.

A maximum-security facility is designed based on the premise that all persons are denied access by whatever means. This can be easily visualized if one imagines an impenetrable dome placed over the facility with no ways in or out. The security of the facility would, obviously, be total. Unfortunately, reality does not provide for total and complete security. People have to be involved, and the problem from the security point of view is allowing the right people to become involved.

Those who are allowed access to a maximum-security facility are people determined by management (sometimes with outside guidance) to have a need to do so. Need in this sense is the facility's need, not the individual's. Whatever the facility requires to sustain itself, it needs. Thus there is need for salesmen, for electricians and secretaries, and for management personnel; and there is need for these individuals to have access.

The first step in establishing an effective access-control system is to determine the personnel needs of the facility. Second, personnel needs must be reduced to specific numbers, and third, numbers must be clarified by name, that is, what, how many, who, such as:

1. The facility needs   process workers
2. The facility needs   5   process workers
3. The facility needs   5   process workers named Smith, Jones, Doe, Brown, and Green.

The facility needs the services of Messrs. Smith, Jones, Doe, Brown, and Green; therefore each is allowed access to the facility. The problem with access control is not so much allowing access to authorized personnel as it is denying access to unauthorized personnel and telling the difference between them.

Those individuals allowed access to and within a facility must be authorized as such by facility management and that information communicated to security personnel. Controls must be in place to ensure that only they are allowed access. It should be mentioned that this chapter also covers exit controls in that egress from a maximum security environment or restricted areas requires controls to preclude theft of protected assets or diversion of sensitive information.

NRC REGULATIONS

The regulations of the Nuclear Regulatory Commission (NRC) governing access controls at fixed-site nuclear facilities are quite stringent. Performance capabilities for physical protection systems include the following:

(b.)   Prevent unauthorized access of persons, vehicles and materials into . . . vital areas. To achieve this capability the physical protection system shall:

   (1.)   Detect attempts to gain unauthorized access or introduce unauthorized material across material access or vital area boundaries by stealth or force using the following subsystems and subfunctions:

      (i.)   Barriers to channel persons and materials to material access and vital area entry control points and to delay any unauthorized penetration attempts by persons or materials sufficient to assist detection and permit a response that will prevent the penetration; and

      (ii.)   Access detection subsystems and procedures to detect, assess, and communicate any unauthorized penetration attempts by persons or materials at the time of the attempt so that the response can prevent the unauthorized access or penetration.

   (2.)   Detect attempts to gain unauthorized access or introduce unauthorized materials into material access areas or vital areas by deceit using the following subsystems and subfunctions:

      (i.)   Access authorization controls and procedures to provide current authorization schedules and entry criteria for both persons and materials; and

      (ii.)   Entry controls and procedures to verify the identity of persons and materials and assess such identity against current authorization schedules and entry criteria before permitting entry and to initiate response measures to deny unauthorized entries."[1]

The NRC is quite specific when it comes to access control subsystems and procedures for fixed sites[2]:

(1.)   A numbered picture badge identification subsystem shall be used for all individuals who are authorized access to protected areas without escort. An individual not employed by the licensee but who requires frequent and extended access to protected, materials access, or vital areas may be authorized access to such areas without escort provided that he receives a picture badge upon entrance into the protected area and returns the badge upon exit from the protected area, and that the badge indicates,

    (i.)   Non-employee—no escort required;

    (ii.)   The period for which access has been authorized. Badges shall be displayed by all individuals while inside the protected areas.

(2.)   Unescorted access to vital areas, material access areas and controlled access areas shall be limited to individuals who are authorized access to the material and equipment in such areas, and who require such access to perform their duties. Access to material access areas shall include at least two individuals. Authorization for such individuals shall be indicated by the issuance of specially coded numbered badges indicating vital areas, material access areas, and controlled access areas to which access is authorized. No activities other than those which require access to strategic special nuclear material or to material or to equipment used in the processing, use, or storage of strategic special nuclear material, or necessary maintenance, shall be permitted within a material access area.

(3.)   The licenseee shall establish and follow procedures that will permit access control personnel to identify those vehicles that are authorized and those materials that are not authorized entry to protected, material access, and vital areas.

(4.)   The licensee shall control all points of personnel and vehicle access into a protected area. Identification and search of all individuals for firearms, explosives, and incendiary devices, shall be made and authorization shall be checked at such points. United States Department of Energy couriers engaged in the transport of special nuclear material need not be searched. Licensee employees having an NRC or United States Department of Energy access authorization shall be searched at least on a random basis. The individual responsible for the last access control function (controlling admission to the protected area) shall be isolated within a structure, with bullet-resisting walls, doors, ceiling, floor, and windows.

(5.)   At the point of personnel and vehicle access into a protected area, all hand-carried packages shall be searched for firearms, explosives, and incendiary devices except those packages carried by persons having an NRC or DOE access authorization which shall be searched on a random basis when the person carrying them is selected for search.

(6.)   All packages and material for delivery into the protected area shall be checked for proper identification and authorization and searched on a random basis for firearms, explosives, and incendiary devices prior to admittance into the protected area, except those Commission-approved delivery and inspection activities specifically designated by the licensee to be carried out within material access, vital, or protected areas for reasons of safety, security or operational necessity.

(7.)   All vehicles, except United States Department of Energy vehicles engaged in transporting special nuclear material and emergency vehicles under emergency conditions, shall be searched for firearms, explosives, and incendiary devices prior to entry into the protected area. Vehicle areas to be searched shall include the cab, engine compartment, undercarriage, and cargo area.

(8.)   All vehicles, except designated licensee vehicles, requiring entry into the protected area shall be escorted by a member of the security organization while within the protected area, and to the extent practicable shall be off-loaded in an area that is not adjacent to a vital area. Designated licensee vehicles shall be limited in their use to onsite plant functions and shall remian in the protected area except for operational, maintenance, security, and emergency purposes. The licensee shall exercise positive control over all such designated vehicles to assure that they are used only by authorized persons and for authorized purposes.

(9.)   The licensee shall control all points of personnel and vehicle access to material access areas, vital areas and controlled access areas. Identification of personnel and vehicles shall be made and authorization checked at such points. Prior to entry into a material access area, packages shall be searched for firearms, explosives and incendiary devices. All vehicles, materials and packages, including trash, wastes, tools and equipment exiting from a material access area shall be searched for concealed strategic special nuclear material by a team of at least two individuals who are not authorized access to that material access area. Each individual exiting a material access area shall undergo at least two separate searches for concealed strategic special nuclear material. For individuals exiting an area that contains only alloyed or encapsulated strategic special nuclear material, the second search may be conducted in a random manner.

(10.)   Before exiting from a material access area, containers of contaminated wastes shall be drum scanned and tamper sealed by at least two individuals, working and recording as a team who do not have access to material processing and storage areas.

(11.)   Strategic special nuclear material being prepared for shipment off site, including product, samples and scrap, shall be packed and placed in sealed containers in the presence of at least two individuals working as a team who shall verify and certify the content of each shipping container through the witnessing of gross weight measurements and nondestructive assay, and through the inspection of tamper-seal integrity and associated seal records.

(12.)   Areas used for preparing strategic special nuclear material for shipment and areas used for packaging and screening trash and wastes shall be controlled access areas and shall be separated from processing and storage areas.

(13.)   Individuals not permitted by the licensee to enter protected areas without escort shall be escorted by a watchman, or other individual designated by the licensee, while in a protected area and shall be badged to indicate that an escort is required. In addition, the individual shall be required to register his name, date, time, purpose of visit, and employment affiliation, citizenship, and name of the individual to be visited.

(14.)   All keys, locks, combinations and related equipment used to control access to protected, material access, vital, and controlled access areas shall be controlled to reduce the probability of compromise. Whenever there is evidence that a key, lock, combination, or related equipment may have been compromised it shall be changed. Upon termination of employment of any employee, keys, locks, combinations and related equipment to which that employee had access shall be changed."[2]

PERSONNEL ACCESS AND EXIT

Barriers

The erection of physical barriers is meant to allow access to a facility to only those persons whose presence is necessary to the operation of the facility. The more sophisticated and impregnable the barriers, the more determined the adversary they are designed to protect against. While barriers are designed to impede covert penetration of a perimeter, they also function to channel personnel to and through designated areas.

Construction of barriers to preclude unauthorized entry and to channel personnel is the first physical step to be taken to control access to and within a facility. Once authorized entrances and exits are determined, all other points of access must be protected by barriers. Routes that must be taken to get into the facility must be determined, delineated, and if necessary, protected by barriers. Authorized entrances and exits must be clearly marked as such, as must authorized routes.

Maximum-security facilities should institute access controls at their perimeter. Entry to the perimeter should be by way of the minimum number of entrances. Controls, as described later in this chapter, should be established and maintained at each perimeter access point to ensure that only authorized individuals are permitted entry. No one other than a minimum number of authorized persons should be allowed to roam about freely within a maximum-security environment.

While access control begins at the perimeter, it is required throughout the facility. There may be one or more areas within the perimeter that are designated as restricted, and access to them may be limited to only a few of those persons authorized access to the perimeter. Barriers must be established around each and every area to and through which access is restricted.

Barriers and turnstiles also serve to restrict the movement of traffic into and out of a controlled access area so as to allow identification and, at some facilities, search of personnel or vehicles desiring entry.

Recognition and Identification

"Access control is the identification and entry/exit regulation of individuals through controlled points."[3] Identification of authorized personnel is the key to any access-control system. It was mentioned that personnel whose presence is necessary must be authorized for access by management. A list of those people and the areas to which they have access must be generated, maintained, and updated so that it is current at all times. The list must be kept in the possession of the security organization with a copy maintained by security at each authorized entrance. The names of anyone desiring access should appear on the authorization list. Names of nonemployees such as vendors, contractors, and visitors should also appear if possible. Procedures governing these and similar categories of personnel must be developed to ensure positive control over their access to and movement within a facility.

Anybody who desires access must be identified. At small facilities, personal recognition most frequently establishes positive identity. At larger facilities, this is of limited value. It therefore behooves the maximum-security director to employ a method for positively identifying all personnel. The most common if not universal means is an identification badge.

ID Badges

At a minimum high-security identification badges should disply both a number and a picture of the authorized holder. Additionally, they should be coded to identify the areas to which access is authorized. Color coding is quite common for this purpose; another method uses stripes or similar markers on the badge. In any case, badges should be laminated or sealed in such a way that tampering is readily observable.

Badges should be issued to and signed for by all employees. An appropriate record of issuance should be maintained. If a badge becomes unservicable, it should be replaced as soon as possible. If an employee forgets his, or it is lost or stolen, a temporary badge should be issued for the day or until a replacement is made. Employees should be instructed to report lost or stolen badges to security, who should maintain a permanent list of such badges.

Badges should carry an inscription such as:

> This badge is the property of XYZ Corporation and must be surrendered on demand or on termination of employment. Loss of this badge must be reported.
>
> If found, please drop in any U.S. mailbox. Postage guaranteed: XYZ Corporation, P.O. Box 1234, Waterford, TX 74428

Signature

Whenever possible, employee badges should be retained on site and issued daily by the security organization after verifying the identity of the employee (by personal recognition, badge photo comparison, badge number, etc.). No one should be allowed into a facility unless he is wearing a proper badge. Everyone within the facility should wear his badge at all times. At a maximum-security facility, personnel identification procedures are a necessity, and compliance with them must be a condition of employment.

Other ID-Verification Devices and Methods

A portion of the Personnel Access Control report prepared by Argonne National Laboratory for the NRC deals with three levels of access control, identification, and identity verification. The following tables show methods covering each of these areas; with each level, the degree of security increases[4]:

The biggest problem lies in the area of identity verification. Formulation and use of authorization lists is a relatively simple matter, as is providing authorized individuals with a means of identification. Verifying identity, es-

Table 8-1 Access Authorization Controls—Level I

Manual System	Semi-automated System	Automated System
Pass words	Combination of CTTV and	Keys
Dress codes	manual system	Key cards
Pass badges	Combination or guard of	Cipher-code or
Tickets	CCTV and automated	combination locks
Decals	system	Coin-operated gates
Access lists		Signs
Escorts		

Table 8-2   Access Identification Controls—Level II

Manual Systems	Semi-automated Systems	Automated Systems
Color-coded picture badges	Combination of CCTV and manual system	Key card plus personalized cipher code
Physical description badges or lists		Personalized key card
Personal physical recognition		

pecially when personal recognition cannot be relied on, presents a far greater challenge.

High-security access control depends on absolute identity—a relatively simple concept that becomes complicated in practice. Deception is one way that is often used to defeat an access-control system. A skilled infiltrator may employ many devices and techniques to convince an access-control officer that he is someone who is authorized access.[5] While the danger of surreptitious overt infiltration is real, there are techniques and products to reduce the risk. At a minimum, for entry to extremely sensitive areas identity-verification should be accomplished by a combination of:

1. Identification credentials (picture badge)
2. Comparison of physical characteristics to information kept on file
3. Codes

For entry to the perimeter and areas other than those classified as extremely sensitive, minimum requirements should be numbers 1 and 2 above, that is, identification credentials and comparison of physical characteristics to credentials.

Identification credentials should consist of at least a picture badge bearing a current photo of the authorized individual. There are also many other types of identification credentials.

Table 8-3   Access Identity-Verification Controls—Level III

Manual Systems	Semi-automated Systems	Automated Systems
Badge exchange system	Code and visual entry authorization technique	Fingerprints Holography Minutiae Handwriting Speech Hand geometry

"The photobadge accounts for over 35 percent of all access control ID usage. Organizations using employee IDs include: office complex, 63 percent; hospitals/schools 48 percent; transport and utility companies, 36 percent; small offices, 36 percent; military and government, 31 percent; retail, 30 percent; heavy industry, 28 percent; light industry, 23 percent; and financial, 23 percent.

"Machine-readable cards come in many forms. Printed-circuit cards are the least advanced, used mostly in auto entry gates and elevator access. They are plug-in cards with electrical contacts at one end.

Magnetic stripe cards have grown considerably since 1976, especially in banking. Since the magnetic code can be altered or copied onto another card easily, the mag stripe alone is not secure. Use of a PIN [personel identification number] or photo greatly increases security.

"Magnetic sandwich cards are die cut from three-layer stock in which the middle layer is gamma ferric oxide (magnetic plastic material). This layer is magnetized in a pattern of dots. The reader detects the dot pattern and electrocically analyzes it.

"Microcircuit cards may be held in close proximity to a reader to activate the system and, therefore, are not inserted into a reader. Future application of these cards may be more sophisticated: the cards could calculate financial data for the bearer and could contain high-security features valuable in financial and computer security.

Card-based computer data access systems require a computer terminal operator to insert a valid card into a slot adjacent to the terminal before access to the data bank results.

"Digital locks are rugged, simple devices often used where card or key would be inconvenient. The system's security can be increased with a card, however, and can be integrated into a central reporting and logging system.

"Magnetic keys and tokens contain magnetic rods in grooveless, notchless flat blades. A slot can replace a standard door knob.

"Fingerprints as ID represent an intriguing option for high-security use. These systems analyze aspects of the fingerprint and compare the identification to information maintained in a data base [Figure 8–1].

"Voice analysis for ID is making much progress. One company has a system useful in low-traffic, high-security situations. The user says four or more preselected words into a microphone to gain access.

"Signature recognition has interested many technological companies over the years. Matching completed (static) signatures has not been successful, however, compared with the measurement of writing dynamics.

"Manual card files may not have the high-tech allure of the system described above, but such systems should grow rapidly in demand for the next few years.

"Ultraviolet light has had its mystery, but what's past is past. Used widely in savings banks, the teller places the passbook under a UV light source and compares the glowing signature with the one on the transaction slip.

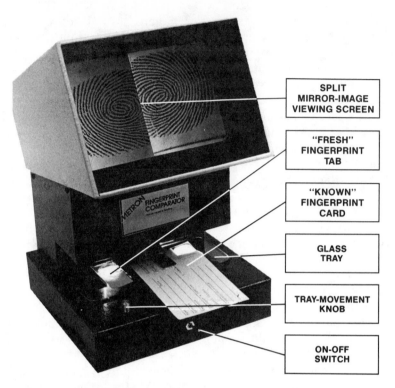

Figure 8-1   Comparator fingerprint system. (Metron Optics, Inc.)

"Scrambled signatures are broken into many marks. A descrambling lens will optically reassemble the signature for comparison with signed document presented for cash or deposit."[6]

For access to the facility, a check should be made of the credential and the holder by a person or system capable of making a comparison. For access to sensitive areas, comparison should include appropriate information kept on file (manual or computer-based system) as well as the credentials being presented. Additionally, a code, whether it be in the form of a key card or combination to a lock, should be required after identity verification but before access is granted.

"The identity of an individual can be verified by determining something about an individual, such as facial features; by determining something possessed by an individual, such as a coded badge; or by determining something known to an individual, such as a numerical code. By using a combination of the above three, identity verification processes, more reliable identity verification can be obtained. Such identification procedures can be accomplished by attendant security personnel or by the use of identification equipment such as video comparator systems."[7]

Access control in a maximum-security environment includes more than personnel authorization, identification, and verification, however. Another essential requirement for access control is a search.

Entry Searches

Prior to authorized admittance to a maximum-security facility, all personnel should be searched for weapons, explosives, and sabotage-related devices. A search should always be a condition of employment and/or access to a facility. The obvious objective is to prevent such interdicted items from being introduced where they can be used to effect destruction and/or theft of assets.[8] Searches of incoming personnel can be accomplished either manually or by the use of equipment that detects the prohibited items. (Prohibited items include, at a minimum, weapons, explosives, incendiaries, alcoholic beverages, radios, cameras, narcotics and/or controlled substances, and personal electronic devices.) The search must be thorough, and prohibited items discovered during a personnel search should be confiscated and retained under security control until the owner leaves, at which time they should be returned, provided return is legal. All illegal items should remain in the possession of security personnel for transfer to local law enforcement authorities.

At facilities where the number of people entering and/or limitations due to lack of resources preclude a search of every person, a random sampling should be taken based on a reasonable percentage determined by security management (or government regulations). The degree of security is, however, diminished when this system is used.

The following actions should be taken whenever detection systems signal the presence of prohibited items[9]:

1.   The individual should be requested to empty his pockets and be rechecked by the detectors.
2.   If this second check is negative, the individual may be allowed to enter.
3.   If the second check is positive, a physical search should be made by an unarmed security officer under observation of another officer.
4.   If an individual refuses to submit to a search, either electronic or physical, or if a prohibited item is found, he should be denied access and appropriate notification (and reports) made.
5.   If an item is found that is not prohibited but is suspicious, the individual should be denied access until a determination can be made by appropriate security personnel that the item presents no threat.

Firearms should always be the first items sought for, regardless of the method used. If metal detectors are employed, they should be able to detect both ferrous and nonferrous metals with at least 90 percent effectiveness.

Metal detectors should also be able to detect a small .25-caliber automatic pistol measuring no more than four by three and one-quarter inches.

"Explosives detectors, whether of the hand-held or portal variety, should be capable of detecting with at least a 90 percent effective detection rate dynamite, TNT, and similar nitrogen-containing compounds in a minimum amount of 200 grams."[10]

All hand-carried packages or items such as lunch boxes should be checked for prohibited items prior to entry to a maximum-security facility. Such searches may be conducted manually, by use of specialized detection equipment, or by x-ray. Again, if prohibited items are found, or if something arouses suspicions, it should be handled as previously suggested.

Exit Searches

Searches of all personnel exiting a facility should also be a condition of employment and/or a condition for entry in the first place. The objective of the exit search should be obvious, but bears stating. It is for the purpose of detecting theft or attempted theft of company assets and/or property. As a general rule, everyone exiting the facility should be searched, as should items being carried out. Again, searches can be manual or electronic.

Other items leaving the facility, for example, trash, must also be checked by a member of the security organization to preclude diversion by this means. Shipments should also be controlled, for example, by a two-man packaging rule, so as to deter diversion by including stolen assets in an authorized shipment for later retrieval or sending stolen assets in an apparently authorized fashion to an off-site location.

VEHICLE ACCESS AND EXIT

Every vehicle entering the confines must be searched for the prohibited items previously mentiond. In many ways, vehicular searches are much more difficult than personnel searches to accomplish effectively simply because the use of detection equipment is more limited and there are more places to hide prohibited items. While detection equipment may be used to search for explosives, the main portion of the vehicular search must be done manually.

As a general rule, only those vehicles necessary to the facility's operation should be allowed access. Employee and visitor parking lots should never be situated within the protected perimeter of a maximum-security facility.

All vehicles should be searched prior to allowing entry. The only exception should be for emergency vehicles when responding to an emergency. Even then, these should be accounted for and logged in, although after the fact. When possible and practical, all vehicles including emergency vehicles should be escorted within the confines of a maximum-security facility by a member of the security organization.

VEHICLE SEARCH AREA CHECK-OFF LIST

Date: _____ Vehicle Make/Model: _____

Lic. Plate (State & No.) _____ Time Search Completed: _____

Officer(s) conducting search: _____

INTERIOR:

— All boxes/bags/suitcases, etc.
— Under seat(s).
— Under instrument panel/dashboard.
— Glove compartment.
— Behind sun visors.
— Arm rests.
— Door/console storage area(s).
  Sleeper section (if applicable)
— Under mattress.
— Under pillows.
— In storage compartments.
— In/under bedding/blankets.
— Behind curtains.

ENGINE COMPARTMENT:

— Underside of hood/tip cab.
— False battery.
— Fender wells.
  Engine
— Top
— Sides
— Underside
  Radiator
— Beside
— Behind
— In front

TRUNK:

— All boxes/bags/cases, etc.
— Beneath carpet or trunk mat.
— Behind & beneath spare tire.
— Any "wells" or other storage spaces
  built into fender wells.

CARGO AREA:

— Climbed inside and checked for
  prohibited articles & personnel.
— Checked under articles in pick-up
  truck bed.

EXTERIOR:

— Under fenders.
— Behind bumpers.
— Behind grill.
— Complete undercarriage.
— Top, sides & bottom of saddle-type
  external fuel tanks.
— Top of truck spare tires racked
  under body.

RANDOM AREAS (Note below)

INSTRUCTIONS:
Officer(s) conducting vehicle searches will execute a vehicle search check-off list form for *every* vehicle which is to be allowed entry into the protected area. All applicable items *will* be checked. Inapplicable items will have the notation "N/A" made to show they were considered and not overlooked. An officer will deliver the completed form to the officer on duty at the Main Gate, who will check the form for completeness *before* allowing the vehicle to enter. If the form indicates a thorough search has been accomplished, the vehicle will be allowed to enter. The form shall be maintained at the main gate for pick-up by security supervisors daily.

Figure 8-2   Vehicle search and check-off list.

Vehicular searches should include at a minimum the engine compartment, trunk or cargo space, undercarriage, passenger compartment, and wheel wells. Admittedly, vehicular searches are difficult to accomplish in a fairly brief time, however, a simple procedure and checklist can expedite the process (Figure 8–2). The use of portable explosives detectors and mirrors can also help to minimize the time involved. (As an aside, vehicles should not only be thought of as a passive threat, i.e., to facilitate the introduction of prohibited items, but as an active threat, i.e., to facilitate forced entry into a facility by crashing through barriers.)

Vehicular searches should include a random element. In other words, they should not always be limited to the same areas of a vehicle. If certain areas of a vehicle are consistently overlooked, such as the fire extinguishers, a potential adversary may recognize the fact and exploit it. Every vehicle search should cover those areas mentioned above plus several others selected randomly by the searcher.

Regardless of the number of personnel involved in a vehicular search, there should always be a security officer observing from a protected area for any indication of duress on the part of a searcher.

Upon exiting the protected area of a maximum-security facility, every vehicle should again be searched for company assets. Depending on the assets involved, detection equipment may or may not be employed. Again, certain basic areas of the vehicle should be searched, as should others selected at random.

OTHER CONSIDERATIONS

Visit Requests

It is always a good idea to schedule appointments and visits ahead of time. Salesmen, vendors, contractors, and the like should never show up unexpectedly at a maximum-security facility. If they do, they should be denied access. Whenever visits are scheduled or otherwise expected, security should be advised beforehand. The same holds true for deliveries and shipments.

Clearance Programs

At facilities where government clearance programs are in effect for all employees, the problem of access authorization is minimized for security management. At those facilities where there are no such programs, however, a background and criminal history check (within legal constraints) should be made prior to authorizing employees (or candidates for employment) access to sensitive areas.

Procedures

Definite access-control procedures should be developed and consistently followed by security personnel. They should be updated and reflect site-specific considerations and requirements (Five sample procedures can be found in Appendices 8–A through 8–E.) Signs should be posted advising personnel of the requirements for entry and exit. Additionally, prior to being admitted to a maximum-security facility for the first time, every person should be briefed on all requirements and sign a statement of understanding, which includes an agreement to comply.

Systems

There are myriad excellent access-control systems and detection aids on the market that can be used effectively to accomplish the tasks inherent in this area of maximum security. While each manufacturer may feel that his product is superior to all others, the ultimate choice of equipment should always be up to the security director. Whatever his choice, it should be based on his needs and requirements.

Appendix 8–A

Procedure for Screening Personnel with Walk-Through Metal Detectors

PROCEDURE

1. The officer assigned to monitor the walk-through metal detector shall, on assuming the post, ensure that the detector cannot be bypassed by personnel entering and that the control panel and its alarm light are shielded from the view of personnel passing through the detector.
2. Items for which the officer will be particularly alert include not only weapons, but cameras and anything that could be used to commit sabotage.
3. Personnel should be asked to remove as much metal from their persons as practicable prior to entering the metal detector. Objects removed shall be placed on the counter for inspection by the officer and may be reclaimed after the person has passed through the detector without generating an alarm.
4. Armed security officers assigned to the site and police officers having site identification badges are not to remove their firearms for the metal detector search when routinely passing through one of the protected area access points. These personnel are to receive a hands-on search on a percentage random basis.
5. Properly identified government personnel and law enforcement officers carrying firearms, or members of the military services carrying firearms on official business who have not been issued a picture badge are not to be asked to remove or surrender their weapons. Before being admitted to the protected area, however, they are to receive a hands-on search. They shall be asked to remove all items from their pockets and to show the person conducting the search the location of their weapon.
6. Personnel should be instructed to pass through the detector individually at a normal walking pace.
7. The flow of personnel through the walk-through metal detector should be regulated to prevent congestion in the area after they pass through the detector.
8. If anyone passing through the detector causes the unit to alarm, he shall be directed to return through the detector. If the alarm is still valid, the

individual shall remove all metallic objects from his person, place them on the counter for inspection, and pass through the detector again. If the alarm persists, he is to be denied access unless he submits to a hands-on search.

9. If an employee refuses to pass through the metal detector or to submit to a hands-on search, he will not be allowed to enter the protected area and the security supervisor will be contacted immediately.

10. If a visitor refuses to pass through the metal detector or to have his personal articles inspected, he shall be denied access to the station and will be asked to leave the site. The area supervisor will be notified.

11. All incoming walk-through metal detectors at security control stations will be checked for sensitivity by the assigned officer at the start of each shift.

12. The required testing will be conducted in the following manner:

a. The tester shall remove all metallic objects from his person.

b. The testing shall be conducted using only the approved nonferrous metal test standard.

c. Tester will locate the approved test standard on the center line of the body at the upper chest level and make seven passes through the detector in the proper traffic direction.

  Note: The tester shall move away from the metal detector more than seven (7) feet before and after every pass-through.

d. Tester will locate the approved test standard on the body center line at waist level and make seven (7) passes through the detector in the proper traffic direction, moving at least three (3) feet from the detector after each pass-through.

e. The last phase of the testing requires the approved test standard be located on the body center line, eight (8) inches above the floor. The tester will again pass through the detector seven (7) times in the proper traffic direction, moving away from the machine the required distance after each pass-through.

f. The unit must detect at least six out of seven times at each position tested.

g. The results of this testing shall be recorded. All malfunctioning equipment must be reported to the area supervisor and a work order prepared.

13. Quarterly, a security shift supervisor will be responsible for testing the walk-through metal detectors using a small revolver as the test source.

14. When a walk-through metal detector becomes inoperative, the operator shall ensure that the percentage of random hands-on searches is increased. The area supervisor is to be notified and a work order is to be written.

SUMMARY

Officers assigned to the walk-through metal detectors must ensure that the apparatus is functioning properly at all times; must remain alert to prevent any unauthorized material or object from being passed around the detector, and must be knowledgable in procedures for operation as well as detector outage.

Appendix 8–B

Procedure for Visual Search of Packages

PROCEDURE

1. Visual searches of all hand-carried packages or objects are required when the x-ray machine at the protected area entry point is not in service and on exit from the protected area.
2. The person carrying the article shall be asked to open the container for the officer's inspection.
3. On entry, visual package searches will be conducted primarily for firearms, explosives, and incendiary devices. Any other prohibited items that may be found during this search shall be isolated from the individual and will be cause for detaining this person at the search station. The officer discovering the prohibited item(s) shall immediately notify his supervisor.
4. When inspecting lunch boxes or bags, the food contained therein shall be handled as little as possible consistent with a thorough inspection of the contents. Thermos bottles may be lifted and gently shaken to check the weight to ensure the bottle is not simply a shell that may contain prohibited items. By gently shaking the bottle the officer can determine if it is being used for its intended purpose and does contain liquid.
   All compartments of briefcases and pocketbooks/handbags must be checked. Any closed containers or cases in these briefcases/handbags are also subject to search.
6. The officer must not merely open a container, glance inside, and think he has conducted a visual search. The visual search requirements are no less stringent than those for the package-search x-ray machine. This means that all containers and their contents must be checked. The search requirement does not apply to hermetically sealed packages containing authorized freight parts or supplies, or packages whose contents would be unusable if opened (e.g., bulk food products, soft drinks, and photographic film). This will require the officer physically to move items around inside the container to ensure that some prohibited item does not lie beneath an accumulation of very ordinary and innocuous items.
7. When conducting this type of search (as in all other duties), a detached but thoroughly professional attitude must prevail. Most individuals will

resent (to varying degrees) this type of search as an invasion of their personal privacy. By projecting a professional manner, compliance and cooperation will be more easily secured.

8.   One must never argue with an individual whose hand-carried articles are being searched.

9.   If an employee refuses to have his hand-carried articles visually searched, that employee shall be refused access and the security supervisor will be notified.

10. If a visitor refuses to have his hand-carried articles searched, he shall be refused access to the protected area and the security supervisor will be notified.

11. Vendors or deliverymen and their packages may be granted access to the protected area only with the written access authorization of an authorized security supervisor.

12. If the vendor or deliveryman refuses to have the package(s) passed through the x-ray machine because of their contents, or whenever the x-ray machine is inoperable, the package(s) will be visually searched for prohibited items. If contraband is found, the same procedure for isolating the packages, detaining the individual, and notifying security shift supervisor applies.

SUMMARY

The requirement for search of all hand-carried packages at the point of personnel access into the protected area loses none of its importance when the change is made from a search by x-ray machine to a visual search. The physical actions required by a visual search will delay the processing of personnel, however, members of the security force must guard against development of an attitude of complacency and expediency. If performance of a thorough and proper visual inspection of all hand-carried articles causes a slowdown, the officer must not perform these duties in a cursory manner simply to avoid inconvenience to waiting personnel.

Appendix 8–C

Procedure for Inspection of Packages Exiting the Facility

PROCEDURE

1. All persons leaving the protected area must submit to a search of packages they might be carrying.
2. Persons attempting unauthorized removal of company property from the facility will be detained and the security supervisor notified.
3. Problems or disputes will be referred to the security supervisor for resolution.
4. A list (which is periodically updated) of persons authorized to sign material passes contains the names of those facility personnel who are authorized to grant permission for removal of items from the facility. Personnel not designated are not allowed to sign material passes.
5. During weekends, holidays, and back-shifts, when persons authorized to approve removal of property from the plant are not available, the security supervisor may grant permission to remove items from the station.
6. The officer(s) on duty at exit points shall be alert to detect surreptitious attempts to pass a package, container, or object that could be (or could contain) company property through the exit without having it examined/inspected as required.
7. The security officer on duty at the exit point shall not activate the remote release for the turnstile if doubt exists on whether any package or object has met the requirements for exit. The officer shall be especially alert during peak exit periods, as attempts at unauthorized removal of material or equipment are most likely to occur during this time when the large volume of exiting personnel could be used to screen a carried object, or when the officer's attention may be more easily diverted.
8. Personnel seeking to remove any material or object that could be construed as company property shall be required to produce a valid material pass that has been signed by an authorized person on the current list.

9.   Lunch boxes, briefcases, pocketbooks, knapsacks, and all other similar objects are to be placed on the counter in front of the exit-point security officer as the person approaches the walk-through metal detector. The officer will examine the item and if it passes his inspection, he shall return it after the owner has passed through the metal detector without the unit alarming.

10.   The turnstile release is not to be activated when the exit-point walk-through metal detector signals the passage of an object that would require a hands-on search. This object could be concealed in a jacket or other innocuous object being carried.

11.   Material passes presented should be checked against the items being removed to ensure that only those that have been authorized are being removed. The officer must be alert for any additions to the property pass which could have been entered after the authorizing person signed the form.

12.   Material passes collected at the exit points shall be controlled for later retrieval by security force supervisory personnel. The officer shall date and sign this form on review before allowing exit.

13.   Whenever material that could be construed as company property is removed or attempted to be removed covertly from the station without authorization, the security supervisor will attempt to resolve the problem with the individual's supervisor or other cognizant individual. In the case of personnel who are not normally assigned to the site such as vendors, deliverymen, representatives from other companies, etc., their supervisors would be at their home base of operations. If resolution cannot be obtained, the questionable material will remain at the facility and a written report will be generated.

SUMMARY

The requirements for and mechanics of package inspection on personnel exit are very clear. As with any security function with which one may be charged, the officer must make sure he is completely familiar with the task requirements, and if he is unsure of some portion of the procedures or when confronted with a new or unusual situation, he must immediately contact his supervisor for instructions.

Appendix 8–D

Procedure for Vehicular Search

PROCEDURE

1. It shall be the responsibility of the driver and passengers of any vehicle or piece of construction equipment authorized entry into the protected area to undergo the required personal searches at the security access point prior to initiation of the required search of the vehicle (or equipment) and prior to entry into the protected area.

2. It shall be the responsibility of the security officer at the vehicle search area to ensure that drivers of any vehicle (or equipment) that has been searched do not enter or have unescorted access to any other vehicle that is in the area awaiting search after they have undergone the required personal search. If the driver leaves the control of the officer he must be reprocessed through the access point.

   a. The officer conducting the search will advise the operator prior to the search that if any contraband or weapons are found during or turned over to the officer by the operator prior to the search, the local police department will be notified. If contraband or weapons are present, the officer will notify the on-duty security supervisor, who will contact the police department advising them of the situation.

   b. Whenever a handgun is found or declared the officer will ask the individual in possession of the weapon if he has a valid state pistol permit. If the individual does, the officer will ask to see it and review it for validity. If the individual does not have or refuses to show the permit, the on-duty security supervisor will be notified.

   c. Security will take possession of any prohibited items, log and place them in the property hold locker, and process the individual and vehicle into the protected area. If the police department chooses not to send an officer to investigate, or if an officer has not arrived by the time the individual and vehicle leave the protected area, the items will be returned to the owner.

   d. The foregoing does not apply to town, city, state, and federal law enforcement officials and security personnel carrying company issued weapons.

> Note: All firearms surrendered for safekeeping must be surrendered to the security supervisor in an unloaded condition.

   e. To prepare the vehicle for search the officer shall have the operator open the hood, trunk, doors, storage compartments, cargo areas, etc.

   f. The search will be thorough and systematic. It will not stop because some item of contraband is found.

   g. To search the vehicle, it is divided into two sections—the passenger side and the driver's side. Beginning at the front of the vehicle, the exterior and then the interior are searched, first on one side, then the other.

3. Areas to check include:

   a. Vehicle interior

     (1) Glove compartment/console storage compartment

     (2) Under seats and between seat and backrest

     (3) Under loose cushions or covers

     (4) In the springs on the back of seats and under seats if they are easily accessible

     (5) Behind sun visors

     (6) Under the dashboard

     (7) In boxes, suitcases, bags, etc., in the passenger compartment, cab, or sleeper

     (8) Sleeper section of tractor cabs, particularly under the bedding and in the storage areas

   b. Engine compartment

     (1) On and under the engine/walls of engine compartment

     (2) Some diesel trucks will be equipped with two batteries. It is necessary to check to ensure that one of these is not an empty case that could contain weapons or explosives. Because removing a battery cap always presents the possibility of getting acid splashed into the eyes, the security officer shall not remove the caps to determine if the battery is genuine. An easier method is to place the bare hand against the outside of the case—if the vehicle has just shut down, both batteries will be warm to the same degree. If one battery is warm and the other cool, further investigation may be required. Another way of checking would be to knock on the case to see if it is hollow.

     (3) If there is a device or apparatus attached to any part of the engine that does not seem to belong, the officer will contact the area supervisor.

   c. Cargo area or trunk

     (1) The officer will climb inside cargo area and physically check for prohibited items, or for individuals attempting to gain undetected access to the protected area

     (2) Under spare tires and trunk mats

        (3)   Inside, behind, or under any items in the bed of a pick-up truck

        (4)   Tool boxes, etc.

             Note: If the cargo area cannot be adequately checked, the protected area gate guard shall be notified and the vehicle shall be treated as a bulk delivery, which requires an armed guard escort.

   d.   Undercarriage

        (1)   Area is inspected for weapons, explosives, or unauthorized personnel, using the handle-equipped mirror provided (may also be used for other restriced areas).

4.   Items for which officers must be alert include:

   a.   Firearms (when any firearm is discovered, the security supervisor shall be notified and shall direct appropriate action).

   b.   Explosives or incidentiary devices that could be used to commit acts of sabotage

   c.   Personnel who have not been processed through an access point

   d.   Any other item considered to be prohibited within the protected area without proper authorization. Such items would include:

        (1)   Cameras, including motion picture and video tape equipment

        (2)   Alcoholic beverages

        (3)   Controlled drugs

        (4)   Dangerous instruments

5.   If any prohibited item (or any item the security officer may be uncertain of) is found during a vehicle search, the officer finding the item shall immediately notify the security supervisor and shall isolate the operator away from the vehicle.

6.   During vehicle inspection the operator must not have access to it until the search is completed and the operator has undergone a personal search at the access point.

SUMMARY

In order to conduct a thorough vehicle search, the officer must use his eyes, ears, and nose as well as his hands. He must be alert for any strange odors or sounds that could indicate the presence of contraband.

Appendix 8–E

Search Procedure Checklist[11]

GENERAL PHYSICAL/HAND SEARCH—
AUTOMOBILE [Figure 8-3]

1. Trunk compartment (including behind seat, storage, etc.)
    a. Luggage, parcels, packages
    b. Tool boxes
    c. Around spare tire
    d. All interior surfaces and voids
    e. Fuel cans and air cylinders (off-load fuel cans and other incendiary materials)
2. Passenger area
    a. Luggage parcels, packages
    b. Under dash
    c. Under seats (visible areas)
    d. Glove compartment and contents
3. Engine compartment
    a. Underside of hood
    b. General fire wall, behind grill, and engine area (look for unnecessary components, type, etc.)
4. Inside bumpers (front and back)
5. General undercarriage and roof (check carefully around fuel tanks)
6. All 4 wheel wells

GENERAL PHYSICAL SEARCH—TRUCK [Figure 8-3]

A. Trucks (general)
    1. Cargo area
        a. Parcel, package, and equipment, etc.
        b. Ceiling, walls, and floor (walk-through)
        c. Noncargo containers, tool boxes, etc. (off-load fuel cans)
    2. Passenger area
        a. Parcels and packages
        b. Luggage

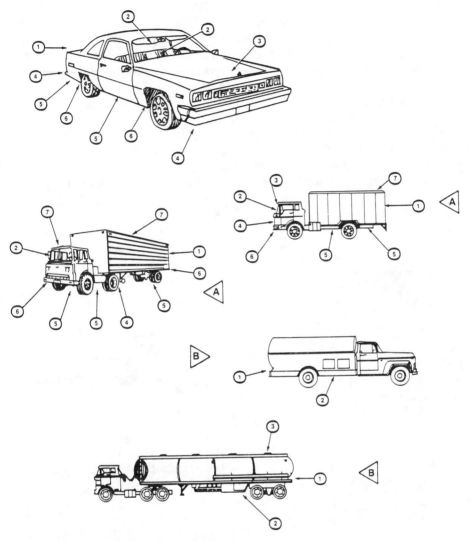

Figure 8-3   General physical and hand search—automobiles and trucks. (U. S. Nuclear Regulatory Commission.)

      c.   Under seat and behind seat (fold up/down seats)
      d.   Sleeper area
  3. Glove compartment and cab storage areas
  4. Engine compartment
      a.   Open hood or cab cover; search readily accessible areas.
  5. General framework, undercarriage, and wheel assemblies, tool boxes, wheel wells, etc. (check around fuel tanks very carefully).
  6. Bumpers, steps, and runningboards

7. Roof or cab and cargo box/trailer
8. External trailer compartment length, depth, etc., to assure that false panels capable of concealing personnel are not built in

The search areas noted below are in addition to those specified for trucks (general)

B. Tank trucks
   1. Hose compartments
   2. Pump compartments
   3. Filler cap area
C. Gas-cylinder delivery truck [Figure 8–4]
   4. Generally between cylinders (assure cylinders only and that cylinders appear normal)

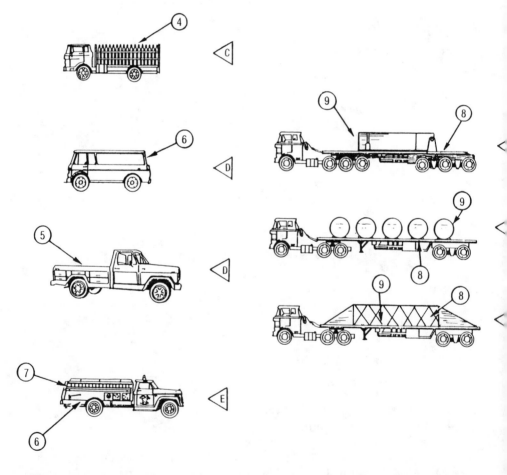

Figure 8-4 General physical and hand search—trucks. (U.S. Nuclear Regulatory Commission.)

D.   Multicompartment service truck
    5.   Each compartment and contents
E.   Emergency vehicles
    6.   Compartments and/or treatment area
    7.   Hose storage area
F.   Cask shipping trailers
    8.   Around cask holding mechanism and special cask trailer apparatus
    9.   Assure casks are sealed.

GENERAL PHYSICAL SEARCH—RAIL CARS [Figure 8-5]

A.   Escorted rail shipments
    1.   Seals on cask or assemblies, etc., which are under escort should be checked prior to release or acceptance.
    2.   All escorted rail cars and locomotives that enter protected area should be observed for abnormalities during pick up and delivery. Shipping car inspection as below when not in custody of couriers (once released or before assumption).
B.   Unescorted rail shipments (cars picked up or delivered)
    1.   Seals on casks, assemblies, or material containers
    2.   Wheels (inside and outside)
    3.   Behind trucks
    4.   Undercarriage of bed, channel and I-beams, side sills, floor supports, and coupling shank
    5.   Around containers, dunnage, equipment, materials, etc.
C.   Box car (in addition to unescorted rail shipment search)
    6.   Interior walls, floor, ceiling, door
    7.   Roof and walkway
    8.   Exterior surface; voids and access panels

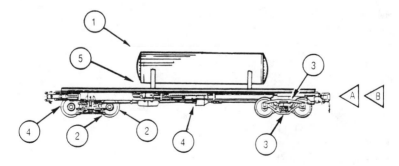

Figure 8-5 General physical search—rail cars. (U.S. Nuclear Regulatory Commission.)

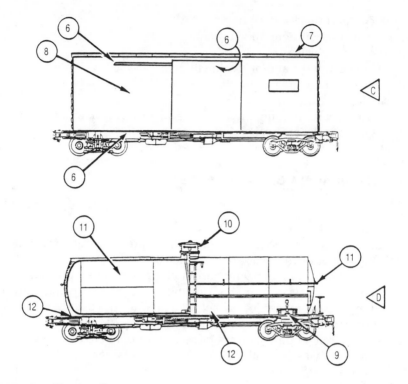

Figure 8-5   *(Continued).*

D.   Tank-type car (inspect carefully and closely in addition to unescorted
      rail shipment search)
      9.   Hose lockers or pump mechanism panels
      10.   Fill-port area and walkway
      11.   Surface of tank for unusual attachments
      12.   Channels and voids created where tank joins carriage or bed

GENERAL PHYSICAL SEARCH—SPECIAL EQUIPMENT [Figure 8-6]

1.   Engine compartments
2.   All storage and tool compartments
3.   Undercarriage (all the way around)
4.   Under seats and cushions
5.   Behind track mechanisms
6.   Battery compartments
7.   All booms and masts
8.   Behind wheels
9.   Fender wells
10.   All roofs

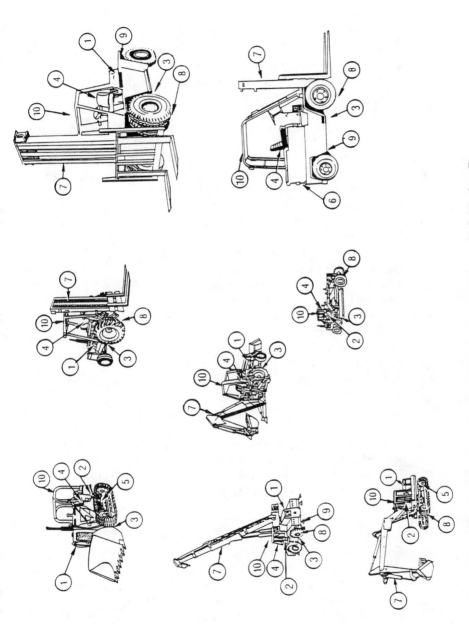

Figure 8-6 General physical and hand search—special equipment. (U.S. Nuclear Regulatory Commission.)

EXTENSIVE PHYSICAL SEARCH—AUTOMOBILE/ PICKUP/STATION WAGON [Figure 8-7]

A. Front section
1. Front license plate and area behind license plate
2. Front directional lights (two locations); examine cover; be alert for indications of recent installation.
3. Front bumper, including inside surface. If bumper is close to auto structure, use an inspection mirror.
4. Between and inside of grill work
5. Headlights (two locations); be alert for indications of recent installation.

B. Side section (both sides—repeat the following on other side of car)
6. Front side lights and lamp cover; be alert for indications of recent installation.
7. Front hub caps; remove and examine cap and wheel and/or inspect for recent removal.
8. Front wheel wells; with the aid of a flashlight and inspection mirror, examine inside of wheel well. Contraband has been found attached by magnets to the inside surfaces of wheel wells.
9. Door handles, and underneath
10. Rear hub caps; remove and examine cap and wheel and/or inspect for recent damage.
11. Rear wheel wells (same as search point #8)
12. Rear side lights (same as search point #6)
13. Window cut-outs; roll windows down and look down into the interior of the door where possible.
14. Surface of doors; open door and examine underside for possible cut-outs.
15. Front side of doors; open door and examine front side of door and adjacent structure of auto for possible cut-outs.
16. Rear side of doors; open door and examine rear side of door and adjacent structure of auto for possible cut-outs.

C. Rear section
17. Rear license plate, and area behind license plate
18. Rear bumper, including inside surface; if bumper is close to auto structure, use an inspection mirror.
19. Tail lights and back-up lights (right and left); inside of lamp covers. Be alert for indications of recent installation.
20. Fuel filler neck; remove cap and examine inside for possible suspension of contraband into the neck. Be cautious of volatile fuel fumes. Confirm presence of gasoline or diesel fuel. Assure no smoking in area while this is done.

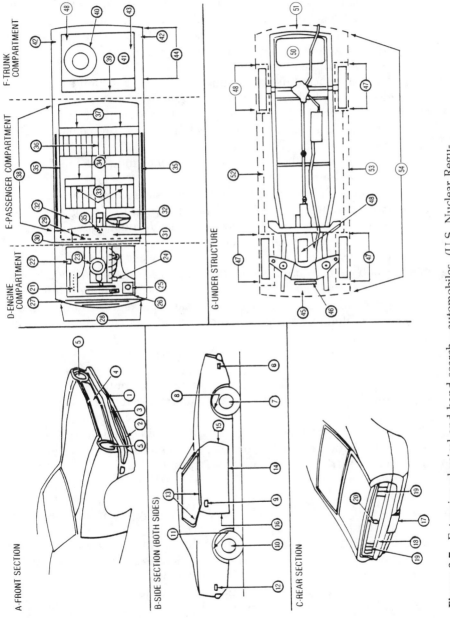

Figure 8-7 Extensive physical and hand search—automobiles. (U.S. Nuclear Regulatory Commission.)

D. Engine compartment
    21. Battery, including area under and around battery
    22. Voltage regulator, including cover for signs of recent installation
    23. Air filter, including indications of recent installation. Examine the thumb-type hold-down nut and area immediately adjacent for signs of tampering. The air filter is not a vital engine part and the inside filtering element can be easily removed and replaced with contraband merchandise.
    24. Oil filter, including indications of recent installation or modification. The oil filter is not a vital engine part and it is possible to modify an oil filter internally so as to bypass the engine oil and leave the interior of the filter hollow for the concealment of contraband.
    25. Windshield-washer liquid container, including the interior with the aid of a flashlight.
    26. Radiator filler neck, and inside for possible suspension of contraband packages. Be extremely careful when removing cap. Wrap hand in a large towel or use an insulated rubber glove and stand back. This is a hazardous operation.
    27. Grill work, including area around and inside of grill
    28. Hood cover and entire engine compartment structural work, and around and under all structural members and engine components for possible attachment of contraband packages. Examine inside of "lightening" holes in stiffener members attached to under surface of hood.

E. Passenger compartment
    29. Glove compartment, including interior and contents
    30. Entire dash panel; with the aid of an inspection mirror and flashlight, examine the entire space behind the dash panel.
    31. Ventilation and heating ducts; with the aid of a flashlight, inspection mirror, and/or the fiber scope, examine the inside of the outlet housing and ducts. Be alert to signs of recent installation. A prime search point.
    32. Floor mats and back side of control pedals, including underside of all floor mats; examine back side of control pedals for attachment of contraband packages.
    33. Front seats, and underneath; with the aid of a flashlight and inspection mirror look up into cushion springs from the bottom.
    34. Bucket seat backs. On most bucket type seats, the inside back panels snap off to expose an area of considerable size.
    35. Ashtrays, removing inside containers to examine contents and space inside of holding structure.
    36. Back seat, including removing it to examine cushions and spring

area (most back seats easily snap out by pulling up on forward edge).

37. Rear seat back, with back seat removed, look up into area behind seat back and auto structure; also check under fold-down seats.

38. Top of passenger compartment including sun visors, mirror, dome light, and header. Examine sun visors and behind the same; behind rear-view mirror, dome light assembly for signs of recent installation; header for slits and bulges.

F. Trunk compartment (and related storage compartments)

39. Trunk roof, including forward and under rear window deck

40. Spare tire; loosen and examine area under tire; be alert to signs of recent work to tire and rim. Check for air pressure.

41. Trunk bottom covering, including underneath.

42. Recessed space behind rear wheel well. Some automobiles have a recess in the area behind the rear wheel well that is usually covered with a cardboard panel and the trunk bottom covering, and gives the trunk a continuous flat appearance.

43. Tail light assembly covers. The lamp assemblies of most tail lights are accessible by removing the back cover, which is located in the trunk; be alert to signs of recent installation.

44. Bottom surface of trunk lid, including inside of "lightening" holes in stiffener members attached to under side of trunk lid

G. Under structure

45. Front gravel panel, including inside

46. Bottom of radiator, and for signs of modification work. The appearance of unusual welds, brazing, soldering, and painting would be an indication of possible installation of false bottoms or compartments. A prime search point.

47. Wheel wells (four locations) including inside surfaces from the bottom

48. Engine oil pan; be alert to signs of recent installation; search same details as #46.

49. Muffler; also be alert to signs of recent installation; search same details as #46.

50. Fuel tank; also be alert to signs of recent installations; search very closely for attached small charges, wires, etc.; search same details as #46.

51. Rear gravel panel, including inside.

52. Right rocker panel, including cut-outs and signs of modification

53. Left rocker panel same as search point #52

54. Entire framework; with the aid of an inspection mirror and portable lighting, examine the entire under framework for the attachment of contraband packages by tape, wire, or magnets.

EXTENSIVE PHYSICAL SEARCH—TRUCK-GENERAL
[Figure 8-8]

A. 1. Bumper and grill work
      a. Attachment of packages to grill work and bumper
      b. Back of license plate, inside of vent openings
  2. Engine area
      a. Check for recently worked screw and nut and bolt fasteners on engine accessory and hose assemblies.
      b. Check for attachment of packages to under side of hood, engine block, steering column, etc. Check radiator only if suspicion demands (open cap with caution).
      c. Inside of cowling surrounding fan blades
      d. Air filter housing
  3. Tire and wheel assemblies for evidence of recent removal. Inspect between dual wheels.
  4. Cab area
      a. Seat cushions
      b. Under seats
      c. Under and behind instrument panel
      d. Inside of glove compartment
      e. Behind stereo-deck assembly; check tapes, speaker housing.
      f. All suitcases and packages
      g. Ash trays
      h. Headliner
      i. Under or behind all foot pedals
      j. Area on top of deck next to front window or windshield
      k. Behind sun visors
      l. Under floor mats
      m. In door panels (roll windows down, shine light into opening)
      n. Inside of vent hoses and outlets
      o. Behind seats
  5. Baggage compartment
      a. Suitcases and packages
      b. Check for packages attached to top of compartment.
      c. Behind insulation and padding on compartment walls
  6. Cab sleeping area
      a. Under mattress
      b. In pillows
      c. Between blanket covers
      d. In ventilation outlets
      e. In headliner area
  7. Battery boxes
      a. In cell compartments (be careful of acid when removing and replacing caps)

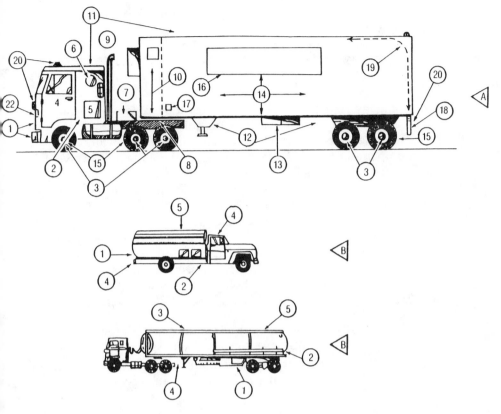

Figure 8-8 Extensive physical and hand search—trucks (General). (U.S. Nuclear Regulatory Commission.)

  b.   Between battery body and wall of box
8. Fifth wheel area (under and around)
9. Trailer refrigeration unit (not on all trailers), all compartments
10. Ice bunker compartment (not on all trailers); access gained by two doors, one on each side, front of trailer. This is a prime spot.
11. Roof—both tractor and trailer for packages attached to roof top; check entire length. Use ladder or mirror on pole.
12. Under entire tractor–trailer for packages attached to structural framework under entire length of tractor and trailer. Note: Information received from various truck drivers suggests that the attachment of contraband packages to the underframe of tractors and trailers is a favorite method of smugglers. Check fuel tanks very closely.
13. Spare part and tire chain compartment (not found on all trailers); outside and inside of packages
14. Interior of trailer

      a. Between side walls, ceiling, and bumper panels (usually plywood)

      b. Check for recently installed screws.

      c. Examine floor for loose flooring and hidden compartments.

      d. Ceiling for attached packages

15. Wheel axles for attached packages
16. Company sign panels (found on most trailers) for contraband concealed in spaces between sign and trailer body
17. Canvas or plastic document pouches, inside and behind
18. Bumper on rear of trailer, including inside of the hollow channels.
19. Trailer—upward-sliding door (not on all trailers), including portion of inside ceiling that is covered by sliding door when door is in open position. Step into trailer and close door, examine ceiling and door track with the aid of a flashlight.
20. Light lenses and reflectors located throughout trailer and tractor. Examine visually with the aid of a light source to determine possible inclusion of contraband in space between face glass and bulb. Also check for recently removed hold-down screws.
21. Externally mounted air filter (on some tractor models) for recent installation
22. External tractor air inlets, including inside for contraband
23. All panels that could conceal personnel, etc. Check thickness of panels. Measure internal depth/length of trailers vs external depth/length. Differences greater than 8 inches are suspect.

EXTENSIVE PHYSICAL SEARCH—SPECIAL TRUCKS
[Figure 8-9]

(The search areas noted are in addition to those specified for trucks—general.)

B. Tank trucks (note: tank trucks, particularly those containing flammables are extremely high-risk sabotage items even without driver involvement)

    1. Hose compartments, removing hoses if necessary. Use flashlight for long cylindrical hoses and compartments.

    2. Pump and storage compartment (top, bottom, sides, doors and contents)

    3. Filler-cap areas

    4. Areas between tank and frame

    5. Assure no unusual attachments to tanks

C. Gas-cylinder delivery truck (gas cylinders are almost impossible to search in large quantities, search carefully)

    6. Between all cylinders

    7. Cylinders for wiring or attachments, all frame platform voids

D. Multicompartment

    8. Each compartment and contents

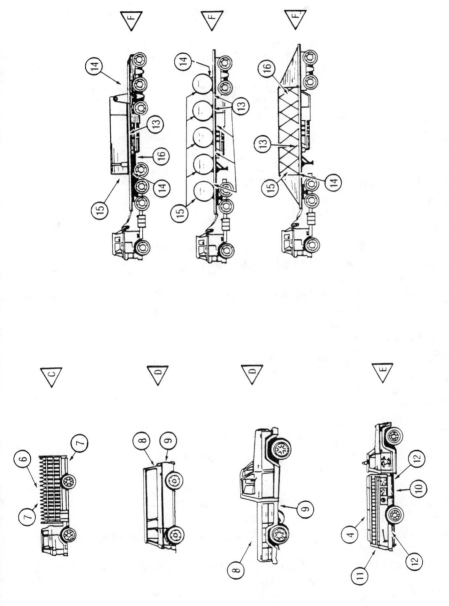

Figure 8-9 Extensive physical and hand search—trucks (General). (U.S. Nuclear Regulatory Commission.)

9.   Voids behind compartments
E.   Emergency vehicles
10.   All compartments and contents
11.   Hose storage areas (draft tubes and fire hoses)
12.   Around special apparatus (mattresses in ambulances, rescue equipment)
F.   Cask shipping trailers
13.   Around and under each cask to assure no attachments, unusual wires, etc.
14.   Cask holding fixtures and stabilizers, inside any voids or hollow areas
15.   Each cask seal
16.   All I-beam and channel structures from both outside and inside

EXTENSIVE PHYSICAL SEARCH—SPECIAL EQUIPMENT [Figure 8-10]

1.   Engine area
    a.   Air and oil filters for authenticity and recent access
    b.   Firewalls and cowling for attachments
    c.   Battery box area
    d.   Radiator content (extremely hazardous check if equipment has been running) only if suspicious or engine is cold
    e.   Tool or spares compartment
    f.   Heater hoses and ducting
    g.   Assure no attachments to engine or housing.
    h.   Hydraulic tank content, remove cap, assure no wires or strings hanging in tank.
2.   Cab or operating area
    a.   Seat cushions
    b.   Under or behind seats
    c.   Tool and storage areas
    d.   Behind visors
    e.   Under floor mats
    f.   Inside and around vent hoses and ducts
    g.   Behind dash and instrument panels
    h.   Parcels and packages (lunch kits, thermos bottles, canned and bottled drinks)
    i.   Fuel tank (no smoking), open and assure gasoline or diesel presence and that there are no wires hanging in tank.
3.   Undercarriage
    a.   Undercarriage framework voids, access panels, channels, and any shelflike areas

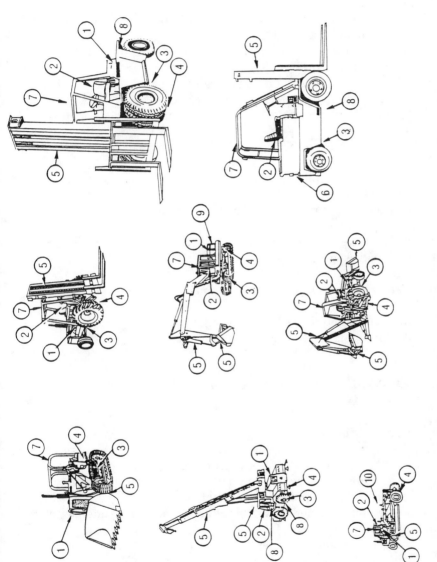

Figure 8-10 Extensive physical and hand search—special equipment. (U.S. Nuclear Regulatory Commission.)

4. Track mechanisms and wheels
   a. Backside of wheels
   b. Between double wheels
   c. Behind track mechanisms and drive wheels
5. Booms, masts, and buckets, etc.
   a. Have booms lowered to check access holes, voids, channels, etc., for items and attachments.
   b. Blades, buckets, blocks, etc., for attachments
   c. Around mast, top of masts, etc.
   d. All tubing that has open ends (use flashlight)
6. Battery compartment (battery-powered vehicles)
   a. Open battery compartment, check around batteries, open cells if appropriate.
   b. Access doors, top, bottom, and sides of compartment
7. Roofs
   a. Tops of roofs, roll bars, roll cages, etc.
8. Fender wells
   a. Inspect with mirror or flashlight as required.
9. Special apparatus
   a. Ballast boxes, compartments, liquid containers, attachment area
   b. Foot pads/stabilizers
   c. Other special apparatus
   d. General hydraulic system, pipes, pumps, valves, reservoirs, etc.
10. Lights
    a. Inspect around lights for recent installation.
    b. Assure lights are functional type (not false).

EXTENSIVE PHYSICAL SEARCH—RAIL CARS
[Figure 8-11]

A. Escorted rail shipments
   1. Seals on cask or assemblies, etc., that are under escort should be checked prior to release or acceptance of the rail car.
   2. All escorted cars, switch engines, etc., that enter the protected area should be observed for abnormalities.
B. Unescorted rail shipments (cars picked up or delivered) and all rail cars not in custody of escorts
   1. Check seals on casks, assemblies, material containers, etc.; assure they have not been subject to tampering.
   2. All wheels (inside and out), using mirror or look through the opposite side.
   3. Trucks and journal-bearing inspection access areas (journal holes), inspect inside of trucks and any voids of shelf area carefully.
   4. Coupler top, sides, and bottom, shelf areas or voids

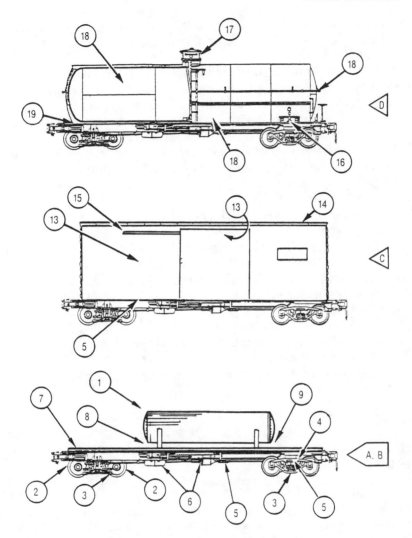

Figure 8-11 Extensive physical and hand search—rail cars. (U.S. Nuclear Regulatory Commission.)

5. All undercarriage beams and supports with a mirror; view from ends, from opposite sides, and/or crouching under the car. Inspect all access holes and voids in the undercarriage. Look at all shelf areas.

6. Brake cylinders, air storage tanks, etc., in undercarriage area to assure that they appear authentic and do not have wires or attachments.

7. Top of the rail car bed, tool boxes or equipment containers

8. Around dunnage and rail car cargo

9. Around casks or special material containers and support mechanism. Check all voids, behind braces, within channel, I-beam and tubular supports.
10. Cooling control instrumentation panels and mechanisms to assure that coolant storage tanks appear authentic without attachments
11. Remove or inspect under tarps and dunnage.
12. If equipment or materials are being shipped on the rail car, inspect them thoroughly (access panels, structure, boxes, etc.).

C.
13. If a box car is used, check interior walls and ceiling; inspect between exterior and interior walls. With mirror and light inspect all voids and access areas.
14. Roof of car
15. Behind sign panels and doors

D. Tank-type cars
If a tank car (fuel oil, LPG, or other chemicals or gas) is to be inspected, check with extreme care both from a personal safety standpoint and from the fact that they contain tremendous potential energy and could be prime targets for sabotage.
16. Hose lockers or pump panels
17. Fill-port area and walkways
18. Overall surface of the tank for attachments of explosive devices, unnecessary wires, etc.
19. Channels or voids where tank joins carriage or bed

NOTES

1. *The Code of Federal Regulations* (Washington, D.C.: 1981), title 10, part 73.45(b).
2. Ibid., part 73.46(d).
3. Deborah Cromer Post, "The Technology of Access Control," *Security World* (October 1980):23.
4. Charles H. Bean and James A. Prell, "Personnel Access Control—Criteria and Testing," *Security Management*:6–7. © 1978. Copyright by The American Society for Industrial Security, 1655 N. Fort Drive, Suite 1200, Arlington, VA 22209. Reprinted with permission from the June 1978 issue of *Security Management* magazine.
5. J. E. Thorsen, "Has 'Absolute Identity' Come of Age?" *Security World* (July 1978):32.
6. *Security Letter* 12, no. 21, part II, (1982) (Adapted from "Access Control and Personal Identification Market," #A943 © 1981 by Frost & Sullivan, Inc., 106 Fulton St., New York, NY 10038.)
7. Nuclear Regulatory Commission, *Entry/Exit Control for Protected Areas, Vital Areas and Material Access Areas* (Washington, D.C.: The Commission, 1980), p. 5.7–2.
8. Ibid.
9. Ibid., p. 5.7–3.
10. Ibid., p. 5.7–4.
11. Nuclear Regulatory Commission, *Vehicle Access and Search Training Manual* (Washington, D.C.: The Commission, 1979), pp. 104–129.

CHAPTER 9

The Security Officer

As important as hardware systems are to the protection of critical assets, the essential element in any and every maximum-security environment is the security officer (the word guard is not used because the duties and responsibilities inherent in providing maximum security are such that it does not adequately recognize and encompass the required diversity).

The Rand report issued in 1972 described the typical security officer as "an aging white male, poorly educated, usually untrained and very poorly paid. He averages between 45 and 55 years of age and has little education beyond the ninth grade and has had a few years of experience in private security."

In contrast, a yet unpublished survey, known as the Hallcrest Report, has found the typical security officer to be:

> A young white male, a high school graduate with probably some college exposure, who has met at least the minimum recommended preassignment training of the task force [on private security]. The median age range is about 33 years and only about 15 percent have not completed high school while 45 percent have had some college. While 65 percent of contract guards felt their pay was too low, they expressed basic job satisfaction. Only about one-fourth of them said they took the job because they were unemployed and couldn't find anything else. In-house guards clearly see a career path with over one-half of them expecting to hold their job until retirement.

There has obviously been much progress made in the last 10 years in the field of security. In the maximum-security environment, however, the caliber of the individual security officer takes on new significance. If the decision is made to provide the highest degrees of security available, it is the result of a determination that high security is necessary. The higher the level of security, the higher the caliber of individuals charged with providing it.

Much of the maximum-security officer's functions revolve around his common sense, judgment, initiative, intuition, intelligence, and perseverance. To find these qualities in suitable proportions anywhere in our society today is an accomplishment of sorts, yet they are all required of persons in this field. The task is made infinitely more difficult given the fact that officers' salaries are traditionally low and the rewards and opportunities for advancement generally are few and far between. Nonetheless, the security officer is the backbone of any security system. It therefore behooves the maximum-security director to recruit, train, and retain the best and highest-caliber personnel possible.

BASIC QUALIFICATIONS

Basic qualifications of security officers can run the gamut from alive and breathing to some of the most stringent requirements required by federal mandate at nuclear facilities. In the maximum security environment, qualifications should at a minimum be those required by the Nuclear Regulatory Commission:

NRC Criteria

"I.   Employment suitability and qualification
A.   Suitability
1.   Prior to employment, or assignment to the security organization, an individual shall meet the following suitability criteria:
a.   Educational development. Possess a high school diploma or pass an equivalent performance examination designed to measure basic job-related mathematical, language, and reasoning skills, ability, and knowledge required to perform security job duties.
b.   Felony convictions. Have no felony convictions involving the use of a weapon and no felony convictions that reflect on the individual's reliability.*
2.   Prior to employment or assignment to the security organization in an armed capacity, the individual, in addition to a and b above, must be 21 years of age or older.
B.   Physical and mental qualifications
1.   Physical qualifications
a.   Individuals whose security tasks and job duties are directly associated with the effective implementation of the licensee physical security and contingency plans shall have no physical weaknesses or abnormalities that would adversely affect their performance of assigned security job duties.
b.   In addition to a above, guards, armed response personnel, armed escorts, and central alarm station operators shall successfully pass a physical examination administered by

---

* It is far more desirable that an individual have no criminal record. (Authors' comment.)

a licensed physician. The examination shall be designed to measure the individual's physical ability to perform assigned security job duties as identified in the licensee physical security and contingency plans. Armed personnel shall meet the following additional physical requirements:

(1) Vision

    (a) For each individual, distant visual acuity in each eye shall be correctable to 20/30 (Snellen or equivalent) in the better eye and 20/40 in the other eye with eyeglasses or contact lenses. If uncorrected distance vision is not at least 20/40 in the better eye, the individual shall carry an extra pair of corrective lenses. Near visual acuity, corrected or uncorrected, shall be at least 20/40 in the better eye. Field of vision must be at least 70 horizontal meridian in each eye. The ability to distinguish red, green, and yellow colors is required. Loss of vision in one eye is disqualifying. Glaucoma shall be disqualifying, unless controlled by acceptable medical or surgical means, provided such medications as may be used for controlling glaucoma do not cause undesirable side effects which adversely affect the individual's ability to perform assigned security job duties, and provided the visual acuity and field of vision requirements stated above are met. On-the-job evaluation shall be used for individuals who exhibit a mild color vision defect.

    b. Where corrective eyeglasses are required, they shall be of the safety glass type.

    c. The use of corrective eyeglasses or contact lenses shall not interfere with an individual's ability to effectively perform assigned security job duties during normal or emergency operations.

(2) Hearing

    (a) Individuals shall have no hearing loss in the better ear greater than 30 decibels average at 500 Hz, 1,000 Hz, and 2,000 Hz, with no level greater than 40 decibels at any one frequency (by ISO 389 "Standard Reference Zero for the Calibration of Purtone Audiometer" [1975] or ANSI S3.6-1969 [R. 1973] "Specifications for Audiometers").

    (b) A hearing aid is acceptable provided suitable testing procedures demonstrate auditory acuity equivalent to the above-stated requirement.

(c) The use of a hearing aid shall not decrease the effective performance of the individual's assigned security job duties during normal or emergency operations.

(3) Diseases. Individuals shall have no established medical history or medical diagnosis of epilepsy or diabetes, or, where such a condition exists, the individual shall provide medical evidence that the condition can be controlled with proper medication so that the individual will not lapse into a coma or unconscious state while performing assigned security job duties.

(4) Addiction. Individuals shall have no established medical history or medical diagnosis of habitual alcoholism or drug addiction, or, where such a condition has existed, the individual shall provide certified documentation of having completed a rehabilitation program which would give a reasonable degree of confidence that the individual would be capable of performing assigned security job duties.

(5) Other physical requirements. An individual who has been incapacitated due to a serious illness, injury, disease, or operation, which could interfere with the effective performance of assigned security job duties shall, prior to resumption of such duties, provide medical evidence of recovery and ability to perform such security job duties.

2. Mental qualifications
   a. Individuals whose security tasks and job duties are directly associated with the effective implementation of the licensee physical security and contingency plans shall demonstrate mental alertness and the capability to exercise good judgment, implement instructions, assimilate assigned security tasks, and possess the acuity of senses and ability of expression sufficient to permit accurate communication by written, spoken, audible, visible, or other signals required by assigned job duties.
   b. Armed individuals and central alarm station operators, in addition to meeting the requirement stated in paragraph a above, shall have no emotional instability that would interfere with the effective performance of assigned security job duties. The determination shall be made by a licensed psychologist or psychiatrist, or physician, or other person professionally trained to identify emotional instability.
   c. The licensee shall arrange for continued observation of se-

curity personnel and for appropriate corrective measures by responsible supervisors for indications of emotional instability of individuals in the course of performing assigned security job duties. Identification of emotional instability by responsible supervisors shall be subject to verification by a licensed, trained person.

C. Physical fitness qualifications. Subject to a medical examination conducted within the preceding 30 days and to a determination and written certification by a licensed physician that there are no medical contraindications to participation by the individual as disclosed by the medical examination guards, armed response personnel, and armed escorts shall demonstrate physical fitness for assigned security job duties by performing a practical physical exercise program within a specific time period. The exercise program performance objectives shall be described in the licensee training and qualifications plan, and shall consider such job-related functions as strenuous activity, physical exertion, levels of stress, and exposure to the elements as they pertain to each individual's assigned security job duties for both normal and emergency operations. The physical fitness qualification of each guard, armed response person, and armed escort shall be documented and attested by a licensee security supervisor."[1]

Additionally, other qualifications may be added as necessary by the facility's security director.

A suggested physical fitness or agility-testing program requires the construction (preferably on site) of an obstacle course. [Construction of the obstacles is well within the capabilities of most site maintenance shops.] This should be designed to measure, among other things, the officer's speed, agility, strength, balance, coordination, and ability to maintain functional capability after arduous activity (Figure 9–1). The suggested course can be laid out on a piece of flat ground measuring only 100 by 50 feet and contains 10 required functions. At station 1, each officer starts by climbing up, over, and down the opposite side of a fixed, double-sided 30 foot ladder. Station 2 consists of three hurdles/barriers that are graduated in height (2, 3, and 4 feet; or 3, 4, and 5 feet; etc.) and spaced approximately four feet apart. At station 3, the officer is required to drag (through use of an attached rope or handle) a 150 pound weight a distance of 15 feet. At station 4 is a 50-pound weight the officer must lift and carry 25 feet. Leaving station 4, he approaches station 5, which is a running broad jump. He must clear a distance equal to his height. Station 6 is a balance beam consisting of a 4 inch × 4 inch × 12 foot beam set one foot off the ground. The officer must walk the length of the beam without falling off. At station 7, he must high-step his way at a double-time pace through a double row of off-set truck tires with 20 inch centers. Station 8 tests his ability to maintain functional capability after ar-

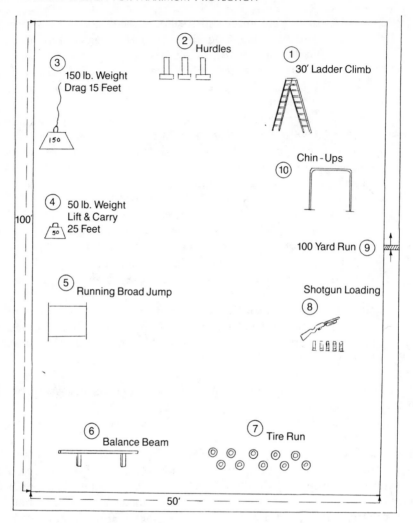

Figure 9-1 Suggested physical agility course.

duous activity by requiring him to load and unload a shotgun with five dummy rounds (rounds are not to be worked through the action to unload). Station 9 is the start of a 100-yard run (once around the perimeter of the obstacle course). Station 10 consists of three full-extension pull-ups on a chinning bar.

The maximum time limit for this physical fitness testing course should be realistically set, taking into consideration the age and physical condition of the officers, and the weather. As specified above, before an individual is allowed to participate in this activity he must recently have undergone a thorough physical exam and been cleared by the examining medical authority. The number of events necessary to pass may also be adjusted. For example, since there are 10 events in the suggested course, a passing score of 70 percent could be established. This would allow personnel with poor upper-body strength to make up for not being able to drag the 150-pound weight or do the three pull-ups. Conversely, if these attributes are considered necessary in all site officers, a 100 percent score could be required for every participant. Failure by an individual to attain that score could be grounds for suspension from duty until such time as he was able to meet the standards. Down-grading to a less demanding (and lower paying) security assignment is another option.

SCREENING

Once candidates meeting the specified qualifications have applied for positions as security officers, it is necessary to verify their application information and conduct interviews, personality inventories, and polygraph tests (depending on location, polygraph testing as a prerequisite to employment is generally illegal in the United States). All of this is essential in screening.

Application information must be verified by conducting a background check of each candidate. At a minimum, this should include:

1. Verification of all employment and unemployment back to the individual's eighteenth birthday
2. Verification of all education, training, and military service back to the individual's eighteenth birthday
3. Verification of all residences back to the individual's eighteenth birthday
4. Checks of at least four character references provided by the individual
5. Criminal history checks of the individual back to his eighteenth birthday

The last is probably the most difficult to accomplish due to the disparity of laws governing release of such information to the private sector.

If the facility is such that government clearance or access authorization is required, verification of all information will also be accomplished by the agency granting clearance.

On successful completion of the background check, each candidate should be interviewed by a personnel manager or someone else knowledgable in personnel functions, the operations manager or supervisor, and the security director or management equivalent. In the case of contractual security, these interviews should be conducted by the contractual security organization. Introduction to the client's representatives may be performed, but interviews of contractual security officers are not recommended (to avoid potential future claims of a coemployer relationship). The client should, however, ensure that his requirements are being met.

As an adjunct to the interview, a candidate's personality should be inventoried. There are a number of tools available for this purpose, such as personality inventories and honesty tests. If legal, a polygraph examination could be conducted. It should be used only as a postinterview step, however, to avoid unnecessary costs. There is no sense in incurring expenses if a candidate has not progressed through the cost-free portions of the selection process.

Once the candidates have qualified for employment and have successfully completed the subjective analysis, selection can be made. It is this final step that personal preferences usually manifest themselves. Regardless of whether or not a candidate is found to be satisfactory, his attitude and philosophy are important considerations. If the individual or individuals responsible for selection of security officers feel that a particular candidate would not be a good choice, that candidate should be rejected. It is seldom wrong to take one's "gut feeling" into consideration, although this may be a luxury one cannot afford. In any event, it is always best for employers to feel as comfortable as possible with their ultimate choices.

TRAINING

Before significant training can commence, it is necessary to identify the specific duties of the security personnel. In the maximum-security environment, certain tasks are essential to the continuity and efficiency of the program and systems. The following functions are essential:

1. Central alarm station (CAS) operator
2. Secondary alarm station (SAS) operator
3. Access control officer
4. Search officer
5. Escort officer
6. Patrol officer
7. Response officer

Depending on the nature of the assignment, some of these functions may be handled by the same person(s). At any fixed post, for example, the officer on duty may be responsible for access control and searches, or patrol officers may be called on to escort visitors.

The Nuclear Regulatory Commission assigns specific performance objectives to the functions listed above:

"1. CAS/SAS Operator
    a. Monitor and operate all phases of the alarm system
        (1) Performance objective/criterion
            CAS/SAS operator shall successfully complete all classroom training related to the use of equipment and tactical considerations and also demonstrate to the satisfaction of the Security Supervisor that they can meet all site procedure requirements in support of the security and contingency plans.

b. Direct response force
   (1) Performance objective/criterion
       CAS/SAS operator shall initiate and coordinate the immediate response to safeguard contingencies demonstrating a thorough knowledge of the site layout.
c. Operate communication equipment
   (1) Performance objective/criterion
       CAS/SAS operator using each item of the existing communication systems shall contact security posts, response force personnel, supervisors, law enforcement authorities, and other on- or off-site assistance organizations with established call signs (i.e., codes, duress signals) to ensure communication security as appropriate.
d. Operate card key system
   (1) Performance objective/criterion
       CAS/SAS operator shall monitor the card key system to detect unauthorized entry attempts; test the system to ensure operability; annotate access logs; evaluate system output data; recognize system malfunction in accordance with manufacturer criteria; and, direct actions to provide interim compensatory measures if system is inoperable.
e. Assess alarms
   (1) Performance objective/criterion
       CAS/SAS operator shall direct response force to specific alarm zones; evaluate response force data to determine if intrusion occurred; use CCTV, when provided, as a secondary method to identify possible intruder and obtain data relative to the adversary within the protected area.

"2. Access control officer
a. Verify visitor/employee identification and access authorization
   (1) Performance objective/criterion
       Access control officer shall establish identity of employees and visitors in accordance with site procedures and determine the authorized access level to specific areas for visitors.
b. Annotate access logs
   (1) Performance objective/criterion
       Access Control Officer shall maintain access logs in accordance with regulations and site procedures.
c. Issue facility identification
   (1) Performance objective/criterion
       Access control officer shall use and maintain authorization lists and issue correct facility badges in accordance with regulations and site procedures.
d. Ensure authorized escorts
   (1) Performance objective/criterion

Access Control Officer shall ensure authorized escort is provided for visitors in accordance with regulations and site procedures; brief escort and visitor on the subject of emergency procedures, areas of access, unauthorized activities, and the responsibilities of the escort.

e. Control of access during security or site emergency
   (1) Performance objective/criterion
        Access Control Officer shall control and access portal during security or site emergencies to only permit access of specifically authorized individuals and off-site emergency response personnel in accordance with regulations and site procedures.

"3. Search officer
   a. Recognize unauthorized materials
      (1) Performance objective/criterion
           Search Officers must be able to recognize materials, found during searches of personnel, packages, and/or vehicles, which are identified in site procedures as being prohibited in protected areas.
   b. Conduct hands on search of personnel
      (1) Performance objective/criterion
           Search Officers shall search personnel for unauthorized materials in accordance with site procedures and shall take action according to these procedures upon finding any unauthorized material.
   c. Conduct hand held or control walk through metal detector search
      (1) Performance objective/criterion
           Search Officers shall be able to calibrate, test, and use hand-held detectors and control persons undergoing walk-through detectors to locate weapons in accordance with regulations and site procedures; and take action according to site procedures upon finding any indication of detection of metal including a weapon.
   d. Conduct hand held or control walk through explosive detector search
      (1) Performance objective/criterion
           Search Officers shall be able to calibrate, test, and use the hand-held or walk-through explosive detector in accordance with site procedures to locate explosive devices or material and to take action according to these procedures upon indications of detecting explosives.
   e. Conduct physical package search
      (1) Performance objective/criterion
           Search Officer shall search packages being taken into the protected area in accordance with regulations and site procedures.

f. Conduct x-ray package search
   (1) Performance objective/criterion
       Search Officer shall calibrate, test and use the X-ray device in accordance with site procedures, to detect any unauthorized material and to react according to these procedures upon finding such material.
g. Conduct vehicle search
   (1) Performance objective/criterion
       Search Officer shall search vehicles, including cab, engine compartment, undercarriage, and cargo area in accordance with regulations and site procedures for unauthorized persons and materials, and take action according to these procedures upon finding such persons or materials.

"4. Escort officer
   a. Conduct personnel escort
      (1) Performance objective/criterion
          Escort Officers must maintain continual and effective observation and control over any visitor; permit access only to authorized areas; insure that unauthorized activities are detected, and notify the CAS/SAS of any unauthorized activity on the part of the visitor.
   b. Conduct vehicle escort
      (1) Performance objective/criterion
          Escort Officers must, in accordance with site procedures involving vehicle access and routes, maintain continual and effective observation and control over both driver and vehicle; lock and secure vehicle if left unattended in protected area; and, ensure that unauthorized materials are not loaded and/or unloaded.

"5. Patrol officer
   a. Conduct patrol of vital/protected areas
      (1) Performance objective/criterion
          Patrol Officer must demonstrate thorough familiarity of site layout; conduct patrol of vital/protected areas to detect unauthorized or suspicious activities; observe, inspect or test security system(s) for deficiencies; respond to and investigate intrusion alarm annunciations by the CAS/SAS; inspect all barriers and security doors for indications of tampering; observe employees and/or visitors for any possible suspicious behavior; and communicate with CAS/SAS and/or other members of the security force, using site-issued equipment, to report findings or initiate further response.

"6. Response officer
   a. Respond to and assess alarms
      (1) Performance objective/criterion

Licensee response personnel must demonstrate a thorough knowledge of site layout; respond to and assess alarm annunciations as directed by the CAS/SAS in accordance with site procedures; investigate unauthorized persons found within protected/vital areas; secure any barrier or security door found unlocked or breached; communicate with CAS/SAS and/or other members of the security force any findings and/or requests for assistance.

b. Conduct searches of protected and vital areas
   (1) Performance objective/criterion
        Response personnel must demonstrate thorough knowledge of site layout; conduct searches of protected/vital areas for unauthorized persons, vehicles or materials in accordance with site procedures; secure and isolate specific areas when directed; inspect vital equipment and components for indications of tampering and/or sabotage.

c. Apprehend and detain unauthorized individuals
   (1) Performance objective/criterion
        Response personnel shall maintain surveillance of suspect until support personnel (either onsite or local law enforcement authorities) arrive unless threat to vital areas or industrial sabotage is imminent. As appropriate detain suspect, using training received in uses of deadly force and legal basis for detention; conduct search of suspect using appropriate method (i.e., hands-on, prone); cuff suspect if necessary."[2]

Once the specific tasks of security officers are defined, it is necessary to develop procedures to ensure that each task is accomplished uniformly, consistently, and in accordance with requirements. These procedures will become the basis for initial training after preliminary orientation.

In the maximum-security environment, basic security officer training after orientation usually starts with the following or similar subjects:

1. Security officer's role ($\frac{1}{2}$ hr)—the role of the private security officer in providing protection at the specific facility
2. Authority of private security officers (1 hr)—legal authority of private security officers (general overview)
3. Report writing ($1\frac{1}{2}$ hrs)—general and site-specific security and situation reporting requirements, documentation, and essentials of a good report
4. Site-specific security systems (4 hrs)—Nature, purpose, and limitations
5. Protection of information ($\frac{1}{2}$ hr)—Protection of security system information
6. Self-defense (4 hrs)—basic concepts of unarmed self-defense
7. Security organization ($\frac{1}{2}$ hr)—explanation of the facility's security organization and operation

8.   Security briefing ($\frac{1}{2}$ hr)—explanation of site-specific security briefing procedures and local law enforcement relationships
9.   Contractor and visitor policy and other topics ($\frac{1}{2}$ hr)—general contractor and visitor policy and other site-related information

The number of hours necessary for initial training is largely dependent on the complexity of the laws and procedures in effect at a particular facility. More training is not necessarily better training. Most security officers' jobs do not require an extensive educational background or a multitude of classroom hours. A common myth prevalent among many people in security and law enforcement is that the basic security officer receives too few hours of instruction, and therefore is inadequately trained. In this day and age, that is seldom the case.

In addition, many people consider security to be the same as law enforcement, albeit on a lesser plane. In reality, both are separate and unique. Depending on a security officer's assignment, completion of many hours of training may not be necessary. Again, depending on the assignment, a few hours of classroom and several hours of on-the-job instruction may be sufficient. The point is to train a security officer for his assignment, but not to overtrain him because it is usually not necessary, it can be costly, and it can lead to an adverse impact on morale (disillusionment).

A second, more advanced phase of training generally follows in the maximum-security environment and should consist of the following or similar subject matter:

1.   Protection of high-risk facilities (3 hrs)—general concepts of protection of high-risk facilities, transport vehicles used, and the commodity being protected; basic response to contingency situations, e.g., bomb threats
2.   Federal guidelines (1 hr)—federal requirements and guidance for the protection of a particular facility, if applicable
3.   Use of nonlethal weapons (3 hrs)—use of batons, riot sticks, chemical agents, and other nonlethal weapons
4.   Basic first aid (8 hrs)—a recognized standard course
5.   Use of force (including deadly force) (2 hrs)—explanation of the legal authority of security officers to use force, including deadly force, to protect the facility
6.   Arrest and detention (1 hr)—legal authority of security officers to arrest and detail individuals
7.   Mechanics of arrest and detention (1 hr)—basic concepts of the mechanics of arrest and detention applicable in a particular jurisdiction
8.   Search and seizure (1 hr)—introduction to the rules, methods, and authority to search and seize property
9.   Assessment techniques (2 hrs) (see Appendix 9–A)—surveillance and assessment techniques in use at the protected facility

10. Communications systems (2 hrs)—site-specific communications systems, their proper use and operation
11. Access-control systems (1 hr)—access control and contraband detection techniques for individuals, packages, and vehicles prior to entry into a facility's perimeter or areas within
12. Duress alarms ($\frac{1}{2}$ hr)—duress alarm operations and procedures (mechanical, audible, and verbal)
13. Alarm station operations (4 hrs)—central and secondary alarm station operations
14. Normal command and control ($\frac{1}{2}$ hr)—security command and control during normal operations
15. Contingency command and control ($\frac{1}{2}$ hr)—security command and control during nonroutine operations
16. Station operations (2 hrs/post)—fixed-post and mobile patrol site-specific operations
17. Search techniques (2 hrs)—search techniques and systems for individuals, packages, and vehicles
18. Escort and patrol responsibilities (2 hrs)—escort and patrol responsibilities, including scheduled tours, fire prevention, and control and safety hazards
19. Contingency response (2 hrs)—site-specific contingency response to confirmed or attempted intrusion, theft or attempts, and other crimes
20. Security during component failure and emergencies (2 hrs)—security systems operations after component failure or power outage and emergencies
21. Equipment testing (1 hr)—security-equipment testing methods and procedures, other than alarm, including assigned personal and post equipment

The numbers in parenthesis after each topic represent the minimum hours of training, depending on the facility, that should be offered. Additionally, more extensive training should be given to response force personnel, and that is covered fully in the next chapter.

Firearms Training

One area that has been intentionally overlooked up to this point involves firearms training.

"There has been much discussion recently on the need for security personnel to be armed. Some proponents of disarming security officers (or not arming them in the first place) argue that the officers' function is to observe and report, not to engage an adversary. The unarmed security officer is expected to summon local law enforcement assistance whenever a crime is observed and let the authorities make the apprehension. (This assumes, of course, the ready availability of local law enforcement authorities.) Conversely, proponents of arming all security officers sometimes argue that firearms are 'tools of the trade' and offer a distinct psychological deterrence thus providing an added 'edge' for the security officer. Opponents of this philosophy counter that the presence of a firearm often tends to exacerbate a situation and could escalate a confrontation to violence. Since it is impossible to predict, with any degree of certainty, which criminal will be deterred and which will be aggravated, by the presence of a firearm, psychological effect associated with the security (and, for that matter, law enforcement) application of firearms should not be used as a basis for the decision to arm or disarm security personnel. The issue must be approached from an unemotional and analytic perspective.

"The basic criterion for arming security personnel at a particular location should always be necessity . . . firearms necessary to the proper performance of the security function? Before this question can be answered, certain considerations must be addressed. A potential threat level must be assigned to the commodity being protected.

Potential Threat Level Inherent to the Commodity

"Every item that requires safeguarding has an inherent threat level. Threat level is defined as the degree of risk associated with safeguarding the particular item or commodity. Certain innocuous items, toasters and blenders for example, have a low threat level. The threat of deadly force being used to steal them is generally absent. Other items, nuclear material munitions, gold, etc. have a high threat level because there is a definite possibility that deadly force could be used to perpetrate their theft.

"When attaching a particular inherent threat level to a certain item, it is wise to consider the geographical and/or physical location of the item— where it is manufactured or located, stored, or transported; the criminal attraction to the item—its desirability and/or convertability to cash; the degree of risk associated with theft versus the rewards of a successful theft (the degree or risk should also be thought of in terms of probability that deadly force could be used against protection personnel. If the penalties for illegal possession of an item are so severe as to suggest that it may be to the thief's advantage not to leave any witnesses, then the use of deadly force in the commission of a theft should be considered a very real possibility); and, the potential consequences of a failure to adequately safeguard the item—hazard to the general public, civil liability, etc.

"Once all of these factors are considered and intelligently evaluated, a threat level can be easily assigned. In any case, arriving at an appropriate threat level ultimately rests on a fair assessment of the risks and a common-sense approach. Emotion should never enter into the decision-making process.

"If the resultant threat level is low, i.e., threat of a particular commodity poses no potential threat to life, then arming security personnel is probably not necessary to effectively perform the security service. The main duty of security personnel is to protect life. If there is no potential danger to life, then firearms are not necessary to protect property.

"When we speak of a threat to life, in this context we must determine that a genuine threat to life exists. It may be generalized threat or it could be a localized threat. A generalized threat to life can be conceived as a threat to anyone, anywhere, at any time prompted by the nature of a particular stolen commodity such as nuclear material. A localized threat to life can be thought of as a threat to persons safeguarding the commodity due to the commodity's value. In either case, if it is determined that a threat to life could be associated with a particular item, good security practice requires that it be safeguarded by all legal means available, including firearms.

Nature of Commodity

"The nature of the commodity being safeguarded is, by far, the most crucial test of necessity for arming security personnel. The following criteria should be satisfied before the decision to arm security personnel is made based on the nature of the commodity.

1. Use could constitute a clear and immediate danger to life.
2. Misuse would constitute a clear and immediate danger to life.
3. Legitimate possession is controlled by law.

Value of Commodity

"The value of the commodity being safeguarded constitutes yet another test of necessity. Satisfying the following criteria may be the basis upon which the decision to arm personnel is based.

1. Value is so high as to suggest that deadly force could be used to effect a theft.
2. Value, while not as high as in number 1, suggests that deadly force could be used to effect a theft due to prevailing circumstances, e.g., geographical location, scarcity of item, receipt of information indicating a theft is planned, etc.

"However, impersonal as it may sound, if the commodity being protected is a person or a facility, the same process should be used.

"Upon the determination that the commodity being protected presents a high threat level, consideration should then be given to arming security personnel entrusted with protection.

Selection and Training of Armed Security Personnel

"Once the decision is made to arm protection personnel, it is not merely a simple act of hanging a gun on someone's belt. Most problems are the result of inadequate selection and training of armed personnel. They are not caused by the mere presence of firearms. Misuse and/or abuse of firearms is a result of inadequate personality, inadequate training, or more likely, a combination of both.

"Every security officer to be armed must be carefully scrutinized and evaluated to ensure that he or she is stable and otherwise suitable to carry a firearm. This can be accomplished via any one of several means currently available to the security practitioner. Ensuring the suitability of personnel to carry firearms is the most important first step of a two-step process. The evaluation process must be constant for as long as an individual is permitted to carry a firearm to ensure continued suitability. Most states require that persons carrying firearms be licensed. Contrary to popular belief, requirements to legally carry a firearm in most states are quite stringent. Application for a handgun permit usually involves an extensive background check and will assist in the evaluation-of-suitability process. Needless to say, any security officer carrying a firearm should be in possession of the necessary permits in accordance with all applicable laws.

"The second step, slightly less important than suitability, is training.

"Good training is the key to safe and effective equipment usage. Since firearms are a piece of security equipment, it logically follows that good training is also the key to their safe and effective utilization. Once the decision is made to arm a suitable security officer, he or she must be thoroughly trained.

"Any program contemplated must be carefully planned. At the minimum, it should begin with a classroom session in which the students will be introduced to the weapon; made completely familiar with its operation (placing particular emphasis on safety); and most importantly, thoroughly indoctrinated in the legal and moral aspects of their use of firearms in the performance of their duties. Equal emphasis in this area should be placed on when and when not to use deadly force. The underlying theme, application of deadly force, is that the use of a firearm would only be justified to protect a life that is in immediate danger and after all lesser means have failed.

"Training must be demonstrative, i.e., the individuals must not merely familiarize themselves with their weapon(s); they must satisfactorily demonstrate competence by achieving minimum qualifying scores on classroom and practical examinations. The practical examination should be a nationally recognized course of fire which is conducted under the supervision of a certified police or security firearms instructor.

"For economic reasons, the use of reloaded ammunition for practice is acceptable; however, for a realistic and accurate evaluation of the individuals' abilities, the qualification course should be fired using the firearms and type of ammunition that will actually be carried on duty.

"Following the satisfactory demonstration of classroom knowledge and practical capability, complete documentation must be maintained. Requalification on at least an annual basis (again with complete documentation) should be a minimum requirement. These training records should be maintained for at least one year following the individuals' termination of employment.

"In conclusion then, it must be remembered that firearms are not a panacea for the protection of assets. They are but one aspect of a security program and, as such, require integration into the overall security program. The decision to arm security personnel must be carefully evaluated with respect to the nature and/or value of the commodity being protected and based on site-specific considerations. If personnel are armed, they must be thoroughly screened and trained!"[3]

The primary purpose of firearms training is to prepare the individual for combat shooting. Anybody charged with the responsibility of carrying a weapon for the protection of life and property must be able to shoot accurately and quickly. He must also have complete confidence in his ability to quickly and accurately assess each situation and, when the use of his sidearm is clearly indicated, take the necessary action to neutralize the threat. Part of the necessary training of each armed officer must involve a thorough understanding of the weapon's inner workings so that early signs of malfunctions may be detected. Cleaning and authorized preventive maintenance procedures must also be a part of firearms training.

It is generally accepted that reasonable force may be used to make an authorized arrest (when arrest powers have been conferred) or for protection of self or another innocent person from attack and injury. Reasonable force is interpreted to mean force that an ordinary, prudent, and intelligent person, with the same knowledge of the situation as the officer possesses, would deem necessary. Consequently, in subduing a disorderly person, only that amount of force necessary to bring the person under control may be used.

The decision to resort to deadly force is the most momentous one any person can make. Deadly force is defined as that degree of force likely to cause death or serious bodily harm. It includes discharging a firearm in the direction of a person, even though there is no intent to kill. Thus it is restricted to self-defense or the defense of another innocent person, when the danger of death or serious bodily harm is imminent. Deadly force must never be used on mere suspicion that a crime, no matter how serious, was committed or that the person being pursued was the perpetrator. When possible, the use of deadly force should be preceded by a clear verbal warning to the individual or group that use of such force is imminent.

A pistol should be kept holstered at all times except to fire in the line of duty, to transfer it to another authorized individual, or to use it during supervised training. It should never be used to threaten, either by removal from the holster or by making a movement toward the holster to create the impression that it will be used.

Warning shots should never be fired for any purpose. They endanger the lives of bystanders and in addition, may prompt a suspect to return the fire on the assumption that he is a target. Another reason for not firing warning shots is that it wastes a limited supply of ammunition that may be needed later.

Because a firearm is a deadly weapon, the following rules must be followed at all times in its handling:

1. Never handle, point or look over the sights of any firearm handed to you without first opening it to make sure it is not loaded. In doing so, check the gun twice—the first time to see if it is unloaded and the second time to see if you were right the first time. If anyone is near, let him see that the gun is unloaded.
2. Never take a revolver out of your holster until you are at the firing line or until you believe the situation has escalated to the point where it will be needed for the preservation of life.
3. On the firing range, never load or cock a firearm unless you are at the firing line, facing the target, and have received the command to do so.
4. While loading the weapon, the muzzle must always be pointing down range. Once loaded, it shall be immediately returned to its holster.
5. Never load a revolver at the beginning of a firing session without checking the barrel for an obstruction. This is accomplished with the cylinder open and empty.
6. Never dry-fire or dry-snap a revolver while waiting your turn behind the firing line.
7. Never turn around on the firing line without having the cylinder open and laying the revolver on the table or returning it to the holster with the hammer down.
8. Never give a revolver to anyone or take a revolver from anyone unless the cylinder has been opened and left open.
9. Never talk while on the firing line except to an instructor.
10. Never go forward or leave your position on the firing line until given the command to do so by the range officer.
11. Never stand at the firing line without aligning yourself evenly with the other shooters.
12. Never fire obsolete cartridges. In case of defective cartridges, the report will not be normal. At such time, immediately stop firing, keep the

muzzle of the weapon pointing down range, and raise your free hand over your head to indicate that you are experiencing a problem and that the attention of an instructor is required.

13. Never carry a revolver cocked.
14. Never leave a loaded weapon unattended or lying about where someone may pick it up.
15. Never draw a revolver from a holster with a finger on the trigger.
16. Never fire a gun in training without wearing some form of hearing protection.
17. Above all else, remember that you must never point a gun at any person unless you are willing to kill that person.

In order to provide all personnel with realistic skills in the use of the service revolver, training should highlight all aspects of combat-style shooting. This involves firing double action (and in some instances, single action), in a variety of positions—crouching, sitting, kneeling, prone, and from behind a barricade, all at various distances. Holding the weapon in both hands is also advocated. Some features of combat shooting are outlined below.

1. Silhouette target—this target presents the life-size silhouette of an adversary, hips to head, facing directly toward the shooter. Various zones on the target have certain values for each hit. Scores are usually expressed as a percentage of the total value.
2. Breath control—any breathing during the actual firing of a round will cause erratic dispersal of the hits. In single action, the shooter should take a deep breath, let out a little, and then hold his breath while he gets off the round. In double-action shooting this same technique is possible; however, it may be more practical for the shooter to hold his breath during a string of shots rather than before each one.
3. Grip (Figure 9–2)—the shooter should grip the revolver firmly with the shooting hand so that the barrel is directly in line with his forearm. In single- and double-action fire, the thumb points downward and the entire hand provides a powerful, convulsive grip on the butt of the gun. Both of these positions are reinforced with the other hand.
4. Double-action fire—the shooter draws the trigger of the revolver all the way to the rear without first cocking the hammer. This involves a much longer trigger stroke than single-action fire. Firing double action also requires changes in grip, trigger finger position, and trigger squeeze.
   a. Grip—as mentioned previously, the grip should be firm with the thumb downward and a strong hold with all fingers. Use of the other hand for extra support is recommended.
   b. Trigger finger position (see Figure 9–2)—instead of pulling with the pad of the first digit, the shooter should grasp the trigger with the crook between the first and second pads of his trigger finger.
   c. Trigger squeeze—the modern double-action revolver has more than

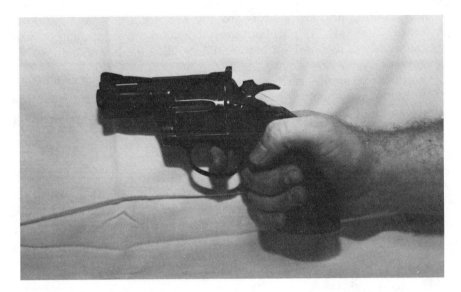

Figure 9-2   Revolver grip. (S. Messemer.)

one stage in its double-action trigger pull. The first stage, constituting about three-quarters of the pull, revolves the cylinder completely to the next round. The shooter can sometimes hear a click when this first stage is reached. At this point, the shooter stops and applies a slow squeeze to the remaining trigger pull. For advanced shooters, this technique is equally as accurate as single-action fire. Under combat conditions at short distances, the shooter should still use a smooth rearward double-action squeeze, but he need not hesitate at the second stage of the trigger pull. For advanced shooters using the two-handed grip, this method is surprisingly accurate.

5. Kneeling position—the kneeling position is assumed from a relaxed, erect, standing position. The foot under the nonshooting hand is moved forward as if to take a step. The shooter then sits on the other heel. The nonshooting hand supports the shooting hand and its elbow is braced on the extended knee.

6. Sitting position—this position is assumed by squatting, dropping the nonshooting hand back for support, and continuing into the fully seated position. The knees are pulled up, the feet spread about a foot apart. The gun is held in the shooting hand, which is supported by the nonshooting hand. Both arms are at full extension and supported by the knees.

7. Prone position—the prone position is assumed by dropping to both knees and facing the target. The upper body then inclines forward; the nonshooting hand and arm support the body on the ground and lower it, under control, to the prone position. As the body inclines forward,

the shooting arm swings forward and keeps the gun pointing down range. The body lies flat, both arms extended toward the target, with the nonshooting hand supporting the shooting hand, and both feet together.

8.   Barricade position—barricade shooting is done from each side of a barricade. When shooting from the right side, the right hand should be used to hold and fire the weapon, with the right eye used for sighting. From the left side, the left hand and eye should be used. In preparation for right-sided shooting, the left foot is advanced to the barricade with the right foot directly behind and spread for balance. Having the opposite foot forward enables the shooter to have maximum protection with good balance. The left hand is then placed against the barricade at eye level, with the fingers up, the palm flat, and the thumb extended to the right to furnish support to the right wrist. For left-sided shooting, the positions are reversed. The revolver must never be rested directly against the barricade, but rather extended past it with the shooting-hand wrist braced by the nonshooting, which in turn is braced against the barricade.

9.   Practical techniques

    a.   Instinctive action—most persons when they are in close combat immediately resort to double-action shooting. This is apparently an instinctive self-defense mechanism that facilitates getting shots off at an adversary as quickly as possible. Double-action shooting should be practiced until the person is able to shoot in this manner with great accuracy.

    b.   Defensive positions

        (1)   Cover—when confronted with a combat situation, an officer should immediately seek cover in order to present as little of his person as possible as a target for the adversary to hit.

        (2)   Crouch—when under fire in close combat (up to seven yards) where cover is not available, the officer should go into a pronounced crouch position and step to his left at the same time he is bringing his gun into position for double-action hip-level shooting.

        (3)   Other positions—at 15 yards or further, a shooter's primary vision switches to his sights. He should drop into a kneeling position and support his shooting hand with his nonshooting hand for better accuracy. The crouch and kneeling positions allow excellent maneuverability. If the situation is such that he feels a gun battle with an adversary might be prolonged and the situation and terrain provide no cover, he should go into prone position, as this gives the adversary a minimum of target to hit, provided the distance is greater than 25 yards.

        (4)   Cross-fire positions—a security officer should, if at all possible, try to station himself in such a position that if any firing of the

weapon is necessary, he will not be caught in the cross-fire of other security officers and the adversary. This is particularly important where two or more security personnel are together.

(5) Counting rounds—during the stress and strain induced by combat, many things are done instinctively; whenever possible, an officer should try to count the number of rounds he fires so that he will be aware of how many he has left.

(6) Firing while running—an officer should not fire his weapon while running. He should stop running, assume whatever position he feels the situation dictates, fire the shot or shots, and then if necessary, continue his pursuit.

10. Firearms qualifications

a. All security force personnel must qualify in the use of the service revolver. Requalification should be at least once a year. The qualification standard for the course which is described below, is 70 percent (210 points out of a possible 300) (Table 9–1). Achievement in excess of the minimum should be recognized as follows:

Marksman—225 to 255 points

Sharpshooter—256 to 280 points

Expert—281 to 300 points

b. Qualification record—a record of officer's qualification in the use of the service revolver should be placed in his official personnel file and a listing of those persons qualified should be maintained in the security office.

Table 9-1 Firearms Qualifications Standards

Stage	Distance (yds)	Position	Number of Rounds	Stage Time (sec)
A	7	Crouch (hip level)	12 (DA)	25
B	15	Crouch (point shoulder)	12 (DA)	30
C	25	Barricade		60 (total)
		(right hand, kneeling)	6 (DA)	
		(right hand, standing)	6 (DA)	
		(left hand, standing)	6 (DA)	
D	50	Barricade		150 (total)
		(prone)	6 (SA)	
		(right hand, standing)	6 (SA)	
		(left hand, standing)	6 (SA)	

DA = double action; SA = single action.

11. Handgun combat shooting
    a. If an officer is called on to use his revolver in self-defense or in defense of an innocent person, he will generally shoot double action. Therefore practice in this type of shooting should be emphasized.
    b. A certain degree of accuracy must be sacrificed for speed in double-action shooting, but with proper training and practice a high degree of proficiency up to approximately 35 yards can be developed.

12. Double-action shooting
    a. Double-action shooting is sometimes referred to as snap shooting. The revolver is cocked and fired in one smooth fast continuous motion of the trigger finger.
    b. Getting a firm grip on the gun as soon as possible is important. Juggling the gun after it leaves the holster is not only unsafe, it results in loss of valuable time.
    c. The grip should be tight with the thumb down, since the trigger pull is approximately three times what it is in single-action shooting.
    d. The wrist and forearm are locked and nothing should move except the trigger finger.
    e. At distances less than 15 yards, the shooter should concentrate his vision on the area of the target he expects to hit.
    f. At distances greater than 15 yards, the shooter concentrates on the target, but picks up his revolver sights in his secondary vision.
    g. For safety in practice, the shooter should keep his finger off the trigger until the weapon is on the target.
    h. It is emphasized that form and accuracy should be developed first; speed comes with practice.

13. Types of double-action shooting
    a. Hip-level shooting
        (1) The shooter on the line assumes a comfortable normal stance.
        (2) On the command to fire, the shooter takes a step with the off-side foot about six inches to the side and six inches forward, and brings his body into somewhat of a crouched position. This position enables him to:
            (a) Move more easily
            (b) Make himself a smaller target
            (c) Withstand a shot from an opponent with less likelihood of falling
        (3) The gun should be drawn forward, dragging the top of the barrel and the front sight along the inside front of the holster.
        (4) With tension on the wrist, the barrel of the revolver will automatically snap up when it clears the holster, bringing the gun out toward and on a line with the target.
        (5) The shooter should be certain he gets a solid grip on the gun with the thumb down before he draws the weapon. Otherwise he will have to shift the gun in his hand, losing valuable time.

(6) The gun should be extended out in front of the shooter to the point where, while fixing his eyes on the target, he can see the gun in his secondary vision.

(7) The elbow should be swung in front of the body and the wrist locked so that the barrell of the gun is an extension of the forearm.

(8) The only motion that should occur while actually firing from hip level is the trigger finger stroking the trigger.

b. Point-shoulder shooting

(1) More accurate results can be obtained at distances further than 15 yards by firing from shoulder level rather than hip level.

(2) It is important that the shooter not change his draw or stance when firing from the shoulder. The draw is the same smooth motion that is used in firing from the hip, but the shooter swings the weapon up to shoulder level.

(3) The shooter places his cheek against his gun-arm shoulder, which will permit him to look straight down his arm across the sights. The time used in bringing the gun to shoulder level will be justified by the increased accuracy at longer distances.

(4) The trigger pull must be a smooth pull straight back so as not to move the shooter's gun out of line. It should not be too slow, nor should it be a quick snap of the trigger.

(5) The shooter should be in a crouch and the arm and shoulder should be locked. The gun must be gripped very tightly with the thumb down on the butt of the weapon.

(6) The shooter should attempt to draw the weapon and assume the point-shoulder position in one motion. Time is lost if not done in this manner.

14. Reloading

a. To reload while on the firing line, the shooter should:

(1) Not move his feet, but pivot at the hips and keep his revolver pointing down range

(2) Lay the revolver in the nonshooting hand while operating the cylinder latch.

(3) Swing the cylinder out with the fingers of the nonshooting hand; the thumb of the nonshooting hand actuates the ejector rod to eject the empty shell casings onto the ground.

(4) Reach into the speed-loader case with the shooting hand at the same time step 3 is taking place, and pick up a speed loader (Figure 9–3) containing six live rounds, or otherwise secure six live rounds.

(5) The speed-loader rounds are aligned with the empty cylinder chambers with the shooting hand as the thumb and middle finger of the nonshooting hand rotate the cylinder. If loading live rounds individually, each round should be inserted at the same cylinder position as it is rotated.

Figure 9-3   Speed loaders. (S. Messemer.)

    b.   When all chambers are aligned with a live round, the speed-loader unlatching mechanism is activated, dropping a live round into each empty chamber; the thumb of the nonshooting hand snaps the cylinder closed. **Do not attempt to snap the cylinder closed with the shooting hand, as damage to the revolver may result.**

    c.   The shooting hand then grips the revolver butt, aligns it with the target, and is supported by the nonshooting hand, and firing is resumed. With a reasonable amount of practice, 12 effective rounds may be fired in 25 seconds or less at 7 yards.

TESTING AND DOCUMENTATION

All training should be documented, and personnel should be tested in each area. Each individual should successfully pass, with at least a 70 percent grade, all examinations prior to completion of each phase of the training program before being allowed to proceed to subsequent phases.

A complete training file for each individual should be set up and maintained, and should include all tests and examination results, as well as firearms qualification records. Training records should be reviewed and updated periodically and should be retained while the individual is employed and for a period of at least two years after employment has terminated.

At least every 12 months, all personnel should be required to successfully complete an annual requalification examination designed to test proficiency with respect to assigned duties. Refresher courses should be given in those areas of demonstrated weakness. The results of requalification testing and training should be retained.

After initial firearms training and qualification, semiannual requalification should be required for each armed security officer. The results, again, should be retained as specified.

Additionally, ongoing training in the form of drills, exercises, scenarios, and penetration tests should be conducted and appropriately documented.

APPEARANCE AND EQUIPMENT

Security officers should always be readily identifiable as such regardless of the environment in which they operate. Most officers are outfitted with a uniform, although some wear coordinated blazers and slacks. In any case, they should always project a professional appearance in dress, attitude, and actions. As was mentioned earlier, the psychology of maximum security is as important as hardware. This fact should not be lost on the officers themselves, supervision, or management.

Just as any craftsman must carry the tools of his trade, so too must the security officer be appropriately equipped. Two basic items, so obvious that they may be overlooked, are a notebook and pen or pencil, which should be the first tools given a maximum-security officer.

He should be equipped with a portable radio and a suitable carrying case. It should be capable of transmitting and receiving on all frequencies in use by the security organization. Under no circumstances should an officer be allowed to carry his radio by hand or in a pocket. Most damage to portable radios is the result of careless handling. This is one area where costs can be kept down with simple emphasis that radios are to be transported in their cases.

Officers should also carry a chemical incapacitating agent. Again, whatever device is used, it should be carried in an appropriate case.

Depending on location and/or circumstances, it may be desirable to issue each officer a baton. As with this and other issued equipment, adequate training must be provided and in some jurisdictions, permits obtained to carry and use it. A flashlight is a key piece of equipment and it should be carried by the security officer all of the time. Some companies offer C-cell flashlights that can also be used as batons.

Each security officer should carry a pair of handcuffs and a key for them. Handcuffs should be kept in an appropriate carrying case.

A set of keys (or key cards) required for the performance of his duties should be issued to each officer. For documentation of required check-stops, a watchman's recording clock (such as those offered by Detex Corporation) could be issued. There are some new and interesting variants of the watchman's clock now on the market that use electronics and radio signals to record mandatory patrols and tours.

Each security officer in a maximum-security environment should be equipped with a personal duress alarm of some sort. At the very least, it

Date: _____

FIREARMS TRANSFER/RECEIPT

Date	Weapon Description (make/model)	Serial number	Time out	Weapon issue receipt signature	Time in	Weapon return receipt signature

Directions: Weapon to be signed for by each officer—receipt upon return acknowledged by receiving supervisor's signature. Start new form daily—previous day form turned in to duty supervisor at end of second shift and becomes permanent record.

Figure 9-4   Firearms transfer receipt.

should have the capability of sending a distress signal when manually activated. Depending on circumstances, it may be desirable to equip each officer with a bullet-resistant garmet. There are several high-quality bullet-resistant vests on the market, as well as sports jackets, raincoats, and windbreakers.

Finally, if personnel are armed, they should be equipped with a sidearm. While the issue is controversial, the best all-around choice for a security sidearm is a revolver, given the degree of firearms expertise possessed by the average security officer. Whatever the choice, sidearm ammunition should be at least .38 special-caliber and standard throughout the security organization so as to facilitate the exchange of ammunition if and when necessary. Armed officers should also carry at least 18 rounds of ammunition in addition to those contained in the sidearm. Extra ammunition can be carried in speed loaders or other devices designed to expedite reloading. Whatever the choice of firearms and ammunition, manufacturer's instructions for safe handling and use should always be explicitly followed.

As part of an overall system of equipment accountability, a receipt of some sort should always be obtained from each officer for each item of issued equipment.

Because of the liability potential inherent in their misuse, firearms should never be allowed off site when the officer to whom they are issued is not on duty. An accounting system should be established that requires each officer to sign for his weapon when coming on duty and ensures its return prior to site departure at shifts end (Figure 9–4).

It is recommended that a weapons count be conducted at the beginning of each security shift and the results entered onto shift records. A thorough inventory by serial number should be conducted weekly, with a report submitted to the security director.

MAINTAINING MORALE AND COMBATTING BOREDOM

One of the most difficult tasks in the field of private security is maintaining the morale of the security organization. This is somewhat easier in a maximum-security setting due to the fact that the commodity being protected is definitely at risk. This can be reaffirmed by the nature and extent of initial and subsequent training. Morale can be maintained by constant training, drills, and exercises. This is most important, as low morale gives rise to complacency, which can be fatal.

A series of training scenarios based on actual potential threats should be prepared and presented to on-duty security personnel during periods of decreased activity. A typical training drill could include a bomb threat, a breach of perimeter security, or theft of a product. Whenever such drills are conducted, all personnel should be advised that a practical training exercise is under way so as to preclude safety lapses. Each training activity should be carefully controlled by the on-duty security supervisor. On its conclusion, a critique should be made and the results documented and retained in the appropriate training files.

Frequent checks should be made by the supervisor of all officers so as to combat the boredom inherent in the job. Whenever anything of significance is discovered by a security officer, he should receive appropriate recognition. Organizing competition between shifts is another morale-boosting technique that can be successful. An annual shift competition consisting of proficiency demonstrations can be held, with the winning shift receiving appropriate recognition. Special projects can be assigned to officers as a means of combatting boredom, improving efficiency, and motivating performance.

It is interesting that the quality of the air breathed while on duty may contribute to the mental alertness and motivation of security personnel. "Normally air contains about the same number of positively charged ions (posions) and negatively charged ones (negions), roughly one to two thousand of each per cubic centimeter. When the total ion concentration (ion level) becomes unnaturally low, or when the ratio of posions to negions becomes seriously unbalanced, the human physiological and metabolic processes are affected."[4] The solution is to provide direct fresh-air ventilation or use a negative-ion generator.[5] This should be a real consideration when faced with the problem of combatting boredom.

Appendix 9–A

ASSESSMENT TECHNIQUES AT A NUCLEAR FACILITY

I. Title: Reporting direct armed attack
II. Objectives
   A. To enable each member of the security force to perform the duties required of an armed officer or unarmed watchman observing an imminent or in-progress direct armed attack on site.
   B. Each officer or watchman will be able to demonstrate through verbal or written exam or by actual physical performance, the proper manner of collecting and relaying necessary information on the attack force.
   C. Each officer or watchman will be familiar with the procedures for notifying proper on-site personnel of the observed imminent or in-progress attack.
III. List of references and materials
   A. 10CFR73.55(c)(4)
   B. NUREG-0674, item 3.5.1
   C. 10CFR73.1(a)
IV. Instruction outline
   Note: Officers shall be made to understand that any point of which they are unsure or which they want clarified should be brought to the instructor's attention immediately rather than waiting until the class is over.
   A. The Nuclear Regulatory Commission requires that the physical protection system at fixed nuclear sites contain safeguards systems to protect against acts of radiological sabotage and to prevent the theft of special nuclear material. It goes on to define radiological sabotage, as "(i) A determined violent external assault, attack by stealth, or deceptive actions, of several persons with the following attributes, assistance and equipment:
      "1. Well-trained (including military training and skills) and dedicated individuals
      "2. inside assistance which may include a knowledgable individual who attempts to participate in a passive role (e.g., facilitate entrance and exit, disable alarms)

"3.   suitable weapons, up to and including hand-held automatic weapons, equipped with silencers and having effective long range accuracy

"4.   hand-carried equipment, including incapacitating agents and explosives for use as tools of entry or for otherwise destroying reactor, facility, transporter, or container integrity or features of the safeguards system, and (ii) an internal threat of an insider, including any employee (in any position)."[6]

It goes on to define the "Theft or diversion of formula quantities of strategic special nuclear materials . . . as (i) A determined, violent, external assault, attack by stealth, or deceptive actions, by a small group with the following attributes, assistance and equipment:

"1.   Well-trained (including military training and skills) and dedicated individuals

"2.   Inside assistance which may include a knowledgable individual who attempts to participate in a passive role (e.g., provide information), an active role (e.g., facilitate entrance and exit, disable alarms and communications, participate in violent attack), or both.

"3.   Suitable weapons, up to and including hand-held automatic weapons, equipped with silencers and having effective long range accuracy

"4.   hand-carried equipment, including incapacitating agents and explosives for use as tools of entry or for otherwise destroying reactor, facility, transporter or container integrity or features of the safeguards systems and

"5.   the ability to operate as two or more teams . . ."[7]

B.   In its initial stages, an armed attack may be overt or covert. Obviously, an overt attack will be more easily detected, although it must be recognized as a possible diversion or feint, especially when it appears no real effort is being made by the attackers to reach a vital or sensitive area, but that their purpose seems to be to create a great deal of sound and fury to engage the greatest number of defenders. A covert attack will be more difficult to detect because the attacking force will usually be a small group of highly trained and very well disciplined personnel who will take great pains to reach their objective without setting off any alarms and by escaping the attention of patrolling guard force personnel, if possible.

C.   All security personnel should be alert for signs that could indicate a direct armed attack is imminent or in progress. Signs of possible imminent attack would include:

1.   One or more vehicles capable of hiding several persons (vans, panel trucks, closed-body delivery trucks, etc.) parked within the isolation zone outside the protected area fence (usually in an area remote from other activities)

2. Personnel (with no apparent reason for their presence) gathering outside the perimeter fence (usually in a remote area)
3. Personnel setting up fence-breaching apparatus, which could include:
   a. Driving a tall vehicle up to the fence for use as a platform from which attackers could leap over the fence into the protected area
   b. Setting up scaling ladders, such as a conventional single ladder leaned against the fence, a production-model large step ladder that would form a stairway up one side of the fence and down the other, or a step ladder made by joining the two halves of a sliding 20-foot ladder. In areas of construction, a seemingly innocent act such as leaving a ladder leaning against the inside of the fence or a piece of equipment parked within the isolation zone inside the fence could be an act of collusion that would enable the adversary force more easily or quickly to gain access
   c. Throwing a large rug or a runner over the fence so that personnel are not hampered by the barbed-wire topping
   d. Placing S-shaped hooks of heavy steel rod into the chain link fence fabric in an ascending line. These are used as steps in scaling the fence.
   e. Carrying large bolt cutters or a portable pack-mounted acetylene cutting torch
   f. The discovery of suspected explosive charges affixed to any section of the fence or a gate in this fence
   g. Discovery of attempted or successful defeat of gate locks
4. Confirmation that large amounts of firearms are present in any spontaneous gathering of protesters. (The protest could be a planned diversion, although its use would be of limited value since local law enforcement assistance is usually available within minutes of any reported such gathering.)
5. Sudden and unexplainable loss of all off-site communications capabilities

D. While a judgment decision is required by the initial observing armed officer or watchman on whether the activity he is seeing could be the initial stages of a possible imminent attack, and observed direct armed attack requires no value decision, only immediate and instinctive action. Signs of direct armed attack in progress include:
   1. Physical destruction of a portion of the fence by an explosive device or through use of tools, including vehicles
   2. Invasion of the controlled entry points by armed personnel who attempt to gain entry through one of these points
   3. Weapons fire

4. The taking of hostages at gunpoint
5. Detection or observation by a member of the security force of one or more unauthorized armed personnel inside the area who are engaged in an act inimical to site operation or the health and safety of personnel

E. When a watchman observes any of the above, he shall:
1. Immediately take cover (if not already in a position that offers cover and concealment)
2. Contact the central alarm station without delay and alert that station to the developing incident
3. Without tying up the radio communications network with unnecessary talk (a natural tendency of personnel who suddenly find themselves in a situation in which the body produces an overabundance of adrenalin), keep the central alarm station informed of the following:
   a. Whether or not penetration has taken place, or it is imminent
   b. Location of the incident
   c. Number of personnel in the armed attack force and a description of the uniforms or clothing worn (as accurate a count as possible without delaying the initial report. If restricted visibility does not allow this, an estimate will do until the correct figure is obtained).
   d. A description and count of the weapons and equipment being carried by the attack force and any supporting personnel who may be providing covering fire or protecting their rear, for example, the following:
      1 Shoulder-fired small arms
         (a) Rifles: automatic, sporting-type, equipped with telescopic sights
         (b) Shotguns: pump action, extended magazine tubes, sawed-off
      2. Handguns
         (a) Revolver
         (b) Automatic
      3. Other weapons
         (a) Knives/bayonets
         (b) Heavy machine guns
         (c) Hand grenades
         (d) Flame throwers
         (e) Shoulder-fired grenade launcher
         (f) Shoulder-fired rockets
      4. Other equipment
         (a) Gas masks
         (b) Boxes, cans, knapsacks

    (c)   Reels of wire

    (d)   Coils of rope with grapnel hooks

    (e)   Communications equipment

    (f)   Binoculars

    (g)   Bullet-proof or military "flak" vests

F.   The watchman shall maintain his position of cover and concealment and continue reporting his observations only until he feels that his position is no longer safe. Under no conditions should a watchman expose himself unnecessarily to an armed attack force.

G. When he can safely to so, this watchman shall leave his position of cover and concealment to meet and direct armed response personnel to the scene of the attack.

H. The duties of an armed officer who observes an imminent attack by an armed force, or one that is already in progress shall be exactly the same as those required of a watchman under the same conditions, with the added responsibility that the officer shall interpose himself between the attackers and any vital equipment or area and do whatever may be required to deny them access to this vital equipment or area.

NOTES

1. *The Code of Federal Regulations* (Washington, D.C.:, 1981), title 10, appendix B, pp. 622–624.

2. Nuclear Regulatory Commission, *Security Personnel Training and Qualification Criteria* (Washington, D.C.: The Commission, 1980), pp. 16–22.

3. Richard J. Gigliotti and Ronald C. Jason, "Should Security Personnel Be Armed?" *Assets Protection* (March-April 1982): 11–13.

4. Charles Wallach, "Posions and Negions Battle for Your Mind," *Security Management*: 50. © 1979. Copyright by the American Society for Industrial Security, 1655 N. Fort Drive, Suite 1200, Arlington, VA 22209. Reprinted with permission from the (March 1979) issue of *Security Management* magazine.

5. Ibid., p. 51

6. *Code of Federal Regulations*, title 10, part 73.1(a).

7. Ibid.

CHAPTER 10

The Response Force

In any maximum-security environment, the people providing security are organized into definitive levels from management to supervision to security force. Each level is further defined by duties and responsibilities. One of the tasks assigned to the security organization is response to contingencies. Contingency, in this context, is defined as any nonroutine occurrence.

Nonroutine occurrences can include a simple event such as an unscheduled alarm, or one of considerable magnitude such as a natural disaster affecting both the facility and surrounding community. A contingency can also be a set of suspicious circumstances.

Contingencies must always generate a response. Depending on circumstances, this can be a check to see that nothing is amiss. In extreme circumstances, the response may be to neutralize a threat to the facility by intercepting and apprehending an adversary. A response to a localized or general disaster may be to rescue survivors and provide medical attention.

In most security organizations, the response function is combined with other duties and responsibilities. In some maximum-security environments, it reserved for, and is the sole function of, selected individuals. Generally, however, the duties of patrolling and response are combined. Response to contingencies should always take precedence over other duties. Caution must be exercised, however, so that security personnel do not succumb to a diversion created to elicit a response for the purpose of neutralizing them.

Those individuals responding to contingencies, whether as a dedicated force or as a part of larger duties and responsibilities, bear a large share of the burden of providing effective security. This is not meant to take away the significant contributions made by other members of the security organization. Response officers, however, must possess characteristics that separate them from their co-workers.

QUALIFICATIONS OF THE RESPONSE FORCE

In addition to meeting qualifications suggested for security officers described in the preceding chapter, individuals assigned the responsibility of response to contingencies must demonstrate certain strengths. Chief among these is sound judgment. As the first responder to a contingency, the officer must be able to exercise good judgment with little or no supervision. As anyone who has spent any time in security or law enforcement knows, most contingency situations are unique; successful resolution, therefore, is a product of good judgment rather than textbook suggestions. Response officers must be motivated and possess self-confidence as well as pride in their accomplishments. They should be dependable and reliable. In addition, they must have the ability to absorb, retain, and effect the extensive training required for the assignment.

Finally, those individuals charged with contingency response must have the ability to remain cool under pressure and the ability to avoid the common pitfall, complacency.

SCREENING

When it comes time to select individuals for patrol and response assignments, the qualities previously mentioned should become part of the selection criteria. Additionally, past experience should be evaluated and taken into consideration, as should past security, law enforcement, and/or military exposure. They should be physically fit and free from any condition that could impede their response or be aggravated by the stress of a contingency situation.

The individual's performance as a security officer must be considered, as should his attitude and commitment to the organization. In some ways the position of response officer can be considered an elevation from that of basic security officer. It may be in the best interests of the security organization to cultivate this image so as to build esprit de corps and demonstrate a career pattern within the organization.

While the requirements as outlined may appear to ask too much in return for the traditionally low rewards offered by a security career, the basic assumption is that there will be officers willing to assume these responsibilities regardless of the rewards.

TRAINING COURSES

Once suitable individuals are selected for a response assignment, yet another phase of training must be accomplished. As a preliminary, the organization and mission of the response force should be explained. Depending on the facility and its requirements, the response force may be a separate entity from the regular operating security force or the two may be integrated. An alternative is to use response force personnel as security officers until a contingency arises, at which time a separate security response team is gathered and assigned to deal with it. Whatever the organization, it must be explained to all personnel. The mission of the response force should also be explained to and accepted by its officers. Simply put, this could be as follows: to respond to and take control of any contingency that poses a risk of injury to facility personnel, visitors, or the general public, or threatens the security of the facility or property being safeguarded, until relieved by proper authority.

This mission can best be fulfilled by highly trained officers. The training that is reserved for response officers should include the following subjects:

1. Adversary groups (6 hrs)—explanation of adversary group operations, motivation, objectives and tactics
2. Sabotage devices, equipment, and disguised weapons (4 hrs)—recognition of sabotage-related devices, equipment, and disguised weapons that might be used against the facility and its personnel
3. Tactical alarm response (2 hrs)—tactical response to, and assessment of, alarm annunciations and other indications of intrusion into and within the protected facility
4. Vulnerability of assets to theft (1 hr)—familiarization with the commodity being protected; vulnerability to, and consequences of, theft of assets or sabotage
5. Use of specialized equipment (2 hrs)—normal and contingency use of specialized protective equipment, including protective masks, night vision aids, and surveillance devices
6. Response force procedures (4 hrs)—procedures and plans governing force activation, operation, and engagement. A sample lession outline, "Response to Bomb Threats," can be found in Appendix 10–A.)
7. Transportation systems (3 hrs)—transportation security organization and operation, types of transport vehicles, other modes of transport, control of area around transports, and normal and contingency site-specific operations for shipment transfers (if applicable)
8. Coordination with local law enforcement authorities (1 hr)—security coordination and cooperation with local law enforcement authorities (LLEA) and current agreements between security and LLEA
9. Alert procedures (1 hr)—explanation of site-specific security and response force alert procedures
10. Response force tactics (8 hrs)—deployment, tactical movements, withdrawal, and disengagement, and use of support fire; cover and concealment; grounds and building searches
11. Civil disturbances (2 hrs)—site-specific response to civil disturbances, e.g., strikes, demonstrations, etc.
12. Theft and sabotage (4 hrs)—response to confirmed theft or attempted theft of assets or sabotage to the protected facility
13. Hostage incidents (4 hrs)—security response
14. Other than security incidents (4 hrs)—security response to emergency situations, other than security incidents such as fires, natural disasters, and safety hazards

If applicable, the following additional subjects should be offered:

1.   Shipment documentation and verification (1 hr)—procedures for verification of shipment contents, documentation, locks, and seals
2.   Shipment delivery and pickup (1 hr)—procedures for same
3.   Isolation of shipment vehicles (1 hr)—techniques and procedures during an on-site contingency situation

Depending on the proximity of medical assistance, the following course may be given:

4.   Advanced first aid and cardiopulmonary resuscitation (24 hrs)—a recognized, advanced first-aid and CPR course

If the security organization has been granted special police powers by an authorized agency or jurisdiction, the following additional training should be considered:

5.   Rights and responsibilities of officers with special police powers (1 hr)—an explanation of the powers vested in special police officers by the law enforcement agency granting such authority, with a clear presentation delineating the jurisdictional boundaries of such authority and its performance limits

Because of the very real possibility that the contingency response force would bear the brunt of any violent action directed against the facility and its personnel, the force should be trained and employed as a team. Only a close-knit organization of such specialists can realistically be expected to perform as required with a better-than-average chance of success and officer survival. As previously indicated, the officers selected for the contingency response force must be the cream of the crop, not just physically, but mentally. It does not help the site, the contingency response force, or the officer involved to have someone with a "hero complex" go charging into a situation that may lead to the serious injury or death of another person or aggravate a static or otherwise controlled situation. The members of the team must be capable of functioning under extreme discipline, yet when an opportunity exists, have the intelligence, initiative, and training to recognize the opportunity and take swift and decisive action to exploit it.

Because of the critical responsibilities placed on these individuals, continual monitoring must be maintained by their supervisors. Any character or behavioral shift or change must be investigated immediately to ensure that the team officers remain physically, mentally, and emotionally qualified for continuation in the assignment.

Courses in Use of Firearms

Each member of the contingency response force must be fully trained in the use of all items of equipment issued to support his role. Firearms are of necessity integral to the contingency response force's equipment. Security management is responsible to ensure that every individual who carries a firearm is suited to do so and trained in the use of the weapon or weapons carried. The following are examples of advanced firearms training courses that would be given in addition to those outlined in the previous chapter, and reflect the greater degree of training necessary for response officers.

Revolvers

To be truly practical, the course must place emphasis not only on accuracy, but on speedy accuracy (Table 10-1). In a life-or-death adversary confrontation the officer will usually be at a disadvantage, as his role is primarily defensive. This disadvantage can be minimized or possibly negated by his quick and accurate fire. Practice must therefore be done on a steady basis. A weekly session at the range for every officer is not considered excessive. As he achieves increasing proficiency, his self-confidence will also increase, with a corresponding improvement in his attitude toward his role.

Once a response force member has progressed to a reasonable level of expertise in this area, he should be subjected to a firearms stress course. A stress course introduces outside stimuli that are not present during routine range qualification. These stimuli tend to reproduce the external influences present in a real-life situation so that the officer can recognize them and adjust his performance to minimize their effects. The officer should run a distance of 100 yards or do strenuous physical exercises (25 sit-ups, 40 jumping jacks, etc.) immediately before going into the firing portion of the stress course. The strenuous activity will simulate having to run to the contingency action site, and his arrival with elevated respiration rate and blood pressure and with adrenalin being introduced into his system. At the line, an instructor is always immediately behind the firer shouting instructions, firing blank cartridges, and in general, adding to the level of tension. For a more realistic approach, the firer should not be wearing hearing protection and should be carrying all the items of equipment with which he would ordinarily respond to a contingency. From a liability standpoint, this may not be desirable; if such a course is offered, waivers of liability should be signed by all participants.

For additional stress and distraction, the instructor may use smoke grenades, noisemakers, and the like to the sides and rear of the shooter, keeping a good safety margin between personnel and any object that could cause injury. Naturally, in order to control the training properly, only one shooter at a time should be allowed to run the stress course. For additional effect, this can be conducted at night using only the rotating lights from a patrol or other emergency vehicle.

Shotguns

The shotgun is probably the single best all-around weapon available to the contingency response force. A 12-gauge pump-action shotgun with cylinder-

Table 10-1   Requirements for Revolver Training

Distance (yds)	Number of Rounds on Each of 2 Targets	Position	Time (sec)
5	3	Strong hand, supported	3
5	2	Strong hand, supported	5
10	3	Strong hand, kneeling	8
10	3	Weak hand, kneeling	10 or 20
12	2	Strong hand, sitting	10 or 20
15	3	Alternating shots, strong hand, standing barricade	10
15	3	Weak hand, standing barricade	12
15	3	Strong hand, kneeling barricade	12
15	3	Weak hand kneeling barricade	15 or 30
20	3	Strong hand, sitting	12 or 30
20	3	Weak hand, sitting	15 or 30
25	3	Strong hand, standing barricade	90
25	3	Weak hand, standing barricade	90
25	3	Strong hand, sitting	90
25	3	Strong hand, prone	90
25	3	Weak hand, prone	90

Targets spaced 4 to 6 feet apart.

bore barrel and extended magazine capacity, loaded with double-00 buckshot is capable of delivering an average of 72 .33-caliber lead projectiles, each capable of incapacitating an adversary. As a comparison, the average 9-mm submachine gun only has a capacity of 32 rounds (Figure 10–1).

In addition to the firepower incorporated into each such weapon, the shotgun's psychological effect is very positive on the individual standing behind it, while the opposite effect is felt by someone staring down its barrel. There have been many recorded instances where the sound of a pump shotgun's action being cycled was enough to convince a miscreant to give up.

Because of the variety of ammunition available, the shotgun is an extremely versatile firearm. In a situation where incapacitation rather than total neutralization is desired, the use of birdshot (No. 4) is recommended as a last resort (Figure 10–2). Maximum nonlethal effect is achieved by "skipping or ricocheting the shot into the adversary's lower extremities. This is accomplished by firing at the ground or pavement in front of an advancing adversary

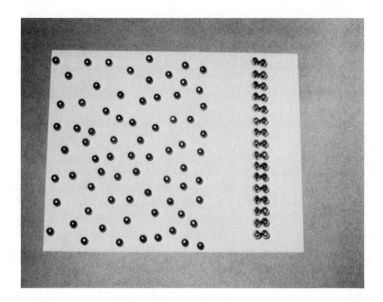

Figure 10-1 72 shotgun pellets (*left*) and 32 9 mm bullets (*right*).

from a distance of 40 to 50 feet so that the shot strikes the pavement approximately 10 to 15 feet in front of the person. Depending on the angle of the shot and the hardness of the surface from which it is deflected, the birdshot will hit the pavement, flatten out, and bounce up to hit the person somewhere in his lower extremities. Usually, the harder the surface from which the shot is "skipped," the less the angle of deflection. In many cases, injuries will not be life threatening, however, as in any situation where firearms are employed, there always exists an element of risk of grave injury or death. Therefore firearms should be used against an individual only to defend the life of the officer or of another person.

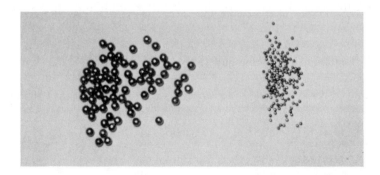

Figure 10-2 00 buckshot and No. 4 birdshot.

There may be situations in which maximum penetration or knock-down power is desired. In these cases, the use of a slug load may be warranted. A shotgun slug is a single, cup-shaped lead projectile that delivers a great deal of energy into a targeted medium. There are other specialty loads available, such as barricade-penetrating tear gas projectiles and aerial flare projectiles.

For practical shotgun training, use of the weapon from the shoulder and hip positions should receive maximum attention. Table 10–2 gives recommended shotgun course requirements.

Firing from the hip position, most shooters will have a decided tendency to fire over the tops of targets. This "climb" increases with every shot, as the recoil is not fully compensated for by the shooter. This can be corrected by instructing him to take an open stance (feet about two feet apart with the weak leg in front) and 60 percent: 40 percent weight distribution front to back. The bottom edge of the shotgun butt should be rested on top of the hipbone and held against the body by the trigger hand forearm. The weak hand should grasp the weapon's forearm stock in a firm grip and, most important, the elbow of this arm should be locked at full extension. This will be somewhat unnatural to the shooter, but it ensures that the weapon is held parallel to the ground. After the first shot, the tendency will be for this elbow to become unlocked. It must not, this is a very important requirement that must be constantly stressed until it becomes second nature on the part of the shooter.

The next requirement is that the shooter, while looking directly at his next target, use his peripheral vision to ensure that the barrel is pointing directly at it (there is a tendency among some individuals to have the weapon pointing to the side of targets; which is sometimes easily corrected by having the shooter reposition his feet).

At the 25-yard line, the shooter may use the sights built into the weapon, but it must be remembered that at both the 15- and the 25-yard lines he has only six seconds in which to fire four rounds, one at each of four targets. With a little practice, this is easily achieved. With advanced shooters, all four rounds can be fired within three seconds and all will be on target. When firing from the shoulder position, the officer can more quickly recover from

Table 10-2   Requirements for Shotgun Training

Distance (yds)	Number of Rounds on Each of 4 Targets	Position	Time (sec) Starting with Empty Chamber
15	4, using 00 buckshot, 1 on each target	Hip	15
25	4, using 00 buckshot, 1 on each target	Shoulder	25

Targets spaced 2 to 3 feet apart.

Table 10-3 Requirements for Rifle Training

Distance (yds)	Number of Rounds on Same Target	Position	Time (min)
100	10	Prone, behind barricade	10
100	10	Kneeling, behind barricade	3
100	10	Standing, off-hand	1
50	10	Standing, off-hand	1

the recoil if he takes an aggressively open stance (weak foot forward about three feet and a 70 percent:30 percent weight distribution front to back). For familiarization, officers should fire the shotgun from their weak side as well as over and around barricades.

Rifles

The choice of a rifle, when one is deemed necessary, has usually been a semiautomatic version chambered for the .223-caliber cartridge. This particular cartridge is small and relatively lightweight, thus allowing the officer to carry a good reserve supply of ammunition. The .223 is, by the way, an extremely efficient round. In addition, the mild recoil and rapidity of fire contribute greatly to quick mastery of the weapon by most officers. A practical rifle course is described in Table 10–3.

To qualify on any of the firing courses thus far outlined, the individual would have to place a minimum of 80 percent of all shotgun pellets and rifle bullets in the black portion of a full-sized silhouette target and achieve a minimum score of 70 percent of the maximum possible total points on the revolver course.

Because it is generally accepted that a situation involving the use of firearms is just as likely to occur during the hours of darkness as daylight, all officers should fire a familiarization course during the hours of darkness (Table 10–4).

The only illumination for nighttime training would be the indirect light from a flashlight, which the officers should not hold or aim. The instructor

Table 10-4 Requirements for Nighttime Firearms Training

Distance (yds)	Weapon	Number of Rounds on Target	Position	Time (min)
15	Revolver	6	Any	1
20	Shotgun	4, using 00 buckshot	Any	1
25	Rifle	10	Any	1

should position this light so that its pattern or reflection "splashes" on the target. To qualify (if that is the requirement) or at least to demonstrate their ability to function effectively under low-light conditions, officers should be able to hit the black portion of a silhouette target with 80 percent of their bullets or pellets.

As with any firearms course, be it handgun, rifle, or shotgun, complete safety indoctrination must be given prior to allowing an officer to fire a course. This must include a safety briefing for each weapon to be fired, and officers should not be allowed to handle any weapon until they have demonstrated their understanding in the safe handling and operation of each one to the satisfaction of the instructor.

Requirements for testing and documentation should be followed as specified in the previous chapter.

RESPONSE FORCE EQUIPMENT

The contingency response force would generally employ the following basic items of equipment:

1. Sidearm with a minimum of 18 rounds of extra ammunition
2. Portable two-way radio
3. Handcuffs with key
4. Speed loaders (or other device designed to expedite reloading)
5. Heavy-duty flashlight
6. Shotgun with a minimum of 10 rounds of extra ammunition

In addition, the following items of specialized equipment may be required depending on such variables as the nature of the item or material being protected, distance from a support facility, availability of a backup force, and the nature of the contingency response force mission (i.e., contain the threat until the arrival of law enforcement authorities or neutralize the threat independently):

1. Tactical ballistic helmet
2. Tactical ballistic vest with inserts for extra protection
3. Rifle with a minimum of 100 rounds of extra ammunition
4. Portable bullhorn
5. Flare gun with at least three flares
6. Self-contained parachute flares
7. Tear gas grenades
8. Protective mask
9. Riot baton
10. Portable, high-power spotlight
11. Set of master keys

12.   Night-vision devices
13.   First aid kit

The site-specific requirements may be such that the response force must be a highly trained, motivated, self-contained, and self-supporting team, provided with the necessary transport, and equipped and prepared to neutralize any threat or number of adversaries with which it is confronted. In this case, exotic specialized equipment may be required such as armored vehicles, power-amplified listening devices; remote-controlled closed-circuit television-equipped robots; bomb blankets, baskets, and transport or detonation vehicles; and fully automatic weapons.

In planning for the necessary acquisitions, great care must be exercised to avoid equipping the force for a mission for which it has not been trained and for which there is no need. At the same time, those items necessary to support the force must be readily available and used in training to ensure total familiarity and qualification of the officers.

At a site where the response force is composed of designated officers who happen to be on duty at the time of the contingency, and who may be assigned to different posts throughout the protected facility, the time wasted in reporting to a central control point to obtain equipment before responding may mean the difference between a problem and a catastrophe. To save precious minutes, it is recommended that emergency response lockers be located in all permanently manned security posts or other suitable areas within the facility (Figure 10–3). Each locker should contain, at a minimum, the following items:

1.   12-gauge shotgun with 15 rounds of 00 buckshot
2.   Rifle with 100 rounds of ammunition
3.   Tactical ballistic helmet with face shield
4.   Tactical ballistic vest with inserts
5.   Riot baton
6.   Parachute flares
7.   Tear gas grenades
8.   Protective mask
9.   Flashlight with fresh batteries
10. Sealed ammunition container with 100 rounds of extra sidearm ammunition, 100 rounds of extra rifle ammunition, 25 rounds of extra 00 buckshot, and 25 rounds of rifled shotgun slug ammunition

All lockers should have a numbered, tamper-indicating seal affixed to the door. They may, as determined by site security management, be equipped with a lock for which each member of the force is issued a key or given the combination. Security supervisors must, on their inspections of each post, check to ensure that the seals on the lockers are not broken or otherwise tampered with.

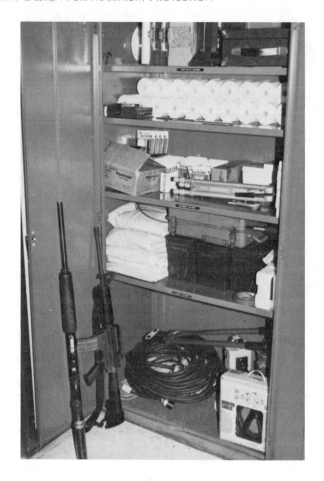

Figure 10-3   Emergency response locker. (S. Messemer.)

A list of its contents can be posted on the locker door if it will not be seen by anyone other than an authorized security officer. If such a list cannot be posted on the outside of a locker, it should be put up inside. On a periodic basis (bimonthly is recommended), a member of security management should inventory the contents of each locker to ensure that nothing is missing. At this time, flashlight batteries should be tested and if necessary replaced, and any expendable item with a known shelf life examined to determine if it should be replaced. All firearms should be examined for serviceability and ammunition checked for signs of deterioration. The results of each inventory should be documented and the locker resealed. The number of the seal or seals used should be recorded and retained.

Appendix 10–A

Lesson Plan

RESPONSE TO BOMB THREATS

I. Length: ½ hour
II. Objectives
    A. The officer will be able to perform the duties required during response to a bomb threat by conducting a search for any suspected destructive device.
    B. The officer will be able to demonstrate, through verbal or written examination or by actual physical performance, the proper manner of searching a room for a destructive device.
    C. The officer will be familiar with the procedures for notifying proper on-site personnel if a suspected destructive device is found.
III. References
    (All references used in the preparation of this lesson should be listed here.)
IV. Procedure
    A. Because of the time element usually involved in a bomb threat, it is imperative that every contingency response officer assigned to a search team proceed with all haste to his assigned search area on receiving his assignment, and after he clearly understands any special instructions that may be given. These may include a description of the device, its time of detonation, specific area in which it has been placed, or other information that may have been received in the threat message. Such information obviously will aid searchers in their duties and must be made known to, and fully understood by, all searchers. Officers will search their assigned post area unless otherwise directed.
        Note: Officers shall be made to understand that any point on which they are unsure or that they want clarified should be brought to the instructor's attention immediately rather than waiting until the class is over.
    B. Personnel shall be instructed that they must not unnecessarily disturb anything. Drawers and doors must be opened very slowly and checked to ensure they are not rigged to act as a bomb-triggering device. Light switches can also be rigged to detonate a device, there-

fore none shall be turned on or off until it has been checked. It is imperative that all members of search teams be sure they have working flashlights equipped with good batteries before they start searching. Switches or controls on machinery could also be rigged to detonate a device, therefore members of search teams shall change no switch or control settings on any piece of equipment.

C. The proper technique for searching any area, from a broom closet to an auditorium, is from the bottom up and from the outside in.

D. On arriving at the designated search area, the first thing the team shall do is to stand still and listen to acquaint themselves with background noises that may be present. This also offers the possibility that if there are no background noises, the sound of a clockwork timing device may be detected.

E. The team leader shall then survey the assigned search area and divide it into equal portions, taking into consideration the amount of furniture and equipment in the space, so that each member's area will take approximately the same time to search.

F. Vital-area search teams shall ensure that all items of vital equipment are checked first. Vital components of a system that may be remotely located should also be carefully searched.

G. The actual search shall be conducted as follows:

1. Team members (usually two persons) start by standing back to back at one end of the room (or assigned space). They then start walking away from each other, searching along the outside wall from floor level to a height of three feet. (If there are rugs in the space, they must be checked as well as the area they are covering.)

2. Once each team member has checked the walls to the predetermined height, he shall work his way into the center of the room (up to the predetermined dividing line), checking all furniture and equipment in this area up to the three-foot search height.

3. On completion of this first sweeping search, the team members shall reassemble at one end of the room or space. They then start back-to-back again and begin the second sweeping search by checking the walls again from the three-foot height up to head-high on the individual searcher. Following this wall search, they then move into the room center again, checking furniture and equipment from the three-foot mark to head height.

4. The third sweeping search is conducted in the same manner as the first and second, however, the searchers now check the walls from head height up to the ceiling. The tops of file cabinets, bookcases, etc., will also be checked, as well as lights, ducts, etc.

     5.   If necessary, a fourth sweeping search will check the area above false or dropped ceilings.

H.   Once the area has been thoroughly searched, signs indicating this should be posted at each entrance to preclude the possibility of other search teams wasting time in going over areas that have already been checked.

I.   Members of the search teams should not use their radios for transmitting messages while inside any building or space. Radio-frequency detonation of an explosive device using electric blasting caps is a possibility. Message transmission from the searchers to the control center should whenever possible be conducted over telephone lines or, if necessary, carried by messenger.

J.   On discovery of a bomb or a suspected bomb, the search team shall:

     1.   Notify the central alarm station or control center by telephone, giving them:

        (a)   The name or location of the space in which the device has been found

        (b)   The exact location within this space where the device is situated

        (c)   As complete a description of the device as possible

        (d)   The name of the searcher who found the suspected device

     2.   Not attempt to move the device or disturb it in any way

     3.   Clear the area immediately of all personnel

     4.   Officers searching fence lines shall be alert for suspicious objects or packages placed adjacent to the fence or attached to the fence fabric, fence posts, gates, etc. Officers assigned to search parking lots shall check under as well as inside vehicles. Any suspicious objects or packages noted shall be reported.

     5.   Officers shall continue searching unless otherwise directed. Just because one suspected device has been found does not mean that there may not be others.

     6.   Once the area has been completely searched, a guard must be posted at all entrances to keep personnel from entering inadvertently.

     7.   The individual who discovered the suspected device shall be prepared to lead bomb disposal personnel to its exact location.

SUMMARY

Assignment of a response officer as a member of a search team places a great deal of responsibility on this individual. Not only must he be extremely careful and conscientious in the manner in which the assigned area is searched, he must be thoroughly familiar with the area itself in order to spot any device or item that does not belong.

CHAPTER 11

Management and Supervision

The successful implementation and effective performance of a maximum-security program is keyed directly to the caliber of management and supervisory personnel employed to oversee security efforts. While such competent, well-educated, and highly trained employees are desirable in all areas of private security, they are essential to an overall safeguards program at a maximum security facility.

Traditionally, former law enforcement officers have been a logical choice to make the transition into private security. Former military personnel have also been thought of as good security personnel. In reality, however, these concepts do not always hold true. Security personnel may have prior law enforcement and/or military experience and this may indirectly benefit them and the organization. A good law enforcement officer or soldier does not, however, necessarily make a good security officer, supervisor, or manager. As earlier stated, security is a unique entity, and more often than not the keys to success in this field are management skill and ability.

When deciding on security management personnel, the first areas of consideration should be the individual's management background or his management potential, followed by prior security experience. Previous law enforcement and/or military experience are third in line of importance.

ORGANIZATION

Because of the sensitivity of most maximum-security operations, a unique and, depending on magnitude, fairly extensive management organization is usually required. The person who is solely responsible for the security program is known by a variety of titles. For our purposes, he is referred to as the security director.

The security director should report directly or indirectly to the chief executive officer (CEO) of the facility. If the reporting relationship to the CEO is indirect, the reporting relationship should be between the security director and a member of the CEO's staff, that is, executive management. In a maximum-security organization there should never be more than two (and preferably just one) levels of management separating the security director from the CEO. Thus while the security director might report directly to a vice president, the former should have clear access to the CEO.

The security director usually oversees the program's administration, operations, and support services. In large facilities he may be aided by deputy directors in each of these three areas. At smaller sites the positions might be shared, for example, the security director taking charge of management and administration and the deputy being responsible for operations and support services.

Operations

The operating functions of the security management organization encompass:

1. Routine day-to-day operations
2. Nonroutine (contingency) operations
3. Investigations

In many organizations there is an individual with overall responsibility for operations and a subordinate who is in charge of investigations or a section that performs investigative chores. In smaller organizations one individual may be responsible for all operational aspects, including investigations.

Administration

The administrative function involves keeping the security program on course by defining the direction to be taken and ensuring that policies are developed and implemented to maintain that direction. Procedures, contingency and crisis management plans, security awareness programs, evaluations and audits of performance, records maintenance, and overall compliance with requirements and mandates are all covered by this area.

Support Services

Maximum security can be broken down into two separate and distinct components: security and security services. Total and complete security, which by the way is an achievable if unrealistic goal, does not allow for production activity. In other words, an effective security organization can provide truly effective security, in the extreme sense, by curtailing all activities that have the potential for creating security breaches. Total security is possible only in a static environment. In reality, however, certain activities must take place. In the maximum-security environment, anything that is required above basic safeguarding can be thought of as service. While security in this context is passive, service is active. Services such as escorting visitors, opening doors, and manning posts that are not essential to protection of the facility but allow for expediency in production activities, are provided to maintain the desired degree of protection (not security). When a facility is in full operation, this concept can be thought of in the following terms: If all activity in a facility were to cease and all nonsecurity personnel were to leave, that level of protection necessary to safeguard the facility and its contents would be described as security. That level of protection that allows the facility to operate can be described as security support service.

Support services can be further delineated as essential and nonessential. The former are necessary for the protection of the facility while it is in operation. The latter are not necessary for the operation but are offered as a convenience to employees. When faced with budget cutbacks and elimination of security personnel, the wise security director will invariably start by reducing the level of nonessential services. Security management provides support services over and above protection, including logistical services. Training, systems and equipment maintenance, specialized equipment and communications support, and special security projects and assignments all fall into the realm of support services.

A suggested management structure for a maximum security facility is as follows:

> Level 1—CEO, vice presidents and executive staff, and security director
> Level 2—deputy directors of operations, administration, and support services
> Level 3—security force and investigations section

Each function encompasses the following areas:

1. Operations—security force, investigations section
2. Administration—policy formulation and implementation, program and procedure development, contingency and crisis management planning, evaluations and audits, records maintenance, compliance with regulations and requirements
3. Support services—special security services, training, systems and equipment maintenance, specialized equipment and communications support, special projects and assignments

All functions must be included in the overall maximum security organization whether or not they are provided by separate individuals or assumed by the security director.

Training

Supervisory personnel should receive the same training as security officers. Additionally, supervisory development programs should be offered through on-site or off-site resources. Management personnel should avail themselves of all training and educational opportunities in areas of security and management.

Admittedly, there has been a definite lack of training opportunities for security supervisors and managers. This has been addressed, however, over the past several years and certain resources are available. The American Society for Industrial Security offers many fine seminars and workshops covering security management and supervision, as do many other professional organizations. Programs are now offered at several colleges and universities. Most institutions have courses and programs in management and supervision that can be quite valuable.

CHAPTER 12

Planning

An effective security program at a maximum-security facility invariably is based on extensive planning. Threat analysis, hardware, and personnel organization are worthless unless they are all blended and shaped into a cohesive program. The format for the successful security program is the overall plan that guides and controls the various components so that each fits together to provide the best possible protection for the facility and its personnel.

The security plan should contain all information regarding safeguards at the protected facility. It should be supported by procedures as well as other plans, such as a training and qualifications plan and contingency plans. The security plan therefore becomes the main guidance document for safeguarding a sensitive facility or community.

The plan must be a formal, written document that has been approved by the highest levels of management and any agencies that may be charged with regulating security. It must contain certain essential information. The U.S. Nuclear Regulatory Commission, in its December 1978 draft of the *Fixed Site Physical Protection Upgrade Rule Guidance Compendium* offers a very valuable standard format and context guide for the preparation of security plans. The following is taken from that source and should prove useful in the planning effort. All or part of it can be modified to suit a particular facility.

"PART I GENERAL ISSUES

"1.0 Overview of site and facility
Describe the general layout of the facility and the surrounding site. Include a map of the entire facility and other maps and illustrations as may be appropriate. Indicate on these maps the locations of physical security systems, subsystems, and major components; also indicate the location of all restricted areas, vital areas, vaults, entry/exit control points, and alarm stations. Describe the relationship between physical security and other activities at the facility.

"2.0 Threats
Affirm the intent to prevent, with high assurance, the theft of special nuclear material (SNM) and to protect against radiological sabotage. . . . For each of the design-reference threats (Chapter 1.0),* de-

---

* Authors' Note

scribe and evaluate the relationship of the . . . threat to the facility and its operations.

"3.0   Local law enforcement agency commitments

Describe the agreements between local law enforcement agencies and the facility security management regarding response and support during contingency events; also describe the liaisons established between the facility security management and the local law enforcement authorities, specifying the officials who perform this function, the frequency of communication, and the nature of these communications. This chapter should include a map showing the location of LLEA facilities in relation to the licensee's facility, and the routes which LLEA personnel might use in responding to an alarm.

"3.1   Size of force

Discuss the number and composition of law enforcement personnel available for assistance and the estimated response time for such personnel to reach the facility. Include in the discussion the number of armed individuals in each complement and the time for each complement to arrive if they are to arrive at intervals.

"3.2   Kind of assistance

Identify the type or kind of assistance that can be provided (such as police power, investigative work, crowd control, or bomb searches) and the kind of equipment available.

"4.0   Contingency plan

Briefly describe the facility contingency plan and relate it to this security plan.

"5.0   Guard force qualification and training

Affirm that a guard force training plan is in effect. Briefly relate the guard force training plan to this security plan.

"6.0   Security management

Describe the structure and management of the security organization, including both uniformed security personnel and other persons responsible for security-related functions. This discussion should include a description of each supervisory and managerial position, including the responsibilities and how lines of authority extend up to facility and corporate management.

"7.0   Quality assurance programs

To provide assurance that the design and procurement of the physical protection system components for a plant are in conformance with requirements and with the design bases and criteria specified by management, a quality assurance (QA) program should be established. Describe the QA program to be established and executed for the physical protection system during the procurement, design, and construction stages.

"8.0   Testing and inspection

Describe the programs to be implemented to regularly and periodically test and/or inspect all physical security system components (equipment, design features, and procedures). Include a discussion of the management of these programs.

"8.1   Tests and inspections during installation

Describe the general procedures for conducting tests and inspections during installation and/or construction of physical protection-related subsystems and components to assure that they comply with their respective design criteria and performance specifications.

"8.2   Preoperational tests and inspections

Describe the general procedures for conducting preoperational tests and inspections of physical protection-related subsystems and components to demonstrate their effectiveness and availability with respective design criteria and performance specifications.

"8.3   Operational tests and inspections

Identify the types of subsystems, number of zones, numbers of components, number of items tested each time, and the frequency and test procedure used to determine physical protection-related subsystems and components are in an operable and effective condition. Also, indicate the functions performed in security force drills, and the frequency and attendance of such drills.

"9.0   Maintenance programs

Describe the programs to provide routine maintenance for all security-related equipment and design features, and to provide emergency repair capabilities for both equipment and design features. Discuss the personnel who will perform these functions, including their training and qualification, whether they are employees of the facility or contract personnel, and the lines of authority from facility management through security management to ensure continued effectiveness of these programs.

"10.0   Security audits

Describe the programs to review periodically the applicability and adequacy of the existing security plan and to assess the compliance of the current performance with existing security requirements.

"10.1   Program audit

Describe the scope, extent, and frequency of planned periodic management audits to review the physical security program of the facility for continued adequacy and effectiveness. Identify by organizational title the persons assigned responsibility for conducting the audits. Affirm that written audit reports will be prepared and submitted to facility management.

"10.2   Compliance audits

Describe the monitoring program established to ensure compliance with existing regulations. Identify by organizational title the persons assigned responsibility for conducting the audits. Affirm that written audit reports will be prepared and submitted to facility management.

"11.0   Security records
Describe the record-keeping programs.

"11.1   Security tours, inspections, and tests
Describe the system for documenting the results of all routine security tours and inspections and of all tests and inspections performed on physical barriers, intrusion alarms, communications equipment, and other security-related equipment.

"11.2   Maintenance
Identify and characterize the records that are kept of all maintenance performed on physical barriers, intrusion alarms, communications equipment, and other security-related equipment.

"11.3   Alarm annunciations
Describe the records system for documenting all alarm annunciations, including false alarms. Also describe the system for identifying the type of alarm, location, date, and time of each occurrence.

"11.4   Security response
Indicate the records that are kept of response by security personnel to each alarm (including false alarm), intrusion, or other security incidents.

"11.5   Authorized individuals
Describe the system for maintaining a record of each individual who is designated as an authorized individual. Indicate whether the record will include the name and badge number of each person so designated, the individual's address, the date of the authorization, its expiration date, the name of the approval authority, and the areas to which access is authorized.

"11.6   Nonemployee access
Describe the system for maintaining a record (register) of each visitor, vendor, or other individual who is not an employee of the facility, with the record showing the individual's name; and the date, time, and purpose of the visit; the individual's employment affiliation and citizenship; the name and badge number of the escort; the name of the individual to be visited; and the name of the person who authorized or approved the visit. Describe the system for maintaining a list of designated escorts.

"12.0   Reports

"12.1   Incidents
Describe the procedures for reporting any incident in which an attempt has been made, or is believed to have been made, to commit a theft or unlawful diversion of assets or to commit an act of sabotage.

"12.2   Unusual
Describe procedures for reporting any unusual occurrences (such as civil disturbances, bomb threats, significant vandalism and demonstrations, or strikes) that may or could have an effect on plant security.

"12.3   Security plan changes

Describe procedures for modifying the security plan.

"13.0   Schedule for implementation

Describe the schedule for implementing the security plan, with special attention to those portions involving new construction, significant physical modification of existing structures, or major equipment installation which will require extensions of time.

"14.0   Redundancy and diversity

Identify the portions of the facility physical security system for which redundant and diverse components are necessary in order to assure adequate performance. In general terms describe the subsystems and components to be used to provide this redundancy and diversity, and how these subsystems and components are redundant and diverse.

"15.0   Security system integrity

Describe how the physical security system will be designed to assure that the integrity of the system is maintained at all times and how the system will exhibit continued resistance to vulnerabilities. This should be a generic discussion of the problem and of the techniques adopted to address it, with only a general description of the measures to be utilized, not a description of the specific components involved (such as the specific line supervisory or tamper-indicating circuitry which will be installed).

"16.0   Security system power sources

Describe the power sources to be used for all physical security-related systems and equipment, including an evaluation of the reliability and vulunerability of each power source. Describe the different emergency power systems (uninterruptible power or other backup power sources) which are to be provided to assure that a power failure will not significantly degrade the physical security system capabilities. This discussion should focus on the power sources as complete systems, rather than viewing them from the perspective of the individual types of equipment to be powered (which will be addressed in part II of the security plan).

"17.0   Alarm stations

Describe the central alarm station (CAS) and the secondary alarm station (SAS) to be installed at the facility. Include their locations on the facility map. Provide a generic discussion of the CAS and of the SAS, which includes all those topics mentioned in the following paragraph.

Describe the types of physical barriers and protective features to be used in the construction of the CAS and the SAS for receiving, assessing, and recording alarm information. Describe the components to be used for communication with security force personnel, on-site response personnel, and other facility personnel and offices. Describe the components to be used for communication with off-site response personnel. Identify the power sources and security programs to be used to assure the continuing operation of the equipment in the CAS and SAS (refer to Chapters 15.0 and 16.0 as appropriate). Describe the procedures for granting access to the CAS and SAS. Describe the command and control personnel, and all other personnel, who will staff the CAS and SAS. Describe all activities to take place in the CAS and SAS under 17.1 and 17.2 respectively.

"17.1   Central alarm station
"17.2   Secondary alarm station

"Part II—Specific System Performance

"INSTRUCTIONS

"This part consists of six chapters, 18 through 23, which parallel the structure of specified performance capabilities. The information to be provided in this section of the facility security plan should describe how the facility physical security system provides the required performance capabilities. These descriptions should be of two types. First, a general description of how the given capability is to be achieved should be given and second, an identification of the specific safeguards components and measures used to implement such a system should be included.

"Equipment descriptions should include manufacturer and model. In the case of design features, such as walls, entry control portals, etc., a basic physical description of the construction or structure should be provided. For procedures, a basic description of the security force actions which constitute the particular procedure should be provided. When a component or configuration of components is used more than once for the same physical security purpose (for instance, at more than one portal) it is only necessary to provide the appropriate information once. The information can then be referenced.

"All redundant and diverse subsystems or components should be identified as such when they are described, with a statement of how these subsystems or components provide redundancy and diversity. The criterion for determining when redundancy and diversity is necessary is: whenever a single adversary action could otherwise so degrade the subsystem or system as to disrupt the required performance capability. Several types of subsystems and systems should possess redundancy and diversity. These include most alarm and detection systems, certain communications links without which effective notification and response communications would not be possible, and alarm stations (a central alarm station—CAS—and a secondary alarm station—SAS).

"18.0   Prevent unauthorized access of persons and materials into restricted areas

Describe the purpose and objective of the measures used to prevent unauthorized access to restricted areas. Relate this to the required performance capabilities.

"18.1   Entry control through restricted area entry portals

For each restricted area, identify the number, location, and type of entry portals, referring to the facility map as appropriate. Treat each vault as though it were a separate restricted area, even if the vault is otherwise considered an item control area within a restricted area, and is entirely within that same area. For each portal, identify and describe all the components required for entry control functions, as described in the following paragraphs. However, in cases where the same configuration of components is to be used at more than one entry portal, the measures need be described only once and may thereafter be referenced.

18.1.1   Entry authorization procedures

Describe the development of entry authorization procedures. Discuss how the lists of authorized personnel for each portal will be developed. Also describe the distribution and maintenance of these lists.

18.1.2   Entry procedures and controls

18.1.2.1   Routine conditions

Describe how routine conditions differ between working and nonworking hours (nights, weekends, and holidays).Identify which portals are to be open and which are to be locked during each of those periods. This discussion should be related to the problem of entry in emergency situations, which is discussed in paragraph 18.1.2.2 below.

18.1.2.1.1   Procedures and controls for personnel entry

For each entry portal, describe how the identification and authorization of each person is to be verified to prevent unauthorized access by deceit. Describe the policies and procedures to be used for the escort of visitors. Discuss the components to be used to detect contraband on authorized personnel at entry control points.

Discuss the procedures and equipment to be used by entry control personnel to notify command and control personnel of the suspected attempt at unauthorized entry. Identify the interim steps to be taken by entry control personnel in the period between notification of security and the arrival of response personnel.

18.1.2.1.2   Procedures and controls for introduced materials

Describe the components to be used to control the introduction of materials by deceit. Describe how the material entry authorizations are to be verified. Describe how the quantity and type of material is to be verified. These descriptions should include the components to be used in the detection of unauthorized materials which are hand-carried by authorized individuals, mailed, or otherwise shipped as part of an authorized shipment. Describe the procedures and equipment to be used by the portal guard for the notification of command and control personnel in the event that the introduction of unauthorized materials is suspected. Identify the interim steps to be taken by access control personnel in the period between notification of security and the arrival of response personnel.

18.1.2.1.3   Procedures and controls for introduction of vehicles

Describe the procedures and equipment used to control the ingress of vehicles into restricted areas, if applicable. Identify the components used to detect unauthorized materials on/in such vehicles, and relate this discussion to section 18.1.2.1.2.

18.1.2.2   Nonroutine conditions

Describe the components to be used for entry control during nonroutine conditions. Discuss how entry control personnel will verify that a bona fide nonroutine condition exists. Describe the procedures to be used for controlling the entry of personnel authorized to enter during each type of nonroutine condition if they differ from those described in paragraph 18.1.2.1.1.

Describe the procedures to be used for the escort

of emergency personnel such as fire fighters and ambulance attendants. Identify the procedures and equipment to be used by the portal officer to notify command and control personnel in the CAS and SAS of a suspected attempt at unauthorized access during nonroutine conditions. Describe the interim actions to be taken between the notification of security and the arrival of response personnel.

18.1.3 Bypass of admittance procedures and controls

Describe the procedures and controls to be used to prevent unauthorized entry through portals by stealth or force (for both open and closed conditions at each portal). Describe the barriers and other components to be used to delay bypass attempts through the portal. Include a discussion of the components to be used to sense unauthorized entry attempts and transmit sensor data to command and control. Identify the equipment and procedures to be used as the CAS and SAS to assess the information. This discussion should include the identification of redundant and diverse components and subsystems to be used to assure that the unauthorized entry is prevented. Describe the actions to be taken to prevent or delay the unauthorized entry attempt from succeeding in the interim between the notification of security and the arrival of response personnel (in those cases where the portal is manned).

"18.2 Entry through the remainder of the restricted area boundary

18.2.1 Detect boundary penetration attempt

Describe the components to be used to detect attempts at unauthorized entry. Identify the components to be used to sense unauthorized entry attempts and to transmit sensor data to command and control personnel. Identify the equipment and procedures to be used at the CAS and SAS to assess this information. This discussion should include the identification of redundant and diverse components and subsystems to be used to assure that unauthorized entry is prevented.

18.2.2 Deter boundary penetration attempt

Describe the barriers and other components to be used to prevent entry through the remainder of each restricted area boundary (i.e., other than at the entry portals). Describe the physical barriers to be used at each restricted area boundary. This description should address the construction of all walls, floors, and ceilings, as well as how ventilation and other openings are to be secured.

18.2.3 Respond to boundary penetration attempt

Describe the immediate actions to be taken between notification of security and the arrival of response personnel. Identify the components to be used to contain unauthorized entry attempts sufficiently to permit the arrival of response forces who will prevent the attempt from succeeding.

"19.0 Permit only authorized activities and conditions within protected areas, material access areas, and vital areas

"19.1 Permit only authorized activities and conditions within protected areas

19.1.1 Establishment of authorized activities and conditions

Define the boundaries of the restricted area, referring to the facility map. Discuss the development of criteria to be used in defining those activities and conditions which are to be authorized and those which are to be prohibited. Describe how lists of authorized activities and conditions are to be developed, maintained, and distributed.

19.1.2 Prevention of unauthorized activities and conditions

Discuss the components to be used to detect unauthorized activities and conditions (include those components to be used to sense unauthorized activities and conditions, and to transmit sensor data to command and control personnel). Identify the equipment and procedures to be used at the CAS and SAS to display the sensor data. This discussion should include the identification of redundant and diverse components and subsystems to be used. Describe any actions which security personnel who may detect unauthorized activities and conditions during routine patrols or tours will initiate in the interim between notification of command and control personnel to the arrival of response forces.

"20.0 Permit only authorized placement and movement of (assets) within restricted areas

Describe the purpose and objective of the measures which are used to control movement and placement of (assets).

"20.1 Establishment of authorized placement and movement of (assets)

Describe the criteria to be used to delineate the authorized placement and movement of (assets) within each restricted area. For each restricted area, discuss the location(s) within which the placement and movement of (assets) is to be authorized, referring to the facility map. Describe how scheduled of authorized placement and movement of (assets) within each restricted area are to be developed, maintained, and distributed.

"20.2 Establishment of current knowledge of (assets)

For each restricted area, describe the components to be used to verify the type, quantity, and location of (assets) within the restricted area. Discuss the procedures to be used to verify the authorization schedules. In the case of multiple restricted areas where the same verification measures are to be used, this information can be referenced.

"20.3   Prevention of unauthorized placement and movement of (assets)

Describe the components to be used to delay the unauthorized placement and movement of (assets) within each restricted area (for example, the containment of (assets) within wire cages when they are between the vault and process machinery). Describe the components to be used to sense unauthorized placement or movement of (assets) and to transmit sensor data to command and control personnel. Identify the equipment and procedures to be used in the CAS and SAS to assess sensor information. This discussion should include the identification of redundant and diverse components and subsystems to be used. For cases in which the unauthorized placement or movement of (assets) is detected by security personnel during routine patrol or escort operations, describe the actions to be taken by these security personnel in the interim between notification of command and control personnel and the arrival of response personnel.

"21.0   Permit removal of only authorized and confirmed forms and amounts of (assets) from restricted areas

"21.1   Control of (assets) removal through restricted area portals

For each restricted area, identify the number, location, and type of portals, including reference to the facility map. For each portal, provide all information required in the following paragraphs. However, in cases where the same configuration of components is to be used at more than one portal, the measures need to be described only once and may thereafter be referenced.

21.1.1   Development of removal authorization procedures

Describe the development of removal authorization procedures. Discuss how lists of authorized personnel, are to be developed, distributed, and maintained.

21.1.2   Administration of removal procedures and controls

21.1.2.1   Normal conditions

Describe how normal conditions differ between regular working hours and nonworking hours (nights, weekends, and holidays). Identify which portals are to be open and which are to be locked during each of these periods. In cases where authorized removal of (assets), scrap, or waste may be limited to certain restricted area portals, these portals should be identified in the appropriate paragraphs below.

21.1.2.1.1   Procedures and control for removal of (assets)

For each portal, describe how the identification and authorization of each person presenting (assets) for removal from the restricted area is to be verified to prevent removal by deceit. Describe how the verification of authorization, type, and quantity of (assets) is to be confirmed. Discuss the components to be used to detect unauthorized removal of (assets). Identify the components to be used to sense unauthorized attempts to remove (assets) from restricted areas and to transmit sensor data to command and control personnel. Identify the equipment and procedures to be used at the CAS and SAS to assess the sensor information. This discussion should include the identification of redundant and diverse components and subsystems to be used.

Discuss the actions to be taken by the portal guard in the interim between notification of command and control personnel and the arrival of response personnel.

21.1.2.1.2 Procedures and controls for scrap removal

For each portal, describe how the identification and authorization of each person presenting scrap material for removal is verified to prevent removal by deceit. Describe how the authorization, type, and quantity of scrap material is to be verified. Discuss the components to be used to detect unauthorized removal of scrap. Identify the components to be used to sense unauthorized attempts to remove scrap from restricted areas and to be used at the CAS and SAS to assess sensor information. This discussion should include the identification of redundant and diverse components and subsystems to be used. Discuss the actions to be taken by the portal guard in the interim between notification of command and control personnel and the arrival of response personnel.

21.1.2.1.3   Procedures and controls for waste removal

For each portal, describe how the identification and authorization of each person presenting waste material for removal from restricted areas is to be verified to prevent removal by deceit. Describe how the authorization, type, and quantity of waste material is to be verified. Identify the components to be used to sense unauthorized attempts to remove waste from restricted areas and to transmit sensor data to command and control personnel. Identify the equipment and procedures to be used at the CAS and SAS to assess sensor information. This discussion should include the identification of redundant and diverse components and subsystems to be used. Discuss the immediate actions to be taken by portal guards in the interim between notification of command and control personnel and the arrival of response personnel.

21.1.2.2   Procedures and controls for removal under emergency conditions

Describe the procedure by which emergency conditions are to be verified by security personnel at each portal. Describe the procedures and equipment to be used to verify the authorization of personnel attempting to remove (assets), scrap, or waste during a bona fide emergency.

21.1.3   Bypass of removal procedures

Describe the procedures and controls to be used to prevent unauthorized removal of (assets), scrap, or waste by stealth or force (for both open and closed conditions at each portal). Describe the barrier and other components to be used to delay bypass attempts through the restricted area portal. Discuss the components to be used to detect attempts to bypass removal procedures and controls. Include those components to be used to sense unauthorized removal attempts and to transmit sensor data to command and control personnel. Identify the equipment and procedures to be used at the CAS and SAS to assess the information. This discussion should include the identification of redundant and diverse components and subsystems to be used. Identify the procedures and equipment to be used at manned portals in the interim between notification of command and control personnel and the arrival of response personnel.

"21.2   Removal of (assets) through the remainder of the boundary

Describe the components to be used to prevent removal of (assets) through the remainder of the restricted area boundary by means of stealth or force. Describe the barriers and other components to be used to prevent unauthorized removal of (assets) including through ventilation, plumbing, and similar systems. Identify the components to be used to sense such attempts and to transmit sensor data to command and control personnel. Identify the equipment and procedures to be used at the CAS and SAS to assess the information. This discussion should include identification of redundant and diverse components and subsystems to be used. In the case of multiple restricted areas where the same configuration of components is used, the information can be referenced. It is not necessary to repeat the information.

"22.0   Provision of authorized access and assurance of detection of and response to unauthorized penetration of the (facility's perimeter)

Describe the purpose and objective of the measures used to control access to the perimeter.

"22.1   Entry control through (perimeter) entry portals

Identify the number, location, and type of entry portals in the perimeter with reference to the facility map. For each portal, identify and describe all the components required for the entry control functions as requested in the following paragraphs. However, in cases where the same configuration of components is to be used at more than one entry portal, the measures need be described only once and may thereafter be referenced.

22.1.1   Entry authorization procedures

Describe the development of entry authorization procedures. Discuss how lists of personnel, material, and vehicles authorized for entry into each portal will be developed. Describe the distribution and maintenance of these lists.

22.1.2   Entry procedures and controls

22.1.2.1   Normal conditions

Describe how normal conditions differ between regular working hours and nonworking hours (nights, weekends, and holidays). Identify which portals are open and which are locked during each of these periods. This discussion should be related to the problem of entry in emergency situations, discussed in paragraph 22.1.2.2 below.

22.1.2.1.1   Procedures and controls for personnel and vehicle entry

For each entry portal, describe how the identification and authorization of each person and each vehicle is verified to prevent entry by deceit. Describe the policies and procedures used for escort of visitors and off-site vehicles.

Identify the methods used to detect, at entry control points, contraband on authorized personnel or in authorized vehicles. Describe the procedures and equipment to be used to notify command and control personnel suspect an attempt at unauthorized entry. Identify the steps to be taken by entry control personnel and the arrival of response personnel.

22.1.2.1.2 Procedures and controls for introduced materials

Describe the components to be used to control introduction of materials by deceit. Describe how authorizations are to be verified. Describe how the quantity and type of materials will be verified. Identify the components to be used to detect the introduction of unauthorized materials which may be hand-carried by an authorized individual, mailed, shipped, or carried on an unauthorized vehicle.

Describe the components to be used to notify command and control personnel in the event that introduction of unauthorized material is suspected. Identify the steps to be taken by entry control personnel in the period between notification of command and control personnel and the arrival of response personnel.

22.1.2.2 Procedures and controls for emergency entry of personnel vehicles

Describe the procedures and controls to be used for controlling entry during emergencies. Discuss how entry control personnel will verify that emergency conditions exist. Describe the procedures to be used for the escort of emergency personnel and emer-

gency vehicles (such as fire trucks and ambulances). Describe the procedures and equipment to
be used to notify command and control and supervisory personnel in the event of an attempt at
unauthorized emergency access. Describe the actions to be taken between the notification of command and control personnel and the arrival of response personnel.

22.1.3   Preventing bypass of entry procedures and controls
Describe the procedures and controls to be used to prevent
unauthorized entry through portals by stealth or force (for
both open and closed conditions at each portal). Describe the
barriers and other components to be used to delay bypass
attempts through the entry portal. Include those components
to be used to sense unauthorized entry and to transmit sensor
data to command and control personnel. Identify the equipment and procedures to be used at the CAS and SAS to assess
this sensor information. This discussion should include the
identification of redundant and diverse components and subsystems to be used. Describe the action to be taken by entry
control personnel to prevent or delay the attempt from succeeding in the period between notification of command and
control personnel and the arrival of response personnel.

"22.2   Entry through the remainder of the (facility's) boundary
Describe the components to be used to prevent entry through the
remainder of the (facility's) boundary. Describe the physical barriers
to be used at the boundary and any isolation zones. The description
of physical barriers should address the construction of all fences and
gates. For buildings which form part of the boundary, describe the
construction of the walls, floors, and ceilings, as well as how ventilation and other openings are to be secured.

Describe the components to be used to detect attempts at unauthorized entry. Identify the components to be used to sense unauthorized
entry attempts and to transmit sensor data to command and control
personnel. Identify the equipment and procedures to be used at the
CAS and SAS to assess the sensor information. This discussion should
include the identification of redundant and diverse components and
subsystems to be used.

Describe the actions to be taken by security personnel who detect
penetration attempts while on routine patrol, escort, or inspection
operations between the time they notify command and control personnel and the arrival of response personnel. Identify the equipment
and procedures to be used to contain unauthorized entry attempts
sufficiently to permit the arrival of response forces who will prevent
the attempt from resulting in theft sabotage.

"23.0   Response

Describe the purpose and objective of response measures to be employed.

"23.1   Communications

23.1.1   Communications with on-site forces

Describe the equipment and procedures to be used by command and control personnel to communicate with on-site security and response forces (this description should be coordinated with the discussion of the makeup of the on-site force in paragraph 23.2.1 below). The information provided here should include all communications with on-site forces which take place after command and control personnel are notified of possible contingency conditions. Describe the equipment and procedures to be used by supervisory personnel to communicate response instructions to the on-site force if these differ from the ones previously described. This description should include identification of redundant and diverse components and subsystems to be used.

23.1.2   Communications with off-site forces

Describe the equipment and procedures to be used by command and control personnel to communicate with off-site response forces (this description should be coordinated with the discussion of the makeup of the off-site forces in paragraph 23.2.2 below). Discuss communications with each local law enforcement agency involved in response activities and communications with all off-site response personnel other than local law enforcement agencies (for example off-duty employees). This discussion should include identification of redundant and diverse components and subsystems to be used.

"23.2   Effective response

This discussion should rely upon and to some extent summarize information provided in the facility contingency plan. While that plan should be referenced for detail, this section should provide an adequate description of the response capabilities.

23.2.1   On-site response

Discuss the personnel who constitute the on-site response force and describe their training (include security personnel and any nonsecurity personnel with response responsibilities). Reference the training plan for training details. Describe the equipment and procedures to be used by on-site personnel in providing an effective response to each of the unauthorized situations discussed in the previous chapters. Explain how the use of this equipment and these procedures result in containment until the off-site response forces arrive.

23.2.2   Off-site response
Discuss the local law enforcement agency personnel (and their training and equipment) who are to constitute the off-site response force. Also describe any other off-site response personnel who may be used for response actions. Include here the approximate time required for off-site forces to arrive at the facility after notification including weather conditions assumed. (Include here detailed aspects of the off-site response capability not discussed in Chapter 3.0 of part I. If the discussion in Chapter 3.0 of part I is already substantially detailed, it may simply be referenced)."[1]

It should be fairly obvious at this point that the NRC guidance takes into consideration every aspect of safeguarding a maximum-security facility. It must be reiterated, however, that the security plan for a particular facility need not include the details suggested. It can, of course, be modified to suit any site-specific purpose. What the NRC guidance does provide is a comprehensive presentation of those areas that must be considered when designing or upgrading the protection plan for a facility.

TRAINING AND QUALIFICATIONS PLAN

The first part of this section should state the qualifications criteria for security personnel employed by or assigned to a particular facility. For example:

1. Native-born or naturalized citizen
2. U.S. high school diploma (or an equivalency certificate) at minimum
3. No convictions for criminal activity
4. At least 21 years of age (or the legal age of majority for the locale)
5. Above average physical condition with no weaknesses or abnormalities, and capable of passing a complete physical examination by a licensed physician
6. 20/20 vision in both eyes, or correctable to 20/20 with glasses
7. No visual color deficiencies
8. Glaucoma or any other progressively degenerative eye disease shall be disqualifying.
9. No disqualifying hearing loss under American National Standards Institute (ANSI) standards as measured by a certified audiologist
10. No history or medical diagnosis of epilepsy or diabetes
11. No history of drug or alcohol addiction
12. No history of psychiatric or psychological treatment, including counseling, and able to satisfactorily pass clinical evaluation by a trained psychiatrist or psychologist

13. List of all diseases and/or injuries incurred during the five-year period preceding employment, showing where and by whom treated, final resolution of the medical problem, and current state of health

14. Capability to maintain function after performing strenuous physical activity (may be demonstrated on the physical agility course specified earlier)

15. No loss of limbs (partial or total amputation of one or more digits may be acceptable and must be individually evaluated to determine if such loss prevents the performance of any aspect of the site required duties)

16. Shall not be agoraphobic

The second section should outline the specific training given to all security personnel. (In the following, an asterisk indicates a practical exercise.)

Sample Training Plan

1. Introduction (1 hr)
   Description: general introduction to the site, its importance, and its personnel structure
   Outline
   A. Orientation
   B. Purpose and function of site
   C. Physical description and layout, including location of vital and sensitive areas
   D. Importance of protecting site, i.e., strategic value; and failure to safeguard, including national security implications and consequences
   E. Personnel organization and structure responsibilities, chain of command and control, and reporting relationships

2. Techniques of physical security (4 hrs)
   Description: discussion of basic security concepts centering on systems normally encountered by security personnel
   Outline
   A. Physical barriers that impede, delay, and control
   B. Access controls for selective admittance, and screening to prevent compromise of safeguards measures, such as disguised weapons
   C. Exit controls to detect theft or diversion
   D. Systems and components: access/exit controls—detection of metals, explosives, and contraband; alarms—operating principles of microwave, sonic, ultrasonic, infrared, passive infrared, seismic, electronic, and others, as well as monitoring, recording, and reporting; communications—radios, telephones (Commercial, Internal, Dedicated), intercoms, codes for operating, contingency, and duress situations (electronic, verbal, and manual gestures and

movements); closed-circuit TV—for surveillance and assessment; lock and key controls—purpose, principles, and safeguards; weapons—nonlethal, such as baton and incapacitating agents, lethal, small arms including handguns, rifles, shotguns, and machine guns, crew-operated (machine gun, mortar, rocket launcher), vehicular weapons systems, and explosives and demolitions; and lighting system, types, purpose, and principles

    E.   Security force purpose, mission, and role

3.   Tour of facility* (2 hrs)

Description: site-specific orientation of the physical layout of the site and facilities with special emphasis on application of general security concepts previously learned

Outline

    A.   Orientation

    B.   Familiarization, i.e., avenues of approach, physical barriers, terrain (advantages and disadvantages), facilities, and resources

4.   On-site administrative requirements (10 hrs)

Description: analysis of site-specific administrative requirements for security personnel

Outline

    1.   On-Site Administrative requirements

        A.   Security force: purpose; mission to protect personnel, assets, and property; organization and structure for every-day operating and contingencies for elements, both operating and response; command and control (chain-of-command); legal authority for apprehension, restraint, detention, arrest, physical force, deadly physical force, search and seizure, crimes and elements, and rules of evidence; deployment for fixed posts, patrols, mobile assignments, response forces, and special assignments (posts and details) (executive protection and mutual aid); philosophy and standards regarding appearance, attitude, interpersonal relationships, code of conduct (disciplinary procedures)

        B.   Physical protection plan, its purpose, briefing, and compliance

        C.   Post orders, their purpose, briefing, and compliance

        D.   Records and reports

5.   On-site systems and equipment (16 hrs)

Description: examination of systems and equipment in use at the site and the operation of each. With the exception of weapons systems, emphasis is on hands-on training and establishing a basis for achieving proficiency in usage.

Outline

    1.   On-site systems and equipment such as

        A.   Access control system, i.e., operation* (recognition of sabotage devices*) and documentation

      B.   Closed-circuit TV, i.e., operation*, and techniques of surveil-lance and assessment

      C.   Alarm system operation, recording requirements, and report-ing requirements

      D.   Communications system operation, routine and contingency codes/call signs

      E.   Lock and key control system operation and documentation

      F.   Lighting system operation

      G.   Weapons system introduction and familiarization (both per-sonal and adversary)

      H.   Personal protective equipment*, i.e., protective masks, bullet-resistant garments, and headgear

6.   Alarm response (4 hrs)

    Description: discussion of appropriate and correct responses to and assessment of intrusion and other alarms

    Outline

    A.   Perimeter alarms

    B.   Interior alarms

    C.   Others, i.e., detectors of metals, explosives, and contraband

    D.   Time constraints

    E.   Response

    F.   Supplemental techniques, i.e., closed-circuit TV and audio aids

    G.   Search techniques* for persons, buildings, vehicles, and terrain

7.   Patrol methods (5 hrs)

    Description: thorough discussion of proper security patrol methods with site-specific and practical application. Considerable emphasis is placed on basic officer survival techniques.

    Outline

    1.   Patrol Methods

      A.   Techniques for point patrols, area patrols (backup personnel), and canine patrols (if applicable)

      B.   Considerations, i.e., cover*, concealment*, backlighting; tact-ical advantages; noise and sound discipline*; communications, (site-specific codes for routine, contingency, and duress situ-ations); challenging* signs, (countersigns, patrol words, and manual methods)

      C.   Clock rounds, (operation of time-recording devices*)

      D.   Ambush avoidance

8.   First Aid

    Description: Standard Red Cross first aid course coupled with a Basic Red Cross cardiopulmonary resuscitation (CPR) course

    Outline

    1.   Includes wounds, specific injuries, shock, CPR, poisoning, drugs and drug abuse, burns, heat injuries, bone and joint injuries, dress-ings and bandages, and sudden illness

9.   Contingency situations
      Definition: intensive and complete treatment of contingency situations
                    most likely to be encountered on site and the correct se-
                    curity force response to each

      Outline
      1.   Contingency situations:
            A.   Security system(s) failure*, including alert procedures, re-
                 sponse, compensatory measures, and recovery
            B.   Confirmed intrusion/attack/diversion/sabotage*, with the same
                 areas of emphasis as above
            C.   Work stoppages/labor disputes, with the same areas of em-
                 phasis as above
            D.   Bomb incidents and threats, including alert procedures and
                 response (recognition and avoidance) to explosive devices and
                 booby traps
            E.   Civil disturbances, including psychology and control of crowds
                 and mobs, alert procedures, response (formations and com-
                 mand and control), and recovery
            F.   Espionage alert procedures, response (investigative activities),
                 and compensatory measures
10.   Firearms (24 hrs)
      Description: complete and demanding course of fire using site-specific
                     weapons and commencing with weapons familiarization,
                     progressing through qualification, and terminating with
                     nighttime qualification

      Outline
            A.   Introduction, with safety briefing, course and range procedures
            B.   Weapons familiarization/use/firing for handguns, rifles, shot-
                 guns, and others
            C.   Weapons qualification firing (day) of the same arms listed
                 above
            D.   Weapons qualification firing (night) using the same weapons
                 listed above
11.   Report writing and documentation (2 hrs)
      Description: Basic instruction in the reports and records required on-
                     site with particular emphasis on the essential elements of
                     good report writing

      Outline
      1.   Report Writing and Documentation:
            A.   Site-specific requirements
            B.   Field notes* and observations
            C.   Basics*, i.e., who, what, when, where, how, why
            D.   Record keeping, including site-specific requirements and pro-
                 cedures

12. Supplemental basic training (16 hrs)
    Description: follow-up course of instruction covering those areas of concern not previously addressed
    Outline
    1.   Supplemental Basic Training
        A.   Nighttime tour of site*
        B.   Rescue operations, such as emergency rescue and transfer*, extrication, and extracting a downed officer*
        C.   Defense against incapacitating agents*
        D.   Traffic Control*, i.e., traffic direction (hand signals), and vehicle stops
        E.   Unarmed self-defense*
        F.   Safety and fire prevention; including hazards, corrective action, and locations of post indicator valves, fire-fighting equipment usage, etc.
        G.   Handling prisoners*
13. On-the-job training (120 hrs)
    Description: 120 hours where each security officer is required to implement the principles, techniques, and procedures learned thus far. Emphasis is on developing proficiency in the use of equipment and systems and achieving competence in the performance of security duties.
    Outline
    None
14. Supervision (4 hrs)
    Description: basic supervisor's course designed to identify and cultivate potential supervisors after initial and secondary training
    Outline
    1.   Supervision
        A.   Principles and qualities of supervision
        B.   Supervisory characteristics and traits
        C.   Supervisory indicators (Tactical supervision)
        D.   Motivation and morale
15. Adversary group operations (4 hrs)
    Description: to acquaint security personnel with the potential adversary groups operating in the site-specific area
    Outline
    1.   Adversary Group Operations
        A.   Profiles
        B.   Motivation
        C.   Objectives
        D.   Tactics
        E.   Force
16. Officer survival (12 hrs)

Description: discussion and practical application of techniques of individual officer survival in situations wherein he may be in danger of death or serious bodily injury

Outline
1. Officer Survival
    A. Individual tactical movements under fire* and use of support fire
    B. Survival, evasion, and escape*
    C. Clandestine tactics and technology
    D. Sniper situations* and countersniper tactics
    E. Ambush situations*, counterambush tactics and ambush survival

17. Adversary actions (12 hrs)
    Description: Instruction in the management of adversary actions directed against the facility or site or its personnel in an attempt to secure a political or tactical advantage

Outline
    A. Hostage situations*, including alert procedures, response, and recovery
    B. Barricaded criminal situations* with the same areas of emphasis as above
    C. Abductions/kidnappings/threats to personnel and against site (alert procedures, response, and recovery)
    D. Contingency planning

18. Weapons qualification under stress (24 hrs)
    Description: series of weapons qualification courses designed to introduce the security officer to stress firing. This module will acquaint the officer with functioning under stress and offer advice and techniques to overcome the obvious disadvantages associated with stress situations.

Outline
1. Weapons Qualification Under Stress
    A. Safety briefing, target identification, and target acquisition
    B. Stress firing course (day)*
    C. Stress firing course (night)*, and with use of artificial light
    D. Firing from moving vehicles*
    E. Firing at moving vehicles*
    F. Principles of ricochet shooting*

19. Supplemental advanced training (6 hrs)
    Description: follow-up course of advanced training subjects not previously addressed in phase III advanced training

Outline
1. Supplemental Advanced Training
    A. Counterinsurgency operations
    B. Infiltration techniques* and defenses

C. Intelligence/information gathering
D. Transport/vehicle security*
E. Protection of classified/sensitive information, i.e., principles of information security and electronic data processing (EDP) safeguards

All of the above subjects will be taught by or verified by security supervision or management. Other personnel may instruct in their areas of expertise.

Each individual will successfully complete (with at least a 70 percent grade) all examinations prior to completion of the training program.

At least every 12 months, all personnel will be required successfully to complete an annual qualification examination designed to test proficiency with respect to assigned duties. The results of training and qualification will be permanently maintained for each individual. Contract as well as proprietary security personnel are subject to the requirements of this training program.

SAMPLE WEAPONS QUALIFICATION TRAINING

Qualification

Each security individual shall fire the handgun, shotgun, and rifle for qualification annually during daylight hours. Guards shall also fire assigned weapons for familiarization annually during hours of darkness.

Handgun

Security personnel shall qualify annually with the handgun on the following prescribed course (Table 12–1) (a modification of that used by the local law enforcement officials statewide); the B-27 target will be used. Minimum qualifying score is 210 points.

Stage 1—7 yards, double action, 12 shots from the crouch position. The 25-second time starts with loaded weapon in holster and includes reloading for the second six-shot string.

Table 12-1   Handgun Qualification Course

Stage	Range (yds)	Fire	Time (sec)	Strings	Shots	Maximum Score
1	7	Rapid	25	2	6	60
2	12	Rapid	90	3	6	90
3	21	Rapid	50	2	6	60
4	25	Rapid	105	3	6	90

Stage 2—12 yards, double action, six shots kneeling, six shots standing left hand unsupported, six shots standing right hand unsupported. The 90-second time starts with loaded gun in holster and includes reloading for two subsequent six-shot strings.

Stage 3—21 yards, double action, six shots standing left hand supported, six shots standing right hand supported. The 50-second time starts with loaded gun in holster and includes reloading for the second six-shot string.

Stage 4—25 yards, double action, six shots, standing left hand from behind barricade, six shots standing right hand from behind barricade. The 1-minute 45-seconds time starts with loaded gun in holster and includes reloading for two subsequent six-shot strings.

Semiautomatic rifle

Security personnel shall qualify annually with the semiautomatic rifle on the following prescribed course (Table 12–2) using the B-27 target. To qualify, the individual must place 80 percent of all rounds within the black silhouette.

Stage 1—100 yards, 10 shots from the prone position.

Stage 2—100 yards, 10 shots kneeling from behind barricade. The 3-minute time starts with chamber empty.

Stage 3—100 yards, 10 shots standing. The 60-second time starts with chamber empty.

Stage 4—50 yards, 10 shots standing. The 60-second time starts with chamber empty.

Shotgun

Security personnel shall qualify annually with the shotgun on the course prescribed in Table 12–3 using the B-27 target.

To qualify each individual shall be required to place 50 percent of all pellets (36 of 72) within the black silhouette.

Table 12-2 Semiautomatic Rifle Qualification Course

Stage	Range (yds)	Fire	Time (min)	Strings	Shots	Maximum Score
1	100	Slow	10	1	10	100
2	100	Timed	3	1	10	100
3	100	Rapid	1	1	10	100
4	50	Rapid	1	1	10	100

Table 12-3   Shotgun Qualification Course

Stage	Range (Yds.)	Fire	Time (Secs.)	Strings	Shots	Maximum Points
1*	15	Rapid	10	1	4	36
2**	25	Rapid	10	1	4	36

*Stage 1 (15 yds., one round fired at each of four separate targets from the hip. The ten seconds time starts with the chamber empty).

**Stage 2 (25 yds, one round fired at each of four separate targets from the standing position. The ten seconds time starts with chamber empty).

Sample Weapons Familiarization Training

Handgun

Security personnel shall familiarize themselves annually with the handgun during hours of darkness by firing 10 rounds from the 25-yard line into the B-27 target. Light from a flashlight may be used.

Semiautomatic Rifle

Security personnel shall familiarize themselves annually with the rifle during the hours of darkness by firing 10 rounds from the standing off-hand position at the 25 yard line. Light from a flashlight may be used.

Shotgun

Security personnel shall familiarize themselves annually with the shotgun during the hours of darkness by firing 4 rounds from the 15-yard line into the B-27 target. Subdued light may be used.

Training

Each security individual will be given weapons training and be instructed in subject areas such as:

1.   Weapons familiarization—introduction to mechanical assembly, disassembly range penetration capability, and firing
2.   Cleaning and storage—weapons cleaning and on-site storage
3.   Weapon firing—day and night firing on designated courses for qualification and familiarization
4.   Weapons handling—introduction to weapons safety in handling

5. Weapons loading—loading, unloading, cleaning, and reloading techniques
6. Drawing the weapon—drawing and pointing the weapon, and situation stimuli
7. Firing techniques—explanation of rapid fire, stress firing, and close-quarter firing techniques

At least once during every 12-month period, armed security personnel will be required to meet qualifications in accordance with the site plan. Practice firing with the weapons will be conducted as appropriate to ensure proficiency.

CONTINGENCY PLAN

The section of the security plan dealing with the facility's response to emergencies, unusual situations, and contingencies is known as the contingency plan.

Nuclear facilities are required to develop and implement a safeguards contingency plan. As its title implies, this deals exclusively with threats to the facility safeguards and is based on a set of 24 threat stimuli provided by the Nuclear Regulatory Commission. Each of the stimuli deals with a safeguards-related contingency.

For non-nuclear facilities, the contingency plan[2] should address every possible situation in which a security response could be generated, including:

Natural disasters	Man-made disasters
Forest fires	Plant fires
Hurricanes	Chemical accidents
Floods	Transportation accidents
Tornados	Public demonstrations/civil disturbances
Winter storms	Bomb threats
Earthquakes	Sabotage
	Radiological accidents
	Nuclear attack

For the most part, the contingency plan should be confined to security responses to incidents as they pertain to safeguarding the facility and its assets. In many facilities, however, the effort expended in writing a plan from the safeguards perspective is usually extended to include overall facility response to contingencies. The following outline is suggested:

   I. Introduction
        Communicate the purpose of the plan and basic actions to be taken by every employee on becoming aware of a contingency situation.
  II. Definitions and abbreviations
      A. Definitions
      B. Abbreviations—list of definitions and abbreviations used in the plan
 III. Scope and applicability
      A. General
          1. A brief description of the facility and its processes with reference to the overview of site and facility sections of the security plan
      B. Scope
      C. Applicability
          1. Compliance with the contingency plan should be mandatory for all personnel while on facility premises.
  IV. Summary of contingency plan
      A. General
          1. Brief summary
      B. Typical contingency scenario
          1. Sample contingency and its effect, including response
   V. Contingencies
      A. Classification
          1. Anticipated potential contingency situations in order of severity, together with appropriate responses to each
  VI. Contingency control organization
      A. Normal organization
      B. Contingency organization
          1. Direction and coordination
          2. Emergency assignments
      C. Additional support/resources
          1. Outside agencies
          2. Corporate resources
          3. Mutual aid compacts
 VII. Contingency response
      A. Activation of contingency organization
      B. Assessment
      C. Corrective actions
      D. Protective actions
      E. First aid
      F. Medical aid
      G. Medical evacuation
      H. Other

VIII.   Facilities and equipment
    A.   Contingency control center
    B.   Communications systems
    C.   Medical facilities
    D.   Damage control equipment and supplies
        1.   Assembly area and control center locations; communications capabilities; first aid and medical supplies; and damage control capabilities

IX.   Maintaining readiness
    A.   Organizational readiness
        1.   Amount and type of training to be given to those involved in the execution of the plan
        2.   Other measures

X.   Resumption of operations
    1.   Considerations on which to base a decision to resume operations
    2.   Procedures and processes to be used to effect a return to work

XI.   Appendices
    A.   Contingency response summary
        1.   General guidelines to be followed in response to each contingency.
        2.   Guidelines for dealing with media coverage of the contingency
    B.   Notification sequence list
    C.   Evacuation plan
        1.   Procedures for a limited or general evacuation of the facility
        2.   Assembly areas and special instructions
    D.   Fire protection plan (optional)
        While attachment of a formal fire protection plan to the contingency plan is optional, every facility should have a formal, up-to-date fire protection plan.

NOTES

1.   Nuclear Regulatory Commission, *Fixed Site Physical Protection Upgrade Rule Guidance Compendium* (Washington, D.C.: The Commission, 1978), pp. 18–51.
2.   Defense Civil Preparedness Agency, *Disaster Planning Guide for Business and Industry* (Baltimore, Md: The Agency, 1978), pp. 1–6.

CHAPTER 13

Coordination with Local Law Enforcement Authorities

All too often, coordination of site operations or contingency plans with local law enforcement officials is an afterthought. The time to consider this matter is not after all the plans have been prepared and approved and are ready for implementation. This approach presents these officials with a fait accompli and solicits their cooperation in ways or with equipment and manpower that they may not be able to provide. It can also quickly erode all prior efforts to build good will between the facility and the local police or other official agencies on whom the site depends for essential protective or assistance services, such as the fire department and ambulance corps.

The careful security planner should, in the preliminary stages of any new site procedure, or a revision of one already in existence, ask himself these questions:

1. Will successful implementation of this plan or procedure require the assistance of the local law enforcement authorities in any way?
2. Based on available knowledge of the local police department's equipment and manpower resources, can they effectively provide the assistance necessary?
3. If they cannot effectively provide the necessary assistance, do the local police have a mutual-assistance agreement with other area law enforcement authorities?
4. If there is a mutual-assistance agreement, what would be the response time and in what numbers can this aid respond to the emergency?

Once it has been determined that the local police have the capabilities necessary to provide requested assistance, either through in-place manpower and equipment or through a mutual-assistance program, the following additional questions should be asked:

1. What are the means of two-way communications available on site that provide a high degree of assurance that communications with local law enforcement officials will be reliable regardless of the contingency?

2.   Which site officials will have the responsibility and authority to initiate a request for assistance from local law enforcement officials?
3.   What special training will be necessary for security and/or local law enforcement authority personnel to ensure the desired response result is achieved?
4.   What if any charges may be assessed against the site for assistance provided?

In a maximum-security setting, there should be several methods for summoning assistance. In addition to commercial telephone lines, the central and secondary alarm stations should have dedicated telephone links (hot lines) with the local police headquarters (provided there is a 24-hour presence there). If the local police department is small and has no night desk person or dispatcher, the hot line should be connected with the nearest state police, sheriff's office, or other agency that is manned around the clock, and which has responsibility for dispatching requested aid for the area in which the site is located. There should also be a direct radio link; this could be as simple as transmitter and receivers located in the central and secondary alarm stations and tuned to police frequencies, or as complex as site and/or police agency rules make it necessary.

PLANNING WITH LAW ENFORCEMENT AGENCIES

In the sit-down planning phase with the local police, the site should provide a list of those officials who have the authority and responsibility to request police assistance. Each individual should have a code name or number that can be checked against the list maintained by the police to verify identity. Naturally, applicable site personnel changes would have to be brought to the immediate attention of the police to ensure that their list is current at all times.

If special training is necessary or would be beneficial, it should be scheduled, with an invitation to the local chief of police for participation by as many of his officers as he feels necessary (or the site may set a realistic limit where necessary). An invitation for police participation in any training that could benefit the department is always a good idea. It builds good will and ensures a cooperative attitude. In an era of lean fiscal budgets, many police chiefs appreciate opportunities to provide relevant training to their personnel at no cost to the department.

If emergency police assistance will require these officials to enter the protected area, the following should be accomplished prior to the necessity for requesting such assistance:

1.   If security clearance is necessary, it should be initiated for all local police who are to be allowed entry.

2.   When required, photo ID badges should be prepared and stored where they will be readily available for issue upon entry.
3.   Officers who will be responding should have frequent familiarization tours of the facility. Danger areas should be pointed out where the use of a weapon, radio transmitter, or open flames could create a severe personnel hazard.
4.   Coordinated training exercises or drills should be conducted so that police and plant security personnel learn to recognize each other and develop their strategies mutually.
5.   Critiques of such exercises between supervisory personnel from both the site security department and the police department will point out areas for change or improvement.

While it is a somewhat delicate subject and one emergency planners would just as soon forget about, some jurisdictions have implemented or are contemplating a monetary charge for their emergency assistance above and beyond the services normally provided to commercial enterprises. As the budgets for police services are cut back, more and more municipalities will begin to consider this seriously. Therefore site planning should bear in mind the fact that local law enforcement assistance may come with a price tag attached.

There are some additional methods whereby cooperation may be obtained from local officials. For example, if the site has a firearms range but local departments do not, the police can be offered free use of the facility (provided a signed waiver is received in advance absolving the site of responsibility for injury or property damage). If the site has a training classroom equipped with audio-visual equipment that is underused, it can be made available to the local department. The police chief and his senior officers can be invited to site celebrations or social events. If the site manufactures consumer goods and has an employee discount purchase program, this courtesy can be extended to the local police; police personnel can be allowed to use company facilities such as a picnic area, beach, athletic fields, and so on.

The chief and/or senior department officers can be invited as guests to fraternal gatherings, such as meetings of the local ASIS (American Society for Industrial Security) chapter; if they express an interest, they can be sponsored for membership. When possible, site personnel can seek to become members, either active or associate, of locally recognized and supported police professional or fraternal organizations, such as IACP (International Association of Chiefs of Police). If any member of the site staff has a great deal of expertise in a subject that would be of interest to police administrators, he can offer to address their group. By the same token, the police officials should be solicited as featured speakers at special security industry gatherings or meetings. Corporate contributions (when properly documented) to police fund raisers are always appreciated. In the case of small police departments, the company may wish to consider purchase and donation of a piece of needed equipment to the local force.

The amount of cooperation that may be obtained from local law enforcement officials is in direct proportion to the amount of time and effort devoted to maintaining a close, personal, and harmonious relationship between the security manager and the local chief of police.

CHAPTER 14

Security in Transit

At some maximum-security facilities, shipment of assets is an integral part of operations. The security director more often than not has responsibility for the protection of assets in transit, that is, direct responsibility or incidental responsibility. There are certain safeguards that should be taken to provide protection from the time assets leave a facility until they are turned over to a recipient who assumes total responsibility for their protection. At facilities where transportation of assets is regulated by a government agency, there are many guidelines in this area as well as regulations to ensure that they are followed. In such cases the security director may have little if any input on the matter. Other facilities, while not bound by legal requirements to safeguard a shipment, sometimes voluntarily assume the responsibility for moral, philosophical, or political reasons.

The suggestions offered herein are intended to assist the maximum-security practitioner in meeting the responsibilities to which he is committed. As with guidelines throughout this book, suggestions represent the minimum safeguards that should be taken.

SECURITY IN TRANSIT

Every shipment of sensitive assets must be planned and should be documented to preclude confusion and after-the-fact attempts to place blame in the event of an accident, theft, or diversion.

While initially a time-consuming effort, planning for shipment security becomes easier after several shipments because of the familiarity that results from repetition. For this reason, extensive planning should go into the first few shipments so that mistakes can be corrected and attention given to areas that were overlooked.

Documenting the planning effort and retaining it on file can certainly be an asset in the event that a problem arises with a particular shipment. It is no secret that critics abound in this world, and there is nothing to indicate that criticism will not be heard if a shipment of sensitive items is lost. Careful planning and documentation can do much to minimize such criticism. The same careful planning and documentation may limit liability if it supports a contention that all reasonable steps were taken to safeguard a shipment, loss of which, for example, could endanger the public. The value of planning in any context cannot be overlooked.

STANDARD OPERATING PROCEDURE

The first step in providing security for the transportation of sensitive assets should always be the development of a standard operating procedure. It should contain the following information: purpose, scope, responsibilities, procedure, records requirements, and attachments (or appendices).

The procedure should specify what types of shipments are to be safeguarded or that all shipments are to be safeguarded. There may be categories of shipments that require additional safeguards depending on their nature; this must be specified.

The following is one example of a transportation security procedure. At a minimum, each suggested safeguard should be included and compliance ensured.

I.   Purpose
    A.   To provide a suitable degree of protection for shipments of company product until protection responsibilities are assumed by the recipient
II. Scope
    A.   It is corporation policy, because of the nature of the product being transported, that protection of shipments be ensured from the time of origination until the time of receipt, or until responsibility for protection is assumed by another agency.
III. Responsibilities
    A.   Security director
        1.   It is the responsibility of the security director to:
            a.   Establish and maintain a current security in transit procedure
            b.   Ensure compliance with the security requirements of the procedure
            c.   Maintain liaison with the shipping department to ensure that the security department is advised of all shipments
            d.   Monitor all shipments to ensure that appropriate security measures have been instituted
            e.   Provide additional safeguards if and when necessary
IV. Procedure
    A.   All shipments will be categorized as follows:
        1.   Category 1 = _____
        2.   Category 2 = _____
        3.   Category 3 = _____
        4.   Category 4 = _____
        5.   Category 5 = _____

B. For all category 1 shipments, the following measures will be taken:
1. An acknowledged order delivery (AOD) or signature service will be requested by the shipping department supervisor.
2. If acknowledgment of delivery is not received when specified, the shipping department supervisor will advise the security department.

C. For all category 2 shipments, the following measures, in addition to those specified in IV B, will be taken:
1. The freight forwarder's management and its security department will be notified.
2. "Nose-loading" of the trailer will be specified.
3. Signature service will be specified.
4. Routing of the shipment will be requested.

D. For all category 3 shipments, the following measures, in addition to those specified in IV B and C, will be taken:
1. Checkpoints will be established and arrival notification requested.
2. Final arrival notification will be requested.

E. For all category 4 shipments, the following measures, in addition to those specified in IV B, C, and D, will be taken.
1. Exclusive use of shipment vehicle will be specified.
2. The trailer will be marked with numbers or letters on its roof; such numbers or letters will be easily visible and readable from low-flying aircraft (they will be at least three feet in height).
3. The shipment vehicle will make no stops except at operating terminals.
4. The trailer will be loaded and sealed.

F. For all category 5 shipments, the following measures in addition to all of those previously specified will be taken:
1. Armed escorts will accompany the shipment vehicle from departure to arrival at its destination.

G. All safeguards measures will be provided by the security department unless otherwise specified.

H. Times of shipment departure will be determined by the security department.

I. Shipments will not be cleared for departure until all specified and additional safeguards have been instituted and verified by the security department.

J. On safe arrival of the shipment, the security director will be advised.

A. Records requirements
A. The following records will be completed and maintained on file by the security department until the safe arrival of the shipment in question, at which time they will be destroyed; no record of a specific shipment may be duplicated:
1. Notice of shipment (attachment A)
2. Shipment checklist (attachment B)
3. Notice of shipment arrival (attachment C)

  B. The security in transit procedure shall be labeled "Company Confidential" and protected accordingly.
VI. Attachments
  A. Notice of shipment
  B. Shipment checklist
  C. Notice of shipment arrival

COMPANY CONFIDENTIAL

Attachment A
Company Confidential
(Not to be duplicated—hand-carry only)

To: Security director   From: Shipping department supervisor
Subject: Notice of shipment   Date:

1. Date of shipment _____
2. Time of shipment _____ (leave blank; to be determined by security department)
3. Destination _____
4. Category of shipment: 1, 2, 3, 4, 5
5. Freight forwarder _____
6. Address of forwarder _____
     Telephone number _____
7. Type of shipment vehicle _____

Attachment B
Company Confidential
(Not to be duplicated—hand-carry only)

Shipment Checklist

Date: _____   Category: _____

Category 1	*Initials*	*Date*
1. AOD requested	_____	_____
2. AOD not received, security advised	_____	_____
Category 2		
3. Forwarder management and security advised	_____	_____

4.   Nose loading specified   _____   _____
5.   Signature service specified   _____   _____
6.   Routing requested   _____   _____

Category 3

7.   Checkpoints established and notifica-   _____   _____
     tion requested
8.   Final arrival notification requested   _____   _____

Category 4

9.   Exclusive use of vehicle requested   _____   _____
10. Roof markings on trailer   _____   _____
11. "No stop" specified   _____   _____
12. Trailer locked and sealed   _____   _____
     Seal number(s) _____

Category 5

13. Armed escorts assigned   _____   _____
     (names, addresses, SSNs, telephone   _____
     numbers)
_____

_____

14. Shipment cleared for departure   _____   _____
     Type _____ Model _____ Year _____
     Color _____ Driver's name _____
     Tractor reg. # _____
     Trailer reg. # _____
     By _____ Date _____ Time _____
15. ETA at destination: _____

Attachment C

To: Security director   From:
Subject: Notice of shipment arrival   Date:

Shipment number _____, which departed on _____,
bearing seal number(s) _____ _____ ar-
rived without incident at its scheduled destination on _____
at _____ pm/am.

Signature _____
Date _____

SHIPMENT SECURITY ORDER

Whenever a shipment is provided with safeguards to ensure its protection and whenever such safeguards include an armed or unarmed escort, a shipment security order should be prepared. It should contain all information pertinent to the protection of that particular shipment.

Company Confidential
Shipment Security Order

Date(s) of shipment: _____
From (departure): _____
To (destination): _____
ETA at destination: _____
Travel route(s): _____ (see attachment) _____

Shipment vehicle information:
Description(s): _____
Special markings: _____
ID number(s): _____
Seal number(s): _____
Cargo: _____

Escort vehicle information:
Description(s): _____
Special markings: _____
ID number(s): _____

Escort personnel:

Name	Address	DOB	SSN	Company

Attachments:
1. Travel route(s)
2. Escort instructions
3. Company-issued equipment
4. Communications information
5. Emergency law enforcement telephone numbers
6. Liaison
7. (Others as necessary)

Company Confidential
Attachment 1
Shipment Security Order

Travel route(s)

(Including layovers, checkpoints, and special instructions)

Route(s)	*Layovers*	*Checkpoints*

Company Confidential
Attachment 2
Shipment Security Order

Escort Instructions

Instructions	*Special Instructions*

Company Confidential
Attachment 3
Shipment Security Order
Company-Issued Equipment

Firearms   *Ammunition*

Type:

Issued to:

Communications equipment

Two-way radios (including CB):
Mobile telephone(s):
Other:

Clothing

Type:

Other

Company Confidential
Attachment 4
Shipment Security Order

Communications Information

Radio codes	Telephone numbers	Special instructions

Company Confidential
Attachment 5
Shipment Security Order

Emergency Law Enforcement Telephone Numbers

Agency	Telephone number

Company Confidential
Attachment 6
Shipment Security Order

Law Enforcement Liaison

Agency	Telephone number	Name	Remarks

Company Confidential
Attachment 7
Shipment Security Order

Other Attachments

(Other attachments listed here and found on subsequent pages)

While most of the shipment security order is self-explanatory, the attachments should be clarified.

Travel Routes

Routes, layovers, and checkpoints should be listed here. Additionally, the freight forwarder's control point and relay manager (and phone number) should be listed for each leg of a journey.

Escort Instructions

Included in the instructions section should be at least the following basic guidelines (those marked with an asterisk (*) should be deleted if escort personnel are not armed):

1. Escorts are to accompany shipment vehicle(s) to destination until turned over to authorized representative as specified.
2. Escorts will stand by with shipment whenever stopped, until loaded, or until responsibility is assumed by authorized representative.
3. In the event of a vehicle emergency, e.g., accident or breakdown, shipment will be safeguarded at all times.
4. In the event of criminal activity directed against shipment, escorts will withdraw immediately from the scene, summon police authorities, and stand by to assist responding law enforcement personnel.
*5. Firearms are strictly for personnel defense, i.e., to protect a life from the imminent use of deadly physical force directed against it.
*6. Only company-issued firearms specified elsewhere in this order are authorized. No other firearms will be taken.
*7. Escorts will comply with all state and local firearms laws and regulations in effect in the state or locality in which they are traveling. Whenever required by law, firearms will be disassembled and stored in the escort vehicle(s).
8. Only stops authorized by the escort team leader (or designee) are permitted and all possible safeguards will be taken whenever shipment vehicles are stopped.
9. At least ____ escorts will remain with the shipment at all times until it is turned over to authorized personnel.
10. Escort personnel will wear a uniquely identifiable symbol or item of clothing and will carry at least two forms of positive identification.
*11. No rounds will be routinely carried in the chamber of any firearm.
12. No alcoholic beverages will be carried in the escort or shipment vehicle(s) or consumed for the duration of the shipment.

Special instructions would include information not found elsewhere in the shipment security order, and could include such things as hotel reservations for escort personnel after shipment has been delivered, and miscellaneous telephone numbers.

Company-Issued Equipment

Included in this attachment should be all equipment issued to escort personnel for their use during a particular shipment.

Communications Information

This section is reserved for radio and/or radio telephone communications information. Radio codes for personnel, duress codes, CB radio information, mobile telephone information, and instructions and other such details should be included.

Emergency Law Enforcement Telephone Numbers

All emergency telephone numbers should be listed of law enforcement agencies and any other agencies as necessary in the area(s) through which the shipment will be traveling.

Law Enforcement Liaison

There are two schools of thought regarding the transportation of sensitive or high-risk items over the nation's highways. One holds that law enforcement agencies should not be advised when this occurs because of the necessity to maintain as absolute a degree of secrecy regarding such shipments as possible. The other school of thought feels that law enforcement authorities should be advised whenever a sensitive shipment is to be routed through their jurisdictions. The latter approach is recommended. Secrecy can be maintained to a certain degree if the shipment is coordinated in advance with the law enforcement authorities through whose jurisdictions it will pass. The security director's initial contact with law enforcement should establish a liaison. It is not necessary to provide any sensitive information at this point other than to advise the agency that a shipment will be passing through and that the agency will be advised just prior to the shipment entering its jurisdiction.

The agency, telephone number, and liaison's name should be listed along with any special notations listed under remarks. Examples of special notations could include firearms laws and requirements for compliance in a particular jurisdiction, unique motor vehicle laws that may be applicable, or other information provided by the liaison.

Other Attachments

Any other attachments to the shipment security order should be listed here and included in the order. Such items as an atlas, equipment checklist, daily expense record, invoices, and delivery receipts may be included.

By following the guidance offered, the maximum-security director can provide the basis for a reasonable degree of protection for his assets while they are in transit. If additional protection is required, he should consult a company specializing in the movement of sensitive items or valuable commodities.

CHAPTER 15

Protection of Proprietary and Safeguards Information

For those facilities that use special manufacturing processes, secret formulas, and exceptionally public-safety-sensitive materials and products, safeguarding of company confidential information and procedures may already be a government required reality, or the necessity for such should be closely examined.

In a maximum-security setting, the types of security-related information that must be protected from unauthorized disclosure include[1]:

1. Details of the physical security plan including all contingency plans
2. Information on the total number of guards employed at the site, including a shift and/or daily break-down
3. Maps, sketches, photos, schematics, blueprints, etc., that show details or the location of physical security barriers
4. Details of the security alarm system, including information on inoperative equipment such as repair requests, work orders, etc.
5. Copies of the security officer post orders or other instructions
6. Site security procedures
7. Information dealing with the emergency response forces, including the composition of off-site forces, their equipment, response time, routes used to reach the site, etc.
8. The names, addresses, and phone numbers of all site personnel
9. Information, reports, pictures, etc., that identify equipment at the site as being vital for the uninterrupted continuance of facility operations, including the provision of physical security services, etc.

Because a disciplined and determined adversary will seek to learn as much about the facility as possible before taking action, he will attempt to obtain this from any available source. This includes detailed plans and specifications for construction, modification, or renovation filed with the local building inspector; copies of the contractor's or subcontractor's working blueprints for installation of intrusion-detection systems; copies of security suppliers invoices for equipment or materials; direct observation; and cultivation of acquaintances with site personnel from whom much of the general information and specific details required can be obtained, either through skillful manipulation or through outright subversion and bribery.

Whenever possible, the information necessary for obtaining a building permit should be as vague as possible under the governing guidelines. Contractors or subcontractors who are involved in the fabrication or installation of security equipment or machinery that is considered vital to safe, secure, and uninterrupted site operations, or that may divulge company proprietary processes, should not be allowed to remove copies of blueprints or other detailed drawings from the site. To prevent the unauthorized copying of such blueprints or plans, the site should prohibit cameras and control access to copiers. When it is not possible or practical for this to be enforced (such as the custom off-site fabrication of bullet-resistant booths, alarm systems, or other intrusion detection devices), the site must ensure that, once the system or equipment is installed, no one, including the designer or installer, is capable of deactivating, using, bypassing, entering, or exiting any part thereof without generating an alarm signal at the central alarm station.

Some adversaries will seek to obtain first-hand information on a site through direct observation. This will usually involve gaining access through subterfuge. Because a maximum-security facility has strict access controls, this ordinarily would be very difficult, however, not necessarily impossible. The identity of all visitor personnel who are to be allowed access should be thoroughly checked and verified. Only those personnel who have an absolute need should be allowed entry into the protected area, and then they should be escorted at all times by an authorized individual who will be responsible for ensuring that they do not have access (visual or otherwise) to any proprietary or safeguards material or item. One method to limit the necessity for processing visitors into the protected area is to set up a visitors' center or other office spaces off site (or outside the protected area) where meetings may take place. This would involve some inconvenience to plant or site officials, but the security benefits far outweigh these inconveniences.

Suppliers of security equipment can be mines of information for an outside adversary. Once the adversary knows what kinds of intrusion-detection system he will be facing, and in cases where the supplier was also the installer where they are located, he can plan how best to enter or carry out his mission with the least chance of detection. In cases where security prohibits an adversary's entry and direct observation, he may seek to cultivate the social acquaintance of site personnel in order to gather intelligence. Through skillful manipulation, an adversary may obtain all or a major portion of the desired information in this manner. In some cases, information may be obtained by bribery, blackmail, coercion, or any other method considered expedient. An employee-awareness program that sensitizes personnel to the necessity for not discussing details about their jobs or physical protection measures would have an effect on adversary intelligence gathering through these means. Such a program would require frequent reinforcement.

Other types of site security information that must be safeguarded include:

1. Details on the guard posts, their locations, physical protection properties, access methods
2. Security officers' defensive positions or areas to which they are to respond for contingency operations
3. Location and details of the security emergency power supply, such as generating capacity, operating endurance, and location of the fuel supply and fuel supply filler, whether the emergency power system is protected by an alarm system, procedures for gaining access to the emergency power equipment, etc.[2]
4. The routes followed by security officers in responding to a contingency or intrusion alarm, and the security officers' routine patrol routes
5. When the material being safeguarded is in a vehicle that is provided with alarm and immobilization capabilities, details of this alarm system and the vehicle immobilization features must also be safeguarded.

In addition, safeguards must be provided for information relative to:

1. The size of the initial emergency response force
2. Types and numbers of weapons with which the security force in general (and response force in particular) are equipped
3. Amount of time necessary for the response force to mobilize, obtain equipment, and respond to the contingency or intrusion site
4. Primary and alternate response routes used by this force
5. Specific plan of action taken by this force on its arrival at the contingency or intrusion scene
6. Details regarding reserve forces, including their availability, response times, whether they are coming from on or off site, weapons and equipment, numbers, duties, etc.[3]

It is suggested that every site with a security information-safeguards program prepare with the aid of an attorney, a document that each employee would be required to sign under oath. It would require that they not divulge safeguards information under penalty of criminal prosecution during the period of their employment and for a set number of years following the termination of such employment.

One of the best methods for ensuring that compromising information is not inadvertently divulged is to restrict such information to only those personnel who have a demonstrated need to know. This approach runs counter to the basic human character makeup of most individuals who have a need to share acquired information or who, when they feel they are being denied information to which others have access are unable to rest until their curiosities have been satisfied. The precept for this requirement is that the fewer the number of persons in possession of sensitive information, the more remote the possibility for a security breach. If a breach should occur, the investigation would conceivably more easily be able to pinpoint the source because of the small number of persons involved.

Whenever safeguards information is not in use it must be afforded proper protection. This would require that it be placed in a suitable security storage container that is capable of being locked, and which in turn is located within a security-controlled or protected access area. A controlled access area, as defined in the *Code of Federal Regulations*,[4]

> should provide both isolation and access control. The boundaries of the area should be of substantial construction to deter entry or exit through other than the established access control points. Access should be positively controlled by personal recognition, use of keys or card keys, or other comparable means.

When it becomes necessary to transport documents containing safeguards information within the same facility, the document should be prominently marked (top left and bottom right corners of each page) with the caveat, "Company Private ("Safeguards") Information—Do Not Duplicate." This may be supplemented by the requirement "Material Requires Hand-Carried Delivery Only." These and any other necessary instructions should be applied by a rubber stamp with letters at least three-eighths of an inch high and preferably in an ink color that contrasts with the body of the communication or printed material. At no time should such an item be entrusted to an interoffice or intraplant mail distribution system. If the document must be sent outside the facility and there is concern regarding entrusting it to the postal system because of its sensitivity, the use of a member of the security supervisory or management staff as a messenger should be considered. When the material is to be transmitted by a postal or commercial messenger service, it should be placed into an opaque envelope and addressed to the receiving official by name and complete address. The envelope should be prominently marked front and back with the words "Safeguards (or "Company Proprietary") Information" (as applicable), "To Be Opened By Addressee Only." This envelope should then be enclosed in another opaque envelope that is suitably addressed and that carries no security markings. No matter which delivery system is used, a continuous chain of custody, by signature, should be required.

Other methods for transmitting safeguards or proprietary information include telephone, telegraph, teletype, facsimile circuits, and radio.[5] Because of the ease with which most electronic forms of communication may be compromised, personnel must be made aware that they are not to discuss matters as outlined above unless the transmission is routine and the information is contained in a message or coded format that does not compromise safeguards features or response procedures. To avoid the discovery of the code key by an electronics eavesdropper, codes should be changed periodically. This change should be to a completely new code rather than modification of an existing one.

Once a written (or other hard copy) item of safeguards or company proprietary information has served its purpose, it should be destroyed to avoid the unnecessary accumulation of outdated though still damaging papers. Destruction may be by shredding or burning, although it must be borne in mind that shredding, no matter how thorough, leaves a residue that may, given enough time and patience, be reconstructed. High-temperature burning or destruction by commercially manufactured disintegrators that turn the material into coarse dust are the surest and recommended methods for records disposal (destruction of government classified material must be effected under specific guidelines not mentioned here).

Other residue that is susceptible to espionage or intelligence gathering includes carbon paper, weak or blurred photocopies, typewriter ribbons, and so on. These items, while not usually thought of as being capable of providing information are, in fact, the first places an individual will seek surreptitiously to obtain company proprietary or safeguards information. For this reason, it is suggested consideration be given to establishing a segregated trash disposal repository into which all carbons, poor-quality copies, used typewriter ribbons, and the like may be placed at the end of the business day. This repository is then either securely locked away until the next business day, or immediately taken to the incinerator or other destruction device for disposal. Ribbons in typewriters should also be removed and placed in a security container as they can, under an expert's examination, divulge all that has recently been typed on that machine.

Thus far, the emphasis of this chapter has been on the necessity for providing safeguards for physical security systems and information. There is a very real presence of industrial espionage by business competitors and by foreign intelligence agents. Companies must now more than ever ensure that their high-technology products and manufacturing processes are not compromised or do not fall into the hands of an individual who may ultimately be responsible for their losing the competitive edge in the marketplace, or even worse, provide technical aid to a country whose goals are inimical to the national welfare. It is an established fact that some countries staff their foreign embassies, missions, and consulates with intelligence agents.

While most individuals envision a spy as someone in a trench coat and felt hat (the movie stereotype), this is far from the truth. Most foreign intelligence agents are nondescript individuals who do not attract undue attention as they go about their jobs of gathering available information on technology. They read each and every informational news publication available, trade magazines, papers presented before professional organizations, government publications, company annual reports, and advertising literature. The type and quantity of information they seek has no limits. Anything and everything is collected and forwarded to a central collection and analysis point where experts collate bits and pieces of data into a cohesive picture of something that would be of value to their government. In many cases, the information that has been openly gathered can be restructured into a complete or nearly complete picture of what the originator considers a properly safeguarded process or product. In cases where the missing pieces cannot be puzzled out by the intelligence agency, they will often order their on-scene agent to obtain detailed data to fill in the blanks.

Richard N. Perle[6] describes the Soviet Union's acquisition of high technology through fair means and foul. In many cases, the technology was properly (and innocently) provided in accordance with existing regulations. In cases where there were prohibitions against the export of the data or product to a Soviet bloc nation by the country of origin, ruses were employed whereby the embargoed item was ordered by a nation against which there were no trade sanctions prohibiting receipt of the information or product, and then trans-shipped to the prohibited nation by the cooperative middleman.

Another area that receives little or no attention relative to providing safeguards is the company computer. As with any electronic apparatus, unauthorized access through sophisticated means is an ever-present threat. To prevent such access, many companies have erected radio-frequency shielding around computer rooms to defeat adversary action. In this case, theft of data is not the objective. Instead, as more and more companies entrust their deepest secrets to computers that are programmed to respond to secret codes, the adversary action involves the generation of an electronic signal to scramble the computers' memory banks and make retrieval of the information extremely difficult or even impossible.

Electronic eavesdropping, while illegal in almost all jurisdictions, is a thriving industry. The "bugs" or electronic microphones can be disguised and/or, because of microminiature circuits, made so small that they may be hidden almost anywhere in the space an adversary wants to monitor. As the electronic eavesdroppers become more sophisticated in their equipment and techniques, so too are those individuals who ferret out such devices. At facilities where access cannot be gained to the space where spoken information is available, microwave technology can be employed. If confidential or restricted data are discussed in a room with a window, certain parabolic microphones can be trained on the window from a considerable distance and pick up with a great deal of clarity all that is said within that space. (The window glass picks up the voice vibrations, and these in turn are picked up by the microphone.)

Any ordinary telephone, even one with the handset in the cradle, is capable of efficiently transmitting all verbal communications in a normal-sized room where it may be located, when appropriately bugged by an eavesdropper.

The methods and equipment that must be guarded against go on and on. Any maximum-security facility that believes it may be the target of electronics eavesdropping or other espionage attempts is advised to contact a recognized and reliable authority in the field for assistance. Most security industry periodicals contain information on such assistance. Before making a final selection, all firms or individuals should be checked out to ensure that established companies with proven records of accomplishment are considered.

This is just a brief sampling of guidance for safeguarding proprietary information. It is by no means all-inconclusive, and by itself will not meet all of the requirements of a government-mandated information security program. If additional guidance is desired, or if a facility's proprietary information falls under the purview of a regulatory agency, appropriate government regulations and references must be consulted.

NOTES

1. Nuclear Regulatory Commission, *Protection of Unclassified Safeguards Information* (Washington, D.C.: The Commission, 1982), pp. 1–4.
2. Ibid.
3. Ibid.
4. *The Code of Federal Regulations* (Washington, D.C.: 1982), Title 10, Part 73.2(2).
5. Nuclear Regulatory Commission, *Protection of Unclassified Safeguards Information*, p. 7.
6. Richard N. Perle, "The Soviet Connection," *Security Management*, pp. 106–109. © (1982). Copyright by the American Society for Industrial Security, 1655 N. Fort Drive, Suite 1200, Arlington, VA 22209. Reprinted with permission from the (July 1982) issue of *Security Management* magazine.

CHAPTER 16

Conclusion

With the marvelous technological breakthroughs being made in the field of electronic devices and equipment specifically designed and engineered for security application, the future appears bright. Just 40 years ago, however, we did not have CCTV, microwave intrusion-detection systems were not available, a small portable radio weighed about eight pounds and was used primarily by government agents or the military, the streets of our cities were safe to walk at night, and the average security guard was a white pensioner with minimal formal education and little or no preemployment training in the security field. Our scientists and engineers can point with justifiable pride to their accomplishments since then. The CCTV is commonly used, microwave intrusion-detection systems provide dependable perimeter as well as enclosed-area protection, the weight of portable radios is measured in ounces (and getting lighter every year), walking the streets of most cities after dark is perilous to say the least, and the average security officer, because of demographics, is still white but now has a high school education and quite probably some college. He has received at least some formal training for his security position, is in his early to middle twenties, and sees security as a viable career field. Technology is wonderful—it has made our jobs as security professionals much easier . . . or has it?

Why have these sophisticated security systems become necessary and ever more complicated? Is it simply to satisfy the average American male's fascination with gadgets, or are we as security professionals in an escalating race with those who would take away or destroy what we are paid to protect and safeguard? Technology and knowledge have no politics. For every new and foolproof piece of electronic wizardry, locking device, and concept or procedure that an intelligent and dedicated professional comes up with to aid us in our daily responsibilities, there is an equally intelligent and dedicated professional somewhere busily at work finding a way to subvert, bypass, or in some other way render it useless. If this were not so, there would be no need for the development of increasingly sophisticated systems and methods.

Make no mistake about it—we are engaged in a war. It may be a genteel war where technology is the weapon and stealth is the tactic, but the possibility of violence with attendant personnel injury or loss of life and severe property damage is present. A criminal elite has developed for whom the emphasis is on brains rather than brawn. The members of this group are individuals of above average intelligence, appearance, and education. They are planners who are systematic and methodical in their approach and who can map out strategies that would make a Pentagon planner proud. These are the truly dangerous adversaries with whom we are finding ourselves confronted. The alarm systems, fences, lights, CCTV, and other physical protection devices will prove very effective against a "smash and grab" attack, but a careful planner will probe the defenses looking for a chink in the protective envelope through which he launches his often undetected attack. This is where we must beat him at his own game.

It obviously does no good to find a "chink" after it has been used against us. Careful planning, preparation of comprehensive though not overly complicated procedures for all regular site operations and possible contingencies, integration and education of all other site personnel necessary to support security contigency plans, recruitment and training of the best qualified personnel available, modern intrusion detection and assessment equipment, and a supervisory staff with the training, background, and knowledge to oversee and manage the operation efficiently are of prime importance. All this, however, quickly becomes useless unless it is constantly updated to meet changing requirements and periodically reviewed to ascertain if a major overhaul may be necessary. The personnel and equipment should be frequently tested to ensure that the desired responses will be forthcoming when required. Because ennui can quickly become a problem among personnel who must perform the same job in the same manner every day, it is extremely important that interest and morale be maintained.

As we look forward, we are encouraged, for the security industry is entering a new era in which the professional is finally being recognized and his worth is becoming appreciated. In 40 years, great strides forward have been made, and who knows what the next 40 will bring. Security work has become a career field and more and more colleges and other institutions of higher learning are providing accredited training curricula specifically designed to prepare an individual for a career in the field, and confer a degree upon successful completion. Security is one of the fastest growing industries currently, and there does not appear to be an end in sight.

What kind of technological breakthroughs can we except in the future—will today's chain link fences be replaced with magnetic force fields? Will a twenty-first-century security officer reach for a laser pistol when suddenly confronted with a life-or-death situation? Will holographic projections be used to confront an intruder rather than place a live officer in a position that presents an element of danger? These all sound like science fiction and, in fact, some of it may be just that. But just 40 years ago, nuclear-powered submarines, airplanes that fly faster than the speed of sound, men on the moon, and microwave intrusion-detection systems would have sounded the same. Scientists and engineers have had a tendency to turn today's science fiction into tomorrow's fact.

The future looks bright indeed, but the concepts and practices we presented in the preceding 15 chapters should, with minor modifications, be just as applicable in 2025 AD as they are today. While we have discussed various specific items of hardware and security equipment whenever necessary to make a specific point or clarify the matter under discussion, our intent has been to concentrate on practical methods of improving security protection and on concepts that may be suitable or adaptable for use in certain situations or at specific types of facilities. Even if everyone reading this book only takes away one new idea that will make his job easier, safer, or faster, or that will increase the protection being provided, it was surely worth the effort.

Bibliography

Anderson, R. E. *Bank Security*. Woburn, Mass.: Butterworth Publishers, 1981.

Argyle, Harold J. "Nuclear Security in a Sagebrush Environment." *FBI Law Enforcement Bulletin* (September 1982):6.

Atomic Energy Commission. *General Use of Locks in the Protection and Control of Facilities and Special Nuclear Materials*. Regulatory Guide 5.12. Washington, D.C.: The Commission, 1973.

Attack Resistant Frangible Roof Concepts - Preliminary Tests, Robert J. Odello, Civil Engineering Laboratory, Port Hueneme, CA 93043, CEL-TM 51-78-04, November 1977.

Attack and Bullet Resistant Security Door Assemblies, John L. Squier and Kenneth O. Gray, Civil Engineering Laboratory, Port Hueneme, CA 93043, CEL-TM No. 61-78-9.

Barnard, Robert L. *Intrusion Detection Systems: Principles of Operation and Applications*. Woburn, Mass.: Butterworth Publishers, 1981.

Barrier Penetration Database. Rev. ed. Upton, N.Y.: Brookhaven National Laboratory, 1978.

Barrier Technology Handbook. Albuquerque: Sandia Laboratory, 1977.

Bean, Charles H., and James A. Prell. "Personnel Access Control—Criteria and Testing." *Security Management* (June 1978):6.

Belsaw Bulletin—Locksmith Shop Notes (July 1981):52.

Bopp, William J. *Police Administration—Selected Readings*. Boston: Holbrook Press, 1975.

Brooks, Pierce R. ". . . officer down, Code Three." Schiller Park, Ill.: Motorola Teleprograms, 1975.

Bureau of Standards, Department of Commerce. *Security Lighting for Nuclear Weapons Storage Sites: A Literature Review and Bibliography*. NBS special publication 480-27. Washington, D.C.: The Bureau, 1977.

Caldwell, Harry. *Basic Law Enforcement*. Pacific Palisades: Goodyear Publishing Co., 1972.

Code of Federal Regulations. Title 10. Washington, D.C., 1981.

"Conducting a Lighting Energy Audit." *National Safety News* (February 1982):24.

"Correctional Communication." *Security Industry and Product News* (April 1982):24–28.

Countering Terrorism. Washington, D.C.: Department of State, 1977.

Defense Civil Preparedness Agency. *Disaster Planning Guide for Business and Industry*. Baltimore: The Agency, 1978.

"Exploring The Microworld." *Newsweek*, October 26, 1981.

Fite, Robert A., and Stuart Kilpatrick. "Final Report, Joint Services Perimeter Barrier Penetration Evaluation." Proceedings of the First Annual Symposium, April 29–30, 1976, Washington, D.C.

Frier, John P. "How Much Light for the Shipping Dock?" *Security World* (November 1978):26.

Gigliotti, Richard J. "The Fine Art of Justification." *Security Management* (November 1980):30–34.

Gigliotti, Richard J., and Ronald C. Jason. "Should Security Personnel Be Armed?" *Assets Protection* (March/April 1982):11–13.

Gigliotti, Richard J.; Ronald C. Jason; and Nancy J. Cogan. "What's Your Level of Physical Security?" *Security Management* (August 1980):39.

Grumbach, A. T. "Locks and Locking—Fulfilling Special Locking Requirements." *Security World* (February 1979):39.

Grumbach, A. T. "Locks and Locking—Lock Sophistication." *Security World* (October 1978):55.

Grumbach, A. T. "Locks and Locking—Pertinence." *Security World* (May 1978):34.

Hardening Existing SSNM Storage Facilities. Preliminary report. U.S. Army Material Systems Analysis Activity. Aberdeen: 1979.

"Home Owners in Distress." *Security Industry and Product News* (August 1982):24.

Hopf, Peter S., ed. *Handbook of Building Security Planning and Design.* New York: McGraw-Hill Book Co., 1979.

Kupperman, Robert H., and Darrell Trent. *Terrorism.* Stanford: Hoover Institution Press, 1975.

Lee, Robert P. "Business and Residential Security." Talk given at the Community College of Rhode Island–Knight Campus, October 27, 1981, Providence.

McCalmont, A. M. "Communications Security Devices." *Security Industry and Product News* (March 1980):19.

Military Police Handbook. Field Manual 19-5. Washington, D.C.: Department of the Army, 1975.

Nuclear Regulatory Commission. *Basic Considerations for Assembling a Closed-Circuit Television System.* NUREG-0178. Washington, D.C.: The Commission, 1977.

Nuclear Regulatory Commission. *Entry/Exit Control for Protected Areas, Vital Areas and Material Access Areas.* Regulatory Guide 5.7. Rev. ed. Washington, D.C.: The Commission, 1980.

Nuclear Regulatory Commission. *Fixed Site Upgrade Rule Guidance Compendium.* Washington, D.C.: The Commission, 1978.

Nuclear Regulatory Commission. *Generic Adversary Characteristics. Summary Report.* NUREG-0459. Washington, D.C.: The Commission, 1979.

Nuclear Regulatory Commission. *Perimeter Intrusion Alarm Systems.* Regulatory Guide 5.44. 2nd Rev. ed. Washington, D.C.: The Commission, 1980.

Nuclear Regulatory Commission. *Protection of Unclassified Safeguards Information.* NUREG-0794. Washington, D.C.: The Commission, 1982.

Nuclear Regulatory Commission. *Security Lighting Planning Document for Nuclear Fixed Site Facilities.* NUREG/CR-1327. Washington, D.C.: The Commission, 1980.

Nuclear Regulatory Commission. *Security Personnel Training and Qualification Criteria.* NUREG-0674. Washington, D.C.: The Commission, 1980.

Nuclear Regulatory Commission. *Vehicle Access and Search Training Manual.* NUREG/CR-0485. Washington, D.C.: The Commission, 1979.

Osborne, W. E. "Access Through the Locking Barrier." *Security World* (July 1978):35.

Perle, Richard N. "The Soviet Connection." *Security Management* (July 1982):106–109.

Physical Security. Field Manual 19-30. Washington, D.C.: Department of the Army, 1979.

Post, Deborah Cromer. "Technology of Access Control." *Security World* (October 1980):23.

Rhodes, Richard C. "Technical Notebook: Lock Security, Part I." *Security Management* (March 1978):66.

"Security Idea File: Three Protective Innovations." *Security World* (April 1979):30–31.

Security Letter 12, no. 21, part II, 1982.

Tactical Communications Center Operation. Field Manual 24-17. Washington, D.C.: Department of the Army, 1967.

Tactical Communications Doctrine. Field Manual 24-1. Washington, D.C.: Department of the Army, 1968.

Technical Data Sheet 76-08R. Civil Engineering Laboratory, Naval Construction Battalion Center. Port Hueneme, Calif., 1977.

Technical Data Sheet 77-07R. Civil Engineering Laboratory, Naval Construction Battalion Center. Port Hueneme, Calif, 1979.

Thorsen, J. E. "Considering the Sources." *Security World* (May 1978):44.

Thorsen, J. E. "Has 'Absolute Identity' Come of Age?" *Security World* (July 1978):32.

Wallach, Charles. "Posions and Negions Battle for Your Mind." *Security Management* (March 1979):50.

Wilson, O. W., and R. C. McLaren. *Police Administration.* New York: McGraw-Hill Book Co., 1972.

Index